Springer Texts in Business

MW00484382

More information about this series at http://www.springer.com/series/10099

Macroeconomic Policy is a lively and informative introduction to the diverse doctrines of macroeconomic theory.

Professor Robert E. Lucas, Jr.
Recipient of the 1995 Nobel Prize in Economics

Farrokh K. Langdana

Macroeconomic Policy

Demystifying Monetary and Fiscal Policy

Third Edition

Foreword by W. Michael Cox

 Springer

Farrokh K. Langdana
Rutgers Business School
Rutgers University–Newark
   and New Brunswick
Newark, NJ
USA

ISSN 2192-4333   ISSN 2192-4341   (electronic)
Springer Texts in Business and Economics
ISBN 978-3-319-32852-2   ISBN 978-3-319-32854-6   (eBook)
DOI 10.1007/978-3-319-32854-6

Library of Congress Control Number: 2016938675

Printed on acid-free paper

This Springer imprint is published by Springer Nature
The registered company is Springer International Publishing AG Switzerland

This book engineers a unique stealth approach to learning macroeconomics. Readers will be drawn in through the interconnected sets of policy analyses, fortified by innumerable relevant and imaginative examples, little realizing that they are absorbing an increasingly sophisticated set of macroeconomic tools along the way.

Professor Richard C.K. Burdekin
Jonathan B. Lovelace Professor of Economics
Claremont McKenna College and
Claremont Graduate School
Claremont, CA, USA

To my wife, Mary

Foreword

Macroeconomic policy analysis has been in a state of flux since the early 1970s. Although the casual student of macroeconomics might expect that economists would have come to some agreement in our quest to model the so-called real world, the analysis of macroeconomic policy has perhaps never been so confounding as it is today. Each monetary or fiscal policy event is almost inevitably followed by at least two completely different and conflicting sets of analyses.

Consider, for example, the question of whether government spending affects GDP growth. One can find just about any answer to this question possible—some say it increases GDP, some that it decreases GDP, and some claim no effect. Others go on to claim that the answer depends on whether the economy is a developed one, such as the US, or an emerging ones, like China and India.

Another central source of confusion is the proverbial Phillips Curve, which, as originally conceived, related the unemployment rate to wage inflation. Some researchers have found an inverse relationship between these variables; others have found no link at all. What's more, the economics profession has introduced new and improved variants on Phillips' tradeoff theme—inflation versus unemployment rates, inflation versus GDP growth, inflation versus capacity utilization, and so on. For each of these postulated relationships, virtually any conclusion can be found. And to confound things further, the conclusions appear to change as the economy changes. The statistical evidence from the much-heralded "New Economy" of the late 1990s seems to suggest that rapid GDP is linked more to *low* than high inflation. Will the real Phillips curve relationship please stand up?

Conceivably, there are as many interpretations of economic phenomenon as there are economists to interpret them. All this may be well and good from the standpoint of the passionate researcher, who makes a living in an endless search for the macroeconomic Holy Grail. But for the typical student, less interested in contrast and more interested in conclusions, the result can be a state of confusion as he or she moves from class to class, from book to book, or from publication to publication. Finding the truth for economics students has become a bit of a mystery.

Enter Farrokh Langdana's book, aptly titled *Macroeconomic Policy: Demystifying Monetary and Fiscal Policy*. Not only does the book shine a bright light through the dense fog surrounding economists' centrist position on macroeconomic thought, it does so with a set of tools virtually all readers can handle. The cumbersome mathematics that most modern economists love but most students loathe, are put aside in favor of teaching tools with wider appeal and suitability.

Even economists have recognized that as our profession has aged, our language—both verbal and quantitative—has become more convenient and precise for us, but less accessible and attractive to the general audience. So, what should the economics professor do? Economist Francis Edgeworth, writing nearly a century ago about Alfred Marshall, one of economics' original and first-class mathematicians, said that "Marshall, who desired above all things to be useful, *deferred to the prejudices of those that he wished to persuade* (emphasis added)." In other words, we should speak in the language of our audience, not our profession. Increasingly, the economics profession shuns this communication principle in favor of "rigor," all the while knowing that, as economist Robert Heilbroner said, "Mathematics has given economics rigor, but alas, also mortis."

The Bureau of Labor Statistics estimates that there are roughly 31,000 economists (including economics professors) in the U.S. out of a population of roughly 310 million. This figures out to be one economist for every 10,000 people. Must not it be important to speak to the other 9,999, not just to the one? Of course, and thus this book is written for you, not for economists.

When Richard Alm and I wrote Myths of Rich and Poor, we set out to debunk a series of widely accepted myths that the U.S. was lagging behind economically, and that its citizens were getting progressively worse off. We accomplished the complete dismantling of such myths by presenting systematic overwhelming evidence that the U.S. has been prospering splendidly in recent decades, and we did so using the only tool possible for such a large audience—common sense. The reaction to our book has been tremendous because we spoke eye to eye with folks, not above their heads.

Macroeconomic Policy: Demystifying Monetary and Fiscal Policy takes on an equally important task—to show the reader that modern macroeconomic analysis is systematic, with logical frameworks within which economies can be successfully analyzed, and to do this without the use of overly fancy techniques. The applied and intuitive approach to the theory centers on diagrammatic derivations, using only the minimal techniques necessary to prove its points. While the book approaches analysis primarily via applications and analysis, the vital theoretical underpinnings have not been sacrificed.

As a long-time professor of economics, a practicing economist and an author, the teaching approach that I find most compelling is the "applications method." Begin with an important issue (such as supply-side economics) at least vaguely familiar to just about anybody, set out the central opposing views with the intuition behind each side, then examine the evidence and thrash out the conclusion. That is the best teaching approach because that is the way people think and work.

And thus it is with Prof. Langdana's book, we have a text that is first and foremost applications oriented. That is why MBA and Executive MBA students will find this book indispensable, financial analysts may like to have it on hand as an essential reference, and even a general audience can find it useful.

The overview chapter clearly and concisely states the book's position regarding its focus on intuition and applicability. The notion of allowing the reader the freedom of choice between the Keynesian or the Supply-Side paradigm for developed economies is fresh and radically different from most conventional macroeconomics texts. In addition, it is an honest approach, given that both monetary and fiscal policymakers in Washington D.C. still make policy based on assumptions behind each paradigm.

The author states that he has taken care not to influence the reader toward either paradigm and he has faithfully managed to keep the promise throughout the text. The coverage is carefully balanced, with the excellent chapter on the New Economy (Chap. 10) being especially pertinent to the two-model approach. In the chapter on monetary policy (Chap. 11), Farrokh Langdana and Giles Mellon actually discuss the fact that reserve requirements are not binding any more in the United States. This is one of very few texts that has managed to cogently explain how the conventional textbook explanation of open market operations and the "money multiplier" has substantially changed in several major economies.

The simulated "media articles" following each chapter are vital to this text and to truly analyzing macroeconomic policy in general. It rapidly becomes evident through the clarity of exposition why the author has been consistently rated so highly as a teacher.

Dr. W. Michael Cox

Dr. W. Michael Cox is Director of the O'Neil Center for Global Markets and Freedom in the Cox School of Business at Southern Methodist University, and coauthor (with Richard Alm) of the highly acclaimed *Myths of Rich and Poor: Why We're Better Off Than We Think* (nominated for a Pulitzer Prize). He is formerly Senior Vice President and Chief Economist at the Federal Reserve Bank of Dallas, where he served for 25 years. Dr. Cox is a regular contributing columnist for Investor's Business Daily. In addition to being a frequent guest on CNN, Fox News, Voice of America and National Public Radio. He is past President of the Association of Private Enterprise Education, a CATO Institute Adjunct Scholar, senior fellow at the National Center for Policy Analysis, and senior fellow at the Dallas Fed's Globalization and Monetary Policy Institute.

Acknowledgments

This book would, quite simply, not have been possible without the assistance and encouragement of many people.

I begin by thanking Prof. Robert E. Lucas of the University of Chicago, the recipient of the 1995 Nobel Prize in Economics, for his comments and suggestions pertaining to my experimental testing of his paradigm-busting "islands" model (Chap. 10). Prof. Lucas' work has been a source of encouragement and inspiration to me as well as to generations of macroeconomists over the last three decades.

Dr. Michael Cox, the former Chief Economist and Senior Vice President of the Federal Reserve Bank of Dallas, and coauthor of *Myths of Rich and Poor: Why We Are Better Off Than We Think,* took time off from his busy schedule to write the foreword for this book, and for that I am most grateful. Dr. Cox is also Professor of Economics at Southern Methodist University, and currently the Director of the O'Neil Center for Global Markets and Freedom in the Cox School of Business. He has drawn upon his experience as economist, professor, banker, and author to eloquently describe the challenges faced in analyzing as well as teaching macroeconomic policy today. In a few short pages he has deftly managed to articulate the very essence of the book.

I remain extremely grateful to my former colleague, the late Professor Giles Mellon at Rutgers Business School with whom I had the distinct honor of coauthoring, most recently, "Monetary Policy in a World of Non-Binding Reserve Requirements." Giles was ahead of his time with his invaluable observation in Chap. 11 in which we "blow the whistle" on the fact that, in reality, central bank open market operations in most developed economies have very little in common with conventional textbook discussions on the subject. This prescient discovery made by Giles has been borne out today when it is now increasingly apparent that movements in Fed funds rates and open market operations really have very little connection with each other—in sharp contrast to conventional textbook explanantions.

I am indebted to my coauthor of two books and a well-cited paper on Confederate financing in the US Civil War, Prof. Richard C.K. Burdekin, the Jonathan B. Lovelace Professor of Economics at Claremont McKenna College and

Claremont Graduate School, for his comments, suggestions, and detailed structural advice related to the draft of the first proposal. Thanks also to Professors Mark Castelino, Leonard Goodman, and Menahem Spiegel for their extremely valuable comments that enabled the proposal to evolve into the first draft.

I am very grateful to my former Executive Vice-Dean, Prof. Rosa Oppenheim, for her extremely useful suggestions pertaining to the organization and content of this second edition. Rosa is the coauthor of Quality Management (McGraw-Hill Irwin), a text that is now in its 4th edition, and she has long mastered the fine art of updating a text to make it current, while at the same time ensuring that the edition is not "dated" or overwhelmed by the additional content.

Many thanks to Prof. Michael Crew, Director of the Rutgers Center for Research in Regulated Industries and author of numerous books in the area of Utilities Regulation, for his support and strategic advice at all stages of the original volume and for steering me to a wonderful working relationship with Kluwer and now Springer Science+Business Media.

The book would not have been completed on schedule and in its final form without the assistance of Prof. Ivan Brick, the Chairman of the Finance and Economics Department at Rutgers Business School. In addition to allowing me the flexibility to work on this project and funding the TAs that helped me with the plots and the data, Dr. Brick also made possible the editorial assistance of my former colleague, the late Prof. Carter Daniel, wordsmith par excellence, by providing funding from The Whitcomb Center for Research in Financial Services. For all this I am most thankful.

Prof. Daniel and my wife, Mary Langdana, deserve a special note of thanks for patiently and laboriously proofreading the manuscript—not once, but several times, often at very short notice. I deeply appreciate their efforts.

My Dean and dear friend here at Rutgers Business School, Prof. Lei Lei has been a source of encouragement, friendship, leadership, and assistance since she and I joined Rutgers so many years ago. To her, I remain grateful for so much— from teaching in Rutgers EMBA many years ago, to the China connection for RBS, to becoming our Dean and propelling RBS to even greater heights.

Two of my former students, Wenjeng Lee and Amir Razzaghi, provided me with copies of their excellent notes from my macroeconomics classes at Rutgers Business School. These notes were invaluable in ensuring that the sequence and intensity of my classroom discussions were faithfully captured in this book. I am particularly grateful to my TAs, Prachi Joglekar and Olga Sorokina, for assistance with many of the plots and to Prachi, in particular, for the index for this 3rd edition.

Many of the questions discussed toward the end of each chapter have been asked in class, and I thank all my students in the MBA and Executive MBA programs in the US, China, India, Iceland, Singapore, and France for their contributions. In addition, some of my former students have made extremely valuable comments and suggestions on the early drafts of the chapters, most of which have been incorporated. I owe a special note of thanks to former students Michael Perron for his excellent insight into the Keynesian nature of the yield curve, and Sarah Boltizar for her suggestions pertaining to the figures in Chap. 5. Other students such as Reginald Crisanto, Nadia

Karalnik, and Omkar Paratkar have made valuable and lasting contributions and they have been acknowledged directly in the text.

Over the years, many former and current students have kindly supplied me—and continue to supply me—with some truly excellent articles from major news publications for which I remain grateful. These articles have allowed me to widen my resource net and include as much relevant and current material as possible. Facts from these articles have been included in several chapters.

The assistance provided by the Rutgers computer support staff, Mahmoud Ahmed, Joe Bassano, Bernice Fair, Shevon Jackson and Kevin Pagan, is also much appreciated. Many of my IT-related requests were off-working hours, on holidays and often late at nights, and this team has always been on hand to extricate me from IT meltdowns that threatened to devour whole chapters at a time, or website issues that could have cut off the Rutgers EMBA program from the rest of the world.

I am very grateful to Lorraine Klimowich, my Editor at Springer, for her encouragement, suggestions, assistance, and advice that resulted in the smooth completion and positioning of this third edition. Lorraine has also been most patient with my myriad queries pertaining to the development and promotion of this edition and the final format of the plots and graphs, and for that I remain most grateful.

My parents in Bombay, Zarrin and Keki, instilled in me a thirst for reading, a quest for knowledge, and a sense of humor from my very early childhood. It was only many years later that I came to truly appreciate the significance of this aspect of my upbringing, and I thank them both for this. My mother, in particular, hammered in me the work ethic that ensured that I completed all projects that I began; without this embedded discipline, this volume would, quite simply, not have happened.

I am so grateful to my son, Christopher Jennelle, statistician extraordinaire, for the many spirted policy-related discussions pertaining to the notion of government regulation, versus Adam-Smith-like incentives to ensure the right free market results in our economy.

My dear friends Kathleen Harmon and Prof. Lewis Kerman have always been there with me with unconditional help and support over all these years. I will always be grateful for their friendship and their kindness.

Above all, I remain most grateful to my wife, Mary. Not only was she one of the two proofreaders for the whole original manuscript as mentioned above, but for much of her married life, she has graciously endured a perpetually distracted husband, his nocturnal working hours on the computer, and the sight of manuscripts stacked obtrusively in almost every part of the house. She endures all this to allow books like this to be published. In addition she has always ensured that in all my economic analyses, I never forget the real human cost of bad macro, and that my readers and I not be desensitized by the colored lines on the board, and in this book. She is primarily responsible for my setting the "tone" of this book to making certain that my students and my readers fully appreciate the power of "good macro" and the devastating, harsh, and poignant reality of "bad macro" on us all. This is partly why all three editions of *Macroeconomic Policy: Demystifying Monetary and Fiscal Policy* have been dedicated to her.

Contents

About the Author

Dr. Farrokh K. Langdana is a professor in the Finance/Economics Department at Rutgers Business School, New Jersey. In addition to this textbook, he is the author of four other books; two research-oriented volumes coauthored with Prof. Richard C.K. Burdekin, the Jonathan B. Lovelace Professor of Economics at Claremont McKenna College, and a text on International Trade and Global Macropolicy with former EMBA student, Peter Murphy, President and CEO of DC Safety. He has also published several articles pertaining to macroeconomic policy and macroexperimentation.

Dr. Langdana is currently the Director of the globally ranked Executive MBA (EMBA) program at Rutgers Business School, as well as the Academic Director of the Rutgers International Executive MBA programs, worldwide. He teaches Macroeconomic Policy as well as International Trade and Global Macroeconomics in the EMBA program as well as in the full-time and part-time (Flex) MBA programs at Rutgers Business School.

In addition to being the recipient of the Warren I. Susman Award for Excellence in Teaching (Rutgers University's highest teaching award), Prof. Langdana has also been awarded the Rutgers Business School's Paul Nadler Award for Teaching Excellence, the Horace dePodwin Research Award, over 15 Executive MBA Teaching Excellence Awards and over 30 Rutgers MBA teaching awards. In addition to teaching in the US, Prof. Langdana has also taught Executive MBAs in China (Beijing and Shanghai), Singapore, France, India, and Iceland.

Professor Langdana is a graduate of the Indian Institute of Technology (Kanpur), and he has an MBA (Finance) and a Ph.D. in Economics from Virginia Tech, in Blacksburg, Virginia.

Professor Langdana can be contacted at Langdana@Business.Rutgers.edu, and his macroblogs and videos can be found at Business.Rutgers.edu/Langdanamacro (scroll all the way down, please).

For more information pertaining to the Rutgers Executive MBA Program and its rankings, please visit EMBA.Rutgers.edu

Chapter 1
Introduction and Overview of the Third Edition

In recent times, authors of macroeconomics texts have faced a series of daunting challenges. The primary challenge lies in the very nature of the subject. Monetary and fiscal policies influence wages, employment, inflation, output, interest rates, and exchange rates and affect virtually all individuals in emerging as well as in developed economies. The applicability and pervasiveness of macroeconomics have never been in doubt. In fact, it is these very aspects that pose the major challenges to authors of texts pertaining to the analysis of monetary and fiscal policies.

Texts that cater primarily to current global macroeconomic events, focusing on the real-world implications of macroeconomic policies on employment, inflation, etc., immediately run into one serious challenge. Given the rapid pace of macroeconomic change and the frequency of global macroeconomic crises, such texts often become outdated by the time they appear. In fact, the greater the emphasis on actual current events, the greater the likelihood of the textbook becoming "dated," and hence the shorter its shelf life.

Another challenge is that theoretical models that drive macroeconomic policy are usually complex time-series models involving significant familiarity with mathematical and statistical techniques. Texts that attempt to incorporate large tracts of cutting edge theory have been received favorably by researchers and students in PhD programs. But, such texts have not done so well with practitioners such as financial analysts and MBA students, where the focus is on learning how to analyze the implications of actual fiscal and monetary policies, rather than the construction and development of theoretical/mathematical models. This mutual exclusivity has thus compartmentalized macroeconomic texts into generally two groups based on either the emphasis on research or on policy analysis.

Finally, perhaps the most daunting challenge faced by authors of macroeconomics texts is that in several developed economies, such as those of the US, Western Europe, and perhaps Japan, two dramatically different macroeconomic models compete for the center stage of macroeconomic policy. In this book,

© Springer International Publishing Switzerland 2016
F. Langdana, *Macroeconomic Policy*, Springer Texts in Business and Economics, DOI 10.1007/978-3-319-32854-6_1

we will describe one of these as "Keynesian/Traditional" and the other as "Supply-Sider/New Classical."

The differences between these two models are anything but academic. In fact, their policy implications are diametrically and fundamentally different. For example, some key issues that produce resoundingly different responses from these two models are as follows:

- Should the government increase spending to promote employment and growth?
- Should the central bank design monetary growth to actively lower/raise interest rates to manage employment and GDP?
- Should the central bank undertake tremendous amounts of money creation to somehow prevent total macroeconomic meltdown in the wake of a deflating asset price bubble?
- Should tax cuts be based mainly on personal income or geared primarily toward businesses?
- Conversely, should tax hikes be resolutely implemented to "do something" about the budget deficit?
- Should the government maintain at least some optimal degree of regulation over business enterprise or is unfettered deregulation and privatization the mantra of growth?

Given these challenges, of either (i) focusing on the applied real-world aspects of policy or on the hard-core theory, or (ii) resolving the two-model issue, the analysis and interpretation of macroeconomic policy have become a largely mystifying process. Individuals grappling with the implications of recent announcements from domestic and foreign policy makers have often been confronted by wildly different analyses, at times in the same publication!

The objective of this book is to demystify macroeconomic policy analysis. Specifically, this book attempts to accomplish this demystification in the following manner:

(1) The primary emphasis of this book will be on practical real-world aspects of fiscal and monetary policy analysis. The book is, first and foremost, an applications-oriented macroeconomic policy analysis guide, designed to cater to individuals who need to analyze fiscal and monetary policies in the context of their personal or professional lives.

All the theory included in the chapters is "must know" theory that is absolutely essential for interpreting policy announcements and analyzing macroeconomic news. Furthermore, whenever possible, the emphasis is on an intuitive, diagram-based approach to the models, with the models themselves gradually increasing in sophistication. For example, the Keynesian multiplier effect is first introduced in Chap. 4, then discussed in detail in the context of the ISLM–ADAS model in Chap. 9, and then again in Chap. 10 in the context of the Keynesian explanation of the New Economy. Similarly, the Classical Model is first introduced in Chap. 4, then in an ISLM–ADAS framework in Chap. 8, and then again in Chaps. 10 and 11 while discussing the New Economy and the monetary policy objectives of the European Central Bank.

One key feature that truly anchors this textbook to the real world is the inclusion of the simulated "media articles" at the end of each chapter. These articles, written by the author and designed to mimic actual articles in periodicals such as the Economist, Wall Street Journal (US and Asian Edition), Business Week, and Financial Times, simulate the form and manner in which macroeconomic "news" is presented to executives and managers in the real world.

The reader should be able to relate the relevant underlined parts of these innovative "articles" to the theoretical course context presented in the current and preceding chapters. The exercises at the conclusion of every chapter are specifically designed to train the reader to relate, interpret, and analyze macroeconomic news as encountered in the workplace. Solutions to these exercises are provided at the very end of each chapter. At times, some of the "solutions" are mostly hints designed to enable readers to arrive at the correct solution by themselves—in fact, some of these hints are even in the form of additional leading questions.

In addition, the book and all the "media articles" are designed to be "time-neutral." All the real-world examples and exercises at the end of the chapters are carefully placed in historical context, and a conscious effort has been made not to allow this text to be dated to a particular era, administration, or country. Furthermore, the book balances macroeconomic policy analyses for emerging economies such as China, India, Central Europe, and South America with developed economies such as the US, Japan, Singapore, and Western Europe. In short, this book is designed to be applicable for readers in both emerging and developed economies.

(2) While this book includes a significant body of theory vital to monetary and fiscal policy analysis, it relegates some of the more quantitative mathematical derivations to texts that cater primarily to research economists. Our focus remains on macroeconomic policy analysis and not on the derivation of theoretical time-series models per se. The mathematical statistical derivations of the theoretical models necessary for research in macroeconomics and integral to PhD education, lie outside the domain of this book.

(3) This book attempts to resolve the Keynesian-Supply Side challenge by explaining exactly how and why two fundamentally different models can indeed legitimately coexist in some economies. Both models are constructed, described, and analyzed in equal detail. This text is careful not to introduce any bias—readers will be presented with the strengths and weaknesses of each model in equal detail.

We will discover that different economies enact policies in radically different paradigms (models) determined by factors such as the nature and sophistication of their labor markets and the quality of information. For example, emerging and transitional economies will be described as "primarily Keynesian" while many developed economies will be described as displaying "supply-side" tendencies.

Interestingly, for some developed economies both models vie for the role of "primary policy model." In these cases, the reader will be presented with all the macroeconomic tools necessary to make the choice of the more suitable model. This text will ensure that no editorial bias creeps into influence the reader to choose one model over the other in economies where the "jury is still out" regarding the operative paradigm.

(4) Each chapter includes discussion questions along with solutions. In over twenty years of teaching MBA and Executive MBA students in the US, China, Singapore, India, Iceland and France, these are the most commonly asked questions pertaining to the respective topics, and their inclusion should go a long way toward demystifying macroeconomic policy.

In summary, the book is designed for individuals who want an applied, hands-on approach to analyzing the effects of macroeconomic policies. The primary audience is MBA and Executive MBA students who have been in the work force long enough to appreciate the importance of monetary and fiscal policies. Intermediate-level undergraduate students will also find this book to be a good supplemental text. Individual investors, analysts, consultants, and in fact anyone who needs to strip away the myths, jargon, and theoretical ambiguity in order to systematically analyze the effects of current and future monetary and fiscal policies will find this text useful.

1.1 Chapter Overview

Chapter 2 begins with an overview of macroeconomic policies and the definitions of key variables such as GDP and inflation. The link between budget and trade deficits, interest rates, exchange rates, and global capital flows is discussed within the context of the National Savings Identity in Chap. 3.

The early groundwork for demand-side stabilization begins with Chap. 4. The first reference to Keynesian macroeconomics is made here along with the concept of the multiplier effect. In the milestone Chap. 5, we discuss key concepts such as the overheating, soft landing, and hard landing of economies. The first overview of the global "subprime crisis" is presented in this chapter with discussions on Quantitative Easing, Tapering, and Hot Capital. This chapter also discusses the measurement of unemployment and the complexities of that particular statistic. Chapter 6 essentially extends the content of Chap. 5 to include the effects of expected risk and inflation on long-term interest rates. The yield curve and the Fisher Effect are included in this chapter. The latter part of Chap. 6 describes the ultimate macroeconomic meltdown—hyperinflation.

The first encounter with the core model underlying macroeconomic policy analysis in this book occurs in Chap. 7. The ISLM–ADAS model is introduced here along with several policy exercises. In this chapter, we introduce an economy where inflation is artificially held constant in order to allow readers to gradually gain confidence with diagrammatic ISLM–ADAS policy experiments. In Chap. 8, we increase the sophistication of the ISLM–ADAS by allowing inflation to change: the Classical paradigm is analyzed here. The Keynesian model follows in the context of ISLM in Chap. 9. This chapter also includes a non-traditional analysis of the Great Depression, along with several exercises pertaining to emerging economy macropolicies.

The supply-sider paradigm is constructed and analyzed in Chap. 10, along with a discussion of the technology-driven New Economy. This chapter includes elements of rational expectations theory, crucial to the development of the supply-side model. The driving influences in this portion of the chapter will be concepts of imperfect and asymmetric information. This capstone chapter also includes significant discussion of the Identification Problem, whereby it is possible to legitimately allow two fundamentally different models to coexist simultaneously. The Keynesian explanation for the New Economy is also presented in this chapter along with a detailed summary of the differences between emerging and developed economies and the Keynesian ("traditional") and supply-sider (New Economy) models.

Finally, Chap. 11 discusses central banks and the role and conduct of monetary policy. The organization and structure of US Federal Reserve System and the European Central Bank are included here. This chapter also includes an update on the current state of reserves in the US banking system and the implication of these reserves on the future conduct of monetary policy. This section on the state of US reserves and the implications thereof incorporates elements of a paper coauthored with Professor Giles Mellon of Rutgers Business School.

Each chapter ends with a section featuring the most common questions asked by students and several simulated "media articles" that will allow readers to relate the theory to real-world macroeconomic news.

Readers may often find serious passages discussing rigorous theory interspersed with livelier, and almost whimsical anecdotal discussions of real-world macroeconomic events. This format, which mimics my teaching style in class, ensures that the "tone" of the book changes often and that readers fully appreciate that the demystification of monetary and fiscal policy is not only important and relevant, but exciting as well.

1.2 What's New in This Third Edition

This edition fully incorporates the global subprime crisis of 2007, and explores the macroeconomic state of the world from what is now referred to as The Great Recession of 2007 to the present. The implications of this crisis continue to this day, and reverberate not just in the US, but globally in both developed Europe and emerging Asia and Latin America.

To fully understand and analyze the macroeconomic state of affairs in our hyper-connected economies, this edition essentially incorporates a greater open-economy approach to macroeconomic analysis. Virtually every chapter has more of a global focus and this is reflected both in the additional theoretical coverage as well as in the articles and examples.

Specifically, the upgrades are the following:

- This edition provides the reader with a more in-depth analysis of global fiscal/monetary/exchange-rate macropolicy. Following the end of the massive, unprecedented money creation by the US and coinciding with the beginning of such monetization by the Eurozone, this edition arms the reader with timely macroeconomic tools designed specifically for global macroeconomic analysis in the post-Subprime-Crisis world. Much of the exchange rate analysis has been moved up to earlier chapters.

- The causes and effects of the Subprime Crisis are explored in a global context at several levels of increasing sophistication, and in three separate chapters. Included here is the author's Broken Rhombus which explains the differences between monetization, open market operations, quantitative easing (listed below), capital investment, government spending, and US Treasury bond auctions.

- Quantitative Easing (QE) adopted by the Federal Reserve as a means of staving off meltdown in the Great Recession is analyzed in detail. QE in Japan, the predecessor of this policy in the US, and QE launched in the Eurozone in 2015, is discussed in detail. This highly controversial monetary policy has been implemented in the Eurozone much to the consternation of monetarily conservative Western Europe, and much to the relief of beleaguered Southern Europe. This conflict of two fundamental macroeconomic paradigms is thoroughly analyzed.

- This edition also includes in-depth discussions of recent monetary policy phenomena such as the Taper, Carry Trades, Debt Limits, Cave Theory, and the "shorting" of national currencies.

- This edition devotes more space to asset price bubbles and efforts made to deflate them. A particular emphasis is on housing and asset price bubbles in the US, India, China, the UK and many countries in the Eurozone.

- The rollercoaster ride of the dollar that began in 2007, followed by its intense appreciation in 2015 is examined in a global context, as are the fluctuations in the other major currencies.

- Significant space is devoted to the currencies pegged to the US dollar, with particular attention to the dollar–yuan and the dollar–euro sagas. The unpegging of the Swiss currency to the euro in 2015 in the wake of the massive "flight to safety" of global hot capital, is visited several times in this edition.

- This edition leverages the author's significant experience in China (teaching there since 1993) and delves into the issues of sterilization by the People's Bank of China and the mechanics of pegging the yuan to a trade-weighted basket of currencies.

- Global oil prices, their sudden fluctuations, and their effects on shale-energy development in the US, are presented in this edition, along with Premier Putin's attempts to desperately shore-up a plunging ruble and capital exodus from Russia.
- This edition includes a thorough overview of the "other" Asian giant, India, following Prime Minster Modi's public declaration of a supply-side approach to Indian macropolicy. This volume also increases the coverage devoted to Southeast Asia centered on Singapore.
- In addition to the conventional measures of unemployment in the US, Chap. 5 will now also include descriptions of measures of unemployment such as U6 that capture marginally employed, discouraged, and involuntary part-time workers.
- Chapter 6 brings in more detail on yield curve inversion and other possible explanations of fluctuations in long-term interest rates. Operation Twist, deployed in the US in the Great Recession, and now possibly in the Eurozone, is overviewed.
- Chapters 3 and 9 include additional coverage on causes and consequences of hot capital flows. In addition to the author's expertise of the Icelandic macroeconomic saga of 2007–08, this edition discusses hot capital outflows from Asia back into the US in 2013, and then again into the US in 2015 following crises in the Eurozone and slowdowns in Asia. The case of Switzerland, struggling in 2015 against massive hot capital inflows, is discussed here.
- Chapter 10 has been expanded to include greater discussion on US macropolicy following the tired and massive Keynesian policies of the Obama Administration. Supply-side policy analyses of German Chancellor Angela Merkel, and macro challenges in the Eurozone, are now updated and discussed in greater depth.
- The fundamentally vital role of macropolicies in fostering innovation is discussed in this edition in Chap. 10. Germany and its vaunted innovation model, along with the South Korean innovation strategy, are analyzed here. Adam Smith is invoked in this edition in the context of government regulation and its effects on innovation and productivity.
- The role of macropolicy in driving and sustaining global supply chains, and creating zones of greater productivity, is overviewed in Chap. 10.
- The final chapter on central banks, Chap. 11, now includes coverage of the "post-subprime mess" in the US from the central bank perspective. This edition also explores how the Liquidity Trap has complicated the effectiveness of US, European, and Japanese monetary policy.

Chapter 2
National Income Accounts

This foundation chapter begins with definitions of key macrovariables and policy instruments essential to macroeconomic policy analysis.

The conventional definition of macroeconomics is the analysis of economy-wide, aggregated variables such as national output, interest rates, employment, wages, inflation, and exchange rates. These are defined as **endogenous** variables, determined by and "within" the macroeconomy. These variables cannot be directly influenced or changed by degree but are a product of the interaction of domestic and global demand and supply pressures.

For example, policy makers cannot simply have a meeting, vote to increase growth from 2 to 3 %, and expect national output to conveniently comply. National output is an endogenously determined variable, and the final change is, instead, a result of simultaneous interactions of consumer and investor expectations, domestic and foreign disturbances (shocks), and, of course, macroeconomic policies.

The macroeconomic policies that influence the endogenous variables are deliberately implemented and directly controlled by policy makers. These policies are considered to be **exogenous**, or determined independently "outside" the model.

The three exogenous policy instruments available to implement macroeconomic policy are changes in tax rates (t), changes in the growth of government spending (G), and changes in the growth of the money supply (M). The first two policy instruments constitute fiscal policy implemented by the government. Changes in the growth of the money supply and, to some extent, in national interest rates are determined and conducted by the nation's central bank, and constitute monetary policy.[1]

In addition to macroeconomic policies, exogenous variables also include "shocks" that unexpectedly slam into the economy. The endogenous macroeconomic variables such as national output, inflation, and employment are influenced, and at times traumatized, by exogenous shocks such as the oil shocks of 1973 and

---

[1]The exact mechanism by which money growth is changed will be covered in detail in Chap. 11.

© Springer International Publishing Switzerland 2016
F. Langdana, *Macroeconomic Policy*, Springer Texts in Business and Economics, DOI 10.1007/978-3-319-32854-6_2

Table 2.1 The macroeconomic "Backdrop"

Fiscal policy	Monetary policy	Shocks
Changes in tax rates (t) Changes in government spending (G) (government controlled)	Changes in money supply (M) and in short-term interest rates (controlled by the nation's central bank)	Wars, weather, oil shocks, terrorism, for example

1979, which resulted in the Great Stagflation in the US, the events of 9/11, and Hurricane Katrina in the United States.[2]

Table 2.1 summarizes the exogenous variables, namely, fiscal and monetary policy instruments, and shocks. The interplay between these variables and factors such as consumer and investor confidence and expectations then determines the host of endogenous macroeconomic variables that we encounter on almost a daily basis in the news.

The following endogenous variables will be represented interchangeably: National output growth = GDP = Y; inflation rate = P; employment rate = n; and interest rates = i.

In addition to the conventional discussion and analysis of macrovariables, one major feature of this book will be the explicit incorporation of the role of **expectations** in formulating and analyzing macroeconomic policy. A key feature introduced below and presented in forthcoming chapters is the concept of "paradigm shifts" where an entire macroeconomic model (paradigm) undergoes a fundamental and unexpectedly drastic change in a relatively short time period.[3]

2.1 Paradigm Shifts: An Introduction

This concept explains how macroeconomic models that may have performed wonderfully in certain periods may suddenly fail within the space of just a few years. It also illustrates how models that are tremendously successful in one economy may be frustrating disasters in another. This book will make the case that paradigm shifts were largely responsible for several major macroeconomic crises.

---

[2]The Great Stagflation is discussed in the context of the "second paradigm shift" in Chap. 10. The US macroeconomic responses following 9/11 and the sub-prime crisis are also included and analyzed in later chapters.

[3]A "model" is simply a well-articulated, theoretical macroeconomic framework. Typically a model includes descriptions (equations) of the goods, money, foreign exchange and labor markets. These markets can be represented and analyzed graphically or mathematically. The major focus of this volume will be on graphical analysis emphasizing the real-world policy aspects of macroeconomics.

The US in the Great Depression of the 1930s and the stagflation of the 1970s, the macroeconomic problems experienced by Japan from the early 1990s to the present, the Eurozone with Western Europe and Southern Europe firmly rooted in two fundamentally different paradigms, and the US in the wake of the sub-prime crisis of 2007–2008, are prime examples that will be discussed in later chapters.

A special feature of this book will be in-depth discussions of the implications and policy prescriptions of each individual paradigm and the linking of these paradigm shifts to the expectations and actions of forward-looking consumers, producers and investors.

Building a Bridge: An Early Intuitive Example Why is macroeconomic policy-making such an imprecise science? With all this computing power at our disposal and with even more accurate and sophisticated data-gathering systems in place, why can't a conventional engineering optimization problem design optimal fiscal and monetary polices that will ensure continuous recovery?

These questions hit at, perhaps, the core of macroeconomic policy design. Prescribing macropolicy is, unfortunately, not an optimization problem like those encountered in engineering. (Having acquired an engineering under-graduate degree, this author remembers agonizing over similar issues in graduate school in macroeconomics). The answer lies in the aspect of macroeconomics that results in paradigm shifts. The following simple example will provide intuition at this early stage. (A more detailed analysis will be presented while studying the JoAnna Grey/Lucas model in Chap. 10.)

A bridge has to be designed to cross a river in Year 1. The design spec-ifications are {A, B, C} where A is the width and depth of the river, B is the load and cycles/second to be experienced by the bridge, and C is the nature of the bedrock, geology, etc. With these specifications, the engineer produces the optimal design, X, which is the blueprint for the bridge.

Now, in Year 5, if another bridge is to be built in a different part of the country, and if, coincidentally, the specifications {A, B, C} are to remain exactly the same, the civil engineer can indeed dust-off blueprint {X} and submit it again. It will work.

However, this procedure would be practically impossible in the world of macroeconomic policy. If a set of "optimal" fiscal and monetary polices {Z} were designed and implemented to improve an economy laboring under the specifications {J, K, L} where J is high inflation, K is high unemployment, and L is low output growth, they may indeed work in Year 1. But, say, in Year 5, if the economy is facing the same problem specified by {J, K, L}, it is more than likely that the set of macroeconomic policies {Z} which were successful in Year 1 would fail or even be counterproductive in Year 5.

The reason is that engineering policy {X} is set against a time-invariant backdrop of nature. Isaac Newton's three laws of motion will always be valid in Year 1 as well as in Year 5. Macroeconomic policy, on the other hand, is

set against a backdrop of individuals who have expectations which are
constantly changing and which are, in turn, functions of the results of past
fiscal and monetary policies.

In our example here, individuals remember the effects of macropolicy {Z}
in Year 1. They remember what happened to interest rates, employment,
exchange rates, etc., soon after {Z} was enacted. So, in Year 5, when they
realize that policies {Z} are about to be implemented again, this time they
indulge in hedging behavior. They anticipate the effects of {Z} based on their
past experience, and they take action to minimize any and all adverse effects
of {Z}. Thus, the cumulative actions of these individuals may end up mini-
mizing or totally negating policy {Z} in Year 5. In this case, a paradigm shift
is said to have occurred. Policy {Z} which may have been a huge success in
Year 1 may now be rendered totally ineffectual in Year 5.

Some examples of such paradigm shifts are presented in Table 2.2.

Until the early 1930s, the US economy was well-represented by the classical
model. Macroeconomic policies dictated by the model and its underlying
assumptions of wage and price changes fit the economy well. However, the
macroeconomic trauma of the Great Depression of 1929–1933 ushered in a shift to
the Keynesian paradigm (named after the British economist, John Maynard Keynes)
that reigned supreme from the late 1930s and was generally considered to be a
globally effective model. The shift from the classical to the Keynesian model is
now labeled Paradigm Shift 1. Macroeconomic policies dictated by the Keynesian
model—activist fiscal and monetary policies—enabled economists to fine-tune
macrovariables such as inflation and output growth with respectable precision.

This macroeconomic Camelot, however, collapsed in spectacular fashion in the
oil-shock decade of the 1970s. The Great Stagflation of the 1970s in the US
(characterized by double-digit inflation and unemployment) ushered in yet another
paradigm shift to the supply-side model, now described as Paradigm Shift 2.

Table 2.2 Paradigm Shifts from the 1930s to the present

Till early 1930s	Late 1930s to late 1970s	Late 1970s to 9/11/2001	9/11/2001 to about 2010	2010 to present
Classical model	Keynesian model	**Developed economies** Supply-side (rational expectationist) **Or** Keynesian **Emerging economies** Keynesian	Keynesian model	**Developed economies** Supply-side (rational expectationist) **Or** Keynesian **Emerging economies** Keynesian

This paradigm, with its theoretical underpinnings in the "rational expectations" models, has policy implications and assumptions that are fundamentally different from its Keynesian predecessor. Here, the roles of government spending and monetary policy in influencing employment and output are minimal at best. The emphasis is on deregulation, tax cuts, and "less government" in general. Adherents of this model, the supply-siders, have claimed responsibility for the US macroeconomic performance of the 1980s till 2001. In fact, as discussed in Chap. 10, the internet-assisted and technology-driven "new economy" has been linked to the deregulatory backdrop of the 1980s.

We will see, however, that in the US, Paradigm Shift 2 is by no means incontrovertible. As discussed in the preceding chapter, since the early 1980s, both the Keynesian and the supply-sider models have been competing for the center stage of macroeconomic policy dominance. Both models claim distinguished and experienced economists and policy makers as adherents. And both seem to be able to "explain" the behavior of key macroeconomic variables reasonably well.[4] It is this two-model coexistence in the US since the early 1980s that has resulted in the conflicting policy analyses, policies, and interpretations discussed in Chap. 1. This duality of models exists only in developed economies such as the US, Western Europe, and Japan. Emerging economies are well described by individual and incontrovertible macromodels to be discussed in detail in later chapters.

Following 9/11 and then the global sub-prime crisis, the whole planet essentially adopted Keynesian macroeconomic policies for the period 9/11/01 to about 2010. Shocks such as 9/11 required an activist and benevolent government to "step up to the line" and to spend on defense and infrastructure. For a rare period in global macrohistory, virtually all economies—mature as well as emerging—adopted Keynesian stabilization policies. After 2010, however, the two-model dichotomy has once again reared its head in the mature economies. Note that emerging economies are all essentially Keynesian.

Each model will be chronologically discussed in the following chapters, beginning with the classical model, followed by the Keynesian and supply-side models, the New Economy, and ending with the world following 9/11 and the sub-prime crisis. For the US economy at present, the reader will have to decide which model— New Keynesian or supply-sider—is most applicable, based on the information and analyses presented in the following chapters. Unlike other texts, which may steer readers towards one of the two models for the US, this book will not impose the author's choice of the "true" US macroeconomic model. While a strong case could be made to indicate that the US had indeed been required to adopt a conventional Keynesian paradigm in the years following 9/11, a consensus for a single model is still conspicuously absent at present. Given that even the governors of

---

[4]The discussion of the time-series generated Identification Problem in Chap. 10 explains how two very different models with drastically different policy prescriptions can legitimately co-exist and explain macroeconomic behavior equally well.

the Federal Reserve are themselves strongly split, it would be pedagogically inappropriate to unequivocally claim one or the other as the dominant macromodel for the US.

2.2   Some Fundamental Definitions

The total value of a country's output is the gross domestic product, or GDP. In the US, this statistic is measured by the Commerce Department. It is defined as the total market value of all final goods and services produced within a given time period by factors of production located domestically.

This seemingly innocuous definition has several interesting aspects. Only final goods and services are included with their final prices inclusive of all taxes. Intermediate goods are not included to avoid the problem of double-counting. For example, an electronic component that is part of a laptop screen is counted in the price of the final laptop. Including it separately at some earlier stage of the production process would simply double-count the component.

Only goods produced (and services rendered) in the current period are included. Unsold inventory is also included with the emphasis on current production, and not necessarily on market clearance. The sale of a used car, or the resale value of a home, for example, would not be a current GDP statistic as these items have already been included in the year in which they were initially produced.

The goods produced and services rendered must be within the current period, and the output must be produced by factors of production (labor, capital, or land), located within the country, hence, gross "domestic" product. This includes output produced (and profits earned) by foreigners and foreign companies in the domestic country, but does not include output produced by domestic citizens abroad. Profits earned by domestic companies abroad are, similarly, not included.

The less widely used gross national product (GNP) statistic measures the output produced by a country's factors of production (domestic workers), regardless of where the production takes place. The following simple example helps differentiate the GDP and GNP statistics. A Japanese company making light trucks in the US would have all its output included in US GDP. However, only the wages of the American workers employed in the truck factory would be included in US GNP.

In late 1999, the Bureau of Economic Analysis (BEA) significantly revised the measurement of GDP. (i) Business software purchases were included in a component of GDP (specifically in the Equipment and Software component of non-residential fixed investment), (ii) government employees' pensions were reclassified as personal savings, and (iii) a new measure of banking output was designed to measure banking productivity gains more accurately. All these revisions may have boosted the annual growth rate of real GDP by as much as 0.4 % annually in the expansion of the late 1990s.

While GDP is one of the most frequently encountered and tracked statistics, it is far from being a perfect measure. By itself, per capita GDP–total GDP divided by the population—says very little about the overall level of pollution, quality of health care, education, government services, financial and legal institutions, etc.[5] In addition the average per capita GDP ignores the vast asymmetry in income distribution experienced in countries where most of the national wealth is concentrated in only a few individuals. In short, the link from per capita GDP to "quality of life" is often tenuous.

A case could be made that GDP is more of a "twentieth century statistic." In our globalized world, driven by technology, companies often offer apps for free, and efficiencies that reduce costs and improve standards of living may be seen as "negatives" in the manufacturing-driven definition of GDP. Article 2.2 toward the end of this chapter, revisits this subject.

Finally, even if per capita GDP were to increase over time, a large portion of this increase could be due to inflation and not to real increases in output. The next logical step, therefore, is to measure national inflation and to determine the "real" or inflation-adjusted output.

2.2.1   Inflation

Inflation is defined as the percentage rate of change of a price index. Two important and frequently encountered price indexes that allow us to measure inflation are the GDP deflator and the Consumer Price Index (CPI). The following examples will best describe these two frequently encountered indexes.

2.2.2   GDP Deflator

The GDP deflator is a nation-wide generalized price index focusing on the change in prices of goods and services that constitute the GDP. This economy-wide index attempts to determine the percentage change in price for all the goods and services produced in an economy.

$$\text{GDP Deflator} = \text{Nominal GDP}/\text{Real GDP}$$

In the following simple example in Table 2.3, the inflation rate is measured from some benchmark or base year in the past (Year 1) to the current time period (Year 5).

In Year 1, country K produced 15 units of X at \$0.20 per unit, and 50 of Y at \$0.22 per unit. In Year 5, as shown below, it produced more of both goods, but the prices also increased. To calculate the real (physical) increase in the value of

---

[5]For example, the boost in GDP obtained by harvesting every tree in the vast forests of the Pacific Northwest in the US would certainly be dwarfed by the ecological disaster that would follow. In fact, historically, economies experiencing phenomenal GDP growth have often also experienced accompanying increases in pollution; Dickensian England is an oft-cited example.

Table 2.3 Real and nominal GDP

Base year (Year 1)	Current year (Year 5)	Real GDP current year (Year 5)
15 of X at $0.20 = $3.00 50 of Y at $0.22 = $11.00	20 of X at $0.30 = $6.00 60 of Y at $0.25 = $15.00	20 of X at $0.20 = $4.00 60 of Y at $0.22 = $13.20
Total = $14.00 Nominal GDP in Year 1 (in Year 1 dollars)	Total = $21.00 Nominal GDP in Year 5 (in Year 5 dollars)	Total = $17.20 Real GDP in Year 5 is $17.20 (using Year 1 prices)

national output, our first task is to measure the rate of inflation and then to sift it out to compute the real inflation-adjusted increase in GDP.

The nominal GDP from the formula is computed by simply multiplying both quantities and prices of each individual good for the particular year in question. Hence, nominal GDPs for Year 1 and Year 5 are $14.00 and $21.00, as presented in Table 2.3. However, computing a growth rate for GDP based on these numbers would certainly overstate the real increase in output. We need to subtract—deflate— the increase in nominal GDP due to inflation.

The next task, therefore, is the computation of the real GDP in the current year. As displayed in the third column, real GDP is computed by multiplying the quantities produced in the current period (Year 5) not with the current prices, but by our base year (benchmark) prices from Year 1. Real GDP is therefore a more modest $17.20 in Year 5. This is the "real" increase in goods and services from Year 1 to Year 5.

The rate of growth of real GDP is defined as the **"growth rate"** of an economy. A decline in real GDP over two consecutive quarters constitutes a **recession**; this is the unofficial, yet widely accepted, definition of a recession.

Plugging the nominal and real GDP into the deflator formula, we obtain:

$$\text{GDP Deflator} = \frac{21.00}{17.20} = 1.22$$

This simple example indicates an inflation rate of 22 % between Years 1 and 5. Alternatively stated, the nominal GDP of Year 5 has to be "deflated" by 22 % to give us the real or inflation-adjusted GDP.

In actual computations performed by the Commerce Department's BEA that calculates and releases GDP figures, all goods and services included in GDP, along with their respective prices, are included in calculating the deflator. This, however, is not a good measure of the inflation experienced by the typical consumer/ worker/family because it includes goods—heavy-duty steam turbines, for example —that are not typical "household" consumption. For this reason, the Fed prefers to use the **personal consumption expenditures index (PCE)** to gauge inflation at the consumer level. The construction of the PCE is similar to that of the deflator, with the big difference being that it includes goods and services only from the consumption category of the GDP—in the next chapter, we will see how GDP is comprised of Consumption, Capital Investment, Government Spending, and Net Exports.

2.2.3 *Consumer Price Index (CPI)*

In marked contrast to the above index that includes all goods produced in the economy, the more familiar CPI tracks only the rate of change in price of a relatively fixed bundle of goods ("market basket") over time. This market basket is designed to represent the typical monthly consumption of a typically urban family of four, and is also referred to as CPI-u.

Initially constructed during World War 1 as a benchmark for adjusting shipbuilders' wages paid by the US government, the index is computed monthly by the Bureau of Labor Statistics (BLS). On a monthly and bimonthly basis, the BLS collects price information of around 96,000 goods and services—everything from mouse pads to mangoes is included. Every month, the Department of Labor sends a team of observers to 23,000 stores in 87 cities to record the most current prices. These items are then placed into eight major expenditure categories to finally produce one price index, the CPI, computed as follows.[6]

$$CPI = \frac{\sum P_i q_0}{\sum P_0 q_0},$$

where
P_i current prices
q_0 "fixed" market basket (consumption bundle)
P_0 base year prices

In the following table, the first column represents the "fixed" market basket composed of 15 of X and 50 of Y. It is the change in price of this consumption bundle over time that will give us the CPI (Table 2.4).

The denominator in the formula is simply the nominal value of the market basket in Year 1 dollars. The numerator is the price of the "fixed" Year 1 basket in Year 5 (current year) dollars. This is computed in the column on the extreme right.

Hence, the CPI is

$$CPI = \frac{17}{14} = 1.21.$$

This indicates 21 % inflation in the fixed market basket from Years 1–5, in this simplified example. Since the CPI measures the cost incurred by a typical family in buying a representative market basket, it is also known as the **cost-of-living** index.

---

[6]The eight categories along with their general expenditure proportions are housing (43 %), food and beverages (15 %), transportation (17 %), medical care (7 %), entertainment (6 %), education and communication (6 %), apparel and upkeep (4 %), and other (about 2 %).

Table 2.4 Computing the CPI

Base year (Year 1)	Current year (Year 5)	To get $\sum P_i q_0$
15 of X at \$0.20 = \$3.00	20 of X at \$0.30 = \$6.00	15 of X at \$0.30 = \$4.50
50 of Y at \$0.22 = \$11.00	60 of Y at \$0.25 = \$15.00	50 of Y at \$0.25 = \$12.50
$\sum P_0 q_0 = \$14.00$	Total = \$21.00	$\sum P_i q_0 = \$17.00$

The rigidity in the composition of the "fixed" market basket has always been known to cause the CPI to overstate the actual inflation rate. In fact, the 1996 Boskin Commission found this amount of overstatement to be as much as 1.1 %.[7]

This overstatement is actually a very significant issue. In addition to measuring inflation, the CPI also measures the change in the cost of living for the urban population of the US, which accounts for approximately 81 % of the total population. It forms the basis for annual benefits adjustments to recipients of Social Security benefits and food stamps, funding for school lunches and other programs, workers whose long-term wage contracts are determined by collective bargaining and non-government sectors that use the CPI as a benchmark for future wage changes. Income tax brackets, interest on inflation-indexed bonds (I-bonds), and exemptions and deductions computed by the IRS are also distorted by overstated inflation.

The overstatement can be primarily attributed to four factors:

(i) **Substitution Bias**

The CPI does not capture the fact that when the price of a particular good increases, consumers quickly shift to a substitute good whose price may not have increased by as much.

(ii) **New Product Bias**

This occurs when new goods and services are introduced into an economy but not yet incorporated into the fixed weights of the market basket. Air conditioners in the 1950s, and mobile phones and laptops in the 1990s, for example, were included years after their introduction. These new products typically experience sharp drops in price within the first few years of introduction, with this initial price decline not being captured by the CPI. In sectors such as consumer electronics and entertainment, avionics, medical technology, and nanoscience (just to name a few), the rate of introduction of new products and services renders even a one-year-old market baskets obsolete.

(iii) **Quality Bias**

It is increasingly difficult, especially in technologically advanced economies, to separate simple changes in price from changes in quality. New video equipment and new medical technology, for example, may be significantly more expensive in the current year, but may easily outperform the corresponding items that constitute a market basket from some earlier base year.

---

[7]Named after Stanford University Professor, Michael Boskin, chairman of the committee. While it was clear for some time that the CPI was overstating actual inflation, the Boskin commission systematically estimated this value.

The BLS does indeed attempt to make adjustments for increases in quality. Inflation in the auto sector from 1967 to the present would have been far higher if this had not been done. Since 1992, the US has also been making quality adjustments for hardware in the information technology (IT) sector. Nevertheless, quality bias, which is linked to the new product bias, remains a challenge for the BLS.

(iv) **Outlet Substitution**

More consumers, both in the US as well abroad, are shopping in outlet malls. Furthermore, sophisticated supply chain management has resulted in generations of discount stores such as Walmart that can sell significantly below standard retail prices. If these stores are not fully represented in the CPI, an upward bias may result in the final inflation figure.

To remedy the bias problem, from 1998 the BLS has switched from updating the weights and composition of the market basket from every ten years to every two years. This shorter period should provide more timely and flexible measure of consumer spending patterns that, in turn, should give us a more accurate measure of inflation. Mobile phones and auto leases were included in a new category in 1998, labeled "education and communication", and personal computers were given a greater role.

This more frequent revision of the composition of the market basket will, hopefully, ensure that the consumption bundle is more in line with current consumption patterns, thereby resulting in a more accurate measure of inflation.

2.2.4 The PCE Deflator: The Index Used by the Fed

Given the recent emphasis on the goal of price stability both in the US as well as in the Eurozone, central banks—despite the popularity of the CPI—have de-emphasized the CPI because of its biases in overstating the true underlying rate of inflation, and have, instead, focused more on the PCE.

In fact, in 2000, the Fed announced a switch to the PCE for three reasons

(i) The PCE is a chain-type index. With advances in sectors such technology, health care, and communications, it was found that many goods produced in the current period (Year 5) were not even in existence in Year 1. Or, alternatively, the base year counterparts of goods in Year 5 (computers, mobile phones, etc.,) were simply not in the same league in terms of productivity and performance.

To remedy this problem, the BEA adopted a chain index for calculating real GDP with the base year now just one year behind the current year. In our simple example, the average of the prices of Year 4 and Year 5 would be used for computing the real GDP in Year 5, instead of the Year 1 prices, as done earlier. Presumably, Year 4 would have more of the items produced in Year 5, and these items would be closer in quality and performance to current items than those produced in Year 1. For the following year (6), a moving average of prices of Years 5 and 6 would be computed as "base year" prices, and so on. Hence, real GDP is now often presented in chained dollars, and the PCE is essentially the rectified equivalent of the GDP Deflator.

(ii)   The PCE is a broader measure of inflation, as it includes more goods and services than the CPI.

(iii) Past values of the PCE can be recalibrated as more sophisticated methods of measuring prices and capturing new data become available.

In 2004, the Fed announced that it would track a sub-category of the PCE called the **core PCE**. The core rate of inflation is simply the inflation measured by the PCE minus price increases (changes) in food and fuel. This is done to sift away the exogenous (external) factors causing inflation and to allow policy makers to focus on the component of inflation caused by domestic endogenous influences such as excess consumer and investor demand. Since mid-2012, the Fed has announced that it will adopt the core-PCE deflator as its preferred inflation measure. After all, as we discuss later in Chap. 5, the endogenous inflation (caused by internal demand pressures) is really the only inflation that central banks can counter with appropriate monetary policy.

We now turn to discussion questions followed by simulated "media articles" in which concepts covered in this chapter will be presented in the form in which macroeconomic information is usually encountered in our professional and personal lives.

2.3   Discussion Questions

The following Q&A section highlights some additional aspects of these inflation indexes.

(1)   *Since both the CPI and the chained-type price index (deflator) measure inflation, why do we often see a "spike" in one and not the other?*
       The deflator includes all goods and services that constitute GDP, but the CPI does not. However, the CPI includes imports, which are not included in the deflator. Typically when oil prices surge, for example, a spike in the CPI is observed while the deflator seems to be unaffected, at least during the particular period. Additionally, the two indexes are not always synchronized; the CPI is measured monthly, whereas the deflator is available only quarterly.

(2)   *Is one index superior to the other? Which index must one use?*
       The CPI suffers from substitution bias, while the PCE index, does not. While this bias has caused the US Federal Reserve to switch from the CPI to the PCE index as its primary gauge for measuring inflation and prescribing policy, the CPI still remains very much alive in that it determines adjustments to social security benefits, pension payments, etc. Furthermore, recent improvements to the CPI's market basket are designed to continuously reduce substitution and outlet biases and to align the CPI more closely with the deflator (PCE).

Generally, very rarely do policy makers examine just one index—CPI or PCE—in isolation. An array of more specialized indexes are also consulted, such as the PPI (producer price index), and the forward-looking CRB (Commodities Research Bureau) index. Other examples include the precious metals index, employment cost index, and the feed-and-seed index. Smaller economies such as Singapore, where foreign trade constitutes a significantly larger proportion of domestic GDP compared to that for the US, would have a greater role for exchange rate influences that affect the price of vital imports such as fuel and food.

(3) *The PPI is another eagerly awaited number. Is it similar to the CPI?*

The PPI is indeed calculated in similar fashion. It measures the wholesale prices of approximately 3500 items and was, in fact, formerly known as the wholesale price index. However, its implications are quite different from those of the CPI and the chained-price deflator. The PPI includes many raw materials and semi-finished goods in the early stage of the supply chain. Therefore, movements in the PPI serve as leading indicators of future price movements at the retail level captured "later" by the CPI and the deflator. This often results in the PPI being one of the more eagerly awaited statistics when expectations of resurgent inflation are high. Another noteworthy index of future inflation is the monthly FIBER (Foundation for International Business and Economic Research). This index focuses on <u>expected</u> labor and raw materials shortages in the near future.

(4) *Should central banks strive for zero inflation?*

Given the fact that—revisions to the market basket notwithstanding—most G7 economies' CPIs tend to overstate the actual cost of living, a zero percent inflation target as measured by the CPI may conceivably correspond to a negative inflation rate in reality![8] These economies would experience deflation with across-the-board average decreases in prices of real estate, stocks, manufacturing, wages, etc., reminiscent of the agony experienced by Japan in the 1990s and into the 2000s, and in the Eurozone in 2015. In later chapters, we will examine how some central banks aim, instead, for stable inflation rates of 1–2 %, rather than potentially deflationary absolute values such as "zero inflation." Unfortunately, though, when banks adopt targets of, say, 2 % (corresponding to actual inflation of, perhaps, 0.5 %), unions and others often tend to misinterpret this as a sign that the central bank is prepared to tolerate a little inflation. They may then push for 2 % wage increases, thereby actually contributing to actual future increases in inflation!

(5) *Finally, since measured inflation tends to overstate the actual cost of living in most economies, does this imply that there is some globally standardized index of measuring inflation?*

While the technique of computing the price indexes in different countries is similar, the market baskets are, unfortunately, not. For example, unlike the

---

[8]The G7 economies are Canada, France, Germany, Italy, Japan, the UK, and the US. With Russia included, we have the G8.

other G7 countries, the UK's retail-price index includes interest payments on home loans. The former Soviet Union did not include many costs of services. Economies like Singapore, that have relatively large trade sectors, have proportionally greater emphasis on traded, exchange-rate sensitive goods such as water, fuel, and food, in addition to re-exports, compared to the US.[9] And Japan's CPI excludes many popular goods such as mobile phones and personal computers. Attempts at convergence are, however, gradually being made—China, for example, switched from using a retail-price index to a more standardized CPI in 2000.

Article 2.2 provides more details pertaining to the choice of deflators in the US, France, and Germany which adjust for quality improvements, particularly in the IT sector.

In the following simulated articles, please comment on/define/explain the underlined phrases/sentences with reference to material from this chapter.

ARTICLE 2.1 CHOOSE YOUR INFLATION TARGET

Fred Burdekin, The <u>New York Ledger</u>[10]

Last week's comments regarding the "right" level of inflation by the Chief Economist of the National Chapter of Certified Accountants have sparked what seems to be a national debate. Even talk-show hosts are in on the act, espousing their personal views on the subject! This newspaper decided to randomly interview some Americans from different walks of life, to get a perspective on what they are thinking on Main Street, USA.

"Why don't they just **(a)** <u>aim for zero inflation? Seems straightforward! Why argue over whether it (target inflation) should be 1 or 2 %? Hey, zero is best!</u>" was Sam Trivenni's comment, as he emerged from his police car in Houston, Texas. Sam is a police veteran of 17 years, and assists wife Judy when he can in her pet grooming business.

---

[9]Singapore's trade sector (imports plus exports and including re-exports) as a percentage of its GDP is often in 160–180 % range, while the US typically has a trade/GDP ratio of 22–25 %.

[10] All "articles" have been created by the author and, as discussed in Chap. 1, are designed to mimic actual reporting of macroeconomic events by the news media. The objective, as discussed earlier, is to allow managers and executives to relate concepts discussed in the chapter to macroeconomic news and analyses presented by the media on a daily basis. The names ascribed to the newspapers and magazines, and to the individuals "quoted" in the articles as well as listed as "authors" are purely fictional. Any resemblance to any existing publication or persons is coincidental. This endnote applies to all "articles" in all chapters of this book.

Mary Etawills of Wills Travels Agency in Blacksburg, Virginia, disagrees. "I'm no rocket scientist, but it seems like some inflation would be good. We want the prices of houses and other assets to go up, don't we?"

The inflation debate affects individuals of all age groups. Edna Winterbauer, resident of Memories Retirement Home in Fayetteville, Arkansas, is con-cerned. (b) "The only increase I ever get in my social security check is cost-of-living. Will zero inflation mean no increases for us retired people? No, I don't like it!"

Mohit Sharma, an IT consultant in San Francisco, takes time out from his latte break at Starbird's to talk to us. He feels that "the indexes are quite confusing. I noticed that (c) often the CPI rises sharply, but the other major indicators do not. Just have

one index and try not to confuse the public." His co-worker, Shifra Bergstrum, added, "I don't even think that the indexes are accurate. I mean, (d) I remember when inflation was 'low' according to the indexes, but it was impossible to afford a house in the Northeast or here on the West Coast? It just doesn't make sense!"

In Colorado, digital spectroscope manufacturer John Zalinsky, who imports electronic components from Asia, went on to say that, "the strong dollar makes my costs of basic electronic components imported from Southeast Asia much lower, and (e) hence, my final product, many steps down the supply chain, is cheaper. This has to decrease inflation. Is this figured in the inflation measurement?" Lots of opinions. Lots of ideas. The debate rages.

ARTICLE 2.2 INFORMATION TECHNOLOGY AND MACRO-DATA

David Mandelstamm, Frankfurt Business Policy Review

Comparing global growth figures has become even more of a challenge in recent years because of the different statistical methods employed by countries to account for changes in quality of output. One major component within this category is the (a) change in the quality of computers.

As the G7 economies have increased capital investment in information technology (IT)

hardware, the magnitude of the potential statistical error in measuring (b) real GDP growth has increased proportionally.

"Measuring the real output of, say, crude oil or coal over time is relatively easy. With computing technology, however, the change in quality every year is so significant that it is really very hard to separate an increase in nominal output or spending between a change in price and a change in volume," remarked Prof. Eugenie Moulin of Tourainne Macroscience Labs, in Tours, France.

Given the massive increases in speed and memory in IT hardware, American statisticians have adopted techniques for adjusting for quality improvements in computers when computing GDP deflators. Within the eurozone, though, only France uses this adjustment technique; Germany does not.

"This adjustment for quality isn't just a matter for statisticians and macroeconomic purists", states Professor Moulin. "This makes a very significant difference."

From 1992 till the present, the (c) price deflator for IT equipment in the US has fallen by over 80 %. In other words, nominal output in the IT hardware sector is deflated by 80 % compared to the amount for 1992 to account for a bias in inflation measurement.

Since Germany does not adjust for this bias, the deflator for IT has shrunk by only 20 %. The implication is that growth in the real IT investment in Germany is understated and so is its real GDP.

In fact, studies by the Macro Institute in Frankfurt (among others) find that if Germany's nominal capital investment in IT were to be deflated by the relatively smaller US GDP deflator, then German investment has grown by an average of 29 % a year since 1992. This is in stark contrast to the 6 % growth figure reported in official government (German) statistics!

(d) Japanese statistics in this area are, in fact, even more distorted. "The Asian economies along with the eurozone economies need to be aware of the measurement differences that exist between their countries and the US, before they design macro-economic policy," states Lord Larry Duncan, a financial analyst an owner of WorldSoft, an IT consulting house based in London.

We find macroeconomic experts everywhere to be well aware of the measurement problems. "No wonder the French statistics (regarding capital investment in IT) look so good!" exclaims Victor Gulli, Senior Economist at Rome's Modigliani Center. "We should all be using the US method which the French have adopted—it just makes sense!" He waves expansively towards his computer sitting beside a window with an amazing view of the Eternal City. "Look, I just bought this last year, and already my teenage son's laptop, which he bought last month, can do more. And he paid less!"

In fact, if American statistical methods were to be applied to the entire eurozone, then its (e) annual growth rate might be at least half a percentage point higher than it has been since the late 1990s.

ANSWERS AND HINTS

ARTICLE 2.1 CHOOSE YOUR INFLATION TARGET

(a) Zero inflation may actually lead to deflation, since inflation is usually over-stated. Deflation is usually symptomatic of an economy in collapse, with average prices of assets falling across the board. Mary Etawills in the fol-lowing paragraph has the right hunch.

(b) This is not just an academic exercise. An inflation-indexed increase is often the only source of increase for those on fixed incomes—correcting the over-stated inflation actually "hurts" these folks.

(c) The CPI includes imports, namely oil. The PCE does not. So when oil shocks slam into the economy, the CPI rises while the deflator remains dormant.

(d) This is average rate of inflation for the whole economy. In some cases, the overall rate of inflation may seem low but could mask high and rising inflation in certain specific sectors. Hence, the increased focus on the notion of spec-ulative asset price (SAP) bubbles in sectors such as IT, the stock market, and in real estate. This will be discussed in Chap. 5.

(e) The PPI would be the relevant statistic here. Please refer to discussions per-taining to the "early-warning" potential of this inflation statistic.

ARTICLE 2.2 INFORMATION TECHNOLOGY AND MACRO-DATA

(a) Which bias is being discussed here?

(b) Business purchases of software are now included in capital investments (I). Clearly, rapid increases in technology and related IT products have unleashed a host of complications in measuring accurate GDP statistics—biases abound.

(c) This is a special deflator for the IT sector, primarily hardware. If the deflator for the US has shrunk by 80 % this means that nominal IT output in the current year has to be deflated now by only 20 % compared to 1992. Why?

(d) Please give an example of these Japanese "distortions" from earlier in the chapter.

(e) As discussed, the annual growth rate of an economy is simply the per capita growth rate of real GDP.

Chapter 3
Budget Deficits, Trade Deficits, and Global Capital Flows: The National Savings Identity

In this cornerstone chapter, the vitally important **National Savings Identity (NSI)**, linking trade and budget balances to global capital flows, interest rates, and exchange rates, makes its first appearance. In many ways, this chapter, linking the "twin deficits" in a fundamentally intuitive manner, sets the tone for macroeconomic policies to be discussed in following chapters.

To some extent, this chapter will be examining past macroeconomic episodes in the US, Europe, and Asia, characterized by record budget and trade deficits. For example, the 1980s and post-9/11 US bond-financed budget deficits, the early 1990s post-unification German experience, the Mexican and Southeast Asian currency crises of the mid- to late-1990s will be explored in detail. The more recent global capital flows beginning with the 2008 subprime crisis (also known as the Great Recession), and the massive "flights to safety" of global capital into the United States and Switzerland since 2014, will be discussed here.

The current US trade and capital flows with China will also be highlighted in this chapter. An NSI analysis of the massive global capital inflows that, in varying degrees, helped to fund the internet-driven economy in the US from the late 1990s, and later the housing bubble, will be a prime focus of this chapter. Using the NSI, we will see how, despite record low national savings and record-high national consumption, the mammoth capital inflows, directly related to the unprecedented US current account deficits (loosely, trade deficits), may have helped finance the so-called "new" economy, the immense increase in fiscal spending on defense and homeland security since 9/11, and household spending on real estate in the US from 2003 to the present. In addition, we will examine the potential pitfalls of large global capital inflows as well as the sudden outflows of "hot capital" such as those that traumatized the Southeast Asian economies in 1997–1998 and then again in the 2010–2015 period.

© Springer International Publishing Switzerland 2016
F. Langdana, *Macroeconomic Policy*, Springer Texts in Business and Economics, DOI 10.1007/978-3-319-32854-6_3

3.1 The National Savings Identity (NSI)

If Y is the value of domestic output (real GDP, from Chap. 2), and if imports of goods and services are denoted as "Imp," the total goods and services available in an economy will be (Y + Imp). This total output is equal to the sum of the private consumption expenditure (C) which accounts for almost 70 % of GDP in the US, capital investment expenditure (I), government expenditure on goods and services (G), and foreign consumption denoted as exports (Exp).

Algebraically, this can be expressed as

$$Y + Imp = C + I + G + Exp$$

Simplifying, we get

$$Y = C + I + G + (Exp - Imp) \tag{3.1}$$

where
Y   National output.
C   Private consumption expenditure (Personal Consumption Expenditure). This is household spending on goods and services but not including household spending on new homes.
I   Capital investment. This includes spending by firms on new plant and equipment, office buildings, machinery, and inventories. This term also includes household spending on new homes.
G   Government expenditure on goods and services.
Exp Exports of goods and services (foreign consumption).
Imp Imports of goods and services.

Capital investment (I) is not to be confused with investing in the stock market and in mutual funds, for example. This latter kind of investing falls under "savings" in macroeconomics. Instead, the "I" in Eq. (3.1) pertains to capital investment as in new construction, purchasing new hardware, housing, and plant and equipment. It usually necessitates the borrowing of loanable funds, and we will soon see how it is closely linked to interest rates.

Since October 1999, in a nod to the internet-driven economy, the Bureau of Economic Analysis (BEA) has redefined capital investment to also include business purchases of computer software. By some estimates, including software purchases in (I) may have boosted annual real GDP growth by about 0.1 % in the late 1990s and early 2000s.

If Y goods and services are produced and sold in this economy, the income obtained from the sale of goods of value Y will be Y dollars. This national income, in turn, is used for private consumption (C), part of it is saved (S), and part is devoured by net tax revenues (T), which are taxes paid minus transfers received.

This is represented algebraically

$$Y = C + S + T \tag{3.2}$$

where
Y   Income from sale of goods of value Y
C   Private consumption expenditure
S   Private savings
T   Net tax revenues.

Simply put, expression (3.1) describes how the available output is distributed, while (3.2) above describes how the income from the sale of the output is divided between national consumption, savings, and taxes.

Equating (3.1) and (3.2) we obtain

$$C + I + G + (Exp - Imp) = C + S + T$$

Simplifying further, we finally get the **National Savings Identity**:

$$(G{-}T) = (S{-}I) + (Imp{-}Exp) \tag{3.3}$$

The term (G − T), the difference between government spending and national tax revenues, represents the national budget balance. If (G − T) is positive, then national budget deficits are incurred as government spending exceeds tax revenues, and if (G − T) is negative, then the national budget is in surplus.[1]

The last term (Imp − Exp), is defined as the current account balance. If (Imp − Exp) is positive, this economy experiences a current account deficit, and a current account surplus if the balance is negative. The current account statistic is reported quarterly and includes trade (exports minus imports) in goods and services, along with global net investment income, and net unilateral transfers (foreign aid or transfers received from abroad). At this point, for notational convenience, investment income and transfers from abroad are subsumed by the term (Exp), while incomes paid (and transfers made) to foreigners constitute outflows of funds, and are included in the term (Imp).

It should be noted that the more familiar "trade balance" reported monthly includes only merchandise trade—goods that clear customs and require paperwork such as bills of lading at ports. The service sector, in which the US has a surplus, while included in the current account balance, is however not fully included in the more familiar trade balance.[2]

---

[1]Some examples of budget deficits are the US budget deficits of the mid-1980s and since 9/11, the Japanese and Belgian budget deficits of the early 2000s. Examples of surpluses are the US surpluses of the late 1990s to 2001, as well as the national balances of most Southeast Asian countries in the late-1990s to the early 2000s.

[2]The current account balance is reported only quarterly unlike the monthly trade balance because services are often intangibles and take time to record accurately. Services do not pass through customs, are harder to measure, and are not reported as frequently as goods crossing international borders.

To appreciate the full potential of the NSI, the next logical task is to explore the fundamental macroeconomic intuition underlying it. The immediate observation is that the two balances—budget and current account—are inextricably linked. We begin by assuming that the domestic economy incurs simultaneous budget and current account deficits; (G − T) and (Imp − Exp) are both positive in (3.3).

Exactly what is the mechanism by which these "twin deficits" are linked? Furthermore, what is the direction of causality? Do budget deficits "cause" current account deficits, or vice versa?

The first step is to examine the left-hand-side of (3.3), and review how national budget deficits are financed. Three broad methods of deficit financing are

1. **Borrowing from Domestic and Foreign Residents**. Here the domestic deficit-incurring government issues (sells) government bonds. In the case of the US, the Treasury is the bond-issuing entity, and the debt instruments (Treasury bills, bonds) are really discount bonds sold at below face value in national auctions. In this case, the interest rate is endogenous and determined by the market supply and demand for domestic government debt at each individual auction. (The concept of "endogeneity" alluded to in the previous chapter, will be explained in the following Sect. 3.1.1.)
2. **Monetization**. Here the central bank is forced to "print money" to pay for outstanding government debt, or is said to "monetize" the deficit. This is clearly not a viable deficit financing option, and detailed discussions of high inflation and hyperinflation in later chapters will bear testimony to the disastrous consequences of rampant monetization.
3. **Debt repudiation**. This is simply a national default on government debt, and, once again, certainly not a viable deficit financing option. (For the sake of completeness, another "option" is the one-time sale of national resources. One example is the sale of gold reserves and oil by Russia following the dissolution of the USSR in the early 1990s. This financing option would be a one-time measure at best.)

3.1.1   Two Crucial Assumptions Underlying the NSI

(1)   Deficits are completely bond financed.

We restrict the following discussion and analysis to the case where national budget deficits are incurred by an economy with responsible fiscal and monetary policy and are <u>mostly if not entirely bond financed</u>, as in the case of the US deficits since the 1980s and in the years immediately following 9/11, the German post-unification deficits as well as most Eurozone deficit financing at the present. (The assumption of responsible macropolicy will be relaxed in later chapters.)

(2) **Fiscal and monetary credibility is sound.**

The central bank has a long-standing reputation of monetary discipline, and will not be pressured by the government to monetize any runaway deficits caused by profligate government spending. The political climate is stable. The national debt is "risk free" or low risk. (The notion of "safe haven" being a distinctly relative status in an increasingly risky world will be addressed.)

At this stage, a short overview of microeconomics is in order. Specifically, the notion of endogenous variables and the shifting of demand and supply curves will be vital to fully appreciate the ISLM-ADAS model which is the "engine room" of this book.

3.1.1.1 Microeconomics Review

The following Fig. 3.1a and b present simple demand and supply plots. As an example, we use the market for the most technologically advanced household communications device—the Ultimate Phone. As prices increase, all other variables staying unchanged, quantity demanded of phones decreases in Fig. 3.1a; as prices increase, quantity supplied increases in Fig. 3.1b, and vice versa. Both the plots depict changes in quantities demanded and supplied for a hypothetical range of prices.

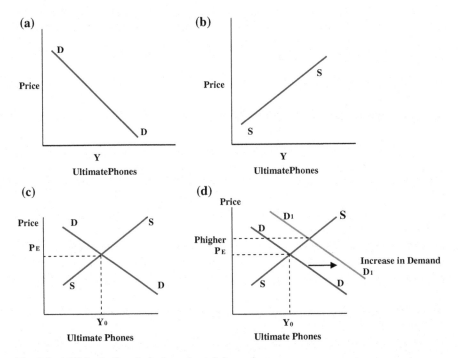

Fig. 3.1 A "lightning" review of supply and demand

Superimposing Fig. 3.1b on to Fig. 3.1a, we get Fig. 3.1c, a simple market-clearing diagram for Ultimate Phones. The market equilibrium price for these phones is given by the intersection of supply and demand—where supply equals demand—denoted by P_E, with Y_0 phones sold, and no unsold inventory or shortage.

This market-clearing equilibrium price is determined "endogenously," or "from within the market" by supply and demand forces. For instance, if all conventional phones were to suddenly become inoperative, there would be an increase in demand for Ultimate Phones at all prices. In Fig. 3.1d, this increase in demand results in a new demand curve located to the right of the existing curve, denoted "Higher Demand." Diagrammatically, the increase in demand translates to a shift to the right in the demand curve, while a decrease in demand causes the demand curve to shift to the left.

In Fig. 3.1d, we have superimposed the original supply curve on this new demand curve, and as a result the equilibrium price (point of intersection) is now higher. Here, prices of Ultimate Phones increased endogenously due to the increase in demand characterized by the rightward shift in the demand curve.

Shifts in both supply and demand curves, or in either of them separately, will affect the endogenous prices of cellular phones. For example, an increase in supply resulting from a massive increase in Ultimate Phone production from global production or imports would shift the supply curve to the right, thereby endogenously driving down equilibrium prices, and vice versa.

While this is a purely "micro" example confining itself to the specific market for phones, in later chapters this concept of endogeneity will be extremely important. The notion that changes in market-clearing "prices" of equilibrium variables are driven by market forces, and not by central planning committees (as in the former Soviet Union), will be applied to macroeconomic variables such as interest rates, exchange rates, GDP, wages, employment, and inflation.

3.1.2 Linking the Twin Deficits

Coming back to the National Savings Identity, we now explore how the budget and current account balances may be linked by the NSI expression

$$(G - T) = (S - I) + (Imp - Exp).$$

By virtue of the assumptions of deficits being bond financed in a safe haven economy, the left-hand-side of the NSI is in fact a demand for borrowing, while the right-hand-side, in equilibrium, constitutes a supply of lending, as presented below.

$(G - T) =$	$(S - I) + (Imp - Exp)$
Demand for borrowing (Demand for loanable funds)	Supply of loanable funds

Fig. 3.2 The National
Savings Identity

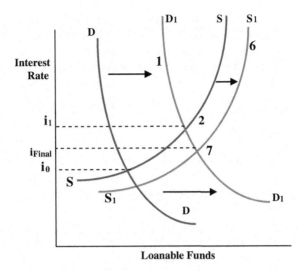

The above Fig. 3.2, presents a market for loanable funds, with the initial interest rate i_0 obtained where demand for borrowing exactly equals the supply of lending. Here i_0 is the endogenously determined equilibrium interest rate prevailing in this economy. The interest rate on risk-free, short-term domestic government bonds could serve as a good proxy for i_0.

The following steps 1–7 present the macroeconomic intuition linking the twin deficits.[3] Steps 1, 2, 6, and 7 are also included in Fig. 3.2.

1. As the central government incurs a budget deficit that has to be financed by borrowing (since we assume no monetization here), the demand for loanable funds increases and the curve DD accordingly shifts to the right to D_1D_1.
2. This increase in demand drives up domestic interest rates to the higher equilibrium, i_1.
3. The time has come to extend our analysis to the global sector. As interest rates of these safe haven domestic government bonds exceed those of other countries, domestic and foreign investors now "switch" to the higher yielding and safe domestic government debt.[4] (Actually, interest rate differences are not the only factors driving global capital flows. As we will discuss later in this chapter, an economy's long-term macroeconomic outlook is vitally important in order to attract global capital.) These investors, who include individuals, life insurance companies, global investment houses, governments, central banks, etc., need to

---

[3]The steps are purely for the purpose of pedagogic intuition. They loosely follow the direction of causality from budget deficits to current account deficits for one particular borrowing cycle.

[4]These are 'real' or inflation-adjusted interest rates. At this point, given no monetization, we assume that the interest rates are indeed real rates. This will be discussed in detail while covering nominal and real rates in Chap. 6.

swap their respective currencies for domestic currency, e.g., yuan or yen or euro for US\$, with the US being the "domestic" country in this example. This excess demand for domestic currency—US dollars—makes this currency "more expensive" in terms of foreign currency in the global foreign exchange markets. That is, the domestic currency appreciates (gets "stronger") relative to foreign currencies. A hypothetical example of US currency appreciation would be

Before step (1) 1 US\$ = 100 units of foreign currency.
After step (1) 1 US\$ = 120 units of foreign currency.

4. With the strengthening of the domestic currency, imports now become "cheaper" for domestic residents, while domestic exports become more "expensive" to foreign consumers who have to exchange more units of their currencies for one unit of domestic currency.
5. Hence, as imports surge and as exports slow, the current account balance (Exp − Imp) decreases and the domestic budget deficit-incurring economy eventually experiences a deterioration in its current account balance. In this scenario, the "twin deficits" are indeed linked. Here, the budget imbalance (G − T) drives the NSI and, by influencing interest rates and exchanges rates, results in a decrease in the current account balance and perhaps eventually in a current account deficit.

During the 1980s and since 2002 for the US and the early 1990s for Germany, for example, the twin deficits did indeed exhibit strong positive covariance for both these economies. Both countries had to resort to large bond issuances to finance their significant budget deficits: the Americans financing the mammoth budget deficits and later, their massive household consumption, and the Germans struggling to finance their post-unification outlays stemming from infrastructure demands of the former East Germany.

6. As the domestic economy amasses cheaper imports, foreigners accumulate deposits of domestic currency. For example, the US accumulates imports from Japan and China, while these two current account surplus countries amass massive dollar deposits. These dollar deposits are then promptly reinvested in the safe haven, high-yielding domestic economy (the US, in this example). That is, the domestic economy incurs a current account deficit but also experiences an inflow of capital—a capital account surplus. This is reflected in move (6) where the inflow results in an increase in the supply of loanable funds, thereby causing the curve to shift to the right from SS to S_1S_1.
7. Finally, thanks to this capital inflow, equilibrium interest rates in the domestic economy are now lowered to i_{Final}. Capital inflows supplement domestic savings (supply of loanable funds), and thereby exert an important ameliorating influence on domestic interest rates.

Almost 40–60 % of the US deficit in the 1980s and post-9/11 periods, and virtually 100 % of US interest expenses on government debt were funded by massive capital inflows associated with the US current account deficits.

The inflow is not just limited to absorbing vast additional amounts of domestic government debt. In fact, from the early 2000s, huge net capital inflows from Asia (mostly Japan and China) have financed auto plants, real estate ventures, mortgage-backed securities (much to their chagrin), and significant portions of the high-skilled labor-intensive manufacturing sector. In fact, one in eight US manufacturing jobs since the late 1990s is in a company owned by a foreign affiliate. In addition, an astounding number of startups in the information technology (IT) sector—particularly in the heyday of the new economy—were funded by mammoth capital inflows tied to the unprecedented US current account deficits.

Under the assumptions made earlier, a country incurring a current account deficit (loosely, trade deficit) will also experience a capital account surplus (net capital inflow). The capital account surplus and the current account deficit are two sides of the same coin. This form of bond financing sounds extremely convenient. The budget-deficit-incurring country experiences a current account deficit but also benefits from capital inflows that serve to keep interest rates lower at home. How long is this sustainable?

At this point, a "sustainable" bond-financed deficit is defined as that which can be rolled over perpetually by issuing additional bonds when the current bonds come due. As per the Dornbusch model of deficit sustainability, as long as the inflation-adjusted (or "real") rate on government bonds is less than the growth rate of the economy, deficits are defined to be sustainable and the NSI bond-financing model can be implemented with impunity.

A "non-sustainable" deficit, however, is that which has exploded out of control and cannot be bond-financed any longer; domestic and foreign investors refuse to absorb any more of this government's debt in their portfolios. A massive monetization becomes inevitable, and this is typically followed by an ensuing and mind-numbing hyperinflation. Here the real interest "lost" on government debt exceeds the growth rate of the economy.[5]

The Dornbusch Model of Fiscal Deficit Sustainability

From: International Trade and Global Macropolicy, Farrokh Langdana and Peter Murphy, Springer, 2014.

Rudiger Dornbusch established that bond-financed budget deficits are sustainable if the Debt/GDP ratio is not growing over time. Let us be sure to distinguish "debt" from "deficit"

Debt = All bonds outstanding from the dawn of time to the present. This is a cumulative number.
Deficit = By default, this is the Federal Budget Deficit, $(G - T)$, and this is an annual number.

---

[5]Seminal work in the area of budget deficit sustainability was done by Sargent and Wallace in their influential 'Some Unpleasant Monetarist Arithmetic', Federal Reserve Bank of Minneapolis Quarterly Review, Winter 1985.

The ability of a government to continuously finance its budget deficits depends not just on the size of the annual deficit, $(G - T)$, but also on interest rates, inflation, and the growth rate of the economy. Interest rates affect a country's cost-of-service debt, which, at a high debt/GDP ratio (above 60–70 %) becomes significant. Inflation—especially, unexpected inflation—reduces the value of the outstanding debt that the government has to pay back. Unexpected inflation erodes the purchasing power of the loans as they mature, hence transferring real purchasing power from lenders to the government. Lenders getting paid back after lending funds to the Treasury for N years finds that now have diminished purchasing power, due to the inflation over the period of the duration of the loan.

Dornbusch determined that:
b^0 = d + (the real purchasing power "lost" by paying interest on government debt − the growth rate of the economy).

We will revisit the notion of real interest rates in detail, later in Chap. 6, when we explore The Fisher effect. As long as $b^0 \leq 0$, bond-financed deficits are defined to be sustainable. In other words if the debt/GDP ratio is 57 % in year 1 and 56.2 % in year 2, and 54 % in year 3, then b^0 is <0, and the stream of deficit financing is sustainable.

If, on the other hand, the debt/GDP ratio were growing over time from, say, 57 % in year 1 to 58.9 % in year 2, and 59.9 % in year 3, the b^0 is >0 and the bond-financed deficits are defined to be "nonsustainable"; very simply this present time-path of deficit financing cannot be sustained. Eventually, domestic and foreign residents will shy away from lending to this country, and the only recourse will be a horrible and crippling monetization.

A loose rule of thumb for G7 economies is that sustainability usually implies a budget deficit/GDP ratio of less than 5 %. Even more stringent, however, is the criterion of the 1991 Maastricht Treaty to qualify for membership in the European Monetary Union (EMU) that specifies a budget deficit/GDP ratio of less than 3 %. Emerging economies, which will be discussed later in the chapter on Keynes, typically have higher sustainability benchmarks with acceptable budget deficit/GDP ratios well in excess of those of their more developed G7 counterparts.

3.2   Possible Negative Aspects of Bond-Financed Deficits

(a) *Crowding Out*

Large bond-financed deficits certainly have their detractors. The most prevalent critique leveled against this form of bond financing is that it "**crowds-out**" private capital investment by large government borrowing.

Ignoring the foreign sector here, the NSI can be written as

$(G - T) = (S - I)$ and re-written as

$$[(G-T)+I] = S \qquad (3.4)$$

where the left-hand-side of (3.4) is the total demand for borrowing. This is now represented as a composite demand for borrowing comprising two components, (i) the government demand for loanable funds $(G - T)$, and (ii) the private sector's demand for loanable funds for capital investment, denoted I and represented by the hatched line in Fig. 3.3. The right-hand-side of (3.4) is the supply of loanable funds, which are national savings, S.

The equilibrium interest rate is determined at i_0, the intersection of the overall demand and supply of loanable funds. Initially, at these interest rates (arbitrarily assumed to be 7 % here), the level of private capital investment is denoted I_0 in Fig. 3.3. This is the private demand for loanable funds at existing overall interest rates i_0.

With the increase in government demand for borrowing to finance budget deficits, the total composite demand curve shifts to the right, as discussed earlier and depicted in Fig. 3.3. This shift, in turn, drives up overall interest rates to i_1 (8.25 % in this example). As borrowing costs rise, the quantity of loanable funds demanded by the private sector falls to I_1 in Fig. 3.3. Here, private capital investment has been "crowded out" of the market place by the large government appetite for the finite pool of loanable funds. Due to the higher interest rates caused by excessive

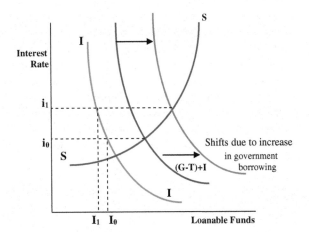

Fig. 3.3 Crowding out

government borrowing, private borrowers are unable to afford the same high level of planned capital investment I_0, and consequently have to cut back to a lower level I_1. The amount by which private capital investment has shrunk, or been "crowded out," is simply $(I_0 - I_1)$.

Proponents of large bond-financed deficits, however, counter that if the conspicuously absent capital inflows associated with the current account deficits are properly included in this analysis, interest rates would indeed be decreased by the capital inflow (as in Fig. 3.2), and the effect on any crowding out ameliorated, if not eradicated.

(b) *Trade Deficits*

Another critique leveled at the NSI-type bond financing pertains to the so-called "deterioration" in the domestic country's export sector. It is argued that such a policy causes jobs to be lost to "foreign competition," not to mention loss of domestic output. In actuality, however, there is no positive correlation between national unemployment and increases in current account deficits.

In fact, episodes of soaring US current account deficits have been characterized by decreasing national unemployment. The then-unprecedented current account and budget deficits of the 1980s were accompanied by strong growth and a virtually full-employment economy. Later, in the early 2000s, the record US current account deficits (this time coinciding with budget surpluses, which we will discuss soon) were accompanied by 30-year lows in the rate of unemployment along with amazingly strong rates of GDP growth that characterized the "new" economy. The US case following 2002 characterized by high budget and trade deficits accompanied by rising unemployment from 2008, will be discussed in later chapters. Other factors currently held dormant in our analysis such as confidence levels, wealth holdings, housing bubbles, and dangerously nonsustainable borrowing come into play since 2002.

The inescapable fact is that free trade does indeed make all trading economies eventually better off. This accounts for the dedication with which many emerging economies (Chile, Mexico, China, Poland, India, Brazil, Vietnam, South Africa, to name a few) are intent on pushing for increased globalization by joining global trading blocks and unleashing the benefits of free trade vis-a-vis their memberships in the World Trade Organization.

What the critics often fail to acknowledge are the effects of free trade on the economy as a whole, and the positive effect of the capital inflows associated with current account deficits. Typically only the merchandise trade deficits (and not even the current account deficits which include more services) become the familiar headline grabbing statistics. Unfortunately, the crucially important attendant capital inflows are hardly mentioned, not fully understood, and usually relegated to the sidelines.

3.3   Two Cases of the NSI: The United States and China

A "US type" economy will be defined to include any safe haven economy that incurs significant fiscal deficit and current account deficits.

A "China type" economy will encompass all reasonably safe haven economies with significant and increasing current account surpluses.[6] In the following discussion, the main difference between the two "types" lies in the current and expected state of their current account balances.

3.3.1   US-Type NSI

We begin by plugging in some hypothetical representative numbers for this class of economies, into the NSI

$$(\mathbf{G{-}T}) = (\mathbf{S{-}I}) + (\mathbf{Imp - Exp}) \tag{3.5}$$

Let $(G - T) = (450)$, a significant budget deficit, and let $(Imp - Exp) = 500$, a large current account deficit. All numbers are assumed to be in billions of US dollars.

$$(450) = (S{-}I) + (500)$$

Quite simply, $(S - I) = (-50)$.

This implies that private demand for loanable funds in this economy outstrips the supply of domestic savings by 50 billion US\$. How is this shortfall in the supply of loanable funds financed?

Rewriting (3.5) we obtain

$$(\mathbf{Imp{-}Exp}) = [(\mathbf{G{-}T}) + (\mathbf{I})]{-}\mathbf{S} \tag{3.6}$$

The first term on the right-hand-side, $[(\mathbf{G - T}) + (\mathbf{I})]$, is the composite demand for borrowing, comprising government demand $(G - T)$ plus private demand, (I). S is the domestic supply of loanable funds.

Once again, plugging in the numbers into the right-hand-side of (3.6), and given that I is 300, and S is 250:

$$(Imp{-}Exp) = [(G{-}T) + I]{-}S = [(450) + 300]{-}250 = 500$$

---

[6]The huge generalization made here is only for the purposes of highlighting polar extremes of NSI applications.

Here, the current account deficit, or more specifically the capital inflow associated with the current account deficit, amounts to 500 billion US$. It is this inflow of funds that finances the shortfall in the supply of loanable funds.

Since 9/11 the large bond-financed budget deficits had necessitated borrowing of around $3 billion a day, with Japan and China being the top two lenders followed by Western Europe. During the Great Recession of 2007–9, total purchases of US Treasury debt by Asia were over five times that bought by Europe with China now leading the list of creditors.

3.3.2 *China-Type NSI*

Here we let the hypothetical sustainable budget deficit be $(G - T) = 30$, and the current account surplus is given as $(Imp - Exp) = -347$. Substituting these values into the NSI we obtain

$$(30) = (S{-}I) + (-347)$$

Therefore $(S - I) = 377$ billion US$.

This is symptomatic of most economies in Southeast Asia that are awash in domestic savings and, on net, are "exporters" of global capital. Given the current account surplus in this example, the outflow is computed to be 377 billion US$. One example of "excess savings" has been the Chinese economy from the mid-1990s to the present.

As we will see in later chapters, one of the main objectives of Chinese macropolicy at the present is to determine how to unleash these excess savings and convert them to Chinese consumption within China to ensure strong growth that will generate enough jobs at home.

3.4   Factors Influencing Global Capital Flows

As stated earlier, **two factors** attract global capital flows to the domestic country

(1) Higher domestic interest rates relative to interest rates in the rest of the world.
(2) Stronger long-term macroeconomic outlook for the domestic country.

Item (1) was discussed in the context of the NSI. The importance of (2) cannot be overstated. Global capital is often dispatched to economies, even regions, which may not necessarily have higher interest rates compared to other nations' domestic bonds, but instead may exhibit impressive growth that is expected to continue into future periods.

In the early to mid-1990s, for example, with the US recovering from its recession of 1990–91, with the European Union wrestling with the demise of its exchange rate mechanism (ERM) and sluggish growth coupled with persistently high unemployment, and with Japan in prolonged recession, the Southeast Asian countries captured the center-stage of global attention. Phenomenal growth rates of over 10 percent annually, low inflation, high employment, stable governments, and rapid increases in infrastructure development, all contributed to massive capital inflows into Malaysia, Indonesia, Taiwan, the Philippines, Singapore, and South Korea. The impressive macroeconomic performance of this region, coupled with the fact that the other traditional destinations for global capital were not factors in the early 1990s, led to unprecedented (and destabilizing) global capital flows into these rapidly emerging economies.

Later, during the Great Recession of 2007–2009, as the US struggled in the throes of its subprime crisis with plunges in both its macro-outlook and its interest rates, once again, emerging economies were awash in massive outflows of capital from the US. Much of this outflow was characterized by "carry trades," where funds are typically borrowed in country A at low rates and then invested (carried) into Country B where interest rates and macro-growth are significantly higher. This, however, has always been a risky proposition. Often, currencies essential to this conversion of capital, as well as the health of economies in both countries A and B are subject to the sudden vicissitudes of fortune that characterize global economies in this hyper-connected world. This brings us to the examination of such highly-sensitive global flows of funds—hot capital—and the macroeconomic devastation that they often leave in their wake.

3.4.1 Hot Capital: The Bane of Emerging Economies

Typically, a hot capital flow is defined as short-term capital flow into an economy, primarily for the purpose of speculative investment. The duration of investment is almost certainly under one year—in fact it could be weeks or even days. Unfortunately, huge amounts of global inflows, primarily of the "hot capital" variety, can become macroeconomic liabilities, as events in Asia were to demonstrate. As discussed in the context of NSI, the inflows were the "flip side" of the current account deficits, and partially helped fund significant portions of the budget deficit. However, the Southeast Asian economies in the 1990s (with the exception of Indonesia) had budget surpluses. Furthermore, most of them had high rates of employment set against a backdrop of almost an oversupply of electronics, automobiles, etc. That is, there was no deficit to finance, nor many huge new capital investments needed in manufacturing.

As capital inflow poured in during the early-mid 1990s, attracted by the impressive growth rates, much of it went into the stock market, real estate, and questionable infrastructure projects such as the longest bridge in the world, the tallest office building in history, or yet another automobile plant. These economies "overheated" (a term we will revisit in great detail in later chapters), with stock markets and real estate assets rising to astronomical prices. It was not uncommon to rent small, efficiency-type apartments in Hong Kong or Singapore in excess of US$ 12,000 per month by 1996–97. A dangerous speculative asset price (SAP) bubble developed.

By the late 1990s, the US recovery powered by the "new" internet-driven and productivity-enhanced economy shifted to a higher gear and was soon joined by signs of recovery in Western Europe. At this point, investors, already apprehensive about the overpriced "bubble" assets of the overheated Southeast Asian economies, pulled capital out from SE Asia and back into the US and Western Europe. This devastating and fairly sudden exodus of capital, referred to as a "hot capital" outflow, was a major factor in the currency crises that traumatized the Southeast Asian economies in 1997–98.[7]

A similar hot capital crisis was experienced by Mexico in 1994. After embarking on an impressive privatization campaign in the 1990s, backed up by significant fiscal and monetary reforms that won global admiration, Mexico was "rewarded" by record capital inflows, primarily from the US. In fact its progressive macroeconomic policies were primarily responsible for enabling President Clinton to push through the North American Free Trade Act (NAFTA). The Mexican central banker, Mr. Miguel Mancera, was legendary in his intolerance for any form of monetization; he epitomized monetary prudence and discipline. The macroeconomic outlook looked rosy indeed, and more capital poured in.

In 1994, however, with the Chiapas Indians in Mexico demanding autonomy and disrupting national transportation, two political assassinations (including that of the prime opposition candidate on live TV), and financial scandals at the highest levels, any notion of Mexico's "safe haven" status was suddenly and fatally damaged. And "safe haven" is indeed a necessary condition for capital flows. With the status gone, so was the hot capital in a dramatic outflow in the last quarter of 1994.

Iceland suffered a hot capital crisis in 2006–2007, fueled largely by 'carry trades.' Rock-bottom interest rates in the US and Japan during the 2005–2006 period resulted in a spate of short-term investment in Iceland's high-yielding government debt, with investors borrowing funds at very low rates in the US and Japan and investing ('carrying') these funds into Iceland (more in Chap. 9). When the Icelandic economy threatened to overheat (defined in Chap. 5), hot capital rushed out, causing downward pressure on the Krona.

The following Fig. 3.4 displays a hot capital outflow and its effects on domestic interest rates.

In Fig. 3.4, domestic interest rates spike sharply from i_0 to i_1 with the sudden exodus of hot capital. This has been clearly evident in Mexico following the outflow of late 1995, as well as in Southeast Asia in 1997–1998. The sharp rise in domestic interest rates traumatizes domestic capital investment, as borrowing costs become prohibitive.

Furthermore, as speculators "dump" domestic assets in their race to unload their speculative investments, the reverse of the earlier NSI story occurs—the domestic

---

[7]One factor was the pegging (or quasi-pegging) of Southeast Asian exchange rates.

Fig. 3.4 Hot capital outflows

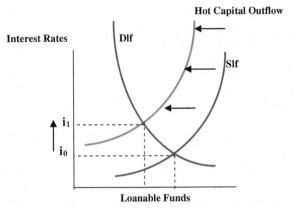

currency collapses as exchange rates weaken. Imports become prohibitively more expensive as the currency gets progressively weaker, sparking increases in inflation (particularly in prices of vital imports such as food and medical supplies), and weakening confidence as the rout continues to escalate.

The devaluation of the domestic currency is often a self-fulfilling prophecy. If domestic and global investors expect the domestic currency to fall further in the future, they will "short" the domestic currency to exploit the arbitrage opportunity. "Shorting" an asset, in the context of this chapter, is exploiting the arbitrage opportunity offered by the knowledge that the asset is very likely to drop in price in the future. Very simply, if 1 unit of domestic currency trades for 10 units of "foreign" currency today, but is expected to trade for only 6 units of "foreign currency" on Day 30, then investors will "short" the currency today. They will buy 10 units of "foreign" currency with 1 unit of domestic currency today, and then on Day 30, they will "come back home" to domestic currency at the rate of 6:1, thus making a 67 % profit. But as more and more investors start selling domestic currency "today" this will often exacerbate the rout in the domestic currency, thereby precipitating its devaluation.

Singapore largely escaped the currency meltdown in 1997–1998 by remarkably prudent monetary policy. Most of the Southeast Asian countries had "managed pegs," or relatively fixed exchange rates with respect to the US currency. (Actually, the Sing\$ was pegged to a basket of currencies with the US being the major component). While the reasons for having "fixed" exchange rates will be discussed in a later chapter, the point here is that inflows in pegged exchange rate regimes translate to direct increases in the recipient country's money supply. If exchange rates were flexible, as in the NSI discussion, the domestic country would experience an appreciation (strengthening) of its currency that would act as a "pressure valve" of sorts and negate the volume of the inflow.

Singapore, under the guidance of its former renowned central banker, Dr. Richard Hu, the head of the Monetary Authority of Singapore, the nation's highly regarded central bank, prudently allowed its currency to float on two crucial occasions to mitigate the incoming flow of funds. In addition, the central bank also countered the inflow with offsetting domestic monetary contraction, thus mini-mizing the destabilizing effects of large inflows of funds overheating its stock market and its real estate sector.

In 2013, India and other Asian economies, along with South Africa, Brazil, and Argentina experience gut-wrenching episodes of hot capital outflows. Following years of near-zero interest rates in the United Sates during the subprime crisis (more on this in later chapters), the US Federal Reserve finally began to announce in 2013 that its massive bond-buyback program that was keeping its interest rates at rock-bottom, was soon to end. This was the now-famous "Taper" which will be disused in the next chapter.

With this news, in anticipation of higher rates back at home in the US, all the carry trades began to "fly back home." This rapid exodus of liquidity hammered the currencies of many of the economies that had housed this hot capital. As capital rushed out and Asian and other emerging countries' exchanges rates plunged rapidly, visions of the ravages of the 1996 Asian crisis were evoked. Of the Asian economies, India and Indonesia, with their significant reliance on external debt, were the most vulnerable.

As currencies plunged, once again their governments pondered the wisdom of allowing such tempestuous inflows hot capital in the first place, and then revisited the Tobin Tax designed by economist James Tobin wherein a country would impose a significant tax and impose controls on capital if it left and rushed back "home" within a specified time period, typically 2–3 years.

China's August, 2015 devaluation accompanied by bleak macroeconomic news regarding its slowing economy, caused a massive exodus of hot capital not just from China, but from much of Southeast Asia into the United States, and to some extent, into Singapore, which also prides itself in being a safe haven. Typically, when one country's currency devalues following a sudden hot capital exodus, its neighboring countries often have to follow suit. Groups of adjoining countries often "cluster" to export similar goods and services given the similarity in their factor endowments, labor skills, and resources. So when one of these economies finds its currency to be devalued following a hot capital outflow, it also finds its exports to be suddenly "cheaper," which translates to the other countries' exports suddenly becoming that much more "expensive." Thus, they too have to weaken their respective currencies to prevent their export markets from being hammered. This is a form of "contagion" that we will revisit in later chapters.

China's slowdown coupled with that of the Eurozone resulted in a highly delete-rious contagion effect on countries that were huge exporters of infrastructure-related commodities such as copper, rubber, zinc, wood, and oil. Economies such as Brazil felt the head-wind of the China slowdown. In September 2015, just one day after Standard and Poor's slashed Brazil's credit rating to junk, the Brazilian real plunged as capital raced out. A frantic injection of $1.5 billion by Brazil's central bank to sell US dollars and buy back its plunging currency, proved futile. Massive government cor-ruption, coupled with a nonsustainable budget deficit/GDP ratio of 9 % caused the real to inexorably fall. All the gains of the long commodity boom that had made the Brazilian economy a darling for global investors were lost.

3.4.2 Factors Influencing Global Capital Flows: The Cave Theory

In addition to higher interest rates and the long-term macroeconomic outlook discussed here, there is yet another determinant of global capital flows. In times of great and grave global crises, capital is often "parked" in safe haven countries. As discussed earlier in this chapter, these are economies characterized by stable governments, and relatively sound fiscal and monetary policies. These are also countries that are relatively immune from global turmoil, and are resilient to exogenous shocks that might make most other countries convulse.

In periods of big macroeconomic/political turmoil, there are times when investors—nations, individuals, institutions—prefer the preservation of principal to uncertain returns. It is at times such as these, that we deploy the "cave" theory. This theory was whimsically formulated by the author of this text, while teaching in Shanghai, at the peak of the Subprime crisis in 2008.

Simply put, if the United States slips into recession, its consumers and institutions and businesses, hunker down and "hide" in the American "cave." As a consequence, consumption and business investment drops. When this happens, and given that the rest of the planet is also facing the same tough macroeconomic head-winds, the malaise spreads to the rest of the world. In similar fashion, the Asians hunker down in their cave, while the Europeans hunker down in their Euro-cave.

When all the major macroeconomic players are hiding out in their respective "caves," the Langdana Cave Theory goes into effect. At this point, in a world of "cave-dwellers," the US cave is seen as the "safest cave," the best shelter from the global storm. Capital will flood in as there will be a massive flight to safety and the US dollar will appreciate. At the peak of the subprime crisis in 2008, when the planet was being buffeted by macro storms, and global investors were huddling in their respective caves, the US had the "best cave." The US experienced a dramatic inflow of "flight to safety" capital which, to this day, has proven to be a major saving grace that has kept its economy solvent. In spite of almost-zero interest rates in the US, a housing market that had crashed, record unemployment and collapsed consumer and investor confidence, and a fractured and ineffective Congress, unprecedented capital inflows poured in when they were needed the most.

Over and over again, the cave theory has been proven correct. In macro convulsions such as when a rogue regime takes power in Africa, a volcano blows apart in Iceland, Greece threatens to default (again), bubbles explode, or oil supplies face disruption (again) in the Gulf, capital rushes into the US, and to some extent, to Switzerland, the other safe haven country.

Switzerland, considered a safe haven, and not being in the straight-jacket of the Eurozone nor even in the European Union, has a strong record of attracting Flight to Safety capital into its "cave." In fact, in the presence of sudden flights to safety into Switzerland, the Swiss have had to limit the appreciation of their currency, the Swiss franc. The rapid capital inflows, combined with the tendency of the Swiss to invest primarily in Swiss sovereign debt (national bonds), tend to appreciate the Swiss franc. And given that the country is largely an export-driven economy, the appreciation in the franc rapidly makes its exports globally uncompetitive. For the Swiss, therefore, the capital inflows have serious negative consequences.

To counter the adverse effects of capital inflows on their exports, they have adopted upper limits on the strength of their currency. If capital inflows tend to strength the Swiss franc beyond the specified upper limit, then the Swiss National Bank (SNB) steps in and artificially weakens the franc by quickly intervening in the foreign exchange markets. The SNB sells Swiss franks and buys other major currencies such as the euro, the US$ and the Japanese yen to rapidly bring the Swiss franc within its specified upper bound.

Hot Capital Outflows: India, 1991 and 2013. By early 1991, India was in a serious balance of payments crisis. At this stage, India could not afford to pay for all its necessary imports; it lacked the foreign exchange (US dollars) to do so. India's biggest export market in the 1980s was the Soviet Union, and with its dissolution went much of India's export revenue, primarily its source of foreign exchange. Coupled with this, the 1991 Gulf war spiked the price of oil, one of India's primary imports. This one-two punch suddenly hammered India's reserves of foreign exchange from $1.2 billion in January 1991 to under half that amount by June. India had only enough foreign exchange for barely three months' worth of essential imports, and was fast approaching a balance of payments default.

Hot capital outflow was rapid and brutal. As the supply of loanable funds shot to the left (see Fig. 3.4), the Reserve bank of India (RBI), India's central bank, spent even more of its very valuable foreign exchange to attempt to buy rupees by selling US dollars and artificially propping up the Indian currency. But, as so often is the case in this futile exercise, this is a losing battle. Typically when policy makers battle endogeneity, the markets always win. Fighting market driven prices and exchange rates is hard, very costly, and mostly futile.

Finally India had to go to the IMF for a loan of $2.2 billion by pledging 67 tons of its gold as collateral. When this became public—the gold constituted India's total gold reserve—an already-weak and embattled government was soon ousted from power by the ensuing outcry, to usher in a more enlightened one. The new government of Prime Minister P.V. Narasimha Rao ushered in badly needed reforms that laid the foundation for the eventual supply-side framework of the later Modi government. (India's macroeconomic liberalization that began in 1991, and its eventual supply-side macropolicy of 2014, will be discussed in detail in Chap. 10.)

The lesson learned by the RBI following the 1991 crisis was that foreign exchange interventions do not work. If a country's exchange rate is dropping as its hot capital rushes out, it is best to not fight the markets. Instead, a more sensible policy would be to allow markets to determine the exchange rates, instead of 'wasting good money after bad' by selling foreign exchange to shore up its plunging currency. This change in macropolicy helped enormously when the India battled yet another exodus of hot capital in 2013.

The hot capital outflow of 2013 was triggered by an announcement from the US Federal reserve that it was contemplating ending its $85 billion a month bond-buyback program. The next chapter will discuss elements of the subprime crisis (the Great Recession) such as Quantitative Easing, the Taper, Bond-buyback, etc. In the context of this chapter, India was, quite simply, attracting hot capital from the US and the Eurozone, in the period 2007–2013.

In the US, with interest rates at rock-bottom and flirting with 0 %—the reason to be discussed in Chap. 4—carry trades were pouring hot capital into India, driving up its property and stock markets. Finally, knowing that it could not simply print $85 billion a month forever, the US announced that it was contemplating a return to eventual normalcy, that is, a "tapering off" of the reckless printing of money, to bring interest rates back into positive territory.

This announcement was a thunderbolt to the emerging economies that had been soaking up the hot capital. The Indian rupee fell 15 % just on the announcement. Capital rushed back to the US, the supply of loanable funds shot to the left as in Fig. 3.4, and the rupee took a hit. Capital controls were enacted by India as well as by Brazil, but with little effect. Currencies of India, Indonesia, Brazil, South Africa, Vietnam, China, Taiwan, and Thailand were pummeled as capital outflows headed back home.

3.5   Discussion Questions

The following questions will highlight and hopefully demystify aspects of budget and current account balances, and their relationships to capital inflows.

1. *Isn't the bond financing discussed here a risky proposition? Isn't the budget-deficit-incurring country essentially being "held hostage" to capital inflows?*

Yes, it is indeed risky if the country is not perceived to be a safe haven, or is simply experiencing a short-term (hot) inflow for speculative purposes. Such an economy could be crippled by sudden outflows and spiking interest rates. However, if the economy is perceived as a true safe haven, then it can be very resilient to temperamental outflows.

The best example, perhaps, is that of the now-famous US Petrodollar I inflows of the 1970s. In spite of an OPEC engineered embargo of oil exports to the US, most of the huge dollar revenues amassed by the oil exporting economies were, surprisingly, funneled back into the US. And this at a time when the US economy was in stagflation, characterized by double-digit inflation, high unemployment, and recessionary output. So, in spite of being in political disfavor with OPEC and undergoing a traumatic stagflation, the petrodollars still found their relatively safest-haven destination.

2. *So then what was Petrodollar II?*

This was the massive inflow into the US after 2006, and it coincided with the global run-up in oil prices. Very simply, the OPEC countries "recycled' their humongous dollar deposits back in the US—only this time they were more discreet. Petrodollar II in the post-9/11 era, was funneled into the US via 'front' corporations (business groups) based in London, and hence, difficult to trace back to the originating sources in the Persian Gulf. After Japan and China, this was the largest inflow into the US.

3. *Isn't the interest paid to foreign investors a source of net wealth loss for the domestic deficit incurring economy?*

This "net wealth loss" has to be weighed against the fact that the capital inflows are indeed lowering domestic final interest rates from i_1 to i_{Final} as we have discussed in Fig. 3.2. Domestic rates certainly would be at the higher interest rate i_1 in a bond-financed deficit incurring economy that was closed to global trade and capital.

4. *There is no denying that while jobs at the national level may be created by capital inflows, specific industries competing with imports do indeed suffer job loss (textiles, steel, apparel, for example). In the context of the NSI, what would happen if the protectionists got their way and disrupted global trade?*

In fact, a similar scenario was almost played out in the US in the mid-1980s and after 2015, and at various times since then attempts have been made to disrupt global trade meetings. In the mid-1980s, the deterioration in the US merchandise trade deficit prompted cries for restricting imports. The US Federal Reserve was keenly aware that any disruption in the trade balance would immediately disrupt the capital account. A sharp cut-back in imports due to trade disruptions would also mean a similar shut down in capital flows. Given the huge budget deficits that were dependent on global capital at that time, such a disruption in capital inflows would have spelled macroeconomic disaster. The supply of loanable funds (in Fig. 3.2) would have rapidly shifted left, spiking domestic (US) interest rates i_{Final} back to i_1, and traumatizing the economy. To preempt this, the famous Plaza Accord of G5 finance ministers (held at the Plaza Hotel in New York) attempted to artificially weaken the US dollar, shrink the current account deficit, and hence ward off the dangerous cries for protectionism.

5. *In the years following the inception of the Euro in 1999, why did the euro steadily weaken with respect to the US dollar (and British Sterling) even though the difference in interest rates between the countries in the Eurozone and the US was fairly constant? And why did it fall precipitously, against the US$ in 2015?*

Once again, it is not just the interest difference but also the long-term macroeconomic outlook that dictates the flow of global capital. The US macroeconomic performance characterized by productivity increases, low inflation, and relatively strong growth from the late 1990s through 2000, clearly outperformed that of the Eurozone with its rigid labor laws and high level of government regulation. Along similar lines, with dismal news from the war in Iraq, an unpopular US President overseas, a US consumer addicted to massive foreign-debt-financed consumption, deflating housing and asset price bubbles, relatively lower interest rates coupled with prospects of trade disruption and higher taxes (by 2008), the US experienced retrenchment of global capital away from the US and towards the euro and India/China. This resulted in a significant rise in the strength of the euro (and other currencies) relative to the dollar as investors parked their funds into what some perceived to be "safer" and higher yielding foreign-currency assets.

By 2014, with prospects of interest rate increases in the US finally in sight, and with Greece, Italy, and other Southern European economies' bloated budgets and fiscal challenges severely straining the very existence of the euro, capital flooded out of the Eurozone into "the best cave," resulting in the ensuing appreciation of the US$ and a relentless crumbling of the euro. With each successive "bailout" of some cash-strapped Southern European economy, and with signs of an eventual resurrection of macroeconomic activity in the US, the euro continued to slip as capital kept flooding out of the Eurozone.

6. *If exchange rates are determined "endogenously" by market conditions (as indicated in the answer to the previous question), then why has there been such a controversy surrounding the euro- and sterling- and dollar-yuan rate?*

China, for a variety of reasons highlighted in the first article in this chapter and later in the book, chose to lock its exchange rate to the US$ till 2005. As Chinese economy grew by an average of 8 % a year for over 30 years, a rate unprecedented in recorded human history, foreign capital flooded in, attracted to China's "long term growth potential." Endogenously, the yuan would have appreciated, but the People's Bank of China (PBoC) artificially prevented this appreciation by locking the exchange rate at 8.24 yuan to a dollar by daily intervention in the foreign exchange markets—buying dollars and selling yuan—till the daily target of 8.24:1 was attained. After 2005, the yuan was allowed to appreciate steadily, but not at a freely-floating endogenously driven exchange. This "artificially lower" exchange rate inspired some calls of "unfair trading practice" that warranted retaliatory macropolicy that would "level the trade field" with China. (More on the China Saga in Article 3.1.)

7. *Isn't it puzzling that several Southeast Asian economies with national budget surpluses (Singapore, for example) began issuing national debt in the early 2000s?*

The market-determined interest rates on long-term government bonds (of duration 10 years, at least) are vital benchmarks that indicate the level of risk that investors take by purchasing long-term government debt. After discussing the Fisher Effect and the yield curve, we will find long-term interest rates on government debt to be invaluable forward-looking indicators of expected <u>future</u> inflation. This information is imperative in enabling the central bank to make effective current monetary policy decisions based on expected inflation in the future. This feature motivates Singapore's issue of 10-year government debt in spite of incurring budget surpluses.

8. *How is it that Japan incurs huge budget deficits through the mid-1990s into 2015, and has virtually zero interest rates for most of this period? Shouldn't rates rise at home in Japan?*

In addition to bond-financing huge government outlays, Japan also indulged in very significant (albeit intermittent) increases in its money supply. In this chapter it was assumed that this was not the case and that large budget deficits were fully bond-financed without any accompanying monetization.

9. *This ties in with the previous question. Where is monetary policy in the NSI? And what about tax rates, consumer confidence, wages, productivity, employment, and inflation? All these are conspicuously absent.*

Yes, they are indeed absent from the NSI discussion presented in this chapter. The NSI is an accounting identity that provides a wonderfully intuitive discussion of fundamental accounting relationships. It is a "broad brush" explanation of the flow of funds and the mechanism linking the budget and current account balances as well as national savings and investments. Its strength lies in the simplicity with which several macroeconomic scenarios can be intuitively analyzed. The equally important details—all the variables listed in the above question, plus some—will be presented in the "engine-room" model of this book, namely, the ISLM-ADAS model. Construction of this fully articulated model beginning in the following chapter will add several layers of sophistication to the discussion presented in this intuitive chapter. In fact, in addition to Japan, witness the US situation by late 2008 and well into 2015; huge deficits during the Great Recession, massive monetization, and interest rates approaching zero.

10. *Finally, what will happen when we have to ultimately pay off all our debt? Sooner or later, we in the United States are going to have to "pay the piper." What happens then?*

There will never be some apocalyptic Day of Macro-Reckoning on which the US, or any debt-incurring country for that matter, will have to "pay off" all its debt in one lump-sum payment. The debt is coming due every day, all the time. A nation's sovereign debt (national bonds) can be 30 days, 3 months, 1 year, and all the way to 30 years in maturity. These government bonds of varying maturities are coming due all the time, and not just on one final day.

In the following simulated media articles, please comment on the underlined parts using material from this and the previous chapter. Use diagrams wherever applicable.

Article 3.1   THE CHINESE YUAN SAGA

Xi Shan, <u>China Macro Review</u>

It is time to look back and review what has come to be known as the Yuan Saga, or if you prefer, the Renminbi Saga. Till 2005, the PBoC had locked (pegged) the yuan to the US dollar by daily and massive foreign exchange intervention. After 2005, the Chinese Central Bank (PBoC) <u>allowed a steady appreciation, with the yuan pegged to a trade-weighted basket of currencies, along the lines of Singapore's 'managed' peg.</u>   **(a)** *Very briefly, how would a central bank peg its currency or allow it to change only gradually?   And fundamentally, why was there upward pressure on the Chinese currency?*

This policy of managed exchange rates against a backdrop of burgeoning <u>current account deficits</u> in the US and Western Europe, unleashed a storm of protest from groups of politicians and trade representatives in the US and Europe. **(b)** W*hy is the current account more accurate than the trade account?* "They are doing this to make their exports cheaper and keep our goods out," complained Ron Wesbury of Morristown Metal Fittings, in Morristown, NJ. "Clearly this is why we in the US have such a big trade deficit with the Chinese!"

However, analysts at Matrix Labs in New Orleans were not nearly as outraged.   In their "Macro Watch" section, the focus was on the very razor-thin profit margins embedded in the Asian supply chains in the late 2000s.   "You have to understand," explained Prof. Federicko Fontana of Matrix Labs, "just a 1% appreciation in an Asian currency is enough for someone like Lands' End or Victoria's Secret, to switch an order for polo shirts or pajamas from China to Thailand. The global supply chains are very nimble now and large multinationals can easily switch source destinations based on short-term exchange rate fluctuations." He added, "by the way, the notion of managing **(c)** <u>the yuan relative to a basket of currencies of nebulous weighs is something the Chinese learned from the Singaporean Central bank—it is really a politically convenient and brilliant system!</u>" *Why 'politically convenient'?*

Others, such as Senator Paulina Orr, remain combative.   On last night's Face the World, the Senator first thanked all her well wishers for their cards while she was hospitalized and then she proceeded to announce her plan to "Retaliate.   It must be a fair playing field!   If the Chinese don't allow the renminbi (Chinese yuan) to appreciate fast as it should, I propose a tax on Chinese imports that will make up the amount by which they are artificially undervaluing their currency. This will rapidly shrink our trade deficit!"

"Not so fast," said Dr. Robert Braunstein, chief economist of Braunstein Vintage Timepieces in New York, "Placing a tariff (tax) on Chinese goods or forcing them to revalue their currency will not shrink our current account deficit. First, keep in mind", explained Dr. Braunstein, gently replacing a rare 18th century Irish clock to the display case in the company museum, "the goods now coming from China will now come from Vietnam, or Thailand, or India. The sectors that we have 'lost' to foreign competition are not coming back here. They are gone. Second, a very significant portion of items coming from China comprise 'intra-industry' trade, mainly components that are part of final products made (and exported) by US multi-national companies. Third, almost 40-50% of the price of most items in the US can be attributed to marketing, transportation and storage. And finally, (d) don't forget the 'pass-through' effect!" *(See below. Given what you have read so far, is this effect a viable option for the Chinese?)*

Cindy Jiang, a researcher in Shanghai Simulations explained this effect to us when we met her for drinks at Cloud Nine in Shanghai. "Essentially, 'pass-through' was what Japan had to do in the post-1985 period after the Plaza Accord. The dollar was artificially weakened in a massive coordinated intervention by the Group of Five (G5) mature economies to ward-off strong protectionism in the US. To maintain market share in the US the Japanese reduced their price of autos thereby negating much of the price increase due to the forced yen appreciation. In essence, they let the exchange rate 'tax' pass-through. More recently, as the US dollar plunged endogenously in 2007-08 following the subprime crisis (presented in detail in Chapters 9 and 11), Eurozone exporters, faced with a strengthening euro, had to adopt the

same strategy."

Simon Du of the Ministry of trade for China agreed to meet us at the South Beauty Szechuan restaurant at the Guomao in Beijing and shifted the discussion to fundamental macro theory. "As we have stated, (e) changing the exchange rate will, by itself, not shrink the US current account deficit with China—there is a fundamental relationship in macro theory that says that this whole thing is about a lack of domestic loanable funds (savings) on the part of the Americans", he explained, carefully sipping his Nine Treasures tea. "As long as this imbalance exists, the US will continue to incur big trade deficits financed largely by us and the Japanese and the British and the mysterious OPEC guys...that's about 2.5 billion dollars a day, right?"

On this note, and against this backdrop, we had some Senators in the US proclaiming that China was buying 'too much' US debt. We met some MBAs from Rutgers Business School at Ling Ling's Pearls and asked them if they agreed. "You really must know your macro to understand this....these politicians forget the capital inflow side of the story. (f) All I can say is that if we limit Chinese purchases of Treasurys, and/or force a drop in the US trade deficit by pushing for a yuan appreciation, we need to be careful for what we ask for—we may see interest rates rising fast in the US!" cautioned class president Melissa Smith.

As the yuan gradually appreciated by late 2007-8 and as Chinese goods became 'more expensive,' another interesting development took place. The nature of Chinese exports changed. Gone were the exports driven primarily by price competitiveness—China is now boosting the productivity and quality of its export sector to be commensurate with the higher prices of exports. Simon Du, nibbling on his watermelon after lunch told us that this development, triggered by the long yuan appreciation since 2005, has **(g)** very important and far-reaching implications for Singapore, Japan and the other countries of Southeast Asia and also for the Western economies. The game has become even more complicated and urgent.

Article 3.2   AFTER EUPHORIA, GERMANS CONCERNED

Lewis Kerman, Bavarian Weekly Review

Setting: Germany in the early 1990s, with the budget deficit increasing dangerously.

It is now almost two years since that magical day when the wall came down. The wall is gone, but has the magic gone too? Today Germans are increasingly worried about the state of their economy. Projected infrastructure spending to modernize the former East Germany has far exceeded even the wildest and most extravagant estimates made just last year. Massive infrastructure expenditures on new telephone lines, sanitation systems, power grids, environmental control, highway repair, nuclear waste disposal, and basic health concerns add up to make the German deficit a whopping 4.8 percent of its GDP.

"This is most worrisome. I see a problem," exclaims Peter Metz, of Madison Securities in Madison, Wisconsin. "If you were to include the Treuhandanstadt, a fund set aside for overhauling obsolete manufacturing Communist-era plants, the budget deficit, according to my numbers, **(a)** will easily be close to 8% of GDP in the very near future. This is not good," he mumbles, nervously fiddling with his tie.

This concern is felt by most Germans—it is most palpable in the former West Germany which will have to subsidize its Eastern half.   To this end, the **(b)** Unity Bonds have helped tremendously, drawing in global capital to help fund the post-unification infrastructure expenses. In fact, the plan is to make Germany a sort of magnet for global funds.

However, Dr. Marie Heinkel, an economist with Bonn Bank, warns, "We Germans will have to understand that with these Unity Bonds, things will change. We have become used to having trade surpluses. **(c)** I will not be surprised to see German trade deficits very soon. This is bound to happen by the laws of macroeconomics." When asked if she felt that this was a problem, she nonchalantly (and enigmatically) replied, "Look at **(d)** the American experience with large budget deficits and learn—what is the expression? You can't eat your cake and have it too?" And with that and an "auf wiedersehen", she jumped into a cab and was gone.

However, not all aspects of the bond financing by foreign lenders are worrisome to most Germans. "It is good that foreigners are pumping money into our economy. This is a good thing because there is a lot of cleaning up left to do," says Manfred Hartmann, as he takes orders in his third-generation delicatessen in downtown Frankfurt. "But **(e)** the country loses since we have to pay all this interest to these foreign lenders. I'd rather borrow at home and keep the interest at home," and then with an abrupt change of subject, "Here, try this bratwurst—family recipe".

The large and growing budget deficits just don't sit right with the Germans. We went to the countryside to interview the rural folks, and met Aida Spiegel, 78, happily retired with her four dogs in her glass-blowing studio 45 miles from Aachen. "My parents taught me never to go into debt. See, they were in the hyper-inflation. So I have always balanced my checkbook. **(f)** If I, a retired librarian, can have the discipline to do this, our government must—should—be able to balance its budget. I am never late with my house or car payments. This big budget deficit now and borrowing from the people, I don't like that".

The predominant emotion two years ago was euphoria. Now it is replaced by uncertainty. Aida and her dogs, Manfred in his deli, Marie at her bank, and Peter in Madison all wait and hold their breaths.

ANSWERS AND HINTS

ARTICLE 3.1 The Chinese Yuan Saga

(a) Actually one of the primary functions of most central banks today is foreign exchange (FX) intervention. We will see later that the policy of artificially undervaluing one's currency, while 'good' for exports in the short run, comes at a tremendous price—more in Chap. 9.

How is a currency managed? Please see the answer to question 6 in this chapter.

Why the appreciation? Note that it is not just interest rates that drive capital inflow.

(b) Describe a fundamental difference between the trade deficit and the current account deficit.

(c) Hint: A 'hard' peg is, say, 10 of A's currency locked (by A) to 1 unit of B's currency. With this system, any deviation in A's currency would be instantly noticed; a hard peg offers no wiggle room. A managed peg, in contrast, is against a basket of currencies and in addition, it allows for a specified range of daily fluctuation too.

(d) The final import price of a good incorporating not just the exchange rate but also the original price of the imported good (in foreign currency) is known as the 'real' exchange rate.

(e) Explain how an inflow is linked to a trade imbalance, using NSI with diagrams.

(f) Use NSI discussion. Please include diagram here.

(g) This pertains to the Lifecycle theory of trade; first, manufacturing, then high-end knowledge-intensive manufacturing, services and R&D.

ARTICLE 3.2 After Euphoria, Germans Concerned

(a and b) The percentage in (a) is ominous, and (b) is the NSI discussion.

(c) Again, this sequence has been discussed in detail. What are these "laws of macroeconomics" cited by Marie Heinkel?

(d) One could conclude that Marie perceives the resulting current account deficits to be problematic. Critically evaluate her concern. Give examples.

(e) Discuss Manfred's concern. Use diagrams.

(f) Aida is comparing her personal financing with that of the government's bond-financed deficits. Is she not incurring any personal "deficits"? Critically evaluate this comparison.

Chapter 4
Aggregate Demand: Setting the Stage for Demand-Side Stabilization

This chapter marks the first step toward the construction of the ISLM/ADAS model which will power macroeconomic analyses in the chapters to come. At this stage we have completed an intuitive overview of the broad links between global capital flows, fiscal, and trade imbalances, and their effects on interest rates and exchange rates.

The national savings identity (NSI), with its remarkable ability to provide an intuitive understanding of a range of diverse macroeconomic scenarios, was explored in the previous chapter. However, as highlighted in the discussion questions of Chap. 3, the NSI, in spite of its versatility and intuitiveness, suffers from a conspicuous lack of detail. The role of the central bank and monetary policy is completely missing. Similarly absent are tax rates and national tax policy, along with consumer and investor confidence. Key variables such as wages, employment, GDP growth, and inflation, are also missing from our analysis in Chap. 3.

To incorporate the above, construction begins on a fully equipped, sophisticated, and well-articulated macro model—the "engine-room"—known as the ISLM–ADAS. The first step explains, derives, and explores the economy's aggregate demand (AD) curve which is the key component in macroeconomic demand-side stabilization.

4.1 Demand-Side Stabilization

In the economy depicted in Fig. 4.1, AD at this stage is loosely defined as the total demand for all goods and services, and aggregate supply as "total output supply." Initially the economy is in equilibrium at some stagnant or recessionary GDP growth rate Y_{low} (presumably accompanied by high unemployment) and rate of price increase P_0.

From a purely diagrammatic perspective, how can this GDP growth be jump-started?

© Springer International Publishing Switzerland 2016
F. Langdana, *Macroeconomic Policy*, Springer Texts in Business and Economics, DOI 10.1007/978-3-319-32854-6_4

Fig. 4.1 Demand-side
stabilization: jump-starting

In Fig. 4.1, if the AD curve could somehow be shifted to the right by designing and implementing the right combination of fiscal and monetary polices, we could stimulate the economy to get to Y_{high} (presumably with lower unemployment). The "cost" of this policy involving a rightward shift in AD is a higher equilibrium rate of inflation (P_{high}), with the obvious benefits being greater GDP growth and more jobs.

This is the first example of demand-side stabilization. The emphasis is on combinations of fiscal and monetary policies that shift the AD curve to the right, in this simple example.

Another scenario is depicted in Fig. 4.2 where we find an economy suffering from high inflation and GDP growth racing out of control. Here, the "problem" is one of high inflation, and to alleviate this situation we resort to another diagrammatic exercise.

In this case, appropriate fiscal and/or monetary polices would result in a leftward shift in AD, taking the economy to $P_{moderate}$ and to a lower, and perhaps more manageable, rate of GDP growth. In this example, unemployment, presumably very low or non-existent to begin with, will actually increase as the GDP growth is deliberately slowed down to $Y_{moderate}$.[1]

Both these shifts in the AD, caused by fiscal and/or monetary policies, constitute macropolicies that attempt demand-side stabilization. These polices primarily came into effect following a paradigm shift after the Great Depression and were later labeled as mainstream Keynesian stabilization policies. It was John Maynard Keynes who in the 1930s first propounded the idea to use combinations of discretionary fiscal and monetary polices to fine-tune the economy by shifting the AD curve.

An ideal situation would perhaps lie somewhere between the extremes depicted by Figs. 4.1 and 4.2 with the economy characterized by moderate inflation and sustainable GDP growth. This scenario will be discussed in Chap. 5.

---

[1]In the following chapter, the concepts of engineering soft-landings for overheated economies, and of jump-starting moribund output will be discussed.

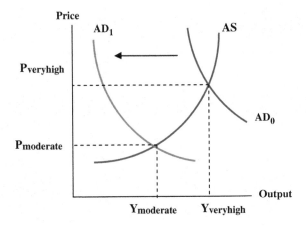

Fig. 4.2 Demand-side stabilization: soft landing

4.2 Business Cycles

A stylized business cycle is presented in Fig. 4.3. The peaks are, of course, periods of recovery and the troughs are recessions. The trend rate of growth is the inflation-adjusted real rate of growth of average GDP.

The objective of demand-side stabilization is to "flatten" business cycles by attempting to make periods of recovery less vigorous, and by making recessions less severe. A more stable planning horizon is preferable to a wildly fluctuating economy, especially when it comes to making long-term capital investments that come "on line" many years into the uncertain future.

The next step is to determine exactly how the AD can be shifted to accomplish demand-side stabilization and flatten business cycles by increasing growth in recessions or slowing down growth and, hence, bringing inflation down, as presented in Fig. 4.4.

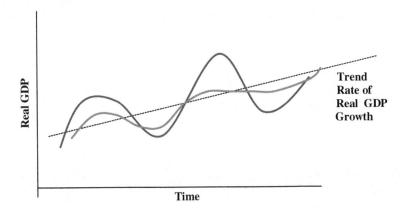

Fig. 4.3 "Flattening" business cycles

Fig. 4.4 Demand-side
stabilization

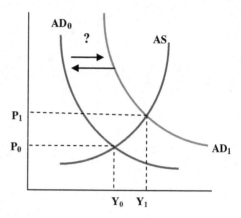

In order to <u>shift</u> the AD to implement demand-side stabilization, we must know exactly <u>what underlies this curve</u>, and how it is derived. The next few pages pertain directly to attaining this objective.

4.3 Variables Underlying the Aggregate Demand: Introducing the Goods Market

This process begins with an examination of the goods market. The condition for equilibrium in this market is actually an expression that we are familiar with:

$$Y = C + I + G + (Exp - Imp)$$

In Table 4.1, three scenarios in a hypothetical goods market are presented.

In row 1 (scenario 1), the value of output produced is 625, while the total planned expenditure composed of all the components, namely, domestic consumption (C), domestic capital investment expenditures (I), government consumption (G), and net foreign consumption (Exp–Imp), add up to 675.

$$C + I + G + (Exp - Imp) = 675$$

Table 4.1 The goods market

Y value of output	C	I	G	(Exp–Imp)	Total planned expenditure and change in output and employment
625	475	50	125	25	675 increase
750	550	50	125	25	750 no change
875	625	50	125	25	825 decrease

In this case, since planned expenditure (675) exceeds the value of output, (625), suppliers respond to this excess demand in the goods market by increasing output and, hence, employment.

In the second row, the value of output in the goods market is 750, which equals total planned expenditure.

$$C + I + G + (Exp-Imp) = 750$$

In this case, the goods market is said to be exactly in equilibrium. Y is indeed equal to C + I + G + (Exp–Imp), there is no excess supply or demand, and there will therefore be no change in output supplied or employment.

Finally, in row 3, planned expenditures (825) are less than the value of output supply (875). Here suppliers respond to this excess supply condition by reducing output and, hence, employment.

These three goods market scenarios constitute the goods market, a crucial component of the fully-articulated model. Plotting output (Y) along the horizontal axis and the components of expenditures, C + I + G + (Exp–Imp), along the vertical axis, we find that all the points where Y will equal C + I + G + (Exp–Imp) must lie on the hatched 45° line. In fact, the hatched line is simply the locus of all possible points of equilibrium in the goods market.[2]

We now plot the three scenarios, three points on the vertical axis being 675, 750, and 825, and the three corresponding points on the horizontal axis being 625, 750, and 875. Plotting these three sets of points, we obtain the expenditure line in Fig. 4.5. This line intersects the hatched 45° line at E_0 which represents the goods market equilibrium at 750.

The goods market equilibrium simply indicates that 750 units of goods produced would be exactly bought-up by 750 units of planned expenditures. At E_0 there is no shortage of goods or unsold inventory. But E_0, by itself, tells us nothing about the overall level of unemployment in the economy.

At this point, a simple yet extremely important hypothetical exercise is in order. We are given that at E_0, in spite of the goods market being in equilibrium, the unemployment rate is a hefty 25 %. What could be done to alleviate this unemployment?

According to the classical paradigm, the model in operation at the time of the Great Depression in the US, nothing could or should be done.[3] The classical economists believed in "natural" rates of output and unemployment which were not amenable to any sort of discretionary macropolicy.

---

[2]We assume here that both axes have the same scale.

[3]This classical belief is not nearly as preposterous as it sounds. Their paradigm was successful, well articulated, and did in fact represent the pre-Depression era quite well. It was the paradigm shift ushered in by mistakes made in the Great Depression that rang the death knell of the classical model with its notions of natural rates of employment and output growth; more on this subject in Chap. 9.

Fig. 4.5 The goods market

It was Keynes who threw a cat among the classical pigeons by propounding an actual discretionary role for fiscal and monetary policy in influencing the key macrovariables.

In our example, this would diagrammatically translate to moving the expenditure line up (using fiscal and/or monetary policies) so that it would intersect the 45° line at some higher point. As displayed in Fig. 4.6, this shift would take the goods

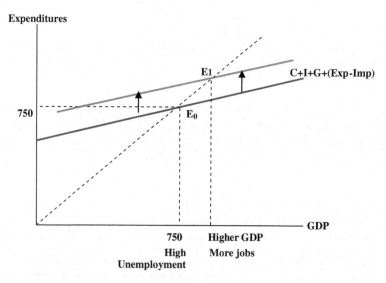

Fig. 4.6 The goods market: the brilliance of Keynes

market to a new and higher equilibrium at E_1, corresponding to a lower unemployment rate.

Keynes pointed out that E_0 was just one equilibrium point in the goods market, and not necessarily the only one, and certainly not the optimal one given the high unemployment in existence at E_0. Instead of assuming E_0 as fixed and inviolate, he proposed activist macroeconomic policies that would shift the expenditure line upward to yield a new and higher equilibrium E_1, resulting in a higher level of employment.

An increase in any of the components of the expenditure line C, I, G, Exports, or a reduction of Imports, can shift the line up. However, as discussed in Chap. 2, the only three policy instruments we have at our disposal are changes in government spending, tax rates, and changes in the money supply which in turn affect interest rates.

By increasing G, for example, the expenditure line moves up and a new equilibrium is established at E_1, as presented in Fig. 4.6. In this situation, large government outlays "jump-start" economies out of recessions.

The shift in the expenditure line presented in Fig. 4.6 will translate to a rightward shift in (P, Y) space discussed earlier in Fig. 4.1 and later in this chapter and the following one.

China from the late 1990s well into the 2000s had to aim for around 8 % GDP growth to absorb the increase in the number of new workers entering the job market.[4] This policy of **bao ba** (guaranteed eight percent) was de-emphasized in the early 2000s by Premier (and former central banker) Zhu Rongji, when it was found that some state and local officials may have been tempted to doctor final statistics under pressure to hit the target. Unfortunately, by 2015, after Zhu's protégés had run out, the role of targets has again been emphasized by the Chinese government.

Another example of large government spending to move the expenditure line to some higher equilibrium E_1 is the US infrastructure spending on dams, power generation, roadways, etc., in the post-Depression years and well into the 1970s and proposed again in late 2008. We will discuss these cases and others in Chaps. 5 and 7.

4.3.1 Analyzing the Components of Aggregate Demand

The next step is to formally link the goods market to demand-side stabilization policies. We begin by moving to a higher level of sophistication to determine the specific composition of the variables that constitute the individual components of aggregate demand, C, I, and G.[5]

---

[4]This included farm workers as well as former employees of state owned enterprises (SOEs).

[5]At this stage, we temporarily suppress the term (Exp–Imp) to focus primarily on the closed economy.

The consumption function is described by the expression:

$$C = \underline{C} + bY + dW$$

where:

C private consumption expenditure.

$\underline{C}$ The autonomous component of consumption, "autonomous" in that this term is independent of income (Y). In this book, $\underline{C}$ will also be the term that includes tastes and preferences and, most important, $\underline{C}$ will be the term that captures consumer expectations. In the upcoming macroeconomic analyses, changes in consumer confidence pertaining to the economic outlook in the near-term will be proxied by this term.

For example, a collapse in consumer confidence in anticipation of an impending macroeconomic downturn is represented by a drop in $\underline{C}$. A surge in consumer confidence, on the other hand, translates to an increase in $\underline{C}$. (Later in this chapter we will discuss how confidence is measured.)

Consumer confidence, like investor confidence, is very sensitive to planned increases in future taxes or signs of unemployment. Even a whiff of impending tax increases or indications of impending or actual lay-offs causes consumer confidence to be adversely affected.

In the United States, private consumption, C, is the giant in the equation. As we have noted earlier, C was almost 72 % of Y by late 2008. In fact, in the bleak months and years following 9/11, it was C that was not just keeping the US economy afloat but (with some help from China) keeping the global economy afloat too.

b The marginal propensity to consume (MPC). This is defined as the increase in consumption, C, arising from a unit increase in national income Y. A value of b = 0.90 for the US means that if average national income were to increase by $1, consumers would spend 90 cents of this increase in income and save 10 cents. The MPC is a stable statistic and inherently captures national as well as cultural spending and saving tendencies. While long-term and gradual changes in the MPC do indeed occur, we will hold b fixed in this book for expository convenience.

Values of MPC, while held fixed for individual economies, do vary significantly across countries. Japan's MPC (around 0.3) is significantly less than that of the US which is at the high end (perhaps, around 0.92 by 2015). Even within economies, the values of MPC may vary substantially by generation, or region. For example, some studies have found the Northeastern States in the US to have a higher MPC compared to the Midwest. In Japan, post-war generations have been found to exhibit greater tendencies to consume. This behavior is in stark contrast to that of those who witnessed the trauma following World War II and the virtual eradication of household savings. In fact, single Japanese women today are at the very high end of the MPC spectrum, practically keeping the economy afloat with their formidable levels of consumption!

Y National income. This term is used synonymously with national output and GDP at this point.

d The amount of an increase in planned consumption stemming from a unit increase in wealth (W) is defined below. Here, d is a small number, unlike the MPC for the US. It may even be as low as 0.2; a \$1 change in wealth does not result in a significant accompanying change in consumption, since investors (consumers) understand the enormous variability in the values of their wealth holdings.

W National wealth holdings. This term includes stock market/mutual fund portfolios and other financial assets. Real estate holdings may also be included.

The celebrated and controversial "wealth effect" takes place when huge increases in the values of individuals' stock market portfolios and stock options coupled with, perhaps, significant appreciation in property prices inflate wealth holdings W. This expectation of future gains may induce individuals to increase consumption in the current period, and to lead a more extravagant lifestyle than their current disposable income would prudently allow. In a sense, the security afforded by future expected income (upon retirement, perhaps), may induce individuals to consume this "future income today". Conversely, a sharp correction in the stock market or a sudden bursting of a real estate price bubble as in the US (and around the globe) in 2007–2008 may have the opposite effect—a negative wealth effect of sorts. In fact, with a large portion of US mortgages being "underwater" since the correction of 2008—that is, value of mortgages exceeding the now lower value of houses—there has been a pronounced negative wealth effect up to the present.

At this stage, we abstract from the wealth component for notational convenience and operate with the simpler version of the consumption function[6]:

$$C = \underline{C} + bY$$

We now examine capital investments, I, in similar detail. The investment function is:

$$I = \underline{I} - fi$$

where:

I Private capital investment (necessitates borrowing) for items such as new plant and equipment, housing, and the growth of new capital stock.

$\underline{I}$ Investment confidence. Along the lines of consumer confidence, this index captures the sentiment of business. The Dun and Bradstreet CEO Index as well as the Index of Leading Economic Activity (LEA) may be considered good proxies for investor confidence. Once again, a positive business (macroeconomic) outlook causes $\underline{I}$ to increase, thus driving up private capital investment and eventually the demand for loanable funds. Conversely, the opposite holds true—a crash in investor confidence sends private capital investment into a

---

[6]Changes in wealth holdings will enter our analysis via accompanying changes in confidence. The confidence term acts as a proxy for changes in wealth holdings such as stock market corrections and run-ups, large swings in real estate prices, etc.

free-fall as in the case of Japan from the late 1990s through the early 2000s (please see box).

In the US, capital investment has really not been a key player from 2000 onwards, when $\underline{I}$ collapsed following the demise of the dotcom bubble, the shock of 9/11, and then the housing and mortgage securities bubble collapses that extended well into the decade.

It should be stressed here that $\underline{I}$ is <u>extremely</u> sensitive to future tax increases as well as to news pertaining to unemployment, even more so than consumer confidence's aversion to future higher taxes.[7]

f The sensitivity (elasticity) of private capital investment to a unit change in interest rates, i. Again 'f' will be held fixed when we begin our ISLM analyses in Chap. 6. Here a unit increase/decrease in interest rates causes private capital investment to *fall/rise* by f, and hence the negative sign.

i Interest rate as defined above. These are assumed to be short-term interest rates, and not to be confused with long-term rates introduced in the following chapter. Here, as interest rates fall, capital investment (private demand for loanable funds) increases, and vice versa.

The main determinant of change in capital investment I is $\underline{I}$ and not interest rates per se. If the business outlook is dismal one to five years into the future, irrespective of how low interest rates may be, investors will be unlikely to pump more funds into private capital investment. In Japan in the late 1990s to the mid-2000s, when interest rates were almost zero percent, and, then later in the US by 2008 when rates were pushed down close to zero, we had perfect examples of this effect. This is similar to a well-known scenario in macro known as a **liquidity trap** where low interest rates prove futile in stimulating capital investment (I) in an economy characterized by dismal macro outlook (low $\underline{I}$).

In fact, from 2008 to 2015, in spite of the tremendous liquidity injected into the US economy exemplified by prolonged low interest rates, there was no significant accompanying explosion of capital investment. With investor confidence staying low due to the higher taxation, excessive government regulation following the subprime crisis of 2008, and global uncertainty, capital investment became a flat-liner. Even with short-term interest rates hovering around zero percent, thanks to the **Quantitative Easing** (to be explained later in the chapter), capital investment remained dead; companies opted to simply sit on sacks of cash and ride-out the uncertainty and high taxes.

While short-term rates are exogenously determined by monetary policy, investor confidence $\underline{I}$, like its counterpart, $\underline{C}$, is endogenous, and determined by investors and consumers who process all current and past information. Both $\underline{I}$ and $\underline{C}$ are very difficult, if not impossible, to change by policy. A recurring theme of this book is that consumer and investor confidence, which may have taken years to build, can indeed be lost "in an afternoon" and policy makers would be unable to stop the collapse.

---

[7]"Taxes" here, include all taxes—federal, state, property, etc. In Chap. 10 we differentiate between business and consumption taxes.

In earlier research done jointly with Giles Mellon in *Confidence Credibility and Macroeconomic Policy* (co-authored with Richard Burdekin), we show that a potential collapse in $\underline{C}$ and $\underline{I}$ can be arrested with rapid and very significant cuts in interest rates (huge increases in M) only—only—in the very early stages of weakening confidence. Any delay only increases the imperviousness of confidence to a belated monetary/fiscal rescue plan.

Before introducing the money market and prior to the derivation of the AD, an overview of the description and measurement of consumer and investor confidence is in order.

Measuring Confidence Two major measures of consumer confidence, derived from large-scale surveys of households, are available in the United States. These are the University of Michigan's Index of Consumer Sentiment and the more familiar Conference Board's Consumer Confidence Index.

The Consumer Sentiment Index, developed by Katona and Mueller (1953), is constructed to measure "those factors which are capable of giving rise to independent variation in the rate of consumer spending and saving, namely, changes in people's perceptions, attitudes, motivations, and expectations."

This index is calculated by processing information from a survey of about 500 households. Survey respondents provide qualitative answers to questions pertaining to current family financial situations, expected financial outlook one year into the future, expected one-year-ahead business conditions, long-term (5-year) expectations of the business environment, and current buying plans for large household durable goods (defined as appliances with a service life greater than 3 years).

The Conference Board's Consumer Confidence Index is constructed in similar fashion. In this case, information is obtained from surveys mailed to about 5000 households every month, with an average response of about 3500 surveys. The questions include topics that pertain to current general business conditions, expected business conditions 6 months into the future, current employment opportunities, and expected household income 6 months into the future.

Comparing the two indexes, the Conference Board survey focuses on shorter-term expectations relative to the Michigan index; participants respond to queries about their perceptions of the economy over the next 6 months as opposed to 5 years. In addition, the Conference Board specifically includes questions pertaining to the respondent's employment and income prospects, instead of the more general "financial condition" questions in the Michigan survey. Basically, labor market news has a greater effect on the Conference Board's index, while the Michigan index is more sensitive to news from the financial markets. For these reasons, the two indexes are not always identical or perfectly correlated.

The Japanese Tankan Index Confidence is measured along similar lines in most G7 countries. The closely watched Japanese Tankan index, initiated in 1961 by the Japanese central bank, is a key quarterly measure of business sentiment and is obtained by surveying 10,000 businesses. The index subtracts the percentage reporting an unfavorable business outlook from those who say that conditions are indeed favorable. Ambivalent ("so-so") outlooks are discarded. A net positive Tankan score indicates an overall optimistic outlook while a net negative score indicates the opposite.

From the bleak 1990s through the serial recessions of the early 2000s, a negative Tankan was, unfortunately, a recurring theme. The bursting of the Japanese stock market and real estate bubbles, the East Asian currency crisis, and the state of large non-performing financial institutions all contributed to the demise of confidence.

The respondents are divided into several categories such as large manufacturers, large non-manufacturers (retailers, builders, realtors, etc.), and small manufacturers. As bank credit for small manufacturers evaporated, and when a 33 % plunge in expected profits was projected, the Tankan went into a record free-fall. At one point, in October 1998, this category's sub-Tankan score fell to an amazingly low level of -57, at that point a record low.

A Singaporean Proxy for Confidence Some economies resort to commonly observed indicators that act as excellent unofficial proxies for formally measured confidence. In fact, these indicators are very readily available and are often extremely accurate. One such example is the use of the Certificate of Entitlement (COE), in the case of Singapore.

The COE is a legal document that must be obtained from the Singaporean government when a vehicle is purchased in the country. Just buying a new car by paying the car dealer the grand total inclusive of taxes, transportation charges, etc., is not enough. In Singapore, one must also obtain "permission" from the authorities to be able to drive this car on Singapore's highly "rationed" roads. The Ministry of Transportation determines the optimum number of vehicles that will operate on the nation's roads without causing the gridlock, pollution, and crippling congestion that plague so many other Asian economies. The "permission", or license, to actually entitle an individual to place another automobile into circulation is the COE.

Every month, the government makes a quota of certificates available to the public. The quota is divided into vehicles of different categories and functions. The number of certificates in each category is determined by the ministry and is based on some pre-determined accepted growth rate of new cars on Singaporean roads, and presumably matched to the rate of growth of new roads, parking spaces, and emissions levels.

Individuals participate in an "auctioning process" and bid on the monthly COE tender either through ATM machines or through car dealers. In this highly regulated environment, obtaining a COE is a significant and non-trivial cost running into thousands of dollars. Circumventing the law by purchasing a car and driving without the COE in this island economy noted for its enforcement of rules, is not an option. The final market-clearing market price of each quota (in the several different classes of automobiles) is, of course, influenced by the existing demand, given a fairly stable growth in supply. COEs become more expensive as demand for new cars increases, and vice versa.

Singaporeans, savvy to the notion of business and personal confidence, have concluded that the price of Certificates of Entitlement (released monthly) is indeed a good proxy of economic outlook and of confidence in the shape of things to come. An expected slowdown, such as the period following the East Asian currency crisis in 1997–1998, resulted in a drop in prices of COEs as demand slumped, and the monthly quota (determined by the government) sold at a significantly lower price. As the economy bounced back after weathering the Asian crisis by 1999, and as confidence in the strength of the economy rose, demand for new cars increased. Given the relatively fixed supply (quota) of available COEs, this increase in demand caused prices of COEs to rise.

Of course, if the supply of licenses (certificates) were to also change, then any change in the final price of COEs has to be interpreted with caution. An increase in the price could either be due to higher demand stemming from increased confidence or, quite simply, to a cut in the supply of new licenses.

At this stage, an examination of the money market is required so that we can proceed with the derivation of the AD curve in order to eventually shift the AD and enact stabilization policies.

4.3.2   A Preliminary Money Market and an Introduction to Quantitative Easing (QE)

Money supply in macroeconomics is defined in real terms, in units of goods. This is done to sift out inflationary effects of currencies of different countries and to reduce money supply to one common denominator, namely, the purchasing power of the money.

The real money supply is: **M/P = Nominal Money Stock/Price level**

M is in units of currency ($) in circulation and P is in units of $/good (the price of a typical market basket). For example: M/P = \$100/\$20 per good = 5 goods (market baskets).

The central bank (Federal Reserve), controls M, defined as the "nominal money stock". The real money supply M/P is a combination of M and P, with M being an exogenous policy instrument, and P determined endogenously by the economy. The real money supply, being independent of the interest rate, is represented by the vertical line in Fig. 4.8.

Money demand is defined as the demand for cash for transactions:

$$\textbf{MoneyDemand} = \textbf{kY} - \textbf{hi}$$

where:

k and h   are constants
Y   national income, GDP
i   interest rate.

The intuition underlying this equation is that, with higher national income Y, the average demand for cash for transactions balances increases. As interest rates rise, however, the "cost" of holding cash balances is the interest rate forgone by not placing this cash in an interest-bearing account. The demand for the amount of cash for transactions decreases, and vice versa. This accounts for the negative sign before the term with the interest rate.

Figure 4.7 displays a money market equilibrium with the equilibrium interest rate at i_0, and real money supply initially at M_0/P_0.

We now perform a simple yet very important experiment; if P_0 were to increase to P_1, with the nominal stock (M) held constant, what would be the effect in the money market presented in Fig. 4.7?

As the price level increases to P_1, the new real money supply falls.

$$M_0/P_1 < M_0/P_0$$

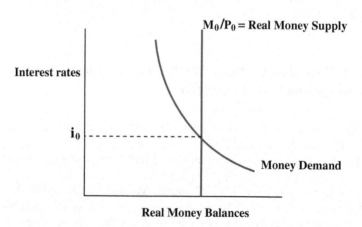

Fig. 4.7 The money market

Fig. 4.8 Deriving the LM

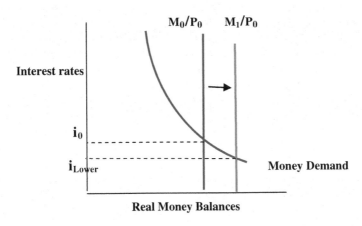

Fig. 4.9 Experiments in the money market

A drop in real money supply is tantamount to a leftward shift (decrease) in the real money supply curve.[8] As real money supply shifts to the left, equilibrium interest rates increase from i_0 to i_1 as depicted in Fig. 4.8. The result of this simple exercise will be crucial in the AD derivation that follows.

Conversely, and increase in money supply from say M_0 to M_1 (Fig. 4.9), would shift the M/P line to the right resulting in interest rates falling from i_0 to some i_{Lower}.

How is money supply increased? We examine this in detail in Chap. 11, but for now we focus on the main method known as **Open Market Operations**. This is the most common method of changing monetary growth in the United States and in other mature economies such as the Eurozone, the UK, and Japan. Very simply, the

---

[8]Shifts in curves were discussed in the microeconomic digression in Chap. 3.

central bank—the Fed, in our case—buys existing US Treasury debt from local banks who are required to carry these bonds in their portfolios. A purchase of a $10,000 Treasury bond from each of the local banks A, B, and C, results in the Fed crediting the local banks with $10,000 each. (Actually there is a money multiplier thanks to the "reserve ratios" involved, but, at this early stage we just treat this as if the local banks obtain $10,000 each from the Fed.) Competition between banks A, B, and C to unload this newly-available money and lend it out, results in a rapid decrease in the short-term rates from i_0 to i_{lower}. These rates that the Fed controls are exceptionally short-term, overnight rates, known as Federal Funds rates. In reality, the Fed and other central banks manage fluctuations of these rates within narrow ± 0.25 % bands.

Important Note: To increase the nominal money stock (M) the Fed bought existing Treasury bonds from the private banks, A, B, and C. This has to be contrasted with the Treasury's auction of new government debt, in Chap. 3, which was necessary to finance new government spending (G). The distinction is important and must be noted and will be revisited in Chap. 11 when we discuss the Broken Rhombus.

The opposite process is true for hikes in short-term rates. Here the Fed requires the local banks to buy back the bonds that they had sold earlier to the Fed. Now the local banks are short of $10,000; money supply has fallen or, shifted to the left, with the result that borrowers now face an increase in interest rates. The local banks have no option; they must abide by the requests of the Fed. These purchases and sales of existing Treasury bonds—Open Market Operations—will be discussed in detail later in Chap. 11. Please note that this process of changing short-term rates via monetary policy is exceptionally fast, and changes can typically be done in under 30 min in the United States.

Following the subprime crisis of 2008, investors, brokers, banks, credit unions, hedge funds, mortgage houses, pension funds, etc., were stuck with the subprime mortgages that went bad when interest rates were nudged up. Borrowers could not make their payments on their dubious mortgages that they really should not have qualified for, in the first place. The collateralized mortgage obligations—basically investment instruments composed of chopped bits of good and rotten mortgages— went sour, leaving holders with literally trillions of dollar of rotting assets. To bail them out, the Fed began an unprecedented, highly controversial and questionable purchase of mortgage bonds worth about $85 billion per month from 2008, with this amount finally "tapering off" by October 2014. It was a mammoth and rampant money creation that beggared the imagination.

The money supply in Fig. 4.9 was shift relentlessly to the right until the interest rates were at zero percent; technically they would have been below zero percent, deep in negative territory, but zero was the floor. That amount of money creation that resulted in technically sub-zero interest rates has been euphemistically referred to as **Quantitative Easing, or, QE**.

And even though rates were stuck at zero (Fig. 4.10), capital investment (I) remained a no-show given the Liquidity Trap discussed earlier. The United States was essentially left with unprecedented money creation, and the investors

QUANTITATIVE EASING (QE)

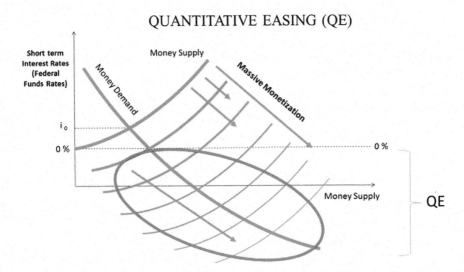

Fig. 4.10 Quantitative easing

and institutions that had made the risky and irresponsible bets on the subprime loans, and had perpetrated the crisis, were essentially bailed out.

In his article in the <u>Wall Street Journal</u>, "Confessions of a Quantitative Easer," November, 2013, Andrew Huszar, one of the prime architects of the Quantitative Easing (QE) Program, did a very bold, and long-overdue *mea culpa*. He wrote:

> We went on a bond-buying spree that was supposed to help Main Street. Instead it was a feast for Wall Street. I'm sorry, America. As a former Federal Reserve official, I was responsible for executing the centerpiece program of the Fed's first plunge into the bond-buying experiment known as quantitative easing. The central bank continues to spin QE as a tool for helping Main Street. But I've come to recognize the (QE) program for what it really is: the greatest backdoor Wall Street bailout of all time.
>
> Andrew Huszar, <u>Wall Street Journal</u>, 11/11/13

He points out that the Fed had planned to buy $1.25 trillion in mortgage bonds in 12 months, and the overall Fed purchase may have topped $4 trillion. In fact, shockingly, he confirms that Wall Street experienced its most profitable year ever in 2009, thanks to money at zero percent which they could lend out at 6 %! And 2010 was almost as good.

What were the effects of this monster increase in monetary growth? More on this in the next chapter, when we analyze the effects of both fiscal and monetary policies on the economy, after developing our model further.

The residual challenges now are how to retract all this liquidity when the time for monetary contraction arises? If inflation were to reappear, or if the US economy were to get some serious traction, then the massive liquidity that is sloshing about in the economy would be inflationary. This undoubtedly was a chief concern for the Federal Reserve in Fall of 2015, when it contemplated the contraction of monetary growth and raising of short-term interest rates for the first time in eight years.

4.3.3 Deriving the Aggregate Demand

Figure 4.11 presents all the components pertaining to the derivation of the AD, developed up to this point.

We start by observing that the goods market is initially in equilibrium at Y_0, the initial equilibrium interest rate is i_0, and the initial price level is P_0. The AD will be derived in the space bordered by the P and Y axes, henceforth referred to as (P, Y) space. The step numbers (in bold below) are also referenced with corresponding numbers in Fig. 4.11.

(1) We begin by plotting the "given" initial point P_0 and Y_0 in (P, Y) space. (The steps numbers are matched in Fig. 4.11.)

(2) P_0 increases to P_1. We now need to determine the final equilibrium Y_1 in order to obtain the second point in (P, Y) space. The two points in (P, Y) space can then be connected to give us the AD curve.

Fig. 4.11 Deriving the aggregate demand curve

(3) As prices increase to P_1, real money supply falls (see the money market diagram) and equilibrium interest rates consequently rise to i_1 as discussed in the simple exercise in Fig. 4.8.

(4) As interest rates increase, capital investment falls, as per our earlier discussion (no change in investor confidence here).

(5) This results in a drop in the expenditures line and a new equilibrium in the goods market at Y_1 that is a lower equilibrium relative to Y_0.

(6) Plotting this point (P_1, Y_1) and joining it to (P_0, Y_0), we obtain the AD curve. (In reality, the AD is a nonlinear function, a rectangular hyperbola, to be exact.)

All points along this AD curve are points obtained by synthesizing the goods and money markets; in fact, each and every point on AD is one where both goods and money markets are simultaneously in equilibrium. Specifically, in Fig. 4.9, The points (P_0, Y_0) and (P_1, Y_1) are simply simultaneous goods and money market equilibria transposed into (P, Y) space. Both these points on the AD have corresponding points of equilibrium in the goods and money markets.

Although the AD reproduced in Fig. 4.12 appears to be just another downward sloping demand curve, it is a whole lot more. There is a tremendous amount of macroeconomic structure underlying this apparently innocuous demand curve. Embedded in the AD are: consumer confidence, investor confidence, government spending, private consumption, capital investment, monetary policy, and tax rates, not to mention a host of global variables such as imports and exports, and foreign GDP, that have been suppressed here.

With the derivation of the AD, a very significant milestone in the analysis and design of macroeconomic policy has been reached. The stage is now set to explore how we can shift this AD to implement demand-side stabilization in the following chapter.

The following section will highlight as well as supplement the information presented in this chapter.

Fig. 4.12 The aggregate demand curve

4.4   Discussion Questions

1. *We have suddenly gone from a very intuitive plane to a more theoretical model. Is this the shape of things to come?*

We have indeed moved to a more theoretical model. In doing so, however, we have increased our level of sophistication. For instance, consumer and investor confidence, the wealth effect, the MPC, monetary policy and the money market, and tax rates (to be discussed soon) were all conspicuously absent in the NSI framework.

As discussed earlier, the NSI was a "broad-brush" accounting framework with tremendous relevance in analyzing international flows of funds, etc., but lacking the domestic details, and particularly missing the existence and role of monetary policy.

In this chapter, we are essentially converging to our final ISLM analysis. With the construction of that model, the "real world" implications and the practicality of our final model will be evident.

2. *Are most measures of confidence adopted in different economies based on survey-generated results? Are the indexes constructed in similar fashion?*

Yes, the method is similar but not identical. We have discussed the Japanese Tankan index in this chapter. Germany's eagerly awaited index for consumer confidence is published monthly by the Munich-based research institute Ifo, referred to simply as the Ifo index. France has a similar index that is released once every other month that includes intangibles such as "quality of life".

In emerging economies, the confidence index may be skewed toward cities and may not be representative of the entire economy. In China, for example, a confidence survey conducted in Beijing or Shanghai, both on the fast-growing Eastern seaboard, may be at odds with the state of the economy in the more agricultural and rural central and western parts of the country. A single confidence survey may not be appropriate for these two structurally different sectors that exhibit vastly different hopes and aspirations, and, most importantly, consumption patterns.

3. *What is the "triple whammy" effect on private consumption?*

Private consumption (C) comprises three elements: consumer confidence, income (actually after-tax income), and wealth holdings (assuming MPC and "d" to be constant).

If the stock market were to undergo a very significant correction, then, according to the much-feared "triple whammy" effect, confidence would fall as wealth holdings collapse with the stock market. Further, if the factor(s) causing the stock market crash were to result in a slowdown in real GDP growth, Y would also fall.

Thus, there is concern that the "triple whammy" of decreases in national income (Y), consumer confidence $\underline{C}$, and wealth (W) would all rapidly conspire to severely curb private consumption.

4. *Are economists in agreement regarding the importance of the role of confidence in designing and analyzing macroeconomic policy?*

Unfortunately, they are not. Those who believe in the importance of the confidence statistic attribute its importance to[9]:

(a) Confidence being a causal factor capable of influencing macroeconomic activity in the near future.
(b) The ability of the confidence term to forecast macroeconomic fluctuations.
(c) The ability of confidence to act as a catalyst, magnifying the effects of macroeconomic shocks.
(d) The confidence index exclusively captures information pertaining to individual's expectations.

Those that do not subscribe to the above sentiment (Fuhrer 1993, for example), find that aside from some idiosyncratic information, the variation in the Michigan Consumer Sentiment Index can be explained by readily available macroeconomic data. That is, any information content provided by the confidence index is already subsumed in the readily available macroeconomic data.

The fact is that while macroeconomic academics remain divided, the confidence indexes, both here and abroad, remain eagerly anticipated by individuals, central bankers and, most importantly, policy makers.

5. *Can confidence be influenced by appropriate macroeconomic policies?*

Both consumer and investor confidence are endogenous, and technically cannot be manipulated by macroeconomic policy. In rare and isolated cases, however, it may be possible to influence confidence with appropriate monetary policy only in the very early stages of a crisis in confidence. (Please see Chaps. 8 and 9 of Burdekin and Langdana 1995, for theoretical details.)

A good example may be Alan Greenspan's prompt action in decreasing interest rates twice in a 2-week period following the collapse of Long Term Capital in Fall 1998 and in the wake of the Asian currency crisis. There is a sense that this preemptive action prevented confidence in the US from collapsing along the lines of the indexes in the stricken East Asian economies. More recently, in a controversial series of policy moves, Fed Chairman Ben Bernanke desperately attempted to save C and I by lowering interest rates to prevent contagion of C, C, I, and I from falling wealth holdings (W), as US housing prices began deflating in 2007. This led to the rampant bond-buy-back program, euphemistically known as Quantitative Easing, which we briefly discussed earlier in this chapter. More details on this subject are forthcoming in future chapters.

---

[9]Please see Confidence, Credibility and Macroeconomic Policy: Past Present and Future, by Richard C.K. Burdekin, and Farrokh K. Langdana, for an in-depth discussion of this subject (Chap. 7).

Article 4.1   SCIENTISTS RATE MACRO CAMP A SUCCESS

By Mike Perron, World Business Review, New York.

Nestled on a hillside with a panoramic view of the Atlantic Ocean, the Macro Retreat conducted by New Jersey based Rutgers Macroscape is getting rave reviews. Designed exclusively to give professionals with non-business backgrounds a hands-on, working knowledge of macro-economic policy analysis, the program has been swamped by an unexpected number of applicants.

Prof. Steve Fountelroy, director of the program, said, "Professionals who have no business background are des-perately in need of information pertaining to how the economy works. Should they pull out of the market? Should they invest some more? This course will give them a very focused yet fundamental working knowledge". He adds, "individuals with non-business backgrounds are having to make very major business decisions today, both at work and in their personal finances. They need to know how the macroeconomy works, and this is where they get the necessary practical information."

Participants attend a 1-week course every 2 months over a 2-year period. "Most of our participants are either engineers, doctors—we have every kind of doctor, even veterinarians— physicists, biotechnologists, rocket scientists, pharma people, IT types, you name it," says general manager, Shelda Megan Wills.

We interviewed some of the participants, and here is a sampling of their comments following the first week's macro course.

Dr. Lenny Hartley, from Omaha, Nebraska, remarked, "I finally understand (a) why consumption does not fall in proportion to a correction in the stock market! And I'm a cardiologist who, until last week had no idea how the economy worked!" He adds, "I am worried about the (b) 'triple whammy', though…"

Gerhard Muller, a bona fide Austrian rocket scientist from Vienna, was confused about investment. "If capital investment increases with lower interest rates, (c) why then did Japan's capital investment not soar when they had those zero rates for all those years in the late 1990s and early 2000s? And the same goes for the US in 2007-15, when interest rates were pushed down?"

"This confuses me too", concurs Meadow Pellagrino, a marine biologist from Daytona, Florida, "and I am also puzzled as to why the (d) classical econ-omists could not come up with Keynes' policies much earlier? Also, if we have equilibrium in the goods market at E_0, (e) shouldn't there be no unemployment at this point, too?"

Jasmine Bhargava, a con-sultant in the biotechnology sector in Cambridge, Massachusetts, loved the design and content of the course. But she feels that she is still not sure "how we can simply 'move up' from one equilibrium point to another. I understand this occurs by increasing government spending. But doesn't this mean that the government borrows x dollars from one group of people and pays the same x dollars to another group?"

At this point, Dr. Fountelroy, interjects, "Excellent question! Store this away as it forms the **(f)** beginning of our session next time! Superb!"

(g) "China and the US clearly enact such polices and maybe now I'll understand the mechanism," exclaims Yong-Suk Choi, a lawyer from San Francisco specializing in US-Far East trade, "but I guess I'll have to wait till next class!"

"You've got us all worked up," laughed Meadow, the marine biologist. "We want to know right away!"

Now this reporter can see why the Macro Retreat has been so successful. The participants can't wait for something they keep referring to as the "engine room"; but maybe that's for a future article!

Article 4.2   CRASHES IN CONFIDENCE AND THE FLIGHT TO SAFETY

Giles Mellon, USA MacroSoft, Inc.

This article extends the NSI analysis by incorporating material from Chapter 3.

It happens every time. Every time the stock market or the housing sector corrects significantly (not just in the US but, really, anywhere), every time bad news roils the headlines, or some emerging economies get hammered by macro-shocks, or Mother Nature lashes out at humankind, some analyst dutifully describes the day's investment as the classic "flight to safety".

MacroSoft sends a team of reporters to understand this ubiquitous phrase. The first and obvious stop is a chat with the macro giant, Professor Lyko, who happens to be speaking at the local architect's conference here in Atlantic City, NJ. We ask her in the coffee break why, typically, US Treasury bonds' interest rates (yields) fall in the so-called "flight to safety".

Lyko replies, between delicate bites of almond-glazed pastry, "The participants of the conference should be able to answer this. There is a massive and sudden increase in the supply of loanable funds into the safe haven country—the United States, in this case, as **(a)** some unseen trigger suddenly deflates consumer and investor confidence. Panicked investors want to 'park' their money in safe-haven assets such as T-bills and T-bonds, and maybe even precious metals. **(b)** This accounts for the drop in yields during a flight to safety; there is often a firming of the US dollar here too."

"And I love that", interjects Michaela Townsend, an architect from Montana, after she washes down her truffle tart with a mocha steamer. "This reassures me and proves to me that we've still 'got it'. We, the US, are still fine in terms of Safe Haven!"**(c)**

We then ask Dr. Ron Farnsworth, the CEO of Investing.Com, why prices of Treasurys typically rise in the flight to safety, and he replies, "Any student of finance will tell you that prices of bonds move opposite to the yield (interest, for now) on bonds."

Prof. Lyko adds, carefully putting aside a plateful of tiny Polish cakes, "Well, the intuitive answer is as follows. There is an auction for **(d)** discounted safe-haven (US) government bonds. In this very simple example, Uncle Sam promises to pay you the face value of $1000 in 3 years. The best bid in the auction today is, say, $950. So the simple 'interest' after 3 years on the $950 that you lent to the government—ignore 'compounding' for now—is ($1000-$950)/$950. **(e)** But if there is panic in the economy due to some crisis in the stock market, in the housing sector, or, say, in Asia, we then have a stampede to the safe haven debt. At this point desperate lenders at the bond auctions are now willing to bid up their best offers for the Treasury bonds to, say, $980. The price has consequently

'risen' and the interest rate (yield) is now 'lower'; ($1000-$980)/$980". This is why, intuitively, bond yields move inversely with their price."

Victor Morales, a CFO of a drafting company based in Chastity, Utah, wonders aloud, **(f)** "So, given what we have heard at this conference, the objective now would be to do damage control by using a rapid and impressively vigorous fiscal and monetary policy mix, right?" Michaela adds, balancing her walnut mousse and strawberries in a very tiny plate, "Yes, we need to go from Eo to E_1 in the goods market—just crank that line up. **(g)** Don't you wish it were really that simple?"

On that whimsically philosophical note, our team of reporters finally reaches the dessert station, whereupon all macroeconomic discussion immediately comes to a delicious halt.

HINTS AND SOLUTIONS

Article 4.1 Scientists rate Macro Camp a Success

(a) This is because 'd', the MPC with respect to a unit change in wealth holdings, is a small number in the consumption function.

(b) The "triple whammy" stems from the extended consumption function (including wealth) and is discussed in the text.

(c) This is because investor confidence, I, was dead in the water, and I is the main driver in the investment function.

(d) They had no reason to come up with a Keynesian prescription because the classical model was performing well till the early 1930s. Remember, as discussed in Chap. 2, macroeconomic models are designed to reflect the reality of the economy they are based in. They are contingent on their particular backdrop and are functions of expectations. As these expectations change, macroeconomic models, unlike the models in physics or engineering, also change, and these transitions are known as paradigm shifts. As these changes occur, new paradigms are ushered in, such as from the classical model to the Keynesian model in the mid-late 1930s.

(e) The goods market equilibrium says nothing about the overall level of employment or unemployment. It simply indicates that the amount produced is exactly equal to planned expenditure, C + I + G + (Exp–Imp), with no excess demand or supply.

(f) Chap. 5 will cover the essence of Keynesian policy prescription. A key Keynesian concept not introduced yet, is the notion of the Keynesian "multiplier" (Chap. 5). Large infrastructure spending will be advocated to reach E_1. The Tennessee Valley Authority (TVA) and the Civilian Conservation Corps (giant infrastructure projects in the US in the years following the Great Depression) are good examples. Massive increases in US government spending on reconstruction and defense, in the wake of 9/11, and then proposed again by President Obama in 2008, could also fall into this category.

(g) Beginning in the late 1990s, China has embarked on an ambitious infrastructure spending campaign on hundreds of miles of new roads, upgraded rail lines, new subway systems and airports, increases in power generation and, of course, the mammoth Three Gorges Dam on the Yangtze river. India is on a similar—though less ambitious—path of boosting productivity via infrastructure growth. In late 2008 China proposed a four trillion yuan expenditure plan to keep growth alive. Eventually, by 2015, it was evident that much of China's government ("fixed asset") spending was, unfortunately, in vast infrastructure projects with diminishing returns to productivity. Examples of ghost cities, ghost ports, train stations with no passengers, and highly subsidized, highly leveraged, and unproductive State Owned Enterprises (SOEs), abound.

Article 4.2 Crashes in Confidence and the Flight to Safety

(a) The final collapse in confidence could come from a variety of sources that could include late breaking news, announcements of new macropolicies, exogenous shocks stemming from political/natural turmoil, or the final bursting of an asset-price bubble to be covered in the following chapter.

(b), (c) relate to the s_{lf} and d_{lf} diagrams from chapter three.

(d) US treasury debt is sold at below face value to the highest bidder (domestic or foreign) at Treasury auctions. In the example provided by Prof. Lyko, the first final bid was $950 for a $1000 face value bond. The bond was therefore sold at a "discount", below final face value, hence "discount bond".

(e) This pertains to one of the factors that attracts capital inflow—domestic safe-haven status. At this time, we side-step issues pertaining to the global mobility of capital. Capital flows vary based on restrictions imposed by different countries, ranging from perfectly mobile global capital to totally immobile.

(f) Note the emphasis on "rapid" and "vigorous" remedial macropolicy—relate this to the discussion on confidence indexes from the chapter.

(g) Refer to the equilibrium points in the goods market diagrams please.

Chapter 5
Demand-Side Stabilization: Overheating, Hard Landing, and SAP Bubbles

In the previous chapter we examined the possibility of a shift in the goods market equilibrium from E_0 to a higher equilibrium E_1, which equated to an equivalent rightward shift in the aggregate demand (AD) curve. This chapter continues the analysis with a discussion of the specific fiscal and monetary policies by which the AD curve can be shifted to enact demand-side stabilization. This will be followed by an in-depth description of overheating, soft landings and hard landings.

In later chapters, we will examine why a significant body of expectations-based research finds demand-side stabilization to be an ineffective policy prescription in some economies since the 1980s.

The following section discusses the first method of shifting AD, namely, a change in the rate of growth of government spending.

5.1 Shifting the AD: Changing Government Spending

Using the example of the goods market from Chap. 4, we now increase government spending from G = 125 to G_1 = 175, an increment of \$50 billion as depicted in Table 5.1.[1]

With the higher level of government spending, the new equilibrium in the goods market is

$$C + I + G_1 + (Exp - Imp) = Y.$$

---

[1] A change in government spending in actual "real world" macroeconomic policy typically implies a change in the real rate of growth of government spending. While macroeconomic variables are obtained from time-series data, in the static example provided here, we resort to a one-step increase in government spending, purely for expository convenience.

© Springer International Publishing Switzerland 2016
F. Langdana, *Macroeconomic Policy*, Springer Texts in Business and Economics, DOI 10.1007/978-3-319-32854-6_5

Table 5.1 Government spending and the goods market

	Y value of output	C	I	G_1	(Exp − Imp)	Change in output and jobs
1	625	475	50	175	25	725
2	750	550	50	175	25	800
3	875	625	50	175	25	875

From Table 5.1, this new higher equilibrium, E_1, is now 875, in row 3. The interesting and important observation here is that a \$50 billion increase in government spending has resulted in an increase in equilibrium GDP in the goods market from 750 (equilibrium from Chap. 4) to a new higher equilibrium of 875, an increase of 125 billion.

This is the essence of a Keynesian stimulus. The final increase in GDP is significantly higher than the government's injection of the additional \$50 billion into the economy. The end result, an increase in GDP of 125, is therefore, a multiple of the injection of G.

This multiplier effect is defined as

$$\textbf{Multiplier effect} = \textbf{change in GDP} / \textbf{change in components of AD}$$
$$= 125/50 = 2.5$$

This is a very powerful (and convenient) result, with strong and obvious implications for government spending. All the government has to do to jump-start an economy is to spend more G, and the whole economy (in this example) experiences an increase in GDP of two and a half times the amount of the increase in government spending!

The next logical step is to determine the mechanism by which this intriguing multiplier effect is generated.[2]

5.1.1 The Mechanism of the Multiplier Effect

The first step is to calculate the marginal propensity to consume (MPC), defined again as the change in national private consumption expenditures stemming from a unit change in national income.

$$\text{MPC} = \text{Change in Consumption} / \text{Change in National Income, denoted Y}$$
$$= (550 − 475)/(750 − 625) = 0.6$$

---

[2]In later chapters, we will examine how this multiplier effect may have "vanished" since the early 1980s in most of the developed economies. But all that is in later chapters—for now, the multiplier effect is alive and well.

Table 5.2 The multiplier effect

Time	Addition to the flow of income	Expenditure
1	50 (initial injection)	$(50)(0.6) = 30$
2	30	$(30)(0.6) = 18$
3	18	$(18)(0.6) = 10.8$
4	10.8...	...
Eventually	...	...
Sum	$50 + 30 + 18... = 125$	

This value of the MPC indicates that in this economy, for every unit increase in national income (Y), consumers increase their spending by 0.60, and vice versa. Thus, 60 % of the initial injection of \$50 billion will be spent, i.e., pumped back into the economy. If the initial increase in G were to be on a high-speed hi-tech transportation system designed to reduce congestion on the highways, then workers in this industry would spend—reinject into the economy—60 % of the \$50 billion, which amounts to \$30 billion. If this amount were to be spent on real estate, for example, then individuals in the real estate sector would, in turn, "recycle" 60 % of \$30 billion back into the economy, and so on.

This sequence of progressively decreasing transactions following the initial infusion of \$50 billion is presented in Table 5.2. As the recipient of each transaction reinjects 60 % back into the economy, this amount is added to the flow of national income. Over successive transactions, by the time the multiplier effect runs its full course, the total addition to the flow of national income should be \$125 billion, the multiplier effect.

The larger the marginal propensity to consume, the greater is the multiplier effect. Conversely, economies with low average marginal propensities to consume (rural China, for example), will experience weak multiplier effects. As we will discuss later in this chapter, large increases in G in such an economy may barely yield any larger increase in GDP.

The multiplier effect relates to the goods market as depicted in Fig. 5.1a. The former goods market equilibrium from Chap. 4, $E_0 = 750$, is increased to $E_1 = 875$. This increase of \$125 billion in equilibrium output (national income) is due to the multiplier effect generated by the \$50 billion increase in government spending.

The relationship **Multiplier = 1/(1 − MPC)** conveniently links the MPC to the magnitude of the multiplier effect. Economies with relatively higher MPCs would benefit from larger multiplier effects compared to those with lower MPCs, even though both economies may have experienced increases in government spending.

The increase in national expenditures, denoted by an upward shift in the expenditure line in the goods market in Fig. 5.1a, translates to a shift to the right in the AD curve (Fig. 5.1b), as national income increases across the range of prices.

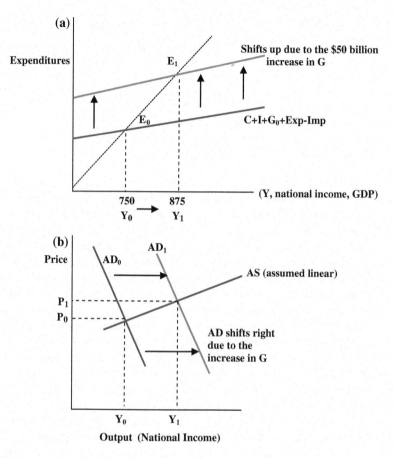

Fig. 5.1 Jumpstarting the economy: fiscal stimulus

Figure 5.2 represents a simple economy with the clockwise flow composed of nominal variables and the counterclockwise flow consisting of real goods and services.

In the counterclockwise cycle, consumers provide labor in labor markets. This labor constitutes a resource (input) supplied by the labor markets to firms that then supply goods and services to the product markets. These products and services are eventually consumed, thereby completing the counterclockwise circle.

The clockwise (nominal) cycle is explained as follows. Consumers incur expenditures on products in the product markets. These expenditures, in turn, are receipts to firms who then incur labor costs in the labor market. The labor costs to firms are incomes to the workers who are also the consumers, thereby completing the cycle.

The more vigorous these clockwise and counterclockwise flows (also referred to as the "income expenditure stream"), the stronger this "engine" runs, thereby

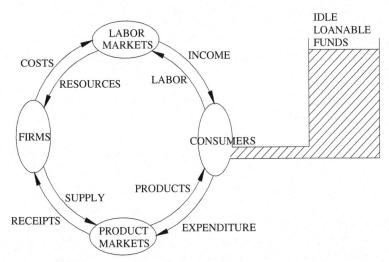

The author is grateful to former Rutgers MBA students Wenjeng Lee and Amir Razzaghi for digitizing the classroom version of this diagram.

Fig. 5.2 The "Engine Room" of the economy

keeping macroeconomic growth strong. Conversely, when clockwise and counterclockwise flows become anemic, the "engine" begins to sputter, leading to a macroeconomic slowdown, or, worse, a recession.

The reservoir affixed to the right of the engine in Fig. 5.2 is a container of "idle" loanable funds. These are potentially loanable funds that, for some reason, have been pulled out of the income–expenditure flows of the economy. The greater the amount of loanable funds in this reservoir, the less vigorous the running of the engine, and the more sluggish the growth of the economy.

During the Great Depression, as banks failed and as entire family savings suddenly evaporated, individuals made "runs" on banks to withdraw whatever savings they could before their banks failed. Liquidity was sucked out of the economy by understandably nervous households.[3] The reservoir was almost full of "idle" funds that were not being injected back into the economy.

At this critical time, Keynes introduced his model. He advocated a strong increase in government spending funded by borrowing idle loanable funds from the general public.[4] In other words, if households and businesses were reluctant to invest in the economy (justifiably, perhaps, given the state of the economy during that period), then the government would do it for them. And most importantly, the injection of government spending would not simply be a one-for-one transfer from lenders to

---

[3]The paradigm shift explanation of the Great Depression, including the liquidity crisis, will be covered in later chapters in detail.

[4]Examples of the US infrastructure spending during that period include the Civilian Conservation Corps and the Tennessee Valley Project.

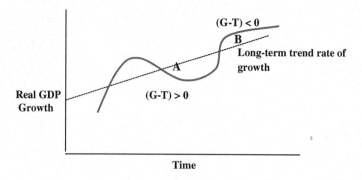

Fig. 5.3 Budget deficits and surpluses over the business cycle

borrowers, but would, instead, jump-start the economy by unleashing multiplier effects. GDP would increase disproportionally, along with employment growth.

This was a shocking policy prescription for that time. Advocating an increase in government spending and even a budget deficit was anathema to the classical economists. As we will discuss later, there was no role for government spending in macroeconomic stabilization in the classical model that existed at the time of the Great Depression. In fact, there was no role for any fiscal and monetary policy in stabilizing output and employment whose rates of growth were referred to as "natural" rates by the Classicists. The very notion that unemployment could be involuntary was incomprehensible in the classical paradigm.

Does this mean that Keynes advocated a string of fiscal deficits every time the economy slowed? Was his policy prescription fiscally irresponsible?

Simply put, Keynes did not advocate continuously increasing deficits. Rather, he advocated a cyclically balanced budget. Figure 5.3 presents a stylized business cycle with the periods of recovery as peaks and recessions as troughs. As the rate of GDP growth begins to decrease, and as the economy goes into recession at point A, Keynes would prescribe an expansionary fiscal policy to jump-start the economy. Government spending would increase and the economy would experience an increase in national bond-financed budget deficits (or decreases in any existing budget surplus).[5]

At point B on the business cycle in Fig. 5.3, once the multiplier effect is well under way and the economy is in recovery at B, government spending is to be cut back to its original rate of growth. This reduction in government spending, coupled with the increase in tax revenues due to the recovery, results in a budget surplus at point B. With a budget deficit at A and a surplus at B, on average the budget would be in balance over the business cycle.

---

[5]Contemporary deficits typically increase rapidly in recessions. The reduction in the national tax base as national income falls, coupled with the additional increase in government spending not just on infrastructure but on unemployment benefits, etc., causes deficits to increase rapidly in recessions. The opposite holds true as well; budget deficits shrink quickly in recoveries.

In fact, at point B, it is indeed imperative that government begins to phase out the new additional spending that it injected at point A. Failure to do so would result in both the government as well as the rejuvenated private sector competing for a relatively finite supply of loanable funds at point B. This competition would drive up interest rates and crowd-out some of the healthy private capital investment at stage B in the business cycle.

While the deficit did not disappear completely—that is, it was not cyclically balanced—over successive business cycles in the United States, the deficit/GDP ratio hovered in the 2.2–2.4 % range from World War II until the mid-1980s. During the mid to late 1980s, however, the deficit burst from this range and rose to 6.1 % of GDP by 1986. A reduction, due to the Gramm-Rudman legislation that stipulated a timetable for automatic spending cuts in very late 1989, was negated by an increase in deficits during the 1990-91 recession (see Footnote 5). By the early 2000s, as tax revenues burgeoned due to strong growth in the late 1990s and as government spending decreased, deficits shrank to finally yield budget surpluses by late 2000s–early 2001s, only to surge back into deficit territory following 9/11 and the war in Iraq.

Keynesian fiscal expansions and contractions will be revisited in detail in the context of the ISLM model in Chap. 7. We now move to the second method of shifting the AD curve—monetary policy.

5.2   Shifting the AD: Changing Monetary Policy

An increase in the rate of growth of the money supply causes interest rates to fall from i_0 to i_1 (Fig. 5.4a), causing capital investment to rise from I_0 to I_1 (in Fig. 5.4b). As capital investments increase, the expenditure line in the goods market shifts up (Fig. 5.4c) and this translates to a rightward shift in the AD (depicted in Fig. 5.4d).

The opposite holds true as well. A contraction in monetary growth results in higher interest rates that act as brakes for interest-sensitive sectors such as construction, and cause capital investments to fall.

There are basically three processes by which the rate of growth of the money supply is changed by the central bank. These will be covered in Chap. 11.[6] At this early stage, we assume that monetary policy is conducted by implementing the most frequently used method in the US—open market operations. All institutions that transact money are required by law to place a certain percentage of their deposits as "reserves" with the central bank. This percentage is known as the reserve ratio. To increase money growth, the central bank (Federal Reserve) in this highly simplified early example, essentially buys government bonds from financial institutions and

---

[6]The three methods by which money supply can be changed are (i) open market operations, briefly introduced in this chapter, (ii) discount rate policies, and (iii) changes in the reserve ratio. More in Chap. 11.

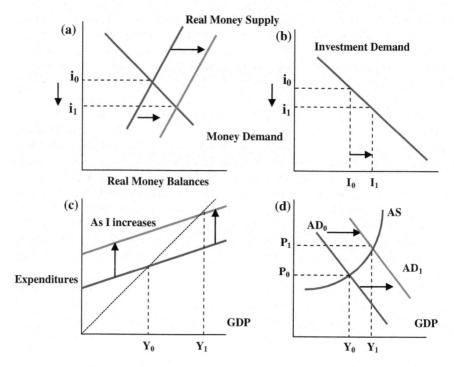

Fig. 5.4 Jumpstarting the economy: monetary stimuli

credits their reserves with this amount. Banks have a greater lending ability thanks to these additional reserves, and competition between banks to make loans quickly results in a decrease in interest rates. To tighten monetary growth, the Fed sells bonds to the financial community, taking in reserves from commercial banks, thrifts, credit unions, etc., and consequently decreasing their ability to make loans. This dearth of loanable funds causes interest rates to rise. (In Chap. 11 we will also discuss how and why in reality, changing monetary growth in most developed economies is actually a lot more complicated than outlined above.)

5.3 Shifting the AD: Tax Policy

We now introduce the tax rate "t" into our analysis. At this stage this is taken to be one nationwide (income) tax rate of t percent.

The consumption function with the introduction of this tax rate t can be written as

$$C_T = C + bY_D \tag{5.1}$$

where:

C_T is the consumption function in an economy with tax rate t
$\underline{C}$ consumer confidence as defined earlier
$\underline{B}$ the marginal propensity to consume (defined earlier)
Y_D is the disposable (after-tax) income.
  This disposable income can be expressed as

$$Y_D = Y - tY \tag{5.2}$$

This simplifies to: $Y_D = (1 - t)(Y)$.
Plug this expression for Y_D into the consumption function:

$$C_T = C + b(1 - t)Y \tag{5.3}$$

From expression (5.3) we observe that an increase in the tax rate t to some higher tax rate t_1 causes private consumption expenditure C_T to decrease. This decrease in consumption causes a drop in expenditures in the goods markets. This, in turn, results in a drop in the goods market equilibrium, and a leftward shift in the AD.

5.4 Summarizing the Three Methods of Shifting AD

The following three policies are designed to shift the AD to the right. In all three cases, expenditures increase, thereby increasing equilibrium output in the goods market and consequently shifting the AD to the right.

Policies that Shift the AD to the Right (presented in Fig. 5.5)

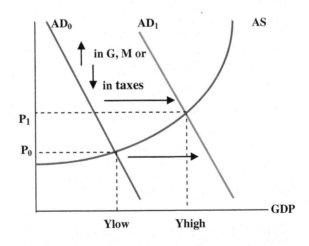

Fig. 5.5 Summarizing policies that shift the AD to the right and jump-start the economy

Fiscal Policy

(1) Increases in government spending (financed by bond-financing discussed in the NSI in Chap. 3).

(2) Cuts in tax rates.

Monetary Policy

(3) Increases in monetary growth and hence decreases in short-term interest rates.

The opposite holds true for policies designed to shift AD to the left: decreases in government spending and monetary growth, and increases in tax rates.

5.5 Unemployment

The next step is to define the **unemployment rate, full employment,** and **full capacity**, in order to fully understand frequently encountered macroeconomic phenomena such as **soft landings** and **overheated economies**.

One of the most frequently encountered and discussed macroeconomic statistics is the unemployment rate. In the US, the unemployment rates are released on the first Friday of each month. The Bureau of Labor Statistics (BLS) constructs a sample of some 65,000 households each month, and interviews them. (An allowance of a maximum of 2500 incomplete interviews is allowed). Each household responds to work-related interview questions pertaining to all family members who are 16 or older. The interview is always conducted during the calendar week that contains the twelfth of the month to allow for cross-sectional intertemporal comparison. Every month, 25% of the households are replaced; thus no household is interviewed for 4 weeks in a row.

A household member is considered **employed** if (i) he/she has worked for at least one hour per week as a paid employee either for someone else or in his/her own business venture, (ii) the individual has worked for at least 15 h per week without pay in a family enterprise, or (iii) the individual is temporarily absent from work due to illness, vacation, legal dispute, etc., even though this may be an unpaid absence.

A person 16 years or older who is not working but is indeed actively looking for work and has made specific attempts to find work during the past four weeks is considered an **unemployed** individual.

Persons not actively looking for work, either because they are discouraged and have given up looking for employment, or simply because they do not want a job, are classified as not being part of the work force. These individuals are not included in the unemployment statistics.

With these criteria, the Civilian Labor Force (CLF) is defined as the population over 16 years of age minus individuals who are, for whatever reason, not actively seeking employment. Alternatively, another definition for the CLF is the total number of individuals employed plus the number unemployed.

The frequently encountered "unemployment rate," is defined as the percentage of the labor force that is characterized as unemployed.

This can be expressed as:

$$\text{Unemployment Rate} = \text{Unemployed}/(\text{Employed} + \text{Unemployed})$$

In terms of the CLF, this is

Unemployment Rate = Unemployed/Civilian Labor Force.

The definition of the unemployment rate is fraught with deficiencies and limitations similar to those affecting the GDP. Since discouraged workers do not "show up" in the reported unemployment rate, as they are not included in the CLF, some analysts believe that the final unemployment rate may not be truly representative of the overall level of job-creation in an economy.

The number of discouraged workers is indeed a significant number. To capture this information and to provide a more accurate assessment of the level of national job creation, the BLS computes six different measures of unemployment, U1 through U6.

- U1 = The percentage of the labor force unemployed 15 weeks or longer.
- U2 = The percentage of the labor force comprised of individuals who have lost jobs or completed temporary work.
- U3 = The official **unemployment rate—the "default" unemployment rate—** where people are without jobs and have been actively looking for work within the past four weeks.
- U4 = U3 + "discouraged workers," or those who have given up looking for work because current economic conditions have led them to conclude that no work is available for them.
- U5 = U4 + other "marginally attached workers," or "loosely attached workers," or those who "would like" to work and are able to work, but have not looked for work recently.
- U6 = U5 + Part-time workers who want to work full-time, but cannot, due to economic reasons (underemployment).

The range between U3, the "default" unemployment rate cited by the media, and U6, the more accurate and realistic picture, is significant. In late 2014, in the US, U3 was 6.3 % while U6 was 12 %.

Another important definition is the **labor force participation rate**. This is defined as the percentage of the total population over 16 that constitutes the civilian labor force:

Participation Rate = Labor force/Population over 16.

The participation rate for the US had been steadily increasing from around 59 % in 1953 into the 68 % range by the late 2000s. However, by late 2015, in the aftermath of the 2008 subprime crisis, the participation rate had fallen back to 62.4 %, the lowest since 1977. The role of labor market deregulation, as well as tax incentives designed to endogenously induce more individuals, mainly women and early retirees, to reenter the labor force and drive up the participation rate, will be the focus of Chap. 10.

It is important to note, that in the absence of information pertaining to the participation rate and to U6, announcements such as, "the good news is that the nation's unemployment rate dropped by 0.2 %," needs to be interpreted very carefully; the announcement, by itself, does not necessarily mean that things are looking up and more individuals are actually at work, and working in jobs that maximize their skills and their education.

Interpreting the Unemployment Rate The fact that discouraged workers are conspicuously absent from the calculation of the unemployment rate is not the only reason that movements in the announced unemployment rate have to be interpreted with care. Another key factor that needs to be considered is the variation in the participation rate and its effect on the unemployment rate.

During periods of strong economic recovery, economies typically experience increases in the participation rate due to surges in the labor force. Longer-term prospects of better, more stable jobs may induce homemakers, for example, to enter (or reenter) the labor force. In periods of growth, companies facing labor shortages may offer better medical benefits, child care, pension plans, prescription drug programs, etc. In this case, the after-tax income along with the benefits may outweigh the cost of lost income while staying at home.

Lucrative job openings may also induce some individuals to postpone higher education or make it attractive for retirees to accept part-time (or even full-time) employment, thereby increasing the participation rate.

While this surge in the number of people entering the labor force and actively looking for employment may be indicative of a strong economy, the unemployment rate may paradoxically rise if these new entrants do not immediately find jobs! The new additions to the labor force have suddenly gone from not being included in the unemployment rate to being classified as unemployed individuals, by merely actively looking for jobs.

However, as the economy continues to prosper, the unemployment rate should decrease as these individuals eventually find jobs.

There are also episodes when individuals enter the labor force and leave quickly if they do not find the "right" job soon. In these cases, a surge in the labor force is followed by a sharp decline, with the unemployment rate mirroring the participation rate.

For emerging economies, measuring and tracking changes in the unemployment rate is a challenge. Performing a sophisticated sampling of households and conducting monthly interviews may not be possible. These countries may not have the necessary tools to accurately track the nationwide civilian labor force. This problem is particularly acute in agrarian economies characterized by small and widely dispersed family farms. Hence, these economies often resort to surveys of demanders of labor—employers—by interviewing small to large businesses. Fluctuations in the level of labor demand for skilled as well as unskilled workers often serve as proxies for the strength of an economy.

In summary, while the unemployment rate is an important indicator of the strength of an economy, its monthly fluctuations need to be interpreted carefully with special emphasis on the underlying factors causing the changes. In addition, caution must also be exercised while comparing unemployment rates globally, as different countries may resort to different measurement tools, similar to the case of the GDP discussed in Chap. 2.

Unemployment is characterized as either frictional, structural, or cyclical.

Frictional unemployment is defined as that rate of unemployment associated with the "normal" working of an economy. This is the residual unemployment that includes individuals currently between jobs and looking for new jobs after being laid-off, or even those who have just entered the work force—after graduating from college, for example—and who may be taking some time to find the job that best matches their interests and qualifications.

Structural unemployment is typically unemployment caused when entire sectors of the local economy shut down—steel, textiles, etc. In this case, there is a serious mismatch between the skills of the workers and the labor demand of a changing economy. Often it is difficult to separate frictionally unemployed workers from structurally unemployed ones. For example, highly skilled laid-off textile workers may be reluctant to accept the jobs that are currently available in the low-wage, manual labor sector.

Cyclical unemployment is that unemployment that fluctuates with the business cycle. Individuals in sectors such as consumer durables, construction, real estate and jewelry may be good examples.[7] Typically the increase in unemployment that occurs during recessions or depressions is described as cyclical unemployment.

Full employment occurs when the unemployment rate is composed mostly of frictional unemployment—cyclical unemployment is not included. Until the mid-1980s, full employment in the US was defined as 6 percent unemployment in the labor force. With the dramatic decreases in unemployment to around 4 % by the late 1990s and early 2000s, this number was lowered to 4 % by many economists.

---

[7]Construction and real estate sectors, while cyclical, typically lag business cycles. Long-term construction contracts, building permits, labor contracts, supplies procurement, etc., are all in place well in advance of the actual construction process. Hence, even though the economy slips into recession, it takes a few months for the building contracts to run their course and for the "momentum" of the sector to wear off and reflect the new mood of the economy.

Later in this chapter, the enormous consequences of this definition will be apparent when controversial issues such as "soft-landings" and "overheated economies" are discussed.

Involuntary unemployment imposes huge costs to society. The value of forgone output resulting from fewer workers is best illustrated by the Great Depression, when GDP fell by 30 % from 1929 to 1933 with unemployment hitting a high of 25 %! In addition to lost output, unemployment imposes serious social and personal costs. Prolonged spells away from work make it hard to get back into the work force and may permanently damage the applicant's job prospects. Unemployment constitutes a waste of resources; experience obtained at the prior job may now be lost to society. Unemployment is also found to be positively correlated with social problems such as alcoholism, theft, drugs, and domestic violence.

Hence, it is hardly surprising that Congress enacted the Employment Act of 1946, declaring that it was in fact the responsibility of the Federal government to "promote maximum employment, production and purchasing power." Full employment had become a formal policy objective in the US.

5.6 Inflation

In Chap. 2, methods of determining the percentage change in prices were discussed in the section on the GDP deflator and the CPI. In this section, **inflation** is defined as a percentage increase in the overall general price level. A **deflation** is an average decline in general prices, as evidenced in the Great Depression in the US in the early 1930s, and in Japan in the late 1990s. **Disinflation** is basically declining rates of inflation. Here prices are, in general, increasing, but by declining successive rates of growth. Examples are the disinflation in the US in the 1980s when the inflation rate fell from slightly over 10 % in 1980 to around 3 % by 1987.

We are now in a position to link changes in the price level with demand-side stabilization which pertains to policies that can shift the AD back and forth, to either stimulate an economy or to bring down dangerously high inflation and growth. This, after all, is the prerequisite to understanding macroeconomic phenomena such as **overheating** and **soft landing**.

The first step is a discussion of the different kinds of inflation, namely, **Demand-pull, cost-push,** and **hyperinflation.** We begin with a discussion of demand-pull inflation, the most frequently encountered form of inflation, in the context of the following policy exercise.

5.6.1 Designing Macroeconomic Policy: An Exercise

Two macroeconomic cases or scenarios, A and B, are represented in Figs. 5.6a, b. Both diagrams assume positively sloped AS curves, which will soon be labeled as "Keynesian" AS curves in the following chapters. This is a major assumption—

Fig. 5.6 Prescribing
demand-side stabilization
policies

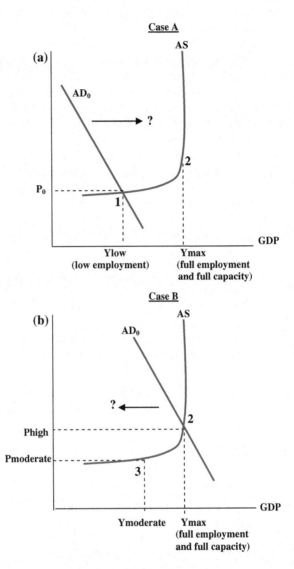

entire macroeconomic paradigms will be differentiated solely based on the shape of
the AS curve in later chapters.

Objective:
In **Case A** you are to prescribe a set of macroeconomic demand-side stabilization
policies designed to move the economy in A from 1 to 2. The starting point 1
represents an economy with a low GDP growth rate accompanied by high unemployment. Essentially, the economy in A is in recession at 1. At 2, you are given
that the GDP growth rate is Y_{max}, the strong rate of growth that exists when the
labor force is at full employment, and where unemployment is mainly of the

frictional type. At this point the economy is also operating at "full capacity," the maximum effective rate of factory utilization.

If policies designed to take the economy to 2 **continue to remain in effect** even after point 2 has been reached, what would be the effect on the economy? Here we explore the ramifications of demand-side policies that cannot be "turned off" and relentlessly continue to influence the economy long after the targets, Y_{max} and full employment, have been attained.

In **Case B**, the objective is to design a fiscal/monetary policy mix to move this economy in the reverse direction, from 2 to 3. The inflation rate at point 2 is a torrid P_{high} corresponding to a very high rate of GDP growth, high capacity utilization, and a very low unemployment rate. Point 3 represents an economy growing at a sustainable GDP rate, with moderate inflation.

Case A:
The economy can be made to hit the target 2 by a combination of:

(i) **Government spending (G) could be increased.** Here, as discussed earlier, this fiscal stimulus generates a multiplier effect that takes the economy to point 2.

(ii) **Tax rates (t) could be cut.** As disposable income (Y_D) increases due to this fiscal stimulus, consumption (C) increases, and this, in turn, drives the economy to point 2.[8]

(iii) **The rate of monetary expansion (M) could be increased**. This monetary stimulus lowers interest rates, spurs capital investment (I), and stimulates growth to reach point 2.

Using Case A, the stage is finally set for a discussion of **demand-pull inflation** by examining the policies prescribed for Case A in Fig. 5.7.

5.6.2 Demand-Pull Inflation

We begin at point 1 in case A with an economy in recession, with low GDP growth (Y_{low}), low inflation rate (P_0), and a high unemployment (low employment) rate which is not explicitly pictured in the diagram.

As demand-side stabilization policies, such as increases in G, cuts in tax rates or increases in M, are put into effect, the economy gets "jump-started" and the AD curve begins to shift to the right along the positively sloped aggregate supply curve as shown below.

Stage One of demand-pull inflation (represented by the intersection of AD_1 and the AS curve in Fig. 5.7) is described as the period in which the economy emerges from its recession. Workers are recalled from layoffs and slowdowns, and plant and

---

[8]As discussed earlier, private sector consumption C is the largest component of GDP—almost 70 % of GDP in the US, and over 60 % in Japan since the late 1990s.

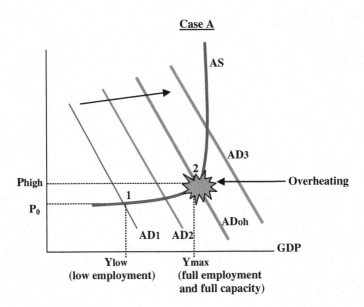

Fig. 5.7 Demand-pull inflation

equipment roars back to life as the economy begins to revive. While rate of GDP growth is strong, inflation in stage one is very low. There is little or no price pressure, as evidenced by the gentle slope of the AS curve in the region denoted as "stage 1" in Fig. 5.7. The intuition supporting little or no acceleration in price growth is that laid-off workers returning to their previous jobs or reentering the civilian labor force do not push for higher wages at this time. The excess capacity of the economy and the abundant supply of raw materials at this early stage also contribute to inflation being fairly dormant in Stage 1.

As the economy continues to grow due to some combination of expansionary fiscal and monetary policies, **Stage two** of demand-pull inflation is reached. As the AD continues to be shifted to the right (AD_2 in Fig. 5.7), due to some combination of government-spending-induced multiplier effects, increases in consumption from tax cuts, or increased capital investment due to lower interest rates, the labor market begins to tighten causing wages to rise. Raw material and real estate costs also increase. In this climate, producers pass on these higher costs in the form of higher prices to consumers. Consequently, strong growth is now accompanied by increasing inflation in Stage two.

In many ways, stage two, given the nature of the AS assumed here, is symptomatic of a healthy, vibrant economy, growing at a sustainable rate, creating new jobs, and incurring moderate accompanying inflation.

However, if AD is pulled still further to the right by ongoing stimulative fiscal/monetary policies, we approach Y_{max} at "full employment" and full capacity. Bottlenecks begin to develop, and the highly skilled and specialized labor market is often the first to exhibit wage pressure. Retaining experienced workers in this climate becomes a challenge. Qualified workers become increasingly harder to find. Larger sign-on bonuses now become necessary along with a host of other perks such as stock options, and so on. And all this occurs despite the fact that newly hired workers may not be as productive as the "first picks" hired in stages one and two.

Raw materials and commodities, beginning with specialized inputs, now also come under excess demand pressure. Overall costs begin to escalate. The output growth for the economy starts rattling against the maximum possible growth, Y_{max}, at "full employment" and close to operating at "full capacity." The growth rate of GDP begins to slowdown due to this combination of operating at (or close to) full capacity with fewer and less-productive new workers.

Accompanying this slowdown is an alarming rise in the inflation rate, driven by higher labor, real estate, and raw materials costs. This increase in inflation could be evidenced either in conventional indices such as the CPI and the GDP deflator discussed earlier, or, more insidiously, in "proxies" of inflation called speculative asset price (SAP) bubbles (described in the following box).

The combination of rapidly increasing inflation against a backdrop of high employment and capacity utilization, and a recently strong period of GDP growth, characterizes an **overheated economy** (at the intersection of AD_{oh} and the AS curve in Fig. 5.7).

For the developed economies, an overheated economy may have a GDP growth rate in the range of 4–7 %, with unemployment as low as perhaps 4 % and overall plant capacity in the range of 85–88 %. Typically, in the US, a benchmark used by economists as a sign of a tight labor market is the point when the number of first-time applicants for unemployment insurance falls below 300,000 per week. (This was indeed the case in the late 1990s, but then as the economy slowed by 2001, the number increased to well above 300,000.)

Emerging economies usually have higher sustainable rates of growth given their lower initial levels of output, employment, and effective capacity utilization. In the case of China and Southeast Asia in the mid- to late-1990s, for example, GDP growth over 10 % would just be considered a comfortable Stage 2. Overheating in China occurred in 1995, when GDP growth roared to over 15 % with inflation raging at nearly 20 % a year, and then again in the late 2000s with growth over 11 %. In 1997–1998, the Southeast Asian economies of Thailand, Indonesia, Malaysia, Singapore, Hong Kong all experienced different degrees of overheating with average annual GDP growth rates in the vicinity of 12 %, and with enormous SAP bubbles in their stock markets, real estate prices, and IT and high-skilled labor sectors. In the UK, escalating real estate prices convinced the central bank in 2000–2001, and later again by 2008, that a nasty SAP bubble, signaling dangerous overheating, was about to pop.[9]

---

[9]Throughout this book, given the inability to display intertemporal effects in the diagrams, the axes represent rates of growth. That is, P_0, Pmoderate, and Phigh are all used interchangeably with "rates of inflation"; their values could be 2, 3 % and a torrid 9 %. Similarly Ylow, Ymoderate and Ymax are used interchangeably with "rates of GDP growth" with values (for example) 0.5, 3 % and a sizzling 8 %.

If, for some reason, the stimulative fiscal and monetary policies that caused the overheating are not decisively checked in time, the AD curve is pulled inexorably to the right **beyond Point 2** (at the intersection of AD_3 and the AS curve in Fig. 5.7). Since no more increases in the growth of GDP are possible, given that we are indeed at Y_{max} at full employment and full capacity, the AS curve rises vertically beyond point 2 as shown in Fig. 5.7.

The continuous and remorseless rightward shift in the AD—demand-pull inflation—rushes up the "vertical leg" of the AS. At this stage, very rapid increases in the rate of inflation are not accompanied by any further increases in employment or output growth that "maxes out" at Y_{max}. The economy staggers into the highly undesirable **Stage 3**, characterized by high and increasing rates of inflation, and no accompanying increase in GDP growth or employment, and closely followed by secondary effects such as inflation- induced collapses in consumer and investor confidence.

Clearly, the objective of prudent macropolicy would be to "slam on the brakes" and somehow arrest the rightward shift in the AD at the **very first hint of over-heating** to prevent the catastrophic Stage 3 from occurring. This is the focus of case B, following the discussion on SAP Bubbles.

SAP BUBBLES AND ASYMMETRIC OVERHEATING. Examples of Speculative Asset Price (SAP) bubbles are the spectacular increases in stock prices, as in the NASDAQ in the US in the late 1990s. The "irrational exuberance" in the US stock market may have led to dangerous SAP bubbles in equities—primarily in the technology sector—and in real estate, contributing to an overheated US economy by 1999.[10] Associated with this bubble were astronomical salaries and benefits that were necessary to attract highly skilled employees in sectors such as Information Technology (IT) and e-commerce, biotechnology, etc., in the US, Ireland and the UK from the mid-1990s till 2000.

Other examples of SAP bubbles are the equity markets of Southeast Asia in the early 1990s, and in Japan in the late 1980s. Housing prices in Singapore, Hong Kong, the US (till 2007), the UK and, of course, Ireland, in the late 2000s, are perfect examples. In the US, the technology bubble of the late 1990s gave way to the liquidity-induced "bubble multiplier," one bubble in dotcoms led to three bubbles by 2006, namely (i) real estate, (ii) mortgage-backed securities driven by the "sub-prime mess," and (iii) a massive bubble in private credit card debt.

Beijing and Shanghai (along with other urban areas in China) incurred dramatic spikes in property prices as personal investment promoted by hot

---

[10]This, of course, is Chairman Greenspan's now-famous comment made in 1996.

capital inflows, excessive liquidity created by the PBoC, runaway specula-
tion, and unfettered bank lending to the private sector surged by late 2014.

Speculative asset price bubbles are considered to be "more dangerous"
because while they may develop in a few specific sectors such as equities, real
estate, commodities, and high-skilled labor, the overall national rate of
inflation as measured by conventional indexes may not be signaling any
proportional escalation of inflation! For example, in the US and Southeast
Asia, as the stock prices, the IT salaries, and real estate prices were in the
stratosphere in the mid to late 1990s, overall rates of national inflation
remained deceptively benign.

For example, when Fed Chairman Alan Greenspan attacked the dotcom
bubble in 2000 with four interest rate hikes, it should be noted that the overall
national inflation rate was only 2.2 %! Dotcoms were SAP bubbling while
the overall economy was not at P_{high}. Similarly, when China had massive
SAP bubbles in housing in the mid-2000s, at times its overall inflation rate
was almost negative! This is the relatively recent phenomenon of **asymmetric overheating;** one sector goes into SAP bubble mode while the rest of
the economy remains benign and calm. These sector-specific bubbles have
made it especially challenging for central banks to isolate them and soft-land
them. Monetary policy is a blunt instrument; a monetary contraction that
pushes short-term interest rates up will hammer the whole economy, not just
the overheated sector(s).

Even if current inflation rates appear benign, and even if SAP bubbles are
absent, inflation warnings could still be triggered by increases in expectations
of impending (future) inflation. Long-term interest rates, for example,
embody investor expectations of future risk and inflation, and are considered
to be key indicators of future inflation. In the following chapter, we will
discuss how and why long-term rates are invaluable forecasters of inflation
that may be "around the corner." Futures prices in commodities and precious
metals, along with other leading indicators, are also other sources of "inflation
warnings" to be discussed soon.

The exercise in Case B presented in Fig. 5.8 prescribes policies designed to
move the economy from 2 to 3. Point 2 is now identified as an overheated economy,
while Point 3 is clearly at some healthy sustainable growth (an "early stage 2") with
inflation at $P_{moderate}$ and output growth at $Y_{moderate}$.

Exactly the opposite policies prescribed for Case A can be now implemented in
Case B. Contractionary fiscal policies in the form of cutbacks in government outlays (spending) and increases in tax rates, or contractionary monetary policy, would
take the economy from 2 to 3 in B. The first policy would generate a negative

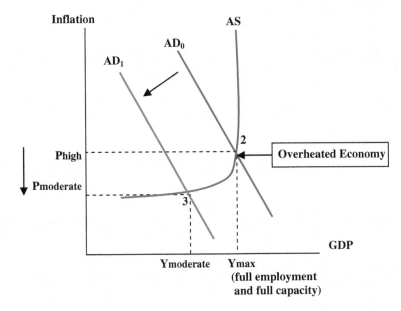

Fig. 5.8 Engineering a soft landing

multiplier effect, the tax increases would decrease after-tax (disposable) income and decrease private consumption, and the central bank's monetary contraction would cause private capital investments to decrease by increasing interest rates. Borrowing costs would then escalate, slowing down interest-sensitive sectors such as construction. All three, or some combination thereof, would decrease AD causing the AD to shift left.

This scenario is the essence of **"engineering a soft landing."** The term can be traced back to the US lunar landing program with references in astronautics journals traced back to the late 1950s. The lunar module had to be designed to "soft-land" on the moon's surface. The phrase was first used in a macroeconomic context in a 1973 Newsweek article. Typically, the tool used to engineer a soft landing is contractionary monetary policy given the relative autonomy and speed with which most central banks can change monetary growth and hence interest rates. Quick, decisive monetary contractions resulting in hikes in short-term interest rates allow central banks to slowdown torrid and unsustainable rates of growth, gently deflate SAP bubbles, and bring inflation down by relieving wage pressure in labor markets where unemployment rates may often be lower than conventional definitions of "full employment". The central bank "cools down" the overheated economy in Case B by slowing the rate of GDP growth Y_{max} to $Y_{moderate}$, and the rate of inflation from P_{high} to $P_{moderate}$.

The US economy in 1994–1995, 1999–2000, and then again in 2006 provides a good example of attempted soft landings. In the latter case in 1999, following six interest rate hikes totaling 1.75 %, the SAP bubble in the technology sector

(NASDAQ) was certainly deflated, the rate of growth of GDP fell from over 5 % to a more sustainable 3 % by early 2001, and then down to less than 1 % by late 2001. First-time unemployment benefit claims again exceeded the benchmark 300,000 per week, implying a slowdown in labor demand pressure. The 13 interest rate hikes in the late Greenspan-early Bernanke era (2006–2007) were aimed at deflating the stubborn SAP bubble in real estate in the US, which then led to the Great Recession of 2007–2014 to be discussed later.

Other examples are the attempts by the Bank of England to deflate what it perceived to be a SAP bubble in housing and stocks in the UK in the late 1990s, the Canadian economy in 2002–2003, and Zhu Rongji's attempt to cool an overheated China in the mid-1990s.[11] From 2003 through 2015, Zhou Xiaochuan, Governor of the People's Bank of China (PBOC), has again been wrestling with what are perceived to be a dangerous SAP bubbles in housing and equities in China.

Needless to say, a soft landing is virtually always a controversial policy move since the monetary brakes need to be applied well in advance of an observed increase in current inflation. Given the nature of this time-lapse between warnings of increases in future inflation and observed increases in prices, central banks sensing inflation in the future often find strong opposition from consumers and investors. These individuals may observe benign rates of contemporaneous inflation and may be lulled into a false sense of complacency. This often places them at odds with policy makers who may be detecting early warnings of upcoming inflation in long-term interest rates in the bond market (this will be discussed later), commodity futures, precious metal futures, wage pressure in skilled labor, and in early SAP bubbles.

If the monetary brakes are hit "too hard" or too long with severe and prolonged interest rate hikes, the soft landing—always a delicate process under the best of circumstances—can quickly become a **hard landing.** This would be characterized by recessions as the rate of GDP growth falls below $Y_{moderate}$, accompanied by general deflation, sharply increasing unemployment, and severely deflated asset prices, not to mention rock-bottom levels of consumer and investor confidence.

One example of a "hard soft-landing" may be the US experience in 2001, or China's experience with growth falling to below expected levels, along with deflation in the wake of the sharp monetary contraction in the mid-1990s aimed at engineering a soft landing.[12]

The box on the following page briefly overviews the pitfalls of a common monetary policy such as that adopted by the Eurozone, against a backdrop of overheating and softlanding discussed earlier.

---

[11]Premier Zhu Rongji was formerly the head of the People's Bank of China. He was primarily responsible for putting policies in place that cooled down a dangerously supercharged Chinese economy in 1994–1995.

[12]The Chinese economy experienced a "hard" soft landing when it was cooled down by Zhu Rongji's aforementioned policies from over 20 % inflation and over 15 % annual GDP growth in 1994 to deflation (or, at most, zero inflation) and just under 8 % growth by 2000.

Two Challenges for the Eurozone: One-Size-Fits-All Monetary Policy and the Stability (and Growth) Pact[13] In January 1999, eleven of the fifteen countries that made up the European Union (EU) agreed to relinquish domestic control over their respective monetary policies to the European Central Bank (ECB) based in Frankfurt. This extremely significant and emotionally charged event was described as the "grand experiment" by the original eleven countries in the Eurozone.

In the context of this chapter, one fundamental macroeconomic drawback of such a one-size-fits-all monetary policy for all 15 member countries (as of 2008), was the fact that at any point in time, it was inconceivable for all of them to be in the same phase of their respective business cycles.

For example, the large economies of Germany, France, and Italy may be in a sluggish early Stage 1, needing stimulus, but the "fringe" economies of Ireland, Spain, and Finland may be dangerously overheating, as was the case by the early 2000s. In this situation, the "fringe" economies would require the ECB to engineer a soft landing by decreasing monetary growth and raising interest rates while the big German, French, and Italian economies would perhaps require the opposite monetary policy—a cut in interest rates! A similar situation arose in 2007–2008, and then, from 2014, when the Southern Eurozone economies of Portugal, Spain, Greece, and Italy were either flat or contracting and France and Germany were, at that time, only concerned with inflation control.

This conflict inherent in the concept of a "unified" monetary policy for all member countries is seen by many economists to be a fundamental flaw in the "grand experiment" of European Monetary Union. Critics of a unified monetary policy claim that if "escape hatches" are not provided for countries to unilaterally engineer soft landings or to jump-start their economies independent of the ECB, the whole common monetary policy experiment may be jeopardized.

Compounding the pressure imposed by common monetary policy, is the fact that the Eurozone countries are also bound by the Stability and Growth Pact which prohibits any unilateral increases in government spending and budget deficit creation beyond specified upper bounds. Violation of aforementioned upper limits could result in very significant national fines (up to 0.5 % of GDP), loss of borrowing privileges, etc. Recently, policy makers in the Eurozone were seriously considering a relaxation of the Stability Pact for exactly the reasons discussed here. However, this was not soon enough to convince Hungary to put its euro adoption plans on hold till 2012, and for Poland to think long and hard about the benefits of early adoption.

---

[13]Please see "ECB: Trials and Tribulations," in Sect. 11.3 (Chap. 11) for more details.

The absence of monetary autonomy in conjunction with the severely curtailed ability of member governments to change (increase) government spending and to generate any multiplier effects leaves policy makers with only one tool to stabilize their domestic economies—changes in domestic tax rates. Given that this is probably the least nimble policy instrument requiring the most time to implement, a rapid unilateral policy response in blocks of nations locked into a monetary union becomes exceedingly difficult.

All skepticism aside, however, the monetary union had plowed remorselessly forward. The gains from the total absence of exchange rate risk within the Eurozone, significantly lower transaction costs, lower long-term interest rates, greater price competition, trade and tourism, more merger activity than ever before, and supposedly greater monetary and fiscal discipline, was thought to someday make the Euro a truly global currency in the not too distant future. But then came the global subprime crisis of 2007, accompanied by falling demand from China, and the whole experiment is under siege with Greece threatening yet another default, and hot capital blowing out of the Eurozone into the United States.

By late 2015, the Southern European economies, beset by nonsustainable budget deficits were pleading unsuccessfully for monetary easing (more M) from the ECB, which would help devalue the euro and spur exports, and also for more eurozone government assistance (more G).

5.6.3   Cost-Push Inflation

Demand-pull inflation is "driven" by stimulative fiscal and monetary policies. If an economy overheats because of a case of over-stimulation, then appropriate policy can be prescribed for a soft landing. In this sense, inflation can be "managed" by macroeconomic policy.

In **cost-push inflation**, however, the inflation is caused by exogenous nonpolicy factors such as oil crises, terrorist shocks, and weather-related events. This inflation, also referred to as "commodity inflation," results in an overall decline in national output productivity, which translates to a leftward shift in the aggregate supply curve, as shown in Fig. 5.9.

Here, at each and every price level, the output supplied decreases. This decrease is perhaps due to the fact that an oil crisis has forced a shift of production toward less efficient fuel sources, and hence toward lower productivity. The AS curve therefore shifts left.[14]

---

[14]In later chapters, the link between productivity shifts in AS curves will be covered. In fact, these shifts will relate to the supply-side model and the new economy paradigm.

Fig. 5.9 Cost-push inflation

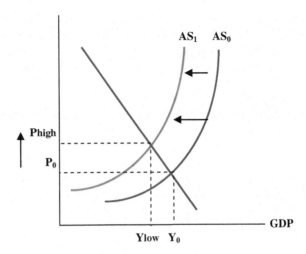

This is the kind of inflation that ravages economies during crises such as oil-shocks, or weather-related crises that ravage most of the agricultural output. Here inflation is found to be **countercyclical.** From Fig. 5.9 we see that as inflation increases in cost-push inflation, GDP growth falls; Y_o falls to Y_{low}. It is the worst of both worlds; high inflation accompanies low GDP growth and the attendant higher unemployment. Since inflation and GDP growth move in opposite directions, cost-push inflation is considered countercyclical.

This is in sharp contrast to demand-pull inflation that is found to be **procyclical.** Earlier in this chapter, as the economy moved from stage 1 to 2 and into over-heating, the rates of growth of inflation as well as GDP both increased. During soft landings, they both decreased. Since rates of change in inflation and output move in the "same" direction, demand-pull inflation is said to be procyclical.

It should be noted here that while commodity prices (grains, energy, precious metals, industrial metals, etc.,) soared by 2007-2008, the resultant inflation was not necessarily a conventional "commodity-driven" cost-push inflation. In fact, the run-up in commodity inflation was really a demand-pull inflation driven by the new equation on this planet—the unrelenting demand for commodities from the pow-ering up Chinese and Indian economies.

To summarize, global commodity inflation that began in the late 2000s was driven by: (i) The excess demand for commodities from superheated India and China, (ii) the resulting rising oil prices that, in turn, further drove up transportation costs (and hence prices) of these commodities, (iii) the huge transition to greater meat consumption from increasingly wealthy China and India which put an increased pressure on larger grain demand from more livestock, (iv) the agro-fuels explosion that necessitated massive corn consumption; corn, incidentally, is the biggest driver of food inflation, (v) the ensuing shift from beef to corn as corn prices soared—the diminished beef supply then caused beef prices to soar, and (vi) finally, and perhaps, most insidiously, another SAP bubble in 'green' technology may be in progress by the late 2000s. Note that, aside from the decline in beef, all the underlying causes are driven by demand-pull forces.

In the following chapter, we will discuss the effect on inflation on long-term interest rates, followed by a description of the ultimate macroeconomic meltdown —**hyperinflation**.

In the mean time, we explore additional economic indicators in some detail. Accurate and reliable measures of inflation and output are imperative to determine if the economy is overheating, if a soft landing is under way, or if cost-push inflation has traumatized the AS curve. While conventional indicators such as the deflator and the CPI were covered earlier, such indicators were "rear-view mirror" indicators—backward looking. The following additional and specialized measures of economic activity, while not exactly forward-looking like the long bonds in the next chapter, are considered particularly important in supplementing the mainstream index-based data, especially in the context of this chapter.

5.6.4   The Index of Leading Economic Activity, napm, and Some "Non-traditional" Indicators

The US Index of Leading Economic Activity is probably the best-known index of impending economic activity in the United States. Developed and published by the United States Commerce Department until the end of 1995. The Conference Board, a private nonprofit group based in New York, was given control of this index in 1996 by the Federal government. A few components were then dropped and others added. Perhaps, one of the more important additions was the addition of the interest rate spread.

Some studies have found that the spread between long- and short-term interest rates is a better predictor of the national business cycle and inflation than most other measures. This finding is, however, controversial, and this topic will be revisited when we discuss the yield curve in the next chapter.

Studies show that the current Conference Board index would have predicted all six U.S. recessions from 1958 to 2015, 3 to 15 months in advance. Emergence from those recessions would also have been predicted correctly from 2 to 8 months in advance.

Ten Components in the Current U.S. Leading Indicator Index

- Average weekly hours in manufacturing
- Initial claims for unemployment insurance
- New orders, consumer goods, and materials
- Vendor performance, slower deliveries
- New orders, nondefense capital goods
- Building permits
- Stock prices, 500 common stocks
- Money supply, M2

- Index of consumer expectations
- Interest rate spread, 10-year T-bonds less the Federal Funds rate.

The manufacturing sector in the United States is well represented by the monthly **Institute for Supply Chain Management (ISM)** index of manufacturing activity. (This was formerly, the National Association of Purchasing Management—NAPM —index). An overall reading below 50 implies a shrinking manufacturing sector, and vice versa. Most US recessions have "begun" with a contraction in manufacturing activity, and hence this is a closely watched index that may signal an impending slowdown in manufacturing, or an imminent recovery.

Another global index that is worth watching is the **Baltic Dry** index managed by the Baltic Exchange in London; its roots go back to the Virginia and Baltick Coffee House in London in 1744. The index tracks dry bulk shipping rates of items such as iron ore, cement, coal, bauxite, cadmium, lumber, and crude oil. Since these inputs are precursors to future production, this indicator is often seen as a good index of future (impeding) economic activity.

However, this predictive ability of the Baltic Dry is effective only so long as the supply of shipping is stable. While the supply of shipping is generally inelastic—it takes two years to get a new ship online and ships, unlike aircraft, are not easily taken out of circulation—the Baltic Dry index could be susceptible to occasional fluctuations in shipping rates based on the supply of shipping.

In general, however, this index is a good indicator of future global economic growth. Note that the Baltic Dry focuses on inputs of real future production transported in bulk carriers, and not on current consumption transported in containers, and hence it should not be used as proxy for container-transported contemporaneous economic activity.

In contrast to the above indexes, the following are interesting examples of some nontraditional indicators used in addition to conventional ones.

Some "Non-Traditional" Indicators[15] **Dr. Clifford Sales**, a physician specializing in treating varicose veins reports, "we use the level of 'pre-paid' (not covered by insurance) cosmetic surgery as a forward-looking indicator. The cost incurred in this treatment is not as prohibitive as other forms of cosmetic surgery ($400/session compared to, say, facelifts at $7,000–15,000). The more expensive 'facelifts' are found to be price-inelastic and economy-neutral (the customers are wealthy), but the demand for varicose vein treatments goes into downturn at least 8–12 months before a full-fledged slowdown hits us." Dr. Sales also finds that the number of patient

---

[15]This box is an exception to the anecdotal write-ups in the book. All the characters are real. These are actual names of students in the Rutgers University Executive MBA program in New Jersey, USA, who responded to a homework exercise in which they had to identify their own sector-specific "indicators." The author remains grateful for permission to quote.

cancellations and no-shows increases months before an "official" recession hits the US. The indicator here would clearly be a leading indicator.

Dan Franzatti, a lawyer working for a leading insurer, states, "Most of the claims I handle are for workers' compensation. Whenever a plant closes or lays off workers, many displaced workers file Occupational Disease compensation claims, usually through the same attorney. Occupational Disease has no specific date of loss, but instead the worker alleges that the time spent at work led to certain disabilities, usually of the repetitive stress type. During the recession of 1990–1991 and then again after 2008, the NJ Division of Labor was absolutely inundated with these claims. With the huge layoffs and closings, the court system was clogged for years! More judges were appointed, and the new courthouse in Newark, built to process claims was swamped!" Dan also notes that often unemployment lags business cycles, and hence the indicator discussed here would be categorized as a lagging indicator.

Jeffrey Herman and his family owns a trucking business. The volume of trucking activity is an excellent concurrent indicator of economic activity. (Fed Chairman Greenspan famously tracked the length of freight cars to gauge the economy.) Jeffrey points out that the profitability of the trucking sector has to be analyzed very carefully. A drop in gasoline prices may be the chief cause, and not an uptick in economic activity. Or, for example, an increase in trucking volume could be due to an "exogenous" factor such as a sharp increase in taxes for passage through the Panama Canal, which would result in freight being routed by land (on trucks) across the United States instead of through the prohibitively expensive Panama Canal.

Scott Mennen, the former Resident Brewmaster at Anheuser-Busch knows a thing or two about beer. Apparently, beer sales are business cycle neutral. He informs us that one discernible variation in beer consumption over business cycles is that in recessions a larger percentage of the beer is consumed at home, and not in bars.

Dave Bishop, employed by a large food company, offers another interesting and related indicator. In the food sector, customers move away from private store labels (generics) and back to higher quality brand items when the near-term outlook looks good. Customers "demand more indulgence" in his company's product lines, with "expensive convenience packaging high on their wish lists" when the economy is humming along, and a slowdown is not in the cards. Capital spending, at least in this sector, is often on the rise in these scenarios. We label his industry's indicator as a short-term leading indicator.

Other "non-traditional" indicators include drops in routine dental visits not covered by insurance, high-end dining, tourism, gourmet coffees, tipping in restaurants, purchases of computer hardware, home furnishings, and consumer durables in general. Items neutral to economic activity include food staples, consumer cosmetics, medium-end dining (diners, family restaurants), and IT (software). While all these are leading and concurrent indicators, movie attendance, in the era before digitized entertainment, was a great indicator—paradoxically, a countercyclical one. As recessions worsened, more individuals went to the movies to escape the reality of the times, as evidenced by the movie boom during the Great Depression!

5.7 Discussion Questions

1. *In demand-pull inflation, growth and inflation go "hand in hand"; they are procyclical. But then how do we explain the fact that we have witnessed substantial and prolonged GDP growth with virtually <u>no</u> rise in inflation, as in the US expansion of the mid-late 1990s?*

There are several explanations. First and foremost, we assumed here that the AS curve was upward sloping (positively sloped) and basically stationary. This is an extremely vital assumption. In later chapters, we will find that supply-siders and New Economy theorists will insist that the curve is crucially affected by corporate tax cuts, productivity gains, and technological breakthroughs that will actually <u>shift</u> the AS to the right.

With a rightward shift in AS the intersection points result in an economy characterized by increases in Y but not necessarily increases in P. Growth without accompanying inflation is the result.

Second, lower global commodity (mainly oil) prices, coupled with a super-strong US dollar served to keep prices of imports low during the 1990s, thus keeping inflation in check.

Third, with increasing amounts of global manufacturing, the additional capacity may result in a rightward shift in the effective Y_{max}. The "kink" may have shifted right as presented in Fig. 5.10, thus keeping conventional overheating at bay. In fact, one reason that Ireland in the late 1990s may have somewhat contained its overheating may be a similar rightward shift in the kink due to large numbers of Irish returning home to a booming Ireland from the UK and the US.

2. *If the policy-making concepts of Stages 1–3 and soft landing are really as intuitive as discussed in this chapter, why cannot policymakers "manage" their economies to comfortably reside in a nice stage 2 on a permanent basis?*

Consistently managing or "fine-tuning" the economy is truly a delicate art, and is often unsuccessful. In fact, perfect soft landings are conspicuous by their limited examples. Monetary policy works with variable lags that can range from 6 to 18 months into the future. Furthermore, it would be naïve to assume that while the central bank is prescribing policy, all other variables remain essentially on well-known and predictable time-paths. The domestic economy could be buffeted

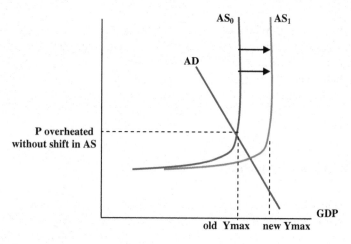

Fig. 5.10 Growth without accompanying SAP bubbles

by a host of factors in the meantime—exogenous shocks, the effects of fiscal policies enacted in the recent past, the state of the global economy, etc.

Furthermore, detecting <u>early</u> and <u>contemporaneous</u> signals of overheating or a soft landing can be very difficult given the plethora of often-conflicting data. Keep in mind that in most economies today, inflation is very asymmetric; overheating manifests itself in SAP bubbles. The overall inflation for the country may be benign, but one (few) sectors could be SAP bubbling out of control. Against the backdrop of low overall inflation, central bankers often have to make the highly unpopular and lonely call of reigning in growth and "ruining the party" by deflating the SAP bubbles before they burst as they did in Japan in the late 1980s.

Finally, and perhaps most damaging to the notion of "fine-tuning," is the claim by the rational expectationists/supply-siders that the AS is <u>vertical</u>, and by definition any attempt to stimulate the economy by fiscal and/or monetary policy is doomed to failure. Picture the AD shifting right in a diagram with a vertical AS curve. The only result would be an increase in inflation with no change in the rate of growth of GDP! This will be the subject of several later chapters when we finally demystify macroeconomic policy-making in developed economies.

3. How do exchange rates and current account balances come into the picture?

It is generally believed that as the central bank increases monetary growth and lowers interest rates to spur growth, the domestic currency will weaken. The intuition is that domestic capital will flow out if foreign interest rates are now higher than the recently lowered domestic rates. This is a <u>very short-term</u> and "knee-jerk" response at best. Exchange rates are determined not just by movements in short-term rates, but more importantly by the current and <u>expected</u> real growth rates of the economies in question as we discussed earlier. If the domestic economy is strong, and real GDP is expected to continue growing, capital will continue to flood into the country to reap investment opportunities. This constant foreign demand for domestic currency will serve to appreciate the domestic currency. If, on the other hand, domestic growth is anemic and the fundamentals are weak, no amount of interest rate increase will attract any significant inflow.

Regarding current account balances, we find current account deficits to increase in periods of strong domestic growth as high domestic incomes result in a greater consumption of imports. On the other hand, current account deficits are typically found to decrease as the economy soft-lands or goes into recession. This is not due to an increase in exports but rather to a decrease in imports brought about by slowing domestic disposable incomes.

4. *Why do employment and real estate lag business cycles?*

This is due to the fact that long-term contracts in employment and construction are often written while the economy is booming. Furthermore, employers are often reluctant to lay off workers at the first sign of slowdown, but instead, they will wait until the recession is incontrovertibly upon them. Along similar lines, they do not recall laid-off workers at the first hint of recovery, but wait until the economy is clearly back on track. Hence, these sectors are found to lag business cycles.

5. *Why are not these alleged SAP bubbles captured by conventional indexes? And when SAP bubbles do exist, why cannot individuals spot the warning signs before the bubble bursts? Why do we need the central bank to be the self-appointed guardian against such speculative crises?*

SAP bubbles may not be fully captured by national inflation indexes such as the deflator and the CPI because speculative bubbles are often confined to very specific sectors, and often to very specific geographic parts of the economy. Typically, bubbles are caused by a surge in liquidity. Rampant monetary creation (perhaps, in response to some past exogenous shocks), results in all the capital rushing to one/few champion sectors in the absence of many investment opportunities. This fuels a run-up in price that escalates as other investors attempt to ride the high-flying asset and desperately bid more for the privilege of doing so.

In addition, with the mature economies moving further away from conventional manufacturing, traditional inflation measures designed to capture increases in costs of raw materials, transportation, storage, and power consumption, etc., may not accurately reflect overheating in a predominantly service oriented economy. In fact, the only hint of overheating in such a service-based economy may be astronomical salaries (plus stock options, flexible hours, child care, etc.,) as employers compete for the dwindling pool of highly skilled workers.

In the following simulated media "articles" please relate all the underlined portions to material presented in this and preceding chapters. Use diagrams liberally, wherever possible.

ARTICLE 5.1 THE EMERALD ECONOMY: PROGNOSIS

Maureen McGovern, Emerald Daily Times

The market for properties in Clover, the capital city of Liredan, is sizzling. In just the last year, some prices have actually doubled. John O'Grady, a 37-year old computer scientist, happily informs this reporter that **(a)** his house has appreciated almost as much as his company's shares!

And as shares have soared, **(b)** so has spending. High-performance luxury cars are everywhere. BMWs clog the streets, and new dealerships dominate busy shopping malls. There is a 9-month wait list for Jaguars. Tourism is roaring. Gourmet dining is all the rage, and imported chefs serving tiny platters of healthy food command rock-star status. Nobody drinks plain old coffee anymore— gourmet coffee is the default option.

Growth in Liredan has been clocked at 8.86% a year, with unemployment at an **(c)** astoundingly low 4.1%. While the current account deficit just reached **(d)** a record high of 4.9% of GDP, the country has also logged a **(e)** budget surplus of 4% of GDP. Inflation, measured by the CPI, is higher at 4.8%, **(f)** up from 4.1% this time last year.

Irene Patterson of Infomacro, a business consulting institute, confides, "all this celebration and rejoicing notwithstanding, we are plain scared. The **(g)** past tax cuts, fiscal spending programs and restructurings which have led to this prosperity may now be cause for serious alarm."

"The current government plan of providing $1 billion in tax cuts, including tax relief on mortgages, is the exact opposite of what we need here now," laments Karl Brenner, economics professor at Cliffside University. "The new immigration law, **(h)** which allows in 250,000 highly skilled workers, primarily in the technology, R&D, engineering, financial analysis and medical services, has helped put a lid on things." He adds, "But the pot will boil over if we stand by and do nothing."

All is not gloom, however. Dr. Kathy Shannon, a veterinarian at Clover Animal Emergency Clinic, is delighted. "We are actually seeing families coming back home. Distant aunts and uncles are not distant any more! Yes, we may be growing too fast and all that, but I believe that the **(i)** increase in national pride is a very good thing. This economy makes us all proud to be from Liredan."

Complicating matters, the metalworkers union and the dockworkers societies **(j)** are demanding yet another cost-of-living increase.   If a desperate government caves in, this will be their third wage increase in 18 months. And this comes at a time when the economy, albeit growing at 8.86%, is tending to (k) "flatten out"—growth has been stuck at 8.84% for this current quarter.

Other concerns abound.

(l) Energy costs have soared along with growth and, just last week, first-time unemployment insurance claims hit their lowest weekly level in 8 years.

Prof. Brenner also warns about the current account deficit. "We remain dangerously reliant on foreigners' willingness to buy our assets. We have become addicted to (m) the inflows that finance our domestic shortfall, and this is perhaps the most dangerous aspect of this economy. We are supposed to be a lucky people—does this good luck extend to macroeconomics?"

Article 5.2   THE   SINGAPOREAN   CONUNDRUM   AND   THE CHINESE CHALLENGE

Prachi Joglekar, Far East Morning Post

Since the time of John Maynard Keynes, economists have long espoused the notion of "multipliers". According to this concept, policy stimuli such as lower interest rates, cuts in tax rates or increases in government spending have effects that ripple through the economy as the "money changes hands". Thanks to each successive individual transaction, the cumulative final outcome would be larger than, or a multiple of, the initial stimulus— hence the multiplier effect.

Singapore has befuddled pol- icy makers. The National Policy Institute, a government-funded committee of empirical fore- casters, has found that the multiplier effects generated in the Singaporean electronics and high-

technology sectors are on the order of 2.4 to 2.8, while those generated in the construction sectors are only 1.4!

This sharp difference has grabbed the national headlines and has focused national attention on the whole notion of such "multipliers". An impromptu national debate is now in progress, and this newspaper has taken the lead in monitoring the range of public opinion. Brief interviews were conducted by our roving team of reporters at Singapore's Changi airport and Orchard Street, and on Wang Fujing street in Beijing.

"You know, I always had a problem with this multiplier thing. You are, after all, borrowing from person A to spend on person B.

(a) <u>The net effect is therefore zero. Right?</u> It all cancels out. So I've never really understood if this multiplier thing is real," says Isaac Goldy, a biotechnologist attending a conference in Singapore.

Thiam Joo Hiu, executive manager of the exclusive Orchard Star Hotel, took time out of her lunch break to tell us, "You know, multipliers are ok. I buy that. I studied all about it. **(b)** <u>But what about the deficits that the fiscal stimuli create? And what about the fact that the interest rates are driven up by government borrowing?</u> That, to me, is the real long-term challenge. I am not losing sleep over why the multiplier is bigger in one industry compared to another."

However, just recently, "the conundrum" of widely different multipliers in Singapore's construction and electronics sectors, may have been solved. Bill Chu and Ashok Govindrajan of Quantonics, a consulting group based in Singapore, find the solution to be "dreadfully trivial". They find that the composition of construction workers is mostly immigrant; Thai, Indonesian, and Malaysian workers on temporary work permits constitute a large part of the construction sector's labor force. These individuals remit most of their disposable income back to their families in their home countries. This simple fact accounts for the lack of any significant construction sector multiplier effect in Singapore relative to the electronics and hi-tech sectors that comprise mostly domestic (Singaporean) workers who "spend their money here at home". Conundrum solved!

And now, we address the Chinese challenge. Policy makers in China have been frustrated in their efforts to stabilize the economy. **(c)** <u>Giant doses of infrastructure spending</u> in conjunction with liberal growth in money creation have yielded sub-par growth. In spite of repeated successively larger doses of stimulation, the final multiplier effect is negligible at best.

We waited till Albert Chung, a computer hardware salesman, finished his Ginger Shrimp at the Great Wall Bistro in Beijing, to get his view. **(d)** <u>"I am no economist, but I would bet that it goes right to the hugely different spending patterns of the two societies</u>—Singaporean and Chinese. And don't forget, even within China, the spending and consumerism that you see in Shanghai and Beijing are not what you see in the western and central parts of rural China. Besides, the Chinese are now worrying about housing expenses, medical benefits, education costs for their kids, and so on."

He may have a point. China certainly has experienced the range of macroeconomic effects, from overheating to a soft hard landing and deflation, and back to growth painstakingly fostered by a combination of fiscal and monetary stimuli. The slogan of Bao Ba, **(e)** guaranteed 8% growth, still resonates with policy makers even though the government has officially shied away from publicly announced targets.

But as long as the multiplier effects are marginal at best, confounded policy makers and analysts will remain huddled over the table.

Article 5.3   ARE WE FINALLY IN A SOFT LANDING? SHOULD WE BE IN ONE?

Al Porcello, <u>Washington Financial Weekly</u>

After seven interest rate hikes, it seems that the Fed may be finally **(a)** slowing the runaway train that is the US economy.

The numbers are just in—it took seven taps on the brakes to bring GDP growth down substantially from 5.1% last quarter to 3.4% in this one. And the stock market has lost over 40% in some sectors, **(b)** primarily in the high flying technology and internet companies.

Housing prices, however, still remain at their stratospheric levels. Even though **(c)** new housing permits fell for the first time in seven years, this month, the number of new houses going on the market **(d)** hit a staggering increase of 4.8% just last month.

"If you ask me, this was one big mistake on the part of the Fed," says Neil Villiers, a marriage counselor we interviewed on the train from New York to Maplewood, New Jersey. "They've slowed the economy down because they were worried about inflation. **(e)** I ask you, where is it! The CPI inflation rate is only 4.1%; it was 4% this time last year. And while growth has slowed, look at unemployment. **(f)** It is still at 3.9%, just slightly above the all-time low we had last year. So they've not slowed anything down but growth. I just wish they would leave well enough alone."

"I agree that inflation must be attacked at all costs," remarks Ruth Zeiss, a receptionist at Fargo Feed and Seed in Fargo, South Dakota. "We had **(g)** some bad recessions when inflation was near 20% back in the oil-crises of the 1970s. But folks forget that nowadays. Anyway, I don't see what the fuss is about now— where is the inflation?"

At Fearless Discount Appliances in Claremont, California, owner Hank Fearless finishes showing a customer a new dishwasher before answering our questions. "It has been desolate here. Desolate for the last 8 months.   **(h)** <u>Ever since interest rates started crawling up, our phones stopped ringing.</u> Nobody wants appliances!   No washers, dryers, fridges, TVs.   Nothing!" He leans over and whisper, "Hey, my name may be Fearless, but I gotta tell you—I'm scared!"

Separately, the Academy for Consumer Confidence once again reported that its confidence index took another tumble, with the index currently **(i)** <u>at its lowest level in three years.</u> Other news appears to be brighter.   The nation's **(j)** <u>current account deficit shrank</u> to its lowest level in six years.

But gloom prevails.   Alex Perone and Susan Fisher, two MBA students in Chicago, are concerned.   "If the government spending cuts that were legislated into effect six months ago finally come on-line, and if the housing market collapses, **(k)** <u>we may stumble into a hard landing</u>,"

worries Alex.   "You know, soft landings are very hard to engineer—if you look back, there are very few successful examples."   Susan adds that she sees, **(l)** <u>"significant inventory building</u> in progress. This implies an impending slowdown."   And durable goods sales (not including capital goods for defense and aircraft) have fallen yet again for the third month in a row.   Susan's wish is that "all this clears up before we enter the job market!"

"The auto market is shutting down," adds Alex. **(m)** <u>"Already 35,000 jobs have been lost</u> in the auto sector since last year. I mean, where does this end?"

As the controversial soft-landing unfolds, debate swirls and concerned citizens put their faith in their policy makers and hope that the economy enters a **(n)** <u>sustainable growth phase with tolerable inflation</u> soon.

Article 5.4   Tax Inversion: Pfizer, Burger King, Obama, Adam Smith and Chinese Walls

© Farrokh Langdana, Rutgers Business School

When US pharmaceutical giant Pfizer made overtures to acquire the British company AstraZeneca, in 2014, it brought the phenomenon of "tax inversion" into the global headlines. Driving this proposed move by Pfizer, and later by Burger King and Chiquita

Banana (among many others), was the fact that in late 2014, the combined state-federal income tax in the US was 40% compared to 21% in the UK. Given that fact that Pfizer had 70% of its cash, amounting to over $35 billion, parked overseas, bringing this money home would be subjecting it to this highly punitive US rate. The overall US tax rate (40%), barring North Korea, is one of the highest on the planet. In addition to the percentage rate, the US is one of very few countries— virtually alone, actually—in taxing worldwide profits whenever they are repatriated to the United States.

In 2014, Burger King decided to place its headquarters in Canada by acquiring coffee-and-donut giant, Tim Hortons, to facilitate its inversion by now making it a Canadian company. This move would result in a savings of $117 million in U.S. taxes by never having to pay corporate income tax on foreign profits if and when it decided to bring the money home to the US. This "could save the company about $275 million from 2015 to 2018, based on a range of Wall Street earnings projections", ("Burger King to Save Millions", Reuters, 12/11/14.)

From a macroeconomic perspective, it makes plain sense to decamp. As tax increases shove the aggregate demand curve to the left and contract the economy/sector, the 'size of the pie' falls. In this context higher, tax rates are simply attempts to obtain 'larger slices of shrinking pies.'

Straight out of this book:

$T = tY$ where T is **tax revenues** ($), t is the **tax rate** (%), and Y is **national (or sector-specific) income** ($). So if the tax rate, t (the slice of the pie), increases, and Y (the size of the pie) falls, the effect on tax revenues, T, is ambiguous. In our discussion here, tax revenues, T could fall.

And as more and more companies flee, we may actually end up with lower tax revenues in the pharmaceutical industry. Examples abound: Michigan-based Perrigo Co., bought low-tax-based Elan Corp. Actavis inverted by buying Dublin-based Warner Chilcott. And Pennsylvania-based Endo Health teamed up with Canadian Paladin Labs to "resurface" in Ireland where the corporate tax rate is as low as 12.5%!

It is not just pharma and Burger King: Chiquita Brands and the music group U2 have both inverted to Ireland, as is Walgreen's in the UK after teaming up with the British pharmacy, Alliance Boots.

The US government responded by leveling accusations of "unpatriotism" at companies that were attempting to invert. Treasury officials took action by changing five sections of the U.S. tax code to make inversions harder and less profitable, and remove some of the benefits that had made the transactions attractive recently, particularly in the pharmaceutical industry.

By Fall 2015, the verdict was in. Regulation did not work. Regulation cannot ever change economic behavior by itself. In the year following the attempt by the Treasury department's tightening of laws to lessen the tax benefits of inversion, "six US companies had inverted, compared to nine the year before", (Obama's Inversion Failure, <u>Wall Street Journal</u>, 9/26, 15). And foreign takeovers of US firms---ultimately having the same positive effect on tax avoidance—boomed. Just in the first nine months of 2015, foreign acquisitions of US companies had exceeded $379 billion, an amount that was approximately double the volume in which US companies were buying foreign rivals. So, once again, higher US tax rates have left us with lower tax revenues, and encouraged the tax-driven offshoring of US business.

The Wall Street Journal (Pfizer's Tax Advantage, 4/29/14) elegantly put it as, "corporate opportunities ought to be driven by business opportunities, and not tax arbitrage. And the goal of US tax policy should be to encourage companies to invest in America, not everywhere else." But, none of this should come as a surprise, really. Adam Smith famously taught us in his <u>Wealth of Nations</u> (1776), that one cannot ever regulate economic behavior. He pointed out that it is all about the right incentive systems; it must "pay" to respond in a certain manner. If it makes tax-related sense to invert, the companies will invert and they *should* invert, charges of "unpatriotism" notwithstanding.

On the other hand, if the well-designed tax and regulatory climate encourages our companies to stay at home, and even entices foreign companies to "invest in America", they will, and they *should* because it makes economic sense! It is all about designing the right incentives that match the goals, and then—ONLY THEN—stepping back and letting the "invisible hand" of Adam Smith perform its economic miracle.

Ultimately, the Chinese say it best when they point out that you cannot build a 50-foot wall to prevent anyone from entering or leaving. They warn you that as soon as you do, someone will invent a 51-foot ladder. Mr. President, tear down the Walls. 51-foot ladders are everywhere.

Article 5.5   Japan Does it Again, 8/2014
Olga Sorokina, <u>Ukraine Financial Weekly</u>

Once again, a tax hike pushes Japan back into recession, just when the country was trying to recover. The three to eight percent (and soon to be 10 percent) tax hike took a heavy toll on household spending, contracting the world's third largest economy by 6.8 percent from April to June. Private consumption (C) dropped by five percent, and C makes up 60 percent of Japan's economy dealing a severe blow.

Japan is in good company. With the United States combined federal-state statutory tax rate of 39.1 percent, we have the highest corporate income tax rates in the developed world. The OECD rate (our competition) is about 25 percent. This has compelled many U.S. companies to relocate their headquarters to lower tax countries.

Below is a very low-intensity tax "primer" to help understand the folly of our policy.

T is <u>tax revenues</u> in **$** or **Yen** or any **currency** of your choice. **T = tY**, where t is the tax rate as <u>a percentage</u>, and **Y** is <u>national income</u>.
So if the tax rate **t** is <u>40%</u> and **national income** is <u>$1,000</u>, then T, tax revenues, will be **$400**.

Now if a government decides that it needs more tax revenues, a la Japan or Obama, it raises the tax rate to say 50%. They expect to get **T = ty =**   (<u>50%</u>)(<u>$1000</u>)= **$5 00** , higher tax revenues.

But very often, this doesn't happen. As soon as the higher tax rates are enacted, or even announced, the economy contracts, and **Y** may fall to <u>$750</u>. Consequently, instead of obtaining <u>$500</u>, the government now gets just (<u>50%</u>)(<u>$750</u>) = **$375** ! The mistake, made over and over again by policymakers, is that **Y** is **NOT** fixed, but endogenous. It shrinks. They are trying to get a larger slice of a smaller pie.

The classic example was during the Great Depression when policy makers raised income taxes to shrink the budget deficit, with the highest bracket going from 25% to 63%. Tax revenues plunged and the budget deficit actually increased instead of shrinking!

Way better to lower taxes (**t**) which would increase economic activity and the national income (**Y**) leading to more tax revenue (**T**), which is the goal in the first place.

SOME ANSWERS AND HINTS

Article 5.1 The Emerald Economy: Prognosis

(a) Sounds like SAP bubbles in the stock market and in real estate are well under way.

(b) Refer to the phenomenon by which consumption is stimulated by increases in stock and real estate prices.

(c)–(f) are examples of an economy that may be _____. Explain why the current account deficit is at a "record high" and why budget deficits tend to shrink when economies go from recessions to periods of recovery.

(g) These are policies contributing to the state of the economy described in questions (c)-(f).

(h) Using an AD-AS diagram, to show how the 'kink' may be shifted.

(i) Soft landings are very hard to engineer, and most unpopular. A booming economy restores pride, and consumer confidence. The general public abhors the idea of deliberately slowing down economic growth that has been so hard to come by.

(j) Wages and prices rise faster as costs increase and bottlenecks develop.

(k) Explain why growth "flattens out" at this stage?

(l) First-time unemployment claims are good measures of labor market tightness. Remember the benchmark number for the US, below which the economy is very likely to overheat?

(m) Explain, using the NSI from Chap. 3.

Article 5.2 The Singaporean Conundrum and the Chinese Challenge

(a) The comment ignores the subsequent injections of funds back into the "engine" of the economy, with each "injection" being determined by the MPC. This, after all, is the essence of the multiplier effect.

(b) Relate this to Chap. 2. If the domestic economy is a safe haven and deficits are "sustainable," then the concern is misplaced. The second half of this quote refers to crowding-out. If government spending is cut back when multipliers are unleashed, the crowding-out effect would be mitigated.

(c) Massive road building, the Three Gorges project, power plants, railways, and the Olympics complex are just some examples.

(d) Compare MPC values for the two economies. Use the relationship between the MPC and the multiplier for China.

(e) Note how emerging economies can sustain higher "minimum speeds" relative to developed economies. An 8 % growth rate would be dangerously incendiary growth for a developed economy.

Article 5.3 Are We in a Soft Landing?

(a) The Fed is in the process of engineering a soft landing. Use diagrams to show how this is being accomplished.

(b)   This is a typical SAP bubble.

(c), (d)   Housing lags business cycles as explained in the chapter. But ominously, new housing permits are falling....

(e)   Comment on the fact that inflation as measured by the CPI may not signal overheating.

(f)   Note that unemployment lags business cycles. Explain why.

(g)   What kind of inflation is Ruth referring to, with mention of oil-shocks? Use diagram.

(h)   Consumer durables are highly procyclical and may be leading indicators given their sensitivity to interest rates.

(i)   Note that private consumption is 60–70 % of GDP in most economies. With $\underline{C}$ falling, C is bound to drop.

(j)   Explain why current account deficits typically shrink during slowdowns and recessions.

(k)   Use a diagram to explain how this may happen. Note the negative wealth effect of a collapsing housing market.

(l), (m)   Both these are symptomatic of a rapidly slowing economy. The auto sector is affected by a decrease in discretionary spending as individuals choose to continue to drive older cars. In addition, the higher interest rates adversely affects car loans. Note how Alex's $\underline{C}$ is influenced by news of job cuts.

(n)   Sounds like stage two of demand-pull inflation. Explain, using diagrams.

Author's Note

Alex and Susan did fine. It took them a lot longer than anticipated, but eventually they both got great jobs. Susan is doing financial analysis for a large pharmaceutical company in New Jersey, and Alex is working in accounting information systems in Baltimore. They meet often.

Unfortunately, the bad news is that Ruth Zeiss lost her job at Fargo Feed and Seed when her company went "on-line" and found that they no longer needed a receptionist. The good news is that she retired and cashed in her pension just before the Fed deflated the SAP bubble.

Hank Fearless did not sell that particular dishwasher that was being demonstrated on the day we walked into interview him. However, three days later, he managed to sell it to a couple remodeling their rental property. Despite that sale, Hank is still afraid.

Neil Villiers, the marriage counselor, reports that his business in Maplewood, New Jersey, is good. "As things slowdown, the brokers and bankers are staying at home a lot more. So their spouses are now going crazy!" Consequently his marriage counseling business is booming. But we do not have a macroeconomic model for that. At least, not in this book.

Chapter 6
Long-Term Interest Rates, the Yield Curve, and Hyperinflation

This chapter introduces the role of intertemporal expectations into our analysis. Effects of current and expected inflation on long-term interest rates will be the focus of the first half of this chapter. This will be followed by a discussion of the ultimate macroeconomic meltdown—hyperinflation.[1]

6.1 Expected Inflation and Long-Term Interest Rates: The Fisher Effect[2]

Long-term interest rates are empirically linked to expectations of future inflation and, risk, and to the real rate of interest by the following expression, known as the Fisher effect:

$$i_{LT} = r + \pi^E$$

where

i_{LT} nominal annual long-term interest rate which is the final interest rate that debtors pay to creditors for long-term loans.[3]

---

[1]While high and rising long-term rates are usually manifested in hyperinflations, the main reason for including hyperinflation in this chapter along with long-term interest rates is to partition the discussion of inflation into two manageable Chaps. (5 and 6) instead of one very large and unwieldy chapter.

[2]Named after Irving Fisher who did seminal research in monetary theory in the early 1920s.

[3]Long-term debt ranges from 5 to 30 years in this chapter. A well-articulated and rich body of theoretical and empirical research exists in the finance and macroeconomics literature in the area of long-term rates and expectations. Our focus here, however, will be primarily on macroeconomic intuition as it pertains to expected inflation and risk. To this end, several simplifying assumptions have been made to highlight the macroeconomic policy-making aspects of this subject without sacrificing the theoretical integrity of the intertemporal models.

© Springer International Publishing Switzerland 2016
F. Langdana, *Macroeconomic Policy*, Springer Texts in Business
and Economics, DOI 10.1007/978-3-319-32854-6_6

r   real interest rate. This is the real return on the loan to the lender and the real cost of the loan to the borrower. This is also the inflation-adjusted rate of return on the loan

π^E expected inflation over the duration of loan. We also subsume general expected risk (such as political risk) into this term

Suppose company ABC needs to borrow $100,000 for 10 years from the general public for additional capital investment. Lenders are interested in undertaking this loan only if they can be better off, in real terms, by at least 10 % at the end of the 10-year period when company ABC pays them back. Both the company as well as the lenders (individual investors, banks, etc.) do their respective macroeconomic analyses and find that inflation over the 10-year duration of the loan is expected to be 8 %.[4]

Hence, lenders will lend to Company ABC for 10 years into the future at:

$$i_{LT} = 10\ \% + 8\ \% = 18\ \% = r + \pi^E$$

Lenders will charge ABC the sum of the real interest that they require ($r = 10\ \%$) plus the expected inflation premium of 8 %. This latter component is simply the amount that lenders need to add to compensate them for the loss in purchasing power of their principal amount due to the 8 % inflation over the duration of the loan.

If this inflation (or general risk) premium were not factored in at the outset, lenders charging just $i_{LT} = 10\ \%$ would find a net real gain of only 2 % in year 10, with inflation having eroded 8 % of the $100,000 loan. In other words, if expected inflation were not added in at the outset, the final real gain to the lender (and the real loss to Company ABC) would be:

$$r = i_{LT} - \pi^E = 10\ \% - 8\ \% = 2\ \%.$$

Hence, if inflation were indeed expected by investors to be 8 % and if the real rate of return is 10 %, then lenders will charge Company ABC the total of 18 % for the 10-year loan. This would be the final i_{LT} demanded by lenders and paid by Company ABC.

The greater the uncertainty, the greater the expected inflation (risk) premium π^E, and hence, the larger the final lending/borrowing rate i_{LT}. It is precisely this expectations-driven feature of long-term interest rates that results in the bond market being a "forward-looking" market.

In general—and particularly in the United States—bond markets are thought to be highly efficient in the speed with which all relevant information is processed effectively by both borrowers and lenders to arrive at an implicit risk premium π^E.

---

[4]For purely pedagogic reasons, we assume just a simple one-shot "interest rate" for the loan duration. In addition, the notion of rational expectations where all investors arrive at similar distributions of expected values given a common information set will be discussed later in Chap. 10 on Pegging and Sterilization.

An i_{LT} term that encapsulates forward-looking uncertainty is a direct product of this efficient information processing behavior on the part of borrowers and lenders. This is why the US bond market has its devoted fans who believe that "bonds know best" and who perceive the bond market to be an "oracle"—a macroeconomic radar, if you will—peering into the not-too-distant-future to accurately determine impending inflation and risk.

In fact, the dictum "bonds know best" is often a very good proxy for general business conditions "just around the corner", and not necessarily valid only in safe haven economies. Take, for example, long-term rates in Russia in the early 1990s following the dissolution of the Soviet Union. The long-term rates were of the order of 1200 % (for medium-term debt), and an i_{LT} of this magnitude sent a very strong cautionary signal to the world community. Such a rate is very likely composed of a real rate of perhaps just 1 % (as an example) and expected inflation/risk premium over the duration of the loan amounting to, perhaps, 1199 %!

Here we have:

$$1200 \% = 1 \% + 1199 \% = r + \pi^E$$

One typical scenario may be that the budget deficit in the above case has become unsustainable, and it cannot be financed by rolling over the debt and by issuing additional government bonds. Domestic and foreign lenders are not forthcoming. As budget deficits stagger into unsustainability, long past the "safe" deficit/GDP ratio of 5 %, a huge monetization becomes inevitable, and, in fact, may already be in progress. Inflation is expected to increase further and spin out of control in the very near future, thereby driving up expectations of inflation to dizzying heights in the current period. Few (if any) lenders would consider lending at long-term rates that primarily consist of huge expected inflation premia.

Long-term rates have "punished" US policy makers, too. In the waning days of the Bush administration in 1990, as the economy slowed into a mild recession, tax revenues shrank fast which in turn led to a rapid burgeoning of the budget deficit. This quickly led to an increase in the deficit/GDP ratio back to the 5 % range, reminiscent of the unsustainability of the mid-1980s. The "macroeconomic radar" implicit in the bond market quickly flashed its warning light. Nervous, efficient, forward-looking bond markets, sensing the increased probability of impending monetization, added an inflation premium that kept long-term rates stubbornly high. As we know, long-term real growth lives and dies by its long-term rates. Capital investment, real estate, and infrastructure are all vitally dependent on low i_{LT} rates. For the Bush administration in 1990, the high i_{LT} rates, spooked by inflation-wary investors, proved to be macroeconomically and politically fatal.

Later, by 2008, the long bonds, much to the relief of long-waiting bond-watchers ("bond vigilantes"), once again flashed their warning as the three SAP bubbles in the US (housing, mortgage-backed securities and credit card debt) began their inexorable deflation. As the US economy contracted, tax revenues shrank. In addition, ongoing government spending on the two wars in Iraq and Afghanistan, increased unemployment benefits, and declining capital inflows resulted in the long bonds flashing a strong 'future inflation' warning. Expectations of future inflation in 2007 in the US were ratcheted up by (i) concerns of future deficit unsustainability, as well as (ii) the next SAP bubble, namely, the commodities bubble in gold, oil, rubber, cement, and, as discussed in Chap. 5, raging food prices.

The long bonds are vitally important within the Eurozone too. The individual member countries can still issue domestic government bonds which embody country-specific risk premia (please see the box on the Maastricht Accord on the following pages). While member countries all share a common currency and common monetary policy as discussed earlier, they do indeed have widely varying domestic fiscal balance-sheets. While some budget deficits range from being well-disciplined *a la* the Stability Pact, others border on unsustainability where their yield curves' long ends, in spite of creative deficit reporting, may give them away.

6.2   The Yield Curve: A Macroeconomic Perspective

Figure 6.1 presents the yield curve that is the time-plot of nominal interest rates on government bonds that range from short-term debt to long-term (30-year) government bonds. The typical yield curve has a positive slope, implying that longer term lending horizons involve greater uncertainty and hence are associated with greater risk premia.

The figure displays an economy where the yield curve has been drifting upward over the last 4 weeks. Here the bond market is signaling higher inflation and/or risk in the very near future as well as in the long run. Both, short- and long-term interest rates are being pushed higher as lenders demand greater compensation for the increased inflation/risk.

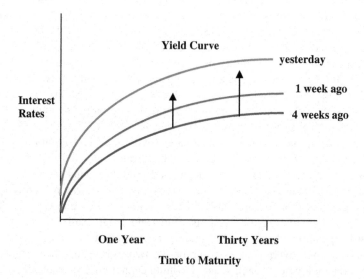

Fig. 6.1 The yield curve signalling an expected increase in future inflation/risk

6.3 Week Ago

If the "long end" of the yield curve (long-term debt of at least 5-year maturity) rises relative to the "short" end, the bond market depicts an economy that is not experiencing inflation at the current time, but is expecting an increase in inflation in the medium to long term. The exact nature of this increase in inflation is determined by macroeconomic analysis. For example, it could be due to an economy on the verge of overheating, with expectations of increasing inflation derived from inventory depletion and early warnings of raw material and high-skilled labor shortages. Or the inflation could be due to impending monetization as a result of budget deficit unsustainability, or even could derive from some other macroeconomic scenario such as cost-push inflation due to an oil shock. The point here is that changes in expected inflation and risk are signaled by an efficient, forward-looking bond market. The underlying interpretations are up to macroeconomic analysis.

While yield curves typically slope "upwards" as in Fig. 6.1, "**inverted**" or downward sloping yield curves are often experienced, with short-term rates higher than the long-term interest rates. Again, several macroeconomic scenarios can explain this.

One scenario examines the case of a central bank that has been tightening monetary growth and driving up short-term interest rates to soft-land a previously overheated economy. As the soft landing progresses and the rates of GDP growth and inflation are cooled down, expectations of inflation and risk fall, thereby driving down long-term rates. Please keep in mind that these expectations of lower inflation in the future as a result of an impending soft landing, are formed "today." As π^E drops, so does the "long end" of the yield curve.

Thus, the "short end" is pushed up due to a contemporaneous monetary contraction (necessary for the soft landing) while the long end drops down due to falling π^E, thanks to an economy expected to cool down in the future. This is why an inverted or "downward sloping" yield curve is often interpreted as a harbinger of macroeconomic slowdown, or worse, a recession. The fear is that the attempted soft landing will not only slow growth and bring down expectations of future inflation, but may go too far and, inadvertently, hard-land the economy into recession. Yield curve inversion will be revisited in Chap. 9 in the contest of the ISLM Keynesian model.

Another reason for inversion could be simply the fact that the demand for long-term borrowing may have gone down. A good example is the US experience in the early 2000s. As the budget deficit shrank to finally go into surplus, and as demand for loanable funds subsequently decreased, long-term rates also decreased, as in our discussion of the National Savings Identity in Chap. 3. In fact, the cutback in the demand for long-term borrowing led to the Treasury's decision in late 2001 to temporarily abolish long-term (30-year) Treasury Bonds.[5]

---

[5]Once again, the discussion here is predominantly "macroesque." A finance text may have an entirely different focus. One must also note that several other scenarios, in addition to the two cited here, can explain an inverted yield curve.

The following two boxes highlight the strong predictive nature of bond markets. The first box is an overview of the Asian experience following the currency crises of 1998, while the second pertains to the Maastricht Treaty of 1991 that established criteria for qualifying member countries to gain membership to the exclusive Eurozone.

The Missing Asian Bond Market Soon after the currency crisis that ravaged Asian economies in 1997–1998, Thailand's central bank governor reflected, "If I could turn back the clock and have a wish list, high in its ranking would be a well-functioning Thai-baht bond market."

Many analysts and policy makers cite the absence of bond markets as a vital ingredient in the meltdown in Asian currencies and the ensuing turmoil. With no bond markets, investors were going in "blind" with no forward-looking macroeconomic radar and were thereby deprived of vital macroeconomic information.

Bond yields of low-risk government securities serve as crucial benchmarks in a host of calculations. For example, in the market for corporate bonds, investors need a benchmark against which a company's risk of defaulting can be gauged. Yields of low-risk government bonds could be regarded as "hurdle rates" that firms should use when appraising investment objectives. Furthermore, government bond yields could serve as reference benchmarks in the derivatives markets also.

The currency crises traumatized savers, perhaps, worst of all. Without bonds, investors planning for retirement had to choose between high-risk equities or low-yielding bank deposits. With banks being shaky themselves, there was really no sensible instrument to plan for retirement. The absence of low-risk government bonds traded in an efficient bond market resulted in a bloated banking sector with banks focusing primarily on short-term lending (unlike bond-investors who may have longer investing horizons). The emphasis on short-term lending led some of Asia's big family owned business empires to favor projects with quicker returns, as opposed to more sensible long-term strategies.[6]

Some business tycoons simply bought their own banks. Lending and borrowing rates came to be determined in a highly inefficient and often corrupt manner. The rates were far from being driven endogenously by market-determined pressures in efficient forward-looking markets with both lenders and borrowers having access to full information. Instead, borrowing and lending rates were determined by expediency and required rates of return on very short-term projects. There was no "macroeconomic radar." There was no mechanism signaling market-determined expectations of impending risk.

---

[6]In fact, if these tycoons sought long-term finance from outside their giant conglomerates, they would have to do so in dollar- or euro-denominated bonds.

The warning lights could not start flashing because they were simply not there.

To rectify this situation, Singapore and Hong Kong moved with great alacrity soon after the meltdown. Singapore began to issue 10-year government bonds to extend the range of the ability of its bond market to "see further." **And this despite a budget surplus!** Hong Kong followed suit; both countries simply invested the proceeds of their long-term bond sales. China also embarked on a similar design and establishment of a sizable government bond market.

Thailand, Indonesia, South Korea and Malaysia began to issue bonds, too. However, these issuances were mainly in response to the budget deficits resulting from their respective currency crisis.

Moving further back in time, the following box highlights the role of long-term rates in qualifying for the monetary union in the countries that constitute the Eurozone. The European monetary union, wherein member countries sacrifice all monetary autonomy and their domestic currencies for a one-size-fits-all monetary policy and the Euro as currency, was labeled "The Grand Experiment." This box includes a brief overview of the "experiment" along with the primary focus on long-term rates.

Long-Term Interest Rates and the 1991 Maastricht Convergence Criteria The Maastricht Treaty, established in late 1991, was a milestone on the long road to European Economic and Monetary Union (EMU). "Maastricht" was the prelude to the adoption of one common currency, the euro, and one common monetary policy to be conducted by the European Central Bank (ECB) in Frankfurt.

Membership in this union of countries—the Eurozone—meant that all aspirant countries needed to get their key macroeconomic statistics "in sync", before they could abandon their currencies and adopt the euro. Countries were required to show strong evidence of fiscal and monetary discipline; one weak link of fiscal or monetary lassitude could jeopardize the integrity of the whole monetary union.

With this objective in mind, several benchmark targets for key macroeconomic statistics were prescribed by the accord. These were the "convergence criteria" that had to be attained by May 1998. At this point, the European Union countries that had successfully qualified for membership to the common currency would be announced. The "convergence criteria" are still valid today, as they apply to new aspirant countries as well:

(i)   Budget deficits have to be under 3 % of GDP. In other words, they
      have to be highly sustainable.
(ii) National debt has to be under 60 % of GDP. Once again this criterion
      is aimed at ensuring fiscal rectitude.[7]
(iii) Inflation cannot exceed the average of the three countries with the
      lowest inflation by more than 1.5 %.
(iv) Long-term interest rates cannot exceed the average of the three
      countries with the lowest long-term rates by more than 2 %.

Low long-term rates imply macroeconomic radar that does not detect
expected inflation risk in the future. Specifically, these oracles of inflation
signal that fiscal discipline (sustainable deficits) has been attained and a
highly inflationary monetization of runaway deficits is not forthcoming.

This last criterion was a particularly important convergence criterion given
that some countries may have resorted to "creative" accounting measures and
unique interpretations of "Maastricht" to attain criteria (i) and (ii). One-time
sales of huge state-owned assets, for example, could significantly reduce the
deficit, conveniently bringing the deficit/GDP ratio under the qualifying 3 %!

If the bond markets are indeed highly efficient in processing
forward-looking information, an endogenously determined (market determined) signal of "low future inflation," signaled by low long-term rates, may
perhaps be a much more reliable indicator of fiscal discipline than published
annual deficit figures.

6.3.1 Negative Real Rates and SAP Bubbles

Rewriting the Fisher effect as: $r = i_{LT} - \pi^{E}$

we obtain the real, or, inflation-adjusted, interest rate.

In this case if expected inflation is larger than nominal interest rates, we end up
with negative real rates. Since the real rate is the actual gain to the lender and actual
loss to the borrower, a negative real rate translates to a real gain to a borrower and a
real loss to a lender. In other words, depositing money in a savings account (becoming a lender) only results in the depreciation of one's savings as the paltry
interest earned is less than the erosion due to the roaring inflation.

Along these lines, a borrower does well in this climate; the value of the principal
at pay-back time is less than it was at the inception of the loan. Lenders pay-back a
loan whose purchasing power has been nibbled away by inflation.

---

[7]In criteria (i) and (ii), if the deficit/GDP ratio fell uniformly towards 3 % and if the debt/GDP ratio
approached 60 % "at a satisfactory rate," the country would also be eligible for EMU qualification.

This climate, characterized by negative real rates, justifiably fosters low savings and heavy debt-driven consumption, and is often the necessary backdrop for consumption-driven SAP bubbles. Perfect examples of SAP bubbles driven by negative real rates are the housing and stock market bubbles in China from early 2003, and in the real estate market in the US from 2003 to 2007.

6.4 Hyperinflations

Hyperinflations are easily the most traumatic of all macroeconomic disasters. The term "hyperinflation" refers not to just a very large increase in the price level, but to a rapid one as well. While there is no formal definition for the term, an economy is said to hyperinflate if inflation is greater than 50 % a month. However, hyperinflations almost never stabilize with final inflation anywhere in that region but instead race uncontrollably past the 50 % mark into stratospheric, inconceivable rates of inflation. For example, in less than 2 years beginning in 1922, the German average price level increased by a factor of 20 billion!

Generations who are unfortunate enough to be struck by the trauma of hyperinflations never forget them. The experience is indelibly seared into public memory. Hyperinflations change lives, policies, and entire generations, and almost inevitably result in a total overhaul of the incumbent government. In this section, we will discuss the causes and eventual remedies of this macroeconomic disaster.

Usually, a hyperinflation is the result of an unsustainable budget deficit. As discussed earlier, and to be revisited again in a later chapter, once the deficit/GDP ratio exceeds an upper bound (around 5 % for developed economies), further bond-financing becomes impossible. Domestic and foreign investors are reluctant to lend more funds to a regime that is perceived to be risky, or to one that has incurred extravagant and irresponsible spending. Such government spending could range from massive infrastructure projects gone awry, to ill-conceived and impulsive fiscal expansion or reckless military spending. The regime may be corrupt; large portions of the increase in spending may end up in their personal coffers or in overseas accounts. A prolonged conflict may be impending or even in progress.

In this situation, "rolling over" the debt that may have just matured, by issuing new bonds, suddenly becomes impossible. To make principal and interest payment on debt, the only option then is to induce or pressure the central bank to simply monetize the debt by "printing money." Typically, in these cases, the central bank does not have a high degree of autonomy. The money creating authority may be subservient to the deficit creating authority, thereby setting the stage for unmitigated money creation to finance giant runaway budget deficits. In fact, in the extreme case, fiscal spending and monetary creation may even be controlled by the same entity![8]

---

[8]Article 6.2, at the end of this chapter, is a shocking and true account of the hyperinflation in Yugoslavia in the 1990s, under Slobodan Milosovic.

6.4.1 The Anatomy of a Meltdown

(1) As severe monetization becomes necessary to finance the giant unsustainable deficits, inflation begins to rise. Consumers "buy now" to beat future price increases. This excess demand on consumption goods drives prices up further.

(2) With increase in inflation, workers demand higher wages to compensate them for rising expenses. These higher wages push up prices and a dangerous wage-price spiral begins to form with wages and prices mutually pushing each other upwards.

(3) As inflation gradually climbs higher, suppliers tend to hoard in anticipation of higher prices in the very near future. This artificially created shortage further exacerbates the excess demand pressure. Inflation now increases very rapidly.[9]

(4) Confidence is continuously plummeting all along. Wages continue to rise along with inflation.

(5) Typically, these countries have a large number of highly inefficient and unprofitable SOEs (State-Owned Enterprises). Examples are steel, power, transportation, mining, and oil. Most owe their very existence to state subsidies, tax credits, subsidized rent, power, transportation costs, and often, guaranteed prices for substandard globally uncompetitive output.[10] As inflation mounts, these SOEs now demand further subsidies, price supports, etc., or else they may threaten general (national) strikes that could cripple the whole country.[11]

(6) The government relents and caves into this pressure from the sizable state-subsidized industry. Further price supports, subsidies, huge cost of living increases to match the rampant inflation, and subsidized housing (to name a few) are provided by the government and financed by yet more monetization! Given the magnitude of the SOEs, this is often a huge and fatal dose of money creation that becomes the proverbial last straw.

(7) Inflation is now completely out of control. Prices may be doubling or even quadrupling between breakfast and lunch time! The economy careens out of orbit, and investor and consumer confidence go into a total free-fall. And all

---

[9]In fact, the severe hyperinflation that ravaged Russia following the dissolution of the Soviet Union was such a serious and crippling problem that hoarders, if caught, would receive the death penalty.

[10]The author hastens to add that not all SOEs are uncompetitive and need to depend on State handouts. Snow Lotus Cashmere, Tsing Tao beer, Magic Panda cellular phones, etc., are high quality world players who also happen to be Chinese SOEs. These enterprises have successfully reinvented themselves to become competitive. Such exemplary SOEs, however, be they in China, the rest of Asia, Europe, or in the Americas, are unfortunately in the distinct minority. According to the Chinese government, its greatest challenge lies in reforming these SOEs and minimizing their drag on the economy without causing a resultant increase in unemployment to destabilize the country.

[11]A "general strike," designed to bring the country to a standstill, is illegal in the United States due to legislation passed by President Truman.

along, as a sinister backdrop, inflation races inexorably upwards until the actual inflation rate becomes a meaningless statistic.

In the Hungarian hyperinflation following World War II, from July 1945 to August 1, 1946, the price level increased from 7964 to an inconceivable $(24)(10^{28})$. In the last 2 months of the hyperinflation, the rates of inflation were $(8.4)(10^5)$ percent and **a staggering $(41.9)(10^{15})$ percent.**

(8) All along, the hyperinflating economy experiences a massive flight of capital as individuals desperately convert domestic savings (and even daily pay-checks) denominated in the ravaged domestic currency to some "hard cur-rency" (US$, euros, even yen), or to precious metals (typically, gold). If a well-functioning bond market had existed, the warning signs would have long been flashing. Irrespective, individuals attempt to somehow preserve at least some modicum of real purchasing power from their life savings.

(9) Typically, the hyperinflating country attempts to stem this hemorrhage of domestic savings by instating capital controls. Often, this measure is of no avail; as savings and nest-eggs shrink rapidly, money floods out of the hyperinflating economy. Illegal secondary markets develop in hard currency and precious metals. The country continues to experience a massive capital exodus.

(10) As individuals convert savings in hyperinflated currency to hard currency or gold, the exchange rate collapses. The domestic currency is progressively worth less and less in terms of hard currency, until, like the inflation rate, the exact rate is irrelevant. Crucial imports such as food, medicine, and fuel, denominated in harder foreign currency, now become virtually unaffordable.

(11) Domestic currency becomes worthless. It loses all value, and its intrinsic paper value may even exceed its face value. Currency may now be used as kindling to light fires (as it was during the German Hyperinflation of 1919–23), or substituted for wallpaper (again, as in the German Hyperinflation).

(12) The economy deteriorates into a barter economy. Goods are traded in informal farmer's markets. The incumbent government is ousted from power. Chaos reigns.

Examples of inflation rates from some classic annualized hyperinflation rates are presented below:

1922 Germany, 5500 %
1985 Bolivia, exceeded 10,000 %
1989 Argentina, 3400 %
1990 Peru, exceeded 7000 %
1993 Brazil, 2400 %
1993 Ukraine exceeded 5200 %
2008 Zimbabwe exceeded 12 million percent inflation (unofficially, the rate was 20 million percent).

Author's Note: The write-up in the following box illustrates the cruel reality and human cost of hyperinflation. This narrative, submitted by my former student Nadia Karalnik (from Russia), was part of a macroeconomics assignment, and is reprinted here in its original form. This is the only instance in this book where all the characters are real.

The Hyperinflation in Russia: The Words of Roza Beydman By Nadia Karalnik, MBA Student, Rutgers University, New Jersey, USA

(At the time this was written, Roza Beydman was just about to become Nadia's mother-in-law.)

Roza immigrated to the United States in 1997. This is a personal story, in Roza's own words, of the events that took place in Russia in the early 1990s, when the country encountered a financial crisis and hyperinflation caused by the instability of the Russian economy.

"I worked very hard my whole life. My husband was an engineer and I was a teacher. Our modest salaries were enough to feed the children and to buy necessities. We always had to be careful with every ruble in order to make sure that every month we could put off (save) some money away. We never trusted that the government will support us once we retired, so we wanted to make sure that we had enough to support ourselves. We managed to collect (save) 15,000 rubles. Considering the fact that in 1990 an average engineer was making 150–200 rubles a month, this was a considerably large sum.

My husband and I both retired in 1986, when we turned 60 years old. Our pensions were 80 rubles a month each. We were very satisfied with our wise decision; the savings really gave us the comfort to be sure that there would be food on the tables today, tomorrow and in the future.

My husband passed away in 1989; he did not live to see the horrors of our falldown.

It was like a bad dream. At first, all food products and clothes disappeared from the stores, and the news about the possible price increases spread very fast around the city. Simple products like sugar and meat became great scarcities. For example, I had to stand in line for two hours to get sugar, and the limit was one kilogram per person. That was the period when money was not the problem. It was simply an issue of what was available for sale.

One day I went to the store and realized that the prices had suddenly increased. The loaf of bread that cost 30 kopeikas for years was now selling for 3 rubles! (100 kopeikas = 1 ruble). Everybody knew that something very bad was happening, but there was just nothing we could do to prevent it. My neighbors told me that the banks are offering high interest rates, so I decided to put half my savings into a savings account. It was only a matter of two weeks before my lifetime savings became worthless. I could now use this money to buy one pair of shoes.

The prices were growing every day and were so high that I couldn't even understand how much everything cost. It became pointless to have rubles; anybody who had a chance to convert rubles to dollars took advantage of it. The exchange rate went from 0.9 rubles per dollar to five thousand rubles per dollar. The dollar became the only valuable currency.

The situation got even worse when they stopped paying salaries and pensions. People who worked in factories were better off; they were paid in the products of the factory. For example, those who worked in the shoe industry were getting paid in shoes. They could then either sell their products or just exchange them for other products at the bazaar.

The elderly people took the hardest hit. Our minimal pension increases could not keep up with every day's inflation. If any of us saved any money, it lost any value and was long gone. We had to start selling personal belongings. Anything that had any value was for sale. The situation in the stores was very different now—the shelves were full of goods and there were no lines anymore. If you had the money, you could buy anything. I had relatives in the United States, and they would send me money every few months through private channels. I would not be able to survive if it wasn't for this assistance. Many old people were starving; they had no choice but to go out on the streets and beg for food and money.

This was a very difficult time in my life. All my life I was a loyal citizen of my country. Even when all my relatives left to go to the United States at the end of the 1980s, I refused to go because I wanted to grow old and die in my mother country.

Unfortunately, this patriotism was gone as soon as the food was gone from my table. The country that cannot provide its citizens with bare minimum necessities is not worth my love and faithfulness. This is the reason why I took the first chance I got to emigrate. Everything that I have just told you seems like a bad dream now; but it was a horrible reality just a few years ago."

Reprinted with the kind permission of Nadia Karalnik.

The story in the box illustrates the ruthless power of macroeconomic policies gone awry. Even if individuals "do the right thing" and work hard, save wisely and invest prudently, errant macropolicy can, unfortunately, eradicate all their accumulated wealth in a matter of weeks. Such is the destructive power of irresponsible macroeconomics.

Our next task is to examine whether hyperinflations can indeed be tamed. If so, how? How can they be prevented? And how challenging is the implementation of such macroeconomic policies?

6.4.2 Hyperinflations: Remedies

Given that unsustainable deficits necessitating tremendous monetizations are typically the underlying causes of hyperinflations, the remedy would then have to address (i) the deficit unsustainability as well as its consequence, and (ii) huge amounts of newly created money in circulation.

First and foremost, the deficit has to be brought back to within its sustainable range by large, difficult spending cuts; item (i) has to be resolved. Government spending cuts could involve significant cuts in salaries of government employees, cuts in pension programs, sharp reductions in subsidies and tax breaks to large state-owned enterprises, and perhaps, most important—privatization of formerly inefficient unprofitable SOEs.

This last item is, perhaps, the most influential in bringing deficits down, as SOEs often consume very significant portions of national tax revenues.[12] Privatization of even a few giant SOEs may result in sharp reductions in national budget deficits, thereby bringing them back into the sustainable range. This policy is, however, beset with challenges. Large-scale privatization would indeed increase national unemployment, as SOEs tend to be characterized by overemployment anyway. As the inefficient companies with outmoded capital stock and globally uncompetitive output are shut down—some for good—unemployment is only exacerbated. Coming in the wake of hyperinflation and macroeconomic collapse, this increase in unemployment is an exceedingly difficult policy to implement.[13]

Often, "austerity measures" required by the IMF as conditions for present and future debt assistance in the form of emergency credit lines, include strong privatization as well as spending-reduction clauses. These ensure that fiscal reform, no matter how unpleasant, is indeed tied to the IMF's short-term financial assistance.

The other side of the equation that needs to be addressed is to somehow roll back the enormous sums of money that are currently in circulation. Compared to the privatization policy just discussed, this, paradoxically, may be the easier policy to implement.

One method to shrink the huge amount of money in circulation is to introduce "new" money. Here the government introduces a new set of notes, with, for example, one million units of the "old" hyperinflated currency now equivalent to

---

[12]During the early 1990s, when the Ukraine was ravaged by hyperinflation, the national mining sector (SOE) was consuming a shocking 50 % of national tax revenues in price supports, subsidies, etc.

[13]China has been nowhere near a hyperinflation since the market liberalization of the 1980s, but nevertheless, the gradual privatization and overhaul of SOEs that happen to be inefficient remain among the government's top priorities. The policy has been to proceed gradually, unlike the Czech Republic and the former Soviet Union in the early 1990s when they performed large-scale national privatizations in just months. The Chinese government plans to merge efficient SOEs with ones that are failing. In this way, the morale, work ethic, and productivity of the "good" SOEs may be transferred to the less successful ones.

one unit of the new currency.[14] Sometimes, the currency is redesigned with the zeros lopped off the old denominations. These conversions only apply to some specified upper limit of accumulated depreciated currency. Not all the depreciated funds can be converted, just a fraction can, and the nation as a whole experiences net welfare loss.

It should be noted here that while the above policy of shrinking the money in circulation is a necessary condition to remedying hyperinflations, it is by no means a sufficient measure by itself. Without fiscal reform in the form of difficult privatization of SOEs, deregulation, and spending cuts that bring budget deficits back into the sustainable range, money supply contraction by itself will be at best a very short-term check on inflation.

To ensure that hyperinflations can never recur, in addition to strong fiscal discipline (which is imperative), monetary autonomy—independence—is vitally important. Institutionally, the central bank needs to be independent of fiscal pressure. Central bankers must be free from pressure by the fiscal authority to monetize away runaway deficits caused by the irresponsible fiscal misadventures of the past. The central bankers' job tenures, as well as the operating budget of the central bank, should not be a function of their degree of cooperation with the government. In other words, the central bank must be secure in its independence to be able to reject pressure from a fiscally irresponsible government to print money and finance away unsustainable deficits.

A large body of empirical macroeconomic research finds enough evidence to substantiate that strong monetary discipline does indeed breed strong fiscal discipline.[15] Strong monetary autonomy is positively correlated with smaller budget deficits since any moral hazard stemming from an implicit monetary "escape hatch" for fiscal profligacy is now removed. Here, governments (the fiscal authority) realize that there is no "friendly" central bank to bail them out of the latest fiscal fiasco by printing more money, and hence greater fiscal restraint is exercised. Consequently, strong monetary autonomy also results in lower levels of inflation and lower long-term interest rates, as fears of expected future monetizations correspondingly subside.

In addition to institutional autonomy, another method is a constitutional and legislative directive ensuring monetary and fiscal discipline. Such a measure may include a constitutionally specified upper limit on inflation and budget deficits with serious penalties for failure. For instance, the Bank of New Zealand Act of 1989 included a clause whereby the Governor of its central bank would be fired if inflation broke through its upper bound of 2 %!

---

[14]Witness four new currencies in Brazil in 6 years in the 1980s.

[15]See Budget Deficits and Economic Performance, Chap. 7, Richard C.K. Burdekin and F.K. Langdana, 1992.

6.5 Monetary Discipline: The Hazards of Pegging[16]

Institutional autonomy may not always be possible. At the other polar end of monetary autonomy, the central bank may simply be an extension of the fiscal arm of the government; the central bank may have been nationalized at some point in the past. Or central bankers may be subservient to the government for renewal of short-term tenures or operating budgets, or may even be subject to "approval" (explicit or implicit) from the fiscal authority before any significant monetary policy can be passed.

In these and other related cases when institutional/constitutional monetary independence does not exist, central bankers often resort to pegging or locking their currencies to those of other countries with strong monetary discipline. In this system, a pegged rate implies either a fixed exchange rate or a narrow range within which the domestic currency is allowed to fluctuate with a "hard" currency of an economy characterized by high monetary and fiscal discipline.

The mechanism by which monetary discipline is attained is as follows.[17] Let the country that seeks to gain macroeconomic discipline be a type-A country. The one with the hard currency stemming from a long history of fiscal and monetary credibility will be the type-B country (the US, for example).

Initially, A pegs its currency to B's at the rate of, say, 4:1. A's central bank ensures that, by daily purchases and sales of the two currencies, the ratio 4:1 is attained.[18] At some time in the future, once again, a familiar dangerous pattern emerges in country A. Its central bankers come under intense pressure from the government of A to increase money growth and to monetize the sizable deficit that is virtually impossible to finance by issuing any more debt.

This time around, however, with the peg in place, if monetization were to be allowed and more units of A's currency were to be printed, the domestic currency would weaken and be less valuable in terms of the harder currency of country B. In other words, the exchange rate may slip from 4:1 to 6:1 if the huge monetization were allowed to take effect. To safeguard the integrity of its well-announced and globally recognized peg, the monetary authority would thus be in a position to legitimately refuse pressure to monetize. (We revisit this topic in Chap. 11 in more detail.)

Examples of exchange rate pegging abound. The East Asian currencies were pegged to the US dollar in varying degrees for most of the 1990s, till the pegs blew apart in 1997–98. Hong Kong, and Singapore have had fairly tight pegs to the US

---

[16]More in Sect. 11.3.5 on Pegging and Sterilization.

[17]This is an extremely intuitive and general explanation at this stage. More detail is reserved for later, after construction of the ISLM model.

[18]Instead of a fixed target rate, this could also be a range. For example, the central bank could ensure that B's currency fluctuates by only ± 2 % with that of A's.

dollar for decades, and the cases of Argentina and Brazil pegging to the US dollar in the 1990s are now legendary. So is the precursor to the Euro, known as the ECU (European Currency Unit), which was part of the ill-fated ERM (Exchange Rate Mechanism) established in the European Union by 12 member countries in 1979.

For attaining monetary autonomy (and indirectly fiscal discipline), pegging is a short-term measure at best. It works well as long as the economies of the type-A country and the type-B country are both in the same phase of their respective business cycles. If, for some reason, B's economy were to overheat, B would be attempting to engineer a soft landing by contracting monetary growth and, hence, by raising its interest rates. This would imply that A would also have to match B's raising of interest rates to keep the exchange rates at 4:1 (to continue the earlier example). This would be fine as long as A also needed to engineer its own soft landing to slow its own overheated economy.

But if A were not overheating but instead slowing down or already in recession, this policy of driving up its own interest rates to ensure that the peg with B remained intact would only exacerbate A's recession! Instead of being jump-started with lower rates, the economy would go into shock as rates now perversely increase!

Policy options at this stage are to either persist with the peg and contract growth in A, or to allow the peg to snap, and to enact the exact opposite monetary policy and revive A's economy by a stimulating dose of lower interest rates.

This was the basic scenario prior to the collapse of the European Exchange Rate Mechanism (ERM) in 1992. The German increases in interest rates following dangerously large unification expenses came at a time when Italy, the UK, and Spain needed the exact opposite monetary policy prescription. These economies were slowing rapidly and they needed a dose of monetary stimulus in the form of lower, not higher, interest rates.

Similarly, in the Asian case in the later 1990s, dangerous SAP bubbles developed, and as the US economy progressively powered up while growth began to slow in East Asia, the overvalued pegs could not be maintained. We will discuss these cases further in later chapters.

More recently, by 2007–2008, as the US progressively lowered interest rates quickly to attempt to stave-off a recession, the economies pegged to the US dollar also had to make corresponding decreases in interest rates to ensure the integrity of their pegs. But these economies—Vietnam, Kuwait, United Arab Emirates, to cite a few—were dangerously overheating at that time! Lowering their rates to mimic US rates would serve only to throw their AD curves further to the right and to aggravate their overheating. The options were to break their pegs and let their respective currencies float, readjust the pegs to more manageable levels, or to continue to maintain the hard pegs and be locked to US monetary policy.

Brazil: A Real Plan After averaging between 15 and 50 % from 1940 to 1980, annual inflation in Brazil exploded into triple digits during the 1980s; from 1980 to 1984, inflation averaged 127 %, and then rose to 475 % from 1985 to 1989.

In the period 1990–1994, inflation went from an annual inflation rate of 2775–2309 %. The growth in process was temporarily checked at times by the repeated introduction of new currencies to "soak up" the vast amount of past monetization—at one stage four new currencies were introduced within six years. But these measures were not accompanied by difficult fiscal reform (privatization, etc.) and hence became temporary and cosmetic measures at best.

Then in 1994, Brazil, following the lead of other Latin American countries suffering the same plight, instated the Real Plan to stabilize its economy. Success was immediate; inflation fell to 73 % in 1995 and then to 2 % by 1998!

The success of the Real Plan can be attributed to the fact that it was a well-announced and adhered-to plan, and, most important, it was accompanied by absolutely necessary fiscal reform. "Announcement" aspects of macropolicy are extremely important. Policymakers must undertake an extensive public education campaign to explain exactly what the planned measures hope to achieve and exactly how key macroeconomic statistics— inflation, employment—will improve, thanks to the bitter medicine. It must be made clear to the general public that the tough measures are a necessary first step to future growth. Further, any and all safety nets (unemployment insurance, job training, etc.) that may be available to displaced workers must be described fully and readily available.

In Brazil, the specific procedures for attaining fiscal and monetary discipline were clearly and repeatedly explained. Monetary discipline was signaled by locking the value of the real to a predetermined consumption bundle, and then pegging the real to the US dollar. In addition, the much harder fiscal reform aimed at privatization and liquidation of large inefficient state-owned sectors, was begun in earnest. Eighteen banks were liquidated during this time. In addition to financial reform, massive deregulation was pursued in industries such as telecommunications, transportation, utilities, and petroleum.

This vital combination of fiscal discipline in conjunction with monetary discipline signaled a determination on the part of Brazil to become serious about macroeconomic reform. This in turn resulted in, perhaps, the most tangible validation of its macroeconomic reform from the global investment community—Brazil began to attract large global capital inflows, the vital ingredient for long-term capital growth.

6.6 Discussion Questions

The following question/answer format serves to highlight some key issues.

(1) **So it is by no means clear that a 5-year government bond paying 25 % interest annually is better for attracting global capital than one that pays 8 %?**

Real rates of return drive global capital flows. The country paying 25 % may have current and expected inflation at 24 %, which results in an inflation-adjusted (real) return of just 1 %. The other country may have inflation at only 2 %, thereby yielding a higher real rate of 6 %.

(2) **Why are tax increases not an option in financing unsustainable deficits? Why must the only options be monetization or debt default?**

Remember, that the deficit is *exposte* tax revenues for the year. There was a certain tax rate t_1 in effect in the economy in year 1. At the end of year 1, after all the tax revenues are collected, the economy in question finds that it has incurred an unsustainable deficit. This is the issue that needs to be addressed. An increase in tax rates to t_2 will only influence the deficit in year 2; it will do nothing to solve the problem in year 1.

(3) **It seems that the same countries continue to experience hyperinflations or high inflations. Is real macroeconomic reform never possible?**

While we do see the "same countries" struggling with hyperinflations over long periods of time, dramatic reform is indeed possible. One example is Germany. Following the trauma of the hyperinflation during the Weimar Republic (1918–22), Germany eventually became Europe's bulwark against inflation. The "legacy" of the hyperinflation was an inflation-phobic central bank in Germany, obsessed with monetary discipline. In fact, the Bundesbank came to be the repository of severe monetary discipline for the whole continent from the 1960s onwards. The French adopted the Franc Fort policy in 1982 by virtually pegging to the D-mark, and saw inflation become a nonproblem by the late 1980s. The ERM discussed earlier, and later the Euro, were strongly influenced by this comforting backdrop of German monetary discipline.

Another example of a country that had reformed its unsustainable ways—albeit briefly—was South Africa in the early 2000s under the leadership of Tito Mboweni, its reformist South African central banker, as discussed in Article 6.1.

Please explain/critique the underlined sentences/phrases in the following "articles" using material from this and preceding chapters. Use diagrams liberally.

ARTICLE 6.1   **TITO MBOWENI AND THE SOUTH AFRICAN RAND**

Uluthu Mbeki, <u>Nairobi Business Journal</u>, (early 2000).

Tito Mboweni, governor of the Reserve Bank of South Africa, may be considered the savior of the rand. Charismatic, effervescent, and fond of pink ties, he explains the bank's workings in the local languages of Sesotho and Zulu.

Unlike his predecessors, he does not believe that the Reserve Bank **(a)** <u>should intervene and artificially support the value of the rand</u>. In a speech to college students last week, he announced that he would let the markets decide the value of South Africa's currency instead of wasting a fortune trying to shore up its value artificially.

Upon hearing this, the markets approved, the people were thrilled, and it is hardly surprising that by the year 2000, South African banknotes are known as "Titos".

Mboweni understood that global investors would inject capital into South Africa only if they were truly **(b)** <u>convinced that serious macroeconomic reform was under way.</u> But changing investor perceptions was a daunting task—most African central banks did not have good records.

Angola's "reforms" included simply lopping off six zeroes from its currency. The head of Congo's central bank was actually arrested for sedition after espousing a tight money policy that included no monetization. And Sani Abacha, the dictator of Nigeria in the late 1990s, had given his central bank a standing order to transfer about $15 million to his Swiss bank account every day.

Against this backdrop, Tito somehow managed a miracle. He pushed through a tight monetary policy and was part of a government plan to advocate smaller wage hikes to the unions, **(c)** to <u>launch major privatization programs, to negotiate free-trade pacts, and to refuse public servants' pay demands</u>.

The markets responded. **(d)** <u>Long-term rates fell from almost 14% to under 10 percent within six months of his taking office.</u>

"It is all about credibility now", said Tijjan Malabar, a staff economist at the Reserve Bank. "There are no fixed exchange rates, no fixed value of gold—it all has to do with the reputation and credibility of a country's fiscal and monetary policies."

But credibility comes slowly; it often takes years to build. We hope Tito has time on his side.

Postscript: *All to no avail. By 2002, the rand had begun to collapse. Capital flooded out of South Africa. Unfortunately, in spite of Tito's earlier example and leadership, the macroeconomic reforms could not combat entrenched interests and did not take hold.*

ARTICLE 6.2   YUGOSLAVIAN DISASTER:
                  A MACROECONOMIC CRIME

Joe Schaffer, <u>Central European Journal</u>

When the government of Slobodan Milosovic was caught ordering the Serbian National Bank to issue $1.4 billion in credits to friends of Mr. Milosovic, the writing was on the wall.[17] This shocking illegal plunder equaled more than half of all new money creation in Yugoslavia in 1991, and proved to be just the tip of the iceberg.

The stage was set for a series of mismanaged and corrupt policies to lead to hyperinflation lasting 24 months, **(a)** <u>the second-highest and second-longest in history.</u> It peaked in January 1994, when the monthly inflation rate was 313 million percent!

Per capita real income fell by around 60% by the time the hyperinflation was over. Food was impossible to afford. Starvation was common. For city dwellers, relatives living in the country with access to farms were often the only source of food.

(b) <u>For weeks on end, all gas stations in Belgrade were closed.</u> Huge piles of domestic currency (dinars) were exchanged for a single German Mark or US dollar; there was an epidemic of capital flight.

By December 1993, 94% of all government expenditures were being financed with newly printed currency, with deficits long unsustainable. Since 1991, the dinar was officially devalued 18 times; 22 zeros were dropped off over time. Just in 1992, there were 5 devaluations, with monthly devaluations often over 99%.

The mint cranked out 900,000 notes a month, but they became worthless just hours after being printed. At one point, a 500 billion dinar note was worth a little over 4 German marks when printed. The currency collapsed on January 6, 1994, and the government officially declared the German mark as legal tender.

In an attempt at reform, the **(c)** <u>central bank introduced a "superdinar" pegged to the Deutsche mark at 1 to 1.</u> In a little over three weeks, an amazing 15 zeros were dropped from the dinar! Inflation did fall from 312 million percent in January 1995 to a negative 6.2% in March, 1995. But without any serious fiscal reform, this proved to be an empty gesture, and by 1998, more than 70 percent of the superdinar's value was gone.

This scenario was a text-book case of a macroeconomic meltdown and a poignant example of great and grave macroeconomic irresponsibility. The economy was already destroyed long before the war began, and an entire generation had been robbed of its hard-earned savings by its own government.

---

[17] Please see the excellent article, "Yugoslavia Destroyed its own Economy," Steve Hanke, <u>Wall Street Journal,</u> 4/28/99, for more details.

ARTICLE 6.3 THE CONTINUING AGONY OF ZIMBABWE, 2007 --?

Jennifer Nepalired, Khatmandu Mountain Sentinel

By August 2008, according to the IMF, Zimbabwe's inflation had reached 12 million percent as the economy continued its rapid deterioration. Earlier, in November 2007, the inflation was 85,000% about the same as that reached by Congo in 1993. Zimbabwe, under the autocratic Mugabe, was the only country to experience so devastating a hyperinflation since the mid-1990s.

Examples of the hyperinflating prices almost border on the ridiculous. By mid-2008, for example, a roll of toilet paper was $175,000 Zimbabwean dollars. The paper was actually sold by the 2-ply sheet at about $600 each, prompting jokes about the $500 currency note!

(a) "The national budget is unimaginably out of control," said our roving reporter, B.G. Garfunkel, on assignment in Zimbabwe. "There are practically no government services and bread, butter, tea, and the basic necessities are now totally out of existence. Gone!"

The government's plan of action? It is twofold, and unbelievable; (i) inflation is to be contained by the expedient measure of simply not releasing the inflation data to the public, and (ii) by legal decree, sellers must bring down prices to government-specified price ceilings or risk imprisonment, or worse!

Simon Punkeen, a Zimbabwan economist who long ago fled the country says that, "introducing new money or decreeing price controls will have no effect as long as the underlying root causes of the hyperinflation are not dealt with!"(b) In fact, Simon reminds us in Milton Friedman's words, "Price controls do not control anything."

(c) Highly skilled workers (doctors, lawyers, engineers, managers) have long since left the country—by some estimates, a shocking 38% of the population has left the collapsing economy over the last 8 years. Many of these individuals now remit money back to their families still trapped at home; by some estimates, a shocking 1/5 of Zimbabwe's current GDP can be attributed to remittances.

The jobless rate may be as high as 80% if you include displaced farmers. The economy has long transitioned to a barter system.

(d) Simon Punkeen points out that the paltry interest on savings (maximum 10%) is dwarfed by the inflation, and this really encourages rapid consumption. Prices are soon expected to quadruple every 2 weeks.

A New York Times, article, "How Bad is Inflation in Zimbabwe?" 5/2/2007, reports: *"Although there is no credible threat to his 26-year rule, Zimbabwe's political opposition is calling for mass protests against the economic situation. So Mr. Mugabe has tightened his grip on power even further, turning the economy over to a national security council of his closest allies. In addition, he has seeded the government's civilian ministries this year with loyal army and intelligence officers who now control key functions, from food security to tax collection.*

At the same time, Mr. Mugabe's government has printed trillions of new Zimbabwean dollars to keep ministries functioning and to shield the salaries of key supporters and potential enemies against further erosion. Supplemental spending proposed early in April would increase the spending limits approved last November by fully 40 percent, and more such emergency spending measures are all but certain before the year ends."

In rural areas, said one official of a foreign-based charity who declined to be named, fearing consequences from the government, even the barest funeral costs at least $6 million, or about $28.50, well beyond most families' means. The dead are buried in open fields at night, she said. Recently, she watched one family dismantle their home's cupboard to construct a makeshift coffin.

"I'll never forget that," she said. "The incredible sadness of it all."

Against this backdrop of pain and suffering, Zimbabwe's rulers seem blissfully oblivious. Mr. Mugabe has just finished construction of his own 25-bedroom mansion in an exclusive gated suburb north of town, surrounded by his henchmen, military aides, and sycophants.

And to cap it all, the government actually claims that it "has a plan" to bring in hard currency to save the country. This would be the 7th plan in 10 years!   Simon Punkeen scoffs, "Seven Plans! **(e)** All the same—print more money and then, some more money!" And he was right—by mid 2008, the government started printing higher denominations of bearers' cheques -- $1 million, $5 million and $10 million -- to help 'solve' the cash crisis.   At this point, prices were doubling every 25 hours.

An IMF report stated that only 13 countries have experienced hyperinflation since 1950, with the average duration of hyperinflation being 17 months. The longest was 59 months in duration, experienced by Nicaragua.

Analysts said the recent decision by the central bank to go on a money printing spree to ease the cash crisis would radically worsen the inflation problem. A loaf of bread in August 2008 was already 1.6 trillion Zim dollars! Prices were doubling every 25 hours at the peak of the hyperinflation in 2008

By mid-2015, Zimbabweans had started exchanging "quadrillions" of local dollars for a few US dollars as President Robert Mugabe's government abandoned its virtually worthless national currency.   A Zimbabwe quadrillion is an astounding 1×10^{15}.

The southern African country started using foreign currencies including the US dollar and South African rand in 2009 after the Zimbabwean dollar was ruined by hyperinflation; full-scale dollarization had taken place in 2009. At the height of the country's economic crisis, Zimbabweans had to carry plastic bags bulging with banknotes to buy basic goods.

From June 2015, customers who held Zimbabwean dollar accounts before March 2009 could approach their banks to convert their balance into US dollars, the governor of the Reserve Bank of Zimbabwe, John Mangudya, said in a statement. Zimbabweans had three months to turn in their old banknotes, which had been selling as tourist souvenirs. "Bank accounts with balances of up to 175 quadrillion Zimbabwean dollars would be paid $5. Those with balances above 175 quadrillion dollars were be paid at an exchange rate of $1 for 35 quadrillion Zimbabwean dollars. It should be noted that "the highest – and last – banknote to be printed by the bank in 2008 was 100tn Zimbabwean dollars. It was not enough to ride a public bus to work for a week." (Reuters, June, 2015.)

The bank said customers who still had stashes of old Zimbabwean notes could walk into any bank and get $1 for every 250tn (tn = trillion) they hold. That meant that a holder of a 100tn banknote would get 40 cents. The bank had set aside $20m to pay Zimbabwean dollar currency holders.

It was the second-worst hyperinflation in history, with the Hungarian hyperinflation being number one. A vast and blatantly obscene macroeconomic crime has been perpetrated against the people of Zimbabwe. A whole generation of Zimbabweans' savings and lives were completely eradicated—stolen---by their shameless government.

Farrokh Langdana is most grateful to his friend and colleague, Prof. Lewis Kerman, for updates on the Zimbabwe Hyperinflation.

ANSWERS AND HINTS

ARTICLE **6.1** TITO MBOWENI AND THE SOUTH AFRICAN RAND

(a)   Central banks can artificially strengthen their currencies by actively purchasing domestic currency and selling foreign currency. (Alternatively, they can deliberately devalue their currencies by doing the opposite.) Such attempts to intervene in foreign exchange markets and to artificially change the value of the domestic currency are very short-term measures at best. Market pressures usually prove to be far more powerful than limited (and costly) central bank interventions.

(b)   High real, or inflation-adjusted, rates are crucial for attracting capital inflows. This fact implies low expectations of future inflation and risk. Expectations of future inflation can be lowered only if domestic and foreign individuals truly believe that deficits will remain sustainable and monetary policy will be tight and disciplined.

(c)   Tito has tackled the most difficult elements. He has said "No" to government workers and officials. He is willing to risk unrest in the streets that will undeniably follow the privatizations and the resulting layoffs. In short, difficult and unpopular fiscal reform is a reality under this regime.

(d)   Bonds know best, and the bond market has rewarded Mr. Mboweni with lower long-term rates. By the Fisher effect (equation presented in the chapter) expectations of future inflation have fallen, given the government's grim determination to undertake serious fiscal and monetary reform. So while short-term rates may have risen due to the tight money policy, long-term rates have actually fallen thanks to lower expectations of future inflation!

ARTICLE 6.2 YUGOSLAVIAN DISASTER: A MACROECONOMIC CRIME

(a) Just a comment here: the largest example of hyperinflation was the Hungarian Hyperinflation in 1945, discussed in the chapter.
(b) With capital flight, domestic currency is sold in exchange for units of foreign (hard) currency. This downward pressure on the domestic currency results in a massive depreciation of the currency and its eventual collapse. All along, imports get progressively more expensive (and, eventually, prohibitive) for domestic residents as the domestic currency drops in value.
(c) This is the relatively "easy" part. Introducing new currency or pegging to strong currency is relatively painless to initiate. The fiscal reform resulting in even greater unemployment is the bitter medicine.

ARTICLE 6.3 THE AGONY OF ZIMBABWE: 2007–?

(a) The budget deficit is long past sustainability, needless to say.
(b) Just introducing new money is not enough, as evidenced in Article 6.2. The 'hard part' is to exorcize the 'cause' of the problem, namely, runaway fiscal spending.
(c) Along with hard capital flight, the country will also hemorrhage highly skilled labor. In fact, the US, Europe and China (Beijing and Shanghai) have benefited from an inflow of highly skilled Zimbabweans fleeing the macroeconomic devastation of their homeland.
(d) Negative real rates only foster greater and immediate consumption.
(e) Zimbabwe is really a "textbook" case of hyperinflation—blatant and relentless monetization on a criminal scale.

Chapter 7
ISLM: The Engine Room

The preceding chapters have included definitions and analyses of discrete components and aspects of the macroeconomy. We discussed the goods market and the multiplier effect in some detail, before exploring overheating and soft and hard landings using AD–AS analysis. The previous chapter included a fairly detailed study of calamitous hyperinflations, and ended with a discussion of the intertemporal and expectational influences underlying long-term interest rates.

In all the previous chapters, almost as a recurring theme, the ISLM model has been referenced and anticipated. This chapter finally introduces "the engine room" and brings us to a stage where we can synthesize and simultaneously analyze all the components of the macroeconomy that have been treated as discrete elements up to this point.

For example, when we increased government spending to generate multiplier effects, *a la* Keynes, one of the effects was an increase in interest rates stemming from an increase in the demand for loanable funds due to additional government borrowing. The resulting negative effect on capital investment was, however, conspicuously absent in the goods-market-multiplier-effect story. The whole channel of influence was simply missing! In another example, while monetary expansion designed to jump-start an economy by decreasing interest rates and increasing capital investment was discussed, the effect of the resulting increase in national income on money demand, feeding back on interest rates, was also missing from our discrete money market story. Not to mention the absence of the confidence terms, the tax rate, the effects of inflation on real money supply, and the influence of the global economy from the various analyses in preceding chapters.

The ISLM model—the mainstay of macroeconomic policy analysis when coupled with (P,Y) space—remedies the above shortcomings and provides us with a well-articulated and sophisticated model that incorporates all the missing "feedback" channels into the analysis of macroeconomic policy.

© Springer International Publishing Switzerland 2016
F. Langdana, *Macroeconomic Policy*, Springer Texts in Business and Economics, DOI 10.1007/978-3-319-32854-6_7

The following sections first derive and then explore the IS and LM curves. We will soon see that the IS and LM curves are simply the goods and money markets placed in (i,Y) space. The derivation will be followed by several full-scale macropolicy exercises introducing and utilizing the whole ISLM model.

7.1   The IS Curve

By definition, the IS curve is simply a plot in (i,Y) space (with interest rates and GDP growth on the two axes) comprising points where the goods market is in equilibrium—here there is no shortage, or excess supply (inventory) in the goods market.

Ignoring the trade sector, the condition for equilibrium in the goods market is[1]:

$$\mathbf{Y = C + I + G} \tag{7.1}$$

Substituting the expressions discussed earlier for consumption, $C = \underline{C} + bY$ and capital investment, $I = \underline{I} - fi$, we obtain:

$$\mathbf{Y = (\underline{C} + bY) + (\underline{I} - fi) + G} \tag{7.2}$$

Simplifying, and solving for i, we get the IS curve[2]:

$$\mathbf{i = A/f - Y(1 - b)/f} \tag{7.3}$$

where $\underline{\mathbf{A}}$ is simply a term for notational convenience comprising consumer confidence $\underline{\mathbf{C}}$, investor confidence $\underline{\mathbf{I}}$, and government spending, $\mathbf{G}$.

On close examination, we find Eq. (7.3) to be a straight line presented in slope-intercept form in Fig. 7.1 with intercept $\mathbf{(\underline{A}/f)}$ and slope $\mathbf{(1 - b)/f}$.

7.1.1   Some IS Exercises

Now that we have derived the IS curve, some IS exercises are in order.

1. *How will the IS curve respond to a collapse in investor confidence?*
   Very simply, as $\underline{I}$ falls, the intercept term $(\underline{A}/f)$ will fall. With no change in the slope (b and f are held constant), the IS undergoes a parallel drop from IS_0 to

---

[1]IS and LM get their names from Keynes' early notation. "IS" stands for investment = savings and "LM" is adopted from his notation for money supply (M) and money demand (L).

[2]The terms **b** and **f** are held constant. As a quick review, from previous chapters we know that **b** is the marginal propensity to consume, while **f** is the sensitivity (elasticity) of capital investment to changes in interest rates.

Fig. 7.1 The IS curve

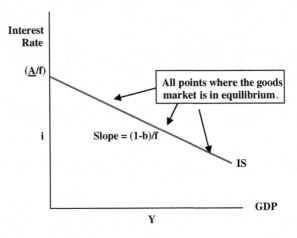

Fig. 7.2 Shifting the IS curve

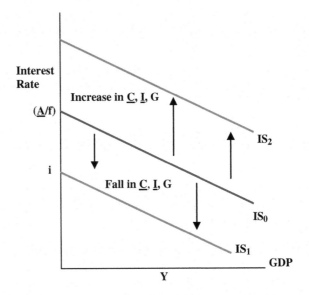

IS_1, as depicted in Fig. 7.2. The opposite holds true: a surge in investor confidence (perhaps due to news of an impending tax cut, or some such uplifting announcement or expectation) will cause the IS to shift up from IS_0 to IS_2, again, without any change in slope.

2. *How would the IS shift with a collapse in consumer confidence, $\underline{C}$?*

   We get the same result. The intercept term falls, dropping the IS curve from IS_0 to IS_1 with no change in slope, since b and f are constant. Similarly, a surge in consumer confidence results in the IS shifting up from IS_0 to IS_2 with no change in slope.

3. *How will changes in government spending affect the IS curve?*
   Increases in government spending G will also increase the intercept term ($\underline{A}/f$), thereby shifting the IS up from IS_0 to IS_2. Cutbacks in government spending outlays will cause the IS to shift down from IS_0 to IS_1 as G drops, decreasing the intercept component. Once again, neither of these shifts will cause the slope of the IS to vary.

As summarized in Fig. 7.2, any combinations of changes in consumer confidence, investor confidence, or government spending will result in a parallel shift in the IS curve.

7.1.2   Introducing Taxes into the IS Curve

Let **t** be some average tax rate prevailing in the economy under consideration. We now define C_T as the after-tax consumption function given by:

$$C_T = C + bY_D \tag{7.4}$$

where Y_D is the disposable (after-tax) income defined as:

$$Y_D = Y(1 - t) \tag{7.4a}$$

Substituting this expression for after-tax income into (7.4), we obtain the consumption function incorporating a tax rate **t**:

$$C_T = C + bY(1-t) \tag{7.5}$$

Using the equilibrium condition for the goods market and the after-tax consumption function, we obtain the expression for the IS curve with taxes.

$$i = A/f - [1 - b(1 - t)]Y/f \tag{7.6}$$

We can see that the intercept term $\underline{A}/f$ is exactly the same as with the IS_0 curve presented earlier in expression in (7.3). But the slope in expression (7.6), $[1 - b(1 - t)]/f$, now includes the tax rate **t**. As displayed in Fig. 7.3, the slope is now larger with the incorporation of the tax rate in IS_t.[3]

4. *If the tax rate were to be increased from some $t_0 = 35$ %, to a higher rate $t_1 = 43$ %, how would the IS be affected?*
   An increase in the tax rate with all other variables held constant would increase the absolute value of the slope, making the IS steeper from $IS(t_0)$ to $IS(t_1)$. The intercept term, however, does not specifically incorporate the tax rate **t**, so in the

---

[3]The absolute value of the slope is taken here. By plugging in some value for t (say, 0.40 for a 40 % tax rate), the comparison between slopes can easily be made.

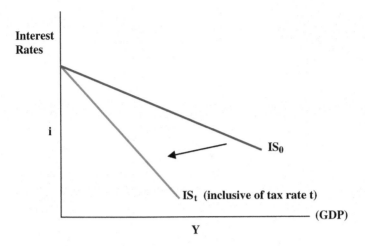

Fig. 7.3 The IS curve with increases in tax rates

absence of any additional macroeconomic changes, the intercept will remain the same. The final result here will be a clockwise pivot in the IS around the same intercept point as displayed in Fig. 7.4.

A tax cut from t_0 to some lower rate t_2 (30 %, perhaps) would decrease the absolute value of the slope term causing the IS to be flatter without changing the intercept term. In this case, the IS pivots counterclockwise from IS(t_0) to IS(t_2) with the cut in taxes.

5. *How would the IS react to increases in tax rates in an economy struggling to recover from a prolonged recession? Or how would an economy, nervously eyeing an approaching slowdown, react to tax increases?*

This extremely important IS exercise will later help explain part of the problem faced by the Japanese economy in the 2000s and then again in 2014–15. After

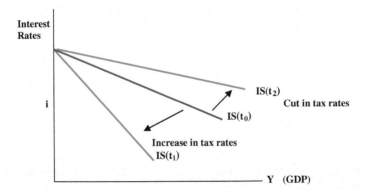

Fig. 7.4 Summarizing IS and changes in tax rates

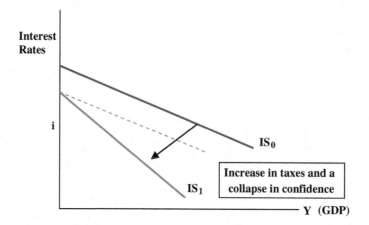

Fig. 7.5 When taxes rise and confidence plunges

struggling to recover from years of stagnation and collapsed equity prices, the Japanese economy was showing a glimmer of recovery in the mid-1990s when the government, despite strong advice from policy makers world wide, increased tax rates in 1996 in a desperate attempt to increase tax revenues. Consumer and investor confidence, just about to stage a comeback, promptly went into free-fall!

A similar and certainly more traumatic case was experienced by the doubling of tax rates during the Great Depression in the United States (to be covered in a following chapter). Later, in 1990–1991, when state taxes in the US were driven up to boost tax revenues, a similar combination of tax increases related to confidence collapses was experienced. In 1990, the state tax increase in the US, in conjunction with several other factors, resulted in the largest 3-month drop in consumer confidence on record.

The IS curve in all these instances experiences a "double whammy" caused by increasing taxes at a time when the economy is exceedingly vulnerable to adverse macroeconomic policy. The intercept term falls as fragile consumer and investor confidence plunges, and the slope gets steeper due to the increase in the tax rate as shown in Fig. 7.5, with IS shifting from IS_0 to IS_1.

The opposite may also hold true. The euphoria generated by a perfectly timed tax cut may cause the confidence terms to soar, lifting up the intercept, and causing the IS to flatten.

7.2   The LM Curve

The LM curve, by definition, is simply a curve in (i, Y) space comprising all points where the money market is in equilibrium. The condition for equilibrium in the money market is simply given by:

Money supply $=$ Money demand

Here money supply is defined as the real money supply in units of goods (as described earlier), and denoted M/P, where M is the nominal money stock denominated in local currency ($), and P is the price of a representative market basket denominated in $/good.

The central bank can indeed control the growth of the nominal money stock M, but the general price level P is endogenously determined within the economy.

Money demand for transactions is now defined as some positive function of national income and a negative function of interest rates:

$$\textbf{Money demand} = \textbf{kY} - \textbf{hi} \tag{7.7}$$

where **k** is the sensitivity (elasticity) of money demand to a unit change in national income **Y** and **h** is the sensitivity of money demand to a unit change in the interest rate **i**. Both **k** and **h** will be held constant here.

The greater the national income, **Y**, the greater the demand for transactions and hence for money, and the greater the interest rate **i**, the smaller the optimum cash balance demanded. The intuition here is that the transactions demand for money increases with greater national income **Y**, while the opportunity cost of carrying money in the form of noninterest-bearing cash is the interest forgone by not investing it in some interest-bearing account, hence the negative sign before the interest term.

Equating real money supply with money demand, we obtain the equilibrium condition in the money market as:

$$\textbf{M/P} = \textbf{kY} - \textbf{hi}$$

Simplifying and solving for i, we obtain the **LM curve**:

$$\textbf{i} = \textbf{(k/h)Y} - \textbf{(1/h)M/P} \tag{7.8}$$

Once again, this is an equation of a straight line with slope **(k/h)**, and negative intercept—**(1/h)M/P,** as presented in Fig. 7.6.

All points on this line represent points in (i,Y) space where the money market is in equilibrium. The slope is positive, and will be held fixed here since k and h are constants. The negative intercept is an algebraic construct, devoid of macroeconomic meaning per se but vitally important in determining how the LM shifts when the nominal money stock or prices change.

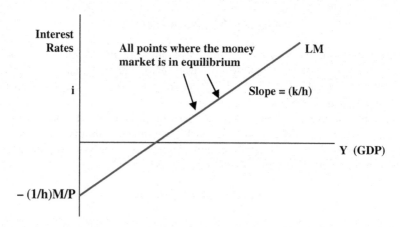

Fig. 7.6 The LM curve

7.2.1   Factors that Shift the LM

What will be the effect on the LM curve of an increase in the nominal money stock, M?

The change in M by the central bank will affect the intercept term. Since this is a negative term, the increase in M would lead the intercept to become a larger negative number (for example, from −40 to −48), thereby decreasing the intercept. With no change in the slope (there is no M in the slope term), the result of an increase in M is a parallel downward, or rightward, shift in LM from LM_0 to LM_1.

A decrease in money growth (decrease in M) results in an upward (leftward) shift in LM and, once again, will not affect the slope as shown in Fig. 7.7.

What will be the effect in the LM curve of an increase in the price level P (an increase in inflation)?[4]

An increase in the price level will cause the ratio M/P to fall, and given the minus sign that precedes the intercept term, we now find the intercept to be 'less negative' (increasing from say, −40 to −30). Again, with no change in the slope, an increase in P results in an upward, or leftward, shift in LM from LM_0 to LM_2.

A decrease in P would cause the LM to incur a parallel shift down (right) as the intercept term decreases in Fig. 7.7.

---

[4]At this stage, we use 'change in price level' interchangeably with 'change in inflation'. When the entire ISLM is put together later in the chapter, we will revisit exactly in what form the data pertaining to P, Y, M, etc., are presented and analyzed.

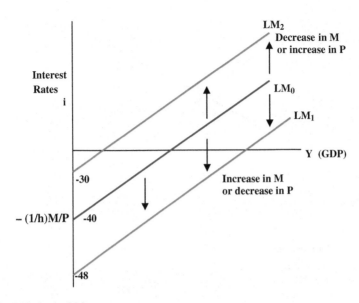

Fig. 7.7 Shifts in the LM curve

> **Important "Rules" for Shifting LM**
>
> (1) **If the ratio (M/P) decreases due to either a decrease in M and/or an increase in P, the LM shifts up (to the left).**
> (2) **If the ratio (M/P) increases due to an increase in M and/or a decrease in P, the LM shifts down (to the right).**
>   **Basically, if the real money supply (M/P), increases, the LM shifts right, and vice versa.**
> (3) **The slope does not change in either case.**

The stage is set for finally superimposing IS onto LM. The intersection point, E_0 at (i_0, Y_0), in Fig. 7.8 is defined as a point where both goods and money markets are simultaneously in equilibrium by virtue of the fact that (i_0, Y_0) lies on IS as well as LM. (Note that the LM axes have been normalized to only focus on nonnegative interest rates.)

In an earlier chapter we synthesized both the goods and money markets to derive the aggregate demand (AD) in (P,Y) space. In terms of our ISLM framework, this simply translates to point (i_0, Y_0) in (i,Y) space transposing to the (P_0, Y_0) point on the aggregate demand (AD) in (P,Y) space as depicted in Fig. 7.9.

Alternatively stated, every point on the aggregate demand curve has a corresponding point in (i,Y) space where both goods and money markets are

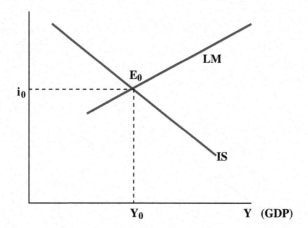

Fig. 7.8 Simultaneous goods-market and money-market equilibrium

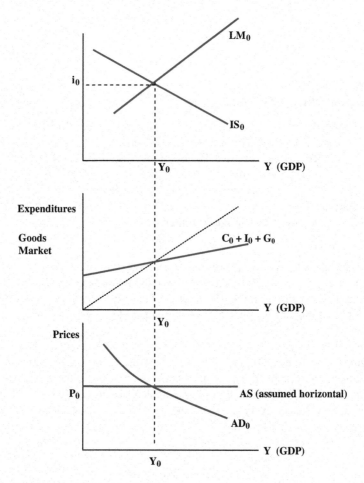

Fig. 7.9 ISLM, goods market and ADAS

simultaneously in equilibrium. Hence, the point (P_0, Y_0) corresponding to goods and money market equilibrium, (i_0, Y_0), "drops down" from the IS and LM intersection point.[5]

The goods market is presented below the (i, Y) space, and it feeds into the IS curve. The IS is, after all, nothing more than the goods market transposed into (i, Y) space.

The aggregate supply (AS) in (P, Y) space is at present assumed to be a horizontal line. This unrealistic horizontal AS is used in this early ISLM chapter purely to facilitate discussion. As we will see next, this clever construction suppresses any inflationary changes stemming from policy changes. This convenient horizontal AS curve will prove immensely beneficial to our early ISLM policy runs by allowing us to deftly abstract from any changes in P whatsoever. (In the next chapter, however, we shed the horizontal AS and incorporate the real thing. The ISLM will then be at its maximum potential for the closed-economy case.)

7.3   ISLM–ADAS Policy Exercises

The stage is finally set for large-scale macroeconomic policy simulations using the ISLM–ADAS model. The following sequence of steps will significantly simplify the analysis.

7.3.1   Survival Guide to ISLM–ADAS Policy Analysis

1. Make all moves in (i, Y) space first. Here any and all shifts/pivots in IS and shifts in LM are to be made. (A summary of all ISLM shifts is presented near the end of this chapter).
2. "Drop down" to (P, Y) space and adjust AD accordingly to conform to the Y just obtained in (i, Y) space. At this stage, we obtain the final values for the rate of inflation (P) and output growth (Y) in the economy in this particular exercise.
3. Ask the question, "Has P (rate of inflation) changed?"
   If the answer is **Yes**, then go back to (i, Y) space and adjust LM till the Y values "line up."
   If **No**, then deftly skip Step 3 and go to Step 4.
4. Close the goods market and the labor market (to be incorporated in the next chapter). Determine how the final values of consumption (C) and private capital investment (I) compare with the original values.

---

[5]This somewhat nonacademic description of the link between the point on the AD and its equivalent point at the intersection of IS and LM will prove immensely useful when ISLM policy exercises are conducted.

5. Present all your results boldly, step back from the diagrams, and analyze the implications of your results.

In "real time," Steps 1 to 4 would all be taking place simultaneously and could span a period ranging from days to months depending on the policies in question, the stage of the economy in its business cycle, and consumer and investor expectations.

Armed with the Survival Guide, we are finally set to perform our first ISLM–ADAS policy exercise.

7.3.2   ISLM–ADAS Policy Experiment I

The purpose is to determine the effect of an increase in government spending on GDP, inflation, private consumption, private capital investment, and interest rates. Once again, we assume a horizontal AS curve in Fig. 7.10.

The economy is initially at some low GDP growth rate Y_0, presumably in need of macroeconomic stimulation from an increase in government spending from G_0 to G_1 in the form of infrastructure building, defense outlays, etc.

Initially, the interest rate is i_0, inflation is P_0, and the rates of private consumption and capital investment are C_0 and I_0.

Following the Survival Guide, **Step 1** occurs in (i, Y) space. As G increases, the IS shifts to the right (up) as the intercept term increases (as in the IS practice exercise). This shift is depicted in Fig. 7.10.

Moving to **Step 2**, we now "drop down" to (P, Y) space so that the AD laterally shifts from AD_0 to AD_1. Remember, the AD is the representation of the intersection of IS and LM transposed to (P, Y) space.

With the completion of Step 2, we now obtain the final rates of inflation (P) and GDP growth (Y) in this exercise. Output growth has now increased from Y_{-0} to Y_1, but inflation is still unchanged at P_0![6] This result is due solely to the fact that the AS curve is assumed to be horizontal, with the specific purpose of artificially suppressing any changes in the rate of inflation. In **Step 3**, the answer to the question "Has P Changed?" is "No," and this allows us to skip to Step 4.[7]

We now "mop up" in the goods market in **Step 4** by ensuring that the equilibrium in the goods market lines up with the final growth rate Y_1 in (i, Y) and (P, Y) spaces. Once again, the expenditure line, the IS curve, and the AD curve are all different representations that include the same goods market with different axes, and hence they must all "line up" at the same Y value.

---

[6]Please note that changes in endogenous variables, as in Y_0 to Y_1, are changes in rates of growth. Y_0 could be 3 % GDP growth, while Y_1 could be 3.9 %, for example. When P_0 stays "the same," this means that the rate of inflation remains unchanged. If P_0 is 2 %, then this means that prices are still growing at an average rate of 2 % at the end of the policy exercise.

[7]The rate of inflation is endogenous and will indeed change in the following chapter when the horizontal AS curve is abandoned for a more realistic one.

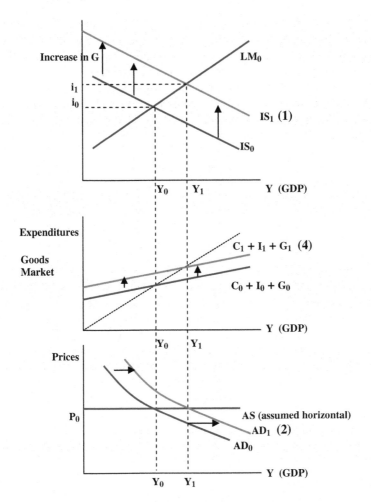

Fig. 7.10 Fiscal stimulus in ISLM-ADAS

Continuing with Step 4 in the goods market, we now determine if C_1 is greater than or less than C_0. We simply plug in the initial and final national income values, Y_0 and Y_1, into the consumption function.

The initial rate of private consumption is:

$$C_0 = C + bY_0$$

And the final rate:

$$C_1 = C + bY_1$$

Since Y_1 is greater than Y_0 as seen in Fig. 7.10, C_1 must therefore be greater than C_0. In other words, since private consumption is a function of national income, and given that we observe an increase in national income arising from the increase in government spending, private consumption must therefore increase.

What will be the effect on private capital investment I?

In this case, we examine the investment function to explore the change in capital investments due to changes in the interest rates that have gone up from i_0 to i_1.

Initially, capital investments are:

$$I_0 = I - fi_0$$

Finally, after interest rates have been driven up by increased government borrowing, from i_0 to i_1, we obtain the level of capital investments as

$$I_1 = I - fi_1$$

Since interest rate i_1 is greater than i_0, and since this increase exerts a negative effect on capital investments, we conclude that capital investments fall from I_0 to I_1.

The **results** are presented in **Step 5**. The increase in government spending from G_0 to G_1 results in an increase in the rate of growth of output (Y). This result should actually be quite familiar as it has been discussed in detail in an earlier chapter— this is the **multiplier effect**, due to an increase in government spending. The increase in consumption from C_o to C_1 is, of course, the mechanism driving this multiplier. The decrease in private capital investment was also discussed in an earlier chapter, and is the **crowding out** due to an increase in bond-financed government spending. Here, government spending jump-started the economy by stimulating consumption, but the increase in G adversely affected private capital investment. The rate of inflation is still P_0, by construction of the horizontal AS.

7.3.3   ISLM–ADAS Policy Experiment II

The central bank, under pressure to "do something" to spur growth, increases monetary growth and lowers interest rates. Show the effect on all key variables. Assume a horizontal AS curve.

Step 1: LM shifts out in Fig. 7.11 as M_0 now increases to M_1 because the central bank increases monetary growth.[8] (The IS remains stationary since there is no change in G or in consumer or investor confidence in this example.)

---

[8]The precise mechanisms by which central banks actually increase money supply and, hence, lower interest rates will be discussed in Chap. 11.

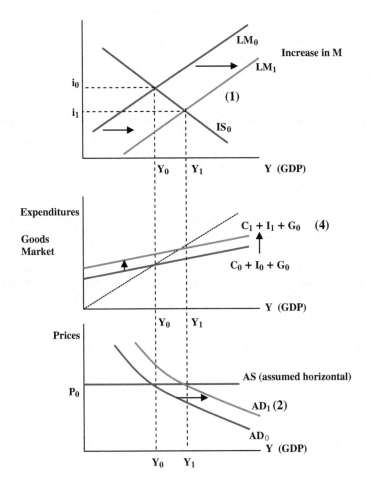

Fig. 7.11 Monitary stimulus in ISLM-ADAS

Step 2: We "drop down" to (P,Y) space and adjust AD until the Y_1 obtained in (i,Y) space lines up with the Y in (P,Y) space. We get the final GDP and price at this stage. Y_0 has increased to Y_1, and once again, thanks to the construction of the horizontal AS, there is no change in inflation; the rate is still P_0.

Step 3: Has P changed? No. So we skip to Step 4.

Step 4: We adjust the goods market by shifting the expenditure line to the right so that the value of Y lines up to be consistent with Y_1.

Is $C_1 > C_0$?

Yes. Since $Y_1 > Y_0$, and since $C = \underline{C} + bY$, consumption will indeed increase as Y increases.

Is $I_1 > I_0$?

Yes. Since interest rates in this policy exercise fall from i_0 to i_1, capital investment given by $I = \underline{I} - fi$ will increase.

Results: The increase in money supply and the resulting decrease in interest rates result in boosting GDP growth from Y_0 to Y_1, increasing consumption from C_0 to C_1, and increasing private capital investment from I_0 to I_1. Inflation is deliberately held constant here at P_0 by construction of the AS.

Policy Challenges in China After successfully cooling down an overheated economy in the mid-1990s, policy makers in China were faced with a more daunting problem—to prevent the soft landing from going "hard." With GDP growth "officially" hovering at 8 percent, barely in accordance with the "bao ba" ("guaranteed" 8 %) growth policy by the early 2000s, policy makers were desperately searching for ways to reignite growth.

However, repeated infusions of mammoth amounts of government spending on infrastructure from the early to mid-2000s well into 2015 did not yield the much anticipated and hoped-for multiplier effects. In fact, the multiplier effect was negligible at best. Large, and fully equipped but deserted "Ghost Cities" in China are grim testimonials to an infrastructure experiment gone bust. How then does one explain this Chinese conundrum?

The explanation lies in the value of the low Chinese MPC. China is essentially a country with two marginal propensities of consumption. The Eastern seaboard with the high-growth zones of development and including the big cities of Beijing and Shanghai, boasts higher MPCs than the rest of the country where the MPC is very low.

In fact, the extreme Western provinces perhaps have a third and lowest tier of MPC. This is hardly surprising given the marked difference between disposable incomes and employment and basic living standards between rural Western and Central China, relative to the dynamic and more prosperous urban Eastern Seaboard.

Lower MPCs imply lower multiplier effects from the expression:

Multiplier $= 1/(1 - \text{MPC}) = 1/(1 - b)$ where b is the MPC.

This explains why an MPC of, say, 0.1, will have a multiplier effect of only 1.1. An increase in government spending equal to 1 million units of currency will result in overall GDP increasing only to \$1.1 million units, for example. This makes Keynesian jump-starting extremely challenging. Until the consumers/citizens in Central and Western China truly believe that better times are ahead, stop hoarding any increase in incomes into their savings, and spend more on consumption, multipliers will remain low.

Diagrammatically (Fig. 7.12) this translates to Chinese IS curves (for the Western and Central regions) being relatively steeper relative to, say, the US type IS curve, since the slope of the IS is $(1 - b)/f$, with b being the MPC. The same vertical increase in the intercept due to the same increase in G will result in a far larger change in Y for a flatter US type IS curve relative to that for the steeper Chinese IS. In Fig. 7.12, the multiplier effect for the US is denoted ΔY (USA), while that for the Chinese IS curve is ΔY (China).

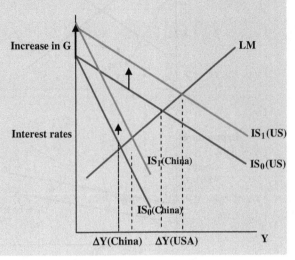

Fig. 7.12 MPC and the multiplier effect

7.3.4   ISLM–ADAS Policy Exercise III: An Increase in Tax Rates

Policy makers in Country K are very concerned. The budget deficit has reached unprecedented proportions. There is a general sense that something "has to be done" to remedy this. Country K has been in the throes of a long recession and is just about to announce its first mildly positive GDP growth.[9] Against this backdrop, policy makers decide that it is time to drastically increase tax rates to generate higher tax revenues, and bring the budget deficit down. (Assume a horizontal AS curve.)

Show the effects on all key macro variables and, in particular, focus on the possible final effect on the budget deficit. Hint: Tax revenues, T, are given by:

$$T = tY$$

where t is the average national tax rate and Y is the level of national income.

---

[9]Recall from a previous chapter that recessions, by themselves, exacerbate budget deficits (G-T). The tax base (T) shrinks as national income falls, and government spending (G), in the form of transfer payments (unemployment insurance, welfare, etc.), increases as jobs dwindle.

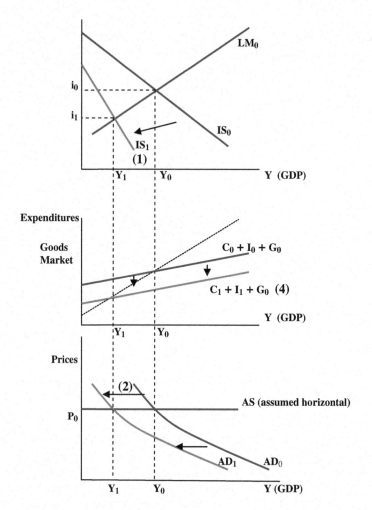

Fig. 7.13 Tax rate increases in ISLM-ADAS

The analysis is presented in Fig. 7.13.

Step 1: Here IS pivots clockwise with the increase in tax rates. In addition, a significant tax increase coming on the heels of an economy just struggling to crawl out of recession will, in all likelihood, traumatize consumer and investor confidence. Both confidence terms, $\underline{C}$ and $\underline{I}$, will fall. The final result on the IS curve is a clockwise pivot due to the tax increase as well as a shift down (to the left) due to the decline in the intercept caused by the fall in confidence triggered by increasing taxes at such an inappropriate time.

The LM will not budge since there is no change in M (or P). The ISLM equilibrium is at Y_1, and i_1.

Step 2: We drop down to (P,Y) space and adjust AD to the left until the Y values are consistent at Y_1. The final GDP growth here has now fallen to a lower Y_1, with prices artificially held constant at P_0.

Step 3: Has inflation changed? No. So we skip to Step 4.

Step 4: Adjust the expenditure line in the goods market so that its equilibrium is at Y_1, consistent with the other two diagrams.

Is $C_1 > C_0$?

No. Since $Y_1 < Y_0$, $C_1 < C_0$ too, by plugging into the consumption function. In addition, consumption falls further because consumer confidence, $\underline{C}$, has also collapsed due to the tax increases. Consumption here is hit by a "double whammy" of lower disposable income (Y_1) and collapsing confidence.

Is $I_1 > I_0$?

It may appear that capital investments should increase since interest rates fell to i_1, but on closer examination this result is unclear since investor confidence, $\underline{I}$, has also collapsed due to the tax increases. In fact, investor confidence, $\underline{I}$, is even more sensitive to current and expected tax increases than $\underline{C}$!

The decline in interest rates in isolation would increase I, but in conjunction with the collapsing confidence the result is now ambiguous—technically it depends on which influence on I is larger. Empirically, however, the influence of $\underline{I}$ tends to "win out." If the macroeconomic outlook looks dismal and further tax increases are imminent, no amount of interest rate lowering will induce investors to borrow for additional capital investment. This situation is one version of the "**liquidity trap**" discussed in earlier chapters, in which no amount of monetary creation and lowering of interest rates—even down to zero—may induce an increase in capital investment if investor confidence has collapsed. Examples abound, from the Great Depression in the US, Japan and Argentina in the early 2000s, and the US again by late 2008.

Results: GDP, interest rates, consumption and capital investments fall, and there is no change in inflation by construction of the AS.

7.3.5 ISLM–ADAS Policy Exercise IV: Simultaneous Increases in Government Spending and Monetary Growth ("Fine-Tuning")

Country K increases government spending to spur growth, but it wants to avoid "crowding out" private capital investment. Hence, it also increases M to lower rates to offset the interest rate effects of the increase in G. Show the effect on all key macrovariables. Once again, assume a horizontal AS curve.

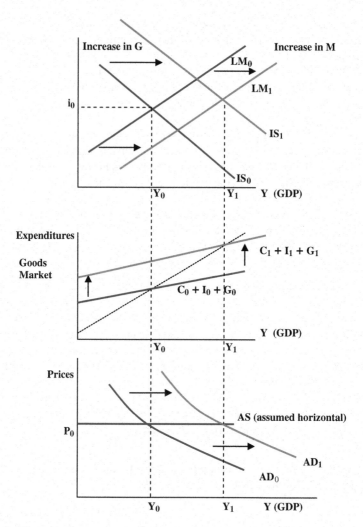

Fig. 7.14 "Fine-tuning" with fiscal and monetary policies

Step 1: As G increases, IS shifts up (to the right) as depicted in Fig. 7.14. And as M is increased, LM also shifts to the right. Here the shifts are coordinated to leave the interest rate unchanged. Note that just the IS shift without an accompanying LM shift would have caused interest rates to rise (as in exercise I) and to crowd out capital investment.

Step 2: Drop down to (P,Y) space and align the Y_1 values by shifting AD. GDP growth has now increased to Y_1 and inflation is still artificially held at P_0.

Step 3: Skip since no change in inflation, and go to Step 4.

Step 4: Adjust the expenditure line in the goods market to be consistent with GDP Y_1. Is $C_1 > C_0$?

Yes, since $Y_1 > Y_0$. By plugging this into the consumption function, we can conclude that $C_1 > C_0$.

Is $I_1 > I_0$?

No change in capital investments here since interest rates are deliberately left unchanged by the joint fiscal-monetary policy mix adopted here. We assume no change in confidence.

Note: Depending on the relative rightward shifts in IS and LM, we technically have an ambiguous effect on interest rates and, hence, on capital investment. The final interest rates could be higher or lower than i_0, depending on the magnitude of the IS shift to the right, relative to that of the LM. In all cases where G and M simultaneously increase, however, Y will increase.

Results: GDP growth increases from Y_0 to Y_1, consumption increases from C_0 to C_1. There was no change in interest rates and, hence, no crowding out of capital investment by policy design in this particular example. Finally, we found no change in inflation by construction of the horizontal aggregate supply curve (AS).

While the primary reason for incorporating the horizontal AS in this chapter has been the deliberate suppression of changes in P, the actual shape of the AS is not completely without "real world" merit. Recalling the discussion on demand-pull inflation from an earlier chapter, Stage 1 inflation was that experienced in the early stages of a macroeconomic recovery. The economy was finally beginning to turn around, presumably after some effective demand-side stimulus, and was characterized by substantial excess labor supply (hence, no wage pressure), excess plant capacity, and raw materials in abundance.

This Stage 1 was characterized by rapidly growing GDP (Y_0 to Y_1) and no significant increase in the rate of inflation (still P_0), and these results are consistent with the AS curve used in this chapter.

7.4 Summarizing IS and LM Shifts

Table 7.1 describes the shifts in IS and LM due to changes in each of the factors in the left-hand column <u>individually</u>, with all others held unchanged.

Table 7.1 A summary of IS-LM shifts

Summarizing IS–LM shifts	IS	LM
Increase in G	Shifts right (up)	No change
Decrease in G	Shifts left (down)	No change
Increase in tax rate	Pivots clockwise	No change
Cut in tax rates	Pivots counterclockwise	No change
Increase in confidence	Shifts right (up)	No change
Decrease in confidence	Shifts left (down)	No change
Increase in money growth	No change	Shifts right
Decrease in money growth	No change	Shifts left
Increase in inflation (P)	No change	Shifts left
Decrease in inflation (P)	No change	Shifts right

7.5 The Global IS

In the following chapters, the IS curve will abstract from the trade sector. However, smaller economies with greater trade sectors relative to their domestic GDPs (Singapore's trade sector including reexports is well over 100 % of GDP) would certainly need to implement an IS that includes exports and imports. A "global IS" is therefore briefly overviewed below.

7.5.1 Global IS: A Brief Overview

Including the [Export–Import] term in the expression for equilibrium in the goods market, we obtain

$$\mathbf{Y} = \mathbf{C} + \mathbf{I} + \mathbf{G} + (\mathbf{Exports} - \mathbf{Imports}) \tag{7.9}$$

Proceeding with the IS derivation, the **global IS curve**, incorporating the trade sector, is

$$\mathbf{i} = [\mathbf{A}/\mathbf{f} + (\mathbf{Exports} - \mathbf{Imports})/\mathbf{f}] - \mathbf{Y}(1 - \mathbf{b})/\mathbf{f} \tag{7.10}$$

In economies such as Singapore, Thailand, and Taiwan, for example, where their trade sectors are significant portions of their respective GDPs, the IS curve must indeed incorporate exports and imports to allow any meaningful macroeconomic policy analysis.

In this case, the net exports term, (Exports–Imports), is now also a component of the intercept term. As depicted in the global IS in Fig. 7.15; the intercept is now [**A/f + (Exports–Imports)/f**].

Fig. 7.15 Global IS

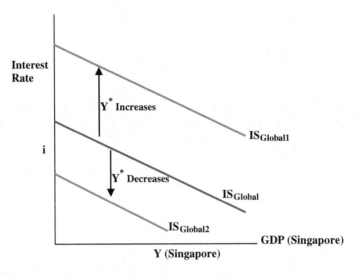

Fig. 7.16 Shifts in global IS due to changes in foreign GDP growth

An increase in exports, stemming from strongly growing foreign economies with healthy national incomes, would increase foreign demand for domestic exports and cause the IS_{Global} to shift up. In Fig. 7.16, the domestic income of the trade-dependent country (Singapore again, and to some extent, even China) is denoted as Y. The income of its big trading partner (the US, for example) is denoted as Y^*. Most of Singapore's electronics and IT exports (89 %) go to the US. As the US economy soars—as Y^* increases—Singapore's exports will increase, since exports are a positive function of foreign national income.[10] This translates to a rightward shift in IS_{Global} to $IS_{Global1}$.

A recession in a large foreign economy, on the other hand, would cause foreign national income to fall, thus resulting in a decrease in foreign demand for the domestic country's exports. In this case, as shown in Fig. 7.16, exports would fall, thereby decreasing the intercept term and causing IS_{Global} to shift down to $IS_{Global2}$.

A perfect example is the effect that China's slowing economy had on commodity and infrastructure-equipment exporting countries. China's rapid growth was great for commodity-exporters like Brazil, Russia (oil), India, Argentina, Australia, and South Africa, but when China slowed by 2015, these countries felt the headwinds of economic deceleration as their exports to China plunged. Torridly growing "high stage 2" economies came crashing down. Hot capital blew out from the commodity-exporting countries and their currencies were strongly depreciated.

Hence, recessions as well as booms can, to some extent, be transmitted globally via the linkages of exports and imports to national incomes. This phenomenon in

---

[10]Along similar lines, Singapore's imports will be a positive function of its own national income, Y.

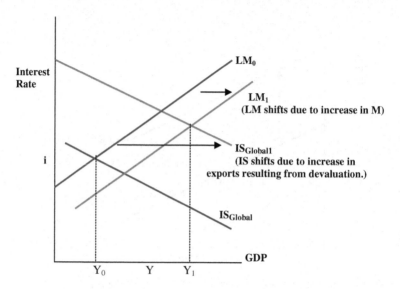

Fig. 7.17 Exchange rate devaluation

which macro-conditions in the home country A can be transmitted via many channels to country B is known as **"contagion."**

Of course, another factor causing shifts in the global IS is the exchange rate. A depreciation, or devaluation of the exchange rate, may make exports "cheaper" in the near term.[11] This is typically accomplished by an increase in domestic monetary growth that weakens the currency by increasing its supply and thus makes it "cheaper" in the global foreign exchange markets. Domestic residents now find their exports to be "cheaper," and their imports now become more "epensive." An appreciation (strengthening) of the domestic currency serves to make exports "more expensive" to foreigners but imports "cheaper" to domestic residents.

A currency devaluation is depicted in Fig. 7.17 by simultaneous shifts in the global IS and the LM. The IS shifts to the right as exports increase, and the LM also shifts to the right as, after all, it is the monetary expansion that results in the weakening of the currency (the devaluation) in the first place. The result presented below is a <u>short-term effect</u> at best, given the eventual increase in inflation, not included in Fig. 7.17. Unfortunately, the short-term results, an increase in national GDP from Y_0 to Y_1 accompanied by an increase in national exports can be dangerously misleading.

---

[11]This is most definitely a very short-term perspective. Devaluations are inevitably inflationary; the increase in monetary growth will finally increase inflation, thereby negating any short-term increases in exports. In fact, as discussed earlier, it was this vicious cycle of devaluations followed by bouts of rising inflation and wages that prompted most of the countries in the European Union to form the Eurozone by adopting one common highly disciplined monetary policy. This topic will be revisited in Chap. 11.

Governments facing reelection may be tempted to pressure central banks to devalue the currency and spur the economy. Unfortunately for citizens, the eventual and inevitable increases in inflation will occur with a lag—after the election. In Europe, after many cycles of devaluations followed by increases in inflation that negated any temporary increases in GDP and exports, the European economies finally decided to peg their currencies to the German currency (and, hence, to German monetary discipline) to preclude any pressure from European governments on their respective central banks to devaluate. The first such attempt was the Exchange Rate Mechanism (the ERM) begun in 1979, where the member countries' currencies were pegged to the D-Mark, followed by the current Eurozone, wherein they relinquish control of their domestic monetary growth to one common European central Bank (ECB) and one common currency, the euro, thereby making unilateral devaluations impossible; more in Chapter 11.

In the US, following the deflating of the housing market and the sub-prime bubble by late 2008, the massive and repeated injections of liquidity by the Fed had led to progressively lower US interest rates. This led to a deteriorating long-term macro-outlook as the US soft-landed, coupled with a fast-dropping US dollar as foreign appetite for our Treasuries diminished. Against this backdrop, investors kept a sharp eye open for the inevitable inflation caused by the loose monetary policy.

While inflation is conspicuously missing from this chapter, the just-described scenario, replete with inflation (both in the goods as well as in the labor market) will be presented from the next chapter onwards.

7.5.1.1 Summarizing Factors that Shift the Global IS[12]

Changes in domestic **government spending, confidence and tax rates** affect the global IS in much the same way as the closed-economy IS. In addition, increases in **foreign national income** ($Y*$) shift the global IS to the right, and vice versa. **Devaluations**, or deliberate weakening of the domestic exchange rates, shift the global IS to the right (along with the LM), and revaluations shift both global IS and LM to the left.

The next chapter incorporates our first "real" AS curve; inflation enters the ISLM–ADAS analysis. But first, the following question–answer format followed by simulated articles should, once again, assist in reviewing the chapter material and clearing up any lingering questions pertaining to the introduction of the "engine room."

---

[12]This discussion of "factors that shift the global IS" in addition to the ones that shift the closed-economy IS cites only two key determinants of shifting, namely, changes in foreign income and devaluation. Other factors also shift the global IS, such as tastes and preferences for imports and exports, etc. These are not included here at this time.

7.6 Discussion Questions

1. *When we increase government spending, G, why do we make the first move in (i,y) space instead of shifting the expenditure line in the goods market, which incorporates G so explicitly?*

   Once again, the sequence recommended by the Survival Guide is purely for convenience. In actuality, all the changes from blue to red lines are taking place simultaneously in all the diagrams over a period of time. Furthermore, the IS curve really **is** the goods market. It is, after all, one and the same thing—the IS line is the goods market represented with different axes, namely, the i and Y axes.

2. *In the example done earlier, when confidence fell following a tax hike, we had to incorporate this into the analysis. In other words, we had to "know" that confidence would fall. Shouldn't the model be giving us that as a result?*

   A more mathematical model would indeed incorporate confidence as an endogenous variable, explicitly dependent on future tax rates, etc. (See Burdekin and Langdana 1999). In this volume, however, we focus on the ready applicability of our analyses and hold confidence exogenous. In other words, we specify if confidence is headed up or down as in ISLM Exercise 3, and then let the model yield the final effects on Y, interest rates, C, I, etc.

3. *Could the analysis all be done mathematically? And, if so, how would this affect the results which are ambiguous and depend on the relative magnitudes of two (or more) shifts?*

   Yes, all the equations could be solved simultaneously, preferably using matrix algebra and Cramer's Rule. The ambiguous terms would remain so; we would have results with algebraic terms whose signs are dependent on relative combinations of elasticities.

4. *The ISLM–ADAS seems well defined and straightforward. Then why are there so many conflicting analyses and policy prescriptions?*

   Unfortunately, the AS curve is not nearly as conveniently "well-behaved" as in this chapter. In the following chapters we will encounter two "real world" AS curves with radically different policy prescriptions and implications. In fact, in some economies, both will be found to be consistent! And this will be shown to be primarily the source of most of the macroeconomic confusion.

   Please critique/explain the underlined sentences and phrases in the following simulated articles using an ISLM–ADAS framework incorporating a horizontal AS curve.

ARTICLE 7.1   A MONETARY PUZZLE IN NIPPONICA

Ishihara Kawanomoto, Far East Economica

Policy makers in the Republic of Nipponica are confounded. Since last year, **(a)** monetary policy has been eased substan-tially, with interest rates virtually at zero percent. And yet, there is no sign of growth within sight. A sense of **(b)** defeatism and gloom pervades the country, particularly in the headquarters of the ruling party headed by Fujimoto Agaji.

The sense of despondency isn't just confined to Nipponica but afflicts the whole region. The **(c)** neighboring countries of DeSarawa, Kwanton, and Uwaji Baru are all in various states of recession or slowdown as their exports sectors have basically shut down due to the sharp decline in Nipponica's economy and in its citizens' desire for imports.

The government seems to be at a loss, and analysts around the globe aren't faring any better. "This is most confusing," says Brian Perry of Hong Kong Global Consulting, "The monetary stimulus isn't jump-starting Nipponica's output at all. **(d)** We should be seeing at least a Stage 1 recovery—but instead, we see more recession!"

Shreedhar Venkatesh of KD-South Asia finds that, "The fact that the real estate sector and the stock markets of Nipponica have both been 'corrected' by over 40 percent during the last year has to figure in the equation."

When this reporter inter-viewed commuters at Wanfuji Station in Wanju, the capital of Nipponica, he heard several possible explanations.

Janet Hara, Director of Marketing for a medical electronics firm explained, "my company **(e)** just laid off 250 workers last week. Every family has at least one family member who has lost his or her job.

"If Akaji doesn't fix this economy, he is out!" Kim Willys, owner of Willys Custom Land-scaping in Wanju said. "So what if interest rates are zero? I don't know of **(f)** anyone who would buy a house in this climate. What's the point? My business is dead."

As the gloom deepens in Nipponica and its neighboring countries, so does the puzzle. **(g)** Why are the lower rates not jump-starting the "engine" of the economy?

ARTICLE 7.2   DISCIPLINE OR DISASTER?

Bryan McCausland, San Antonio Weekly News

Senator Jenkins' campaign has now "gone national". Two weeks ago, he was Senator Who? And now, as the nation gets infected with Jenkins Fever, both major parties have hustled to form Action Committees to deal with this new challenge from "Contender Jenkins" and his grassroots movement that threatens to sweep over them like a veritable prairie fire.

"No, of course we aren't scared," said Todd Gakk, the President's chief political aide, "but we aren't going to ignore what's going on."

'What's going on' is that Senator Jenkins and his rallying cry of Discipline! Discipline! Discipline! has resonated in the country as none other over the last several elections. Last night in Bridgewater, New Jersey, an expected audience of 3,000 turned into a crowd of over 6,000! Over the weekend in Blacksburg, Virginia, a planned rally for 2,500 drew over 10,000, with people driving five hours from Washington, DC!

Here is the Jenkins' Message:

1.   "We need government discipline. A severe red-uction in government spend-ing is long overdue".

2.   "We need fiscal discipline. Let's raise taxes until all this deficit and all this debt is paid for in the next two years". (Deafening roar of approval).

3.   "We need monetary discipline. Greed must be stamped out. Our greed and our excesses in the stock market and in real estate have caused immense over-valuation. The central bank must burst this bubble by tightening money and raising rates....."

4.   "Discipline   is   the   key!" (Thunderous applause).

However, all aren't on board. At the National MBA Conference in Denver, Colorado, Juan Pereira found Jenkins' policies to be "Puzzling. I see them causing recession! Could my analysis be wrong or is Jenkins' policy agenda totally faulty?" he wonders. John Graham, an MBA student from a huge Midwestern university, feels the same way. "I see the Discipline agenda to be strongly contractionary—no doubt in my mind!" Ricard Hu, an Executive MBA from a US program based in Singapore, is even stronger in his denunciation. "These policies remind me of the erroneous policies recommended by the IMF to the Asian countries soon after the 1997-98 crises—totally contractionary and totally wrong!"

So, is Jenkins recommending Discipline or Disaster? Hopefully, as the analysis continues, the hard macroeconomic truth will emerge. In the meantime, the disciples flock by the thousands to the man of the hour.

Use ISLM-ADAS to analyze Senator Jenkins' policies. Remember that the results here are contingent on the horizontal AS curve.

ANSWERS AND HINTS

ARTICLE 7.1 A MONETARY PUZZLE IN NIPPONICA

(a) Show the LM shifting to the right with an increase in M and a resultant decrease in equilibrium interest rates in ISLM space.

(b) Sounds like the confidence terms, C and I, are falling. IS should be shifting left. Clearly, the net effect has been a final drop in equilibrium GDP—Y has been falling. Interest rates are very low due to the combination of a shift in LM to the right and a shift in IS to the left. The AD has shifted significantly to the left to "line-up" with the lower Y in (I,Y) space.

(c) Using a separate ISLM-ADAS framework for the combined neighboring countries, incorporate a global IS, and show how and why Nipponica's falling national income (Y*) affects the economies of its neighbors. That is, this time the "domestic" economies (Y) in the ISLM analysis are Nipponica's neighbors.

(d) Mr. Perry is neglecting the effect of the leftward shift in IS due to the falling confidence in Nipponica. The huge drop in the stock market, referred to by Mr. Venkatesh, has undoubtedly traumatized the confidence terms.

(e) Increasing signs of unemployment are disastrous for consumer and investor confidence.

(f) Capital investments increase with lower interest rates, but fall with a collapse in investor confidence, I. In fact, the influence of investor confidence—especially when it is falling—is usually the dominant effect on capital investment. It seems that Nipponica may be in the throes of a "liquidity trap". Low interest rates, even close to zero, may not help spur capital investment if confidence has hit rock bottom.

(g) Show how a leftward shift in IS due to a collapse in confidence is negating the effects of the rightward shift in LM caused by the monetary expansion.

Chapter 8
The Classical Model

In this chapter, changes in the rate of inflation are finally incorporated into the ISLM–ADAS analysis. This raises the overall level of sophistication of our analysis from Chap. 7 by incorporating a "real world" aggregate supply curve into the ISLM analysis. The stage is also set for an explanation of paradigm shifts between Keynesian and supply-sider models.

We begin by deriving our first fully articulated AS curve: the aggregate supply curve adopted by the classical economists. This AS was the centerpiece of macroeconomic policy in the United States through the Great Depression and into the early 1930s.

The following table presents a time chart tracing the major changes in models—paradigm shifts—that have occurred in the US economy (and generally in developed economies) since the early part of the last century. Each of the models chosen to "characterize" a period of US macroeconomic history indicates a clear and strong consensus on the part of policy makers (the incumbent government) and researchers regarding "the" operative macroeconomic model in question. In cases where there is no clear consensus model, either from the national policy or research perspective, both models are listed as in the third column of Table 8.1.

Each of these models will be described and analyzed in the following chapters chronologically, beginning with the classical model. In periods in which both models simultaneously exist and vie for center stage, both models will be analyzed. Later, (in Chap. 10) after discussing how two models can indeed legitimately coexist, the reader will have to choose the paradigm that, in his/her opinion, best describes the economy in question.

© Springer International Publishing Switzerland 2016
F. Langdana, *Macroeconomic Policy*, Springer Texts in Business and Economics, DOI 10.1007/978-3-319-32854-6_8

Table 8.1 Paradigm Shifts Over Time

Till early 1930s	Late 1930s to late 1970s	Late 1970s to present
Classical Model	Keynesian Model	**Developed Economies** Supply-side (rational expectationist) leading to the New Economy since the mid-1990s **Or** New Keynesian **Emerging Economies** New Keynesian

8.1   Classical Aggregate Supply: Derivation

Before the Classical AS curve can be diagrammatically derived, two additional concepts must be introduced, namely (i) the production function and (ii) the labor market.

The economy's production function is given:

$$Y = f(k, n) \tag{8.1}$$

where output Y is some function of capital k and employment n. We hold the economy's capital stock k constant at $\underline{K}$.

This makes output supply simply a function of its only variable, employment, given by:

$$Y = f(n) \tag{8.2}$$

The production function, a plot of the output produced in (Y, n) space is presented in Fig. 8.1.

The convex shape of the production function in Fig. 8.1 is attributed to the Law of Diminishing Marginal Returns. With capital held fixed, as employment increases, output increases too. After a point, however, additional increases in employment result in increasingly smaller increments in output. In other words, the production function begins to flatten out, resulting in its characteristic convex shape.

After all, with capital stock (the number of machines, for example) held fixed, simply increasing workers will increase output only up to some finite upper limit (Y_{max} in Fig. 8.1), at which point all the capital stock is being maximized (the machines are all being used at maximum capacity).

Dovetailing the production function is the labor market, presented in Fig. 8.2. Labor demand and supply are functions of the **real wage** defined as W/P, where W is the nominal wage (in units of currency, $), and P is the price of a representative market basket, denominated in $/good. The real wage W/P, the ratio of the two, is therefore denominated in units of goods. In other words, the real wage is the real purchasing power of the nominal paycheck W.

Fig. 8.1 The production function

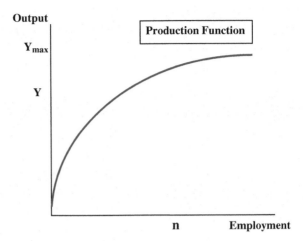

This formalizes the increase in the real purchasing power of one's paycheck upon being transferred (by one's parent company) at the same salary (W) to another part of the country where the cost of living (P)—real estate and insurance, for example—is significantly lower. In this example, the real wage W/P, would increase, and vice versa.

Labor demand intuitively increases as real wages fall (the demand for labor slopes "down"), while labor supply increases as the real wage increases (slopes "up") as in Fig. 8.2.[1] Here the labor market is in equilibrium at a rate of employment n_0 and real wage W_0/P_0.

The crucial assumption made by the classical economists is that nominal wages (W) and prices (P) are fully flexible. That is, if inflation were to increase by say, 3 %, nominal wage growth, by this definition, would also rise by the same amount (3 %). This would in turn leave the ratio, the real wage W/P, unchanged. The same holds true for drops in inflation. Here, by the classical assumption of full wage-price flexibility, nominal wage growth would also fall by the same percentage, thereby leaving the ratio unchanged.

This crucially important assumption will "drive" the derivation and slope of the classical AS curve and will be fundamentally responsible for the implications of fiscal and monetary policy in the classical world. Later, the sudden collapse of this assumption will bring us to our first major (and calamitous) paradigm shift. But first, we derive the classical AS below in Fig. 8.3.

Examining Fig. 8.3, the two figures on the left are the production function on the top and the labor market below. Equilibrium employment in the labor market at n_0 is consistent with employment n_0 in the production function since the rates of employment in these two diagrams must "line up." The initial GDP is Y_0.

---

[1]This is a simplified version of the labor market. Later, in Chap. 10, labor supply and demand will be functions of expected and current tax rates in the supply-sider paradigm.

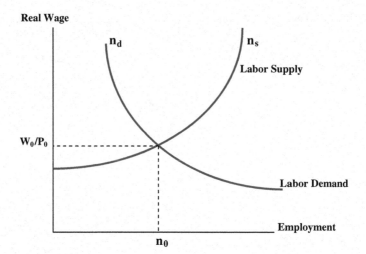

Fig. 8.2 The labor market

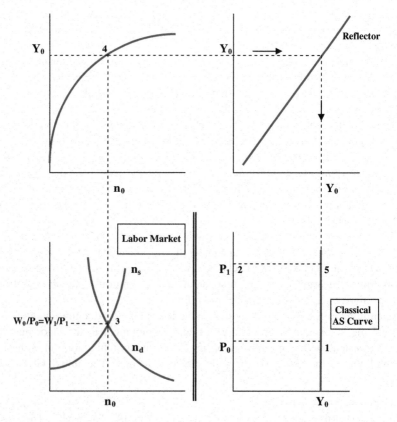

Fig. 8.3 Deriving the classical AS curve

The figure in the top right corner with the Y–Y axes is simply a "reflector" designed to "reflect" values of Y emanating from the production function down by 90° into (P, Y) space in the bottom right of Fig. 8.3, in which the Classical AS is about to be derived.

8.1.1   Derivation Sequence

(The numbers in Fig. 8.3 match the following steps):

1. The first step in the classical AS derivation is to plot the initial "given" point. Initially, GDP is at Y_0 and the price level is at P_0, and this point (P_0, Y_0) is plotted in (P, Y) space.[2]
2. We now allow P_0 to increase to P_1. To keep the derivation simple, let P_0 increase by, say, 50 % to P_1. By the classical assumption, since nominal wages W are fully flexible, W_0 must also increase by 50 % to W_1. The real wage is consequently unchanged with $W_1/P_1 = W_0/P_0$.
3. Since the real wage is unchanged, equilibrium employment (in the labor market) is still at n_0.
4. With employment unchanged, we see that n_0 employment still corresponds to GDP Y_0 in the production function. So, even when P_0 increased to P_1 in Step 2, GDP remained unchanged at Y_0.
5. We plot the new higher price P_1 and the unchanged GDP, Y_0, into (P, Y) space and join this point to the initial point (P_0, Y_0) in order to diagrammatically obtain the classical AS curve in Fig. 8.3

The existence of the double-lined "firewall" between the lower two plots is included to emphasize that the vertical axis in the labor market is different from that in the diagram in the bottom right corner in which the AS has been derived. The "firewall" ensures that lateral transposition of macroeconomic variables does not erroneously take place between these two diagrams.

Also, as in earlier diagrams, all variables are expressed implicitly as rates of growth. For example, Y_0 is the initial rate of growth of GDP, while n_0 is the rate of growth of employment, and so on.

Putting all the markets together for the first time in Fig. 8.4, the ISLM (i, Y) space, the goods market diagram, and the AD curve are identical to those from Chap. 7. The new additions are the production function, the labor market, and, most important, the new, vertical, classical aggregate supply curve. The horizontal AS curve from the previous chapter, introduced for pedagogical reasons, is now replaced by the vertical Classical AS curve.

---

[2]The Y_0 coincides with Y_0 in the production function reflected down into (P, Y) space. The P_0 is not anchored by any lateral location.

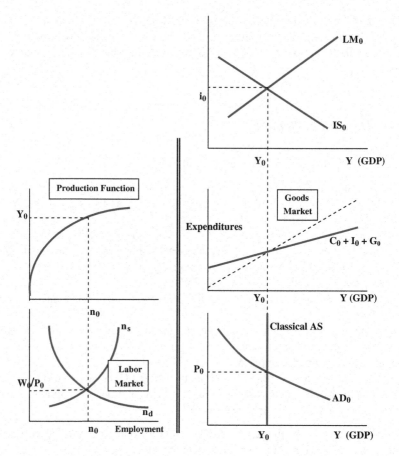

Fig. 8.4 ISLM ADClassicalAS

The crucial assumption driving this economy is the full flexibility of nominal wage growth, and prices. As discussed earlier, the IS and LM curves represent goods and money market equilibria in (i, Y) space, and the AD is simply the representation of simultaneous goods and money market equilibria in (P, Y) space.

8.2 Policy Exercise I: Increase in G

Incorporating the classical AS curve into our earlier ISLM–ADAS framework, we now explore the effect of increased government spending on the key macroeconomic variables.

Once again, we use the survival guide of Chap. 7. The numbered steps below match the corresponding numbers in Fig. 8.5.

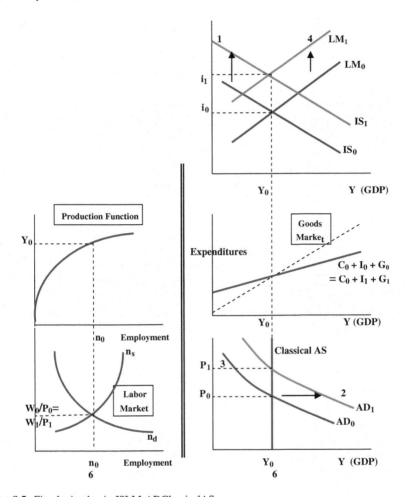

Fig. 8.5 Fiscal stimulus in ISLM ADClassicalAS

1. As G increases, so does the intercept term in the IS, and consequently, as discussed in the previous chapter, IS_0 shifts up (to the right) to IS_1.
2. We "drop down" to (P, Y) space. The aggregate demand, AD_0, shifts laterally by the same lateral shift in IS. This time, though, with the vertical classical AS curve, the new equilibrium—the point where the latest AD curve (AD_1) intersects the AS—is at a <u>higher rate of inflation</u>, P_1, and the <u>same</u> rate of growth of GDP, Y_0.
3. Has P changed? Yes, inflation has changed. Instead of deftly skipping Step 3 and going to Step 4, as we did in the previous chapter, we go back to (i, Y) space and adjust the LM.

4. The increase in price from P_0 to P_1 reduces the ratio (M/P), thereby shifting the LM to the left, as in our discussion in Chap. 7.[3] Equilibrium in (i, Y) space must be consistent with equilibrium in (P, Y) space, and hence the LM shifts left until equilibrium in ISLM space is at Y_0, consistent with the Y_0 in (P, Y) space—the Y_0 must "line up." Final interest rates are now at i_1.

5. We close the goods market. Since the equilibrium here must be consistent with Y_0, the expenditure line will not shift.

   Is there any change in private consumption C?

   No. Since there was no final change in Y (still at Y_0) and since $C = \underline{C} + bY$, there will be no change in C.

   Will there be any change in private capital investment, I?

   Yes. Since interest rates have increased to i_1, and since $I = \underline{I} - fi$, capital investments will fall; $I_1 < I_0$.

   And, finally, government spending has increased from G_0 to G_1, by policy. Therefore, since the expenditure line does not shift and since the final goods market equilibrium is still at Y_0, we can conclude that the increase in G must exactly equal the decrease in I, in order for the total, $C + I + G$, to be unchanged.

   The increase in G has directly resulted in an equal and offsetting decrease in I: this economy suffers 100 % crowding out.

6. **Results:**

   An increase in government spending does not increase Y here. GDP growth stays unchanged at Y_0. Here there is no multiplier effect stemming from an increase in G in an economy with a classical AS. There is no change in private consumption. Interest rates are driven up to i_1 by the increase in government spending. Capital investment suffers 100 % crowding out. Inflation now increases to a higher rate P_1. And in the labor market, nominal wages increase; W_0 increases to W_1 in the same proportion as the percentage increase in prices from P_0 to P_1. Equilibrium employment stays at n_0 in this economy.

In summary, the results are sobering—especially after contrasting them with those for the same policy exercise from the previous chapter. Fiscal expansion does not yield any increase in GDP or employment growth; the only results are higher inflation, higher interest rates, and severe crowding out.[4]

While this discussion could be thought of as a predominantly historical exercise, since the classical model existed before the 1930s, the relevancy of this exercise cannot be overstated. We will soon see that the modern-day supply-siders as well as new economy adherents in the US and Europe also subscribe to a vertical AS curve. In fact, it is commonly referred to as the New Classical AS curve! While this

---

[3]In this case, the ratio M/P_0 fell to M/P_1. There is no change in monetary policy in this example; M stays unchanged.

[4]Contrast this with the result from Chap. 7 incorporating a flat AS. An increase in G resulted in a strong multiplier effect as Y increased along with private consumption C. Conveniently, in Chap. 7 , inflation was conspicuously absent by construction of the horizontal AS.

modern vertical AS curve is obtained from a somewhat different set of conditions, the ISLM exercises in this chapter will indeed apply to these modern curves too.[5]

8.3 ISLM–ADAS Policy Exercise II: Increase in M

Current GDP growth is at Y_0, given to be a sluggish rate. The central bank is under pressure to increase M and reduce interest rates and to "do something" to increase GDP growth. Using an ISLM–ADAS with a classical AS curve, analyze the effects of this monetary expansion.

(The numbers in Fig. 8.6 once again correspond to the following sequence from the ISLM survival guide.)

1. LM_0 shifts to the right as the central bank increases monetary growth from M_0 to M_1. At this stage, the real money supply increases from M_0/P_0 to M_1/P_0, and this causes the rightward shift in LM_0–LM_1. (Since there is no change in government spending G, or in tax rates, foreign income, exchange rates, or in confidence, IS will be unchanged in this exercise.)
2. Dropping down to (P, Y) space, the AD_0 shifts out laterally to AD_1 by the amount of the lateral shift in LM. However, equilibrium in AD/AS space is still at Y_0, given the vertical Classical AS, and inflation has increased from P_0 to P_1.
3. With the change in P, we cannot skip Step 3. LM must now be adjusted until equilibrium in (i, Y) space is consistent with that in (P, Y) space. In other words, the Y_0 in the AD/AS diagram must "line up" with the same value, Y_0, in the final ISLM diagram.
   Since P_0 increased to P_1, the real money supply now falls from M_1/P_0 to M_1/P_1, and this causes the LM to snap back to LM_0 from LM_1.
4. We now close the goods market. Since equilibrium is still Y_0, the expenditure line will not shift. With no change in final Y, private consumption C will not change. And with no change in final interest rates, capital investment I will also not change. There is no change in G, by policy. In the labor market, by the classical assumption, nominal wages will increase in proportion to the increase in the rate of growth of prices; W_1/P_1 will again be equal to W_0/P_0, thereby leaving the real wages unchanged. Equilibrium employment will still be at the rate n_0.

In conclusion, the effect of a monetary expansion, again in stark contrast to the result obtained in the previous chapter, will only be to exacerbate the rate of inflation. Prices and wages will be driven up. There will be no change in GDP growth—no multiplier effect—and no effect on private capital investment. Interest

---

[5]The New Classical AS is also known as the Rational Expectations AS curve. This curve is the "engine-room" of the supply-sider paradigm and will be the subject of Chaps. 10 and 11.

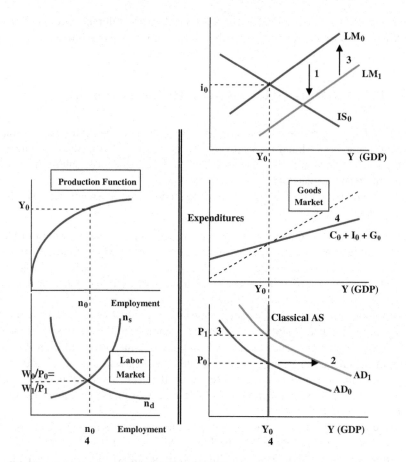

Fig. 8.6 Monetary stimulus in ISLM ADClassicalAS

rates may be temporarily lowered, but as the inflation kicks in and P_0 increases to P_1, the LM snaps back until interest rates are back to i_0.

In fact, as inflation increases, long-term interest rates (not shown in the ISLM analysis) would typically increase, thanks to the Fisher effect discussed in an earlier chapter.[6] And higher long-term interest rates against a backdrop of expected increases in inflation would negatively impact long-term capital growth.

Once again, this result, which may appear chronologically obsolete, has huge contemporary policy implications. In later chapters we will find that the European

---

[6]The interest rates in the ISLM space are short-term (typically 1-year) interest rates.

Fig. 8.7 The Neutrality of
Demand-Side Stabilization in
a Classical AS Economy

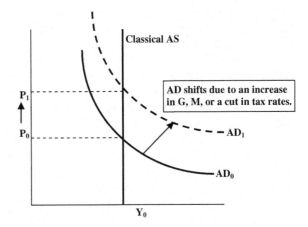

Central Bank adopted a similarly vertical AS curve in the late 1990s—the New
Classical version—as the centerpiece of the theory underlying its monetary policy
objectives for the countries constituting the Eurozone.

8.4   The "Natural" Rates of GDP and Employment Growth

Both the ISLM–ADAS exercises involving expansionary fiscal and monetary
policies and incorporating the Classical AS curve only increased the rate of growth
of domestic inflation (Fig. 8.7). There was no effect on GDP growth or on the rate
of employment. This neutrality of demand-side stabilization on GDP and
employment resulted in the output and employment growth rates being labeled
"natural" rates of growth by the classical economists.[7]

According to the Classicists, attempting discretionary demand-side stabilization
by changing G, M or tax rates would only change the rate of inflation, P. The
"natural" rate of growth in output, Y_0, would remain unaffected by fiscal and
monetary policies. As nominal wages increase in proportion to prices, employment
again stays at the "natural" rate, n_0.

---

[7]This comment anticipates the neutrality propositions proposed by the later rational expectationists
(Robert E. Lucas, Robert Barro) in an era of New Classical macroeconomics that began in the late
1970s-early 1980s.

There is no role for fiscal and monetary stabilization in an economy characterized by a vertical AS curve—shifting the AD by changing G or t or M only affected
nominal variables such as P and W.

This notion of "natural" rates that could not be changed by macroeconomic
intervention was indeed justified in an economy dominated by a vertical classical
AS. However, this notion of nonintervention was to prove macroeconomically fatal
when, during the Great Depression, the model changed—the paradigm shifted—
and, unbeknown to policymakers, the Classical AS swung into the Keynesian
model where fiscal and monetary stabilization are indeed effective.

The next two chapters describe the causes and effects of the shift from the
Classical to the Keynesian model, followed by a description of the macroeconomic
calamity known as the Great Depression.

As per our usual format, the following questions and cases will underscore,
clarify, and review the salient points made in this chapter.

8.5   Discusssion Questions

1. *It is clear that "full flexibility" is the vital assumption responsible for the
   classical AS being vertical. Why did the Classicists make this assumption? How
   could they justify it?*

Going back to the introduction of this book, we have seen that macroeconomic
models—unlike models in physics or engineering, for example—must reflect the
contemporaneous real-world environment in which they are based. Prior to the
1930s, policy makers and researchers witnessed a long period where prices
increased gradually and steadily and nominal wages did indeed increase in proportion.[8] Employment grew at some steady growth rate, n_0. The notion of involuntary unemployment was absent in the Classical world. They simply did not "see"
huge involuntary unemployment because it was not a major feature of their
observed macroeconomic "world."

The assumptions of full nominal wage and price flexibility reflected observed
macroeconomic reality, and these assumptions were crucial to the model and the
model worked—until the assumption of full flexibility of wages and prices came
crashing down in the 1930s.

---

[8]Note that the classicists had no serious experience with <u>falling</u> prices. It was assumed that
nominal wages would also fall in proportion to prices. They were wrong.

2. *If Y_0 could not be changed, how would recessions be cured?*

Once again, there was no role for fiscal and monetary policy in either jump-starting or soft-landing an economy in the classical paradigm. Shifting the AD would affect only inflation. In Chap. 10, when we revisit the vertical AS in the New Classical model of the supply-siders, we will explore how the thrust of macroeconomic policy shifted from changing G and M to focusing on factors such as deregulation, technology, productivity enhancement, and business and personal tax cuts. The objective changed from shifting AD to shifting AS.

3. *In the "real world," typically how long does it take to go from Steps 1 to 4 in the Survival Guide?*

The real-time duration of each exercise depends on the history—the distribution —of consumer and investor expectations, and the location of the economy on its phase of the business cycle. For example, following a monetary expansion, inflation may take longer to increase in Economy A where there is no history of monetary irresponsibility. However, in Economy B, notorious for its monetary looseness, even the vaguest suggestion of a planned increase in M will send inflationary expectations through the ceiling. In this example, Economy B would race from Steps 1 to 4 at a much faster rate than Economy A.

4. *In the exercise in this chapter where M was increased, does the LM actually shift out to the right for a while and then "snap back" as P increases?*

Yes. Inflation follows monetary expansion with a lag. We may actually experience a period with lower interest rates soon after an increase in M as the LM shifts to the right. Inflation will, however, inevitably increase from P_0 to P_1, thereby causing the LM to finally "snap back" to its original position. Once again, the timing of the change in inflation following a change in monetary policy depends on the economy and the macroeconomic situation in question. We will revisit this lag when we discuss Milton Friedman and the role of monetary policy in Chap. 11.

Please explain/critique the underlined sentences/phrases in the following simulated articles using material from this and preceding chapters. Use diagrams liberally including ISLM–ADAS analyses incorporating a Classical AS.

Article 8.1   TAX HIKE PLANNED IN CLASSICO!

Ted Marousas, <u>California Financial Gazette</u>

Late last week, investors at home and abroad were busy digesting the big news from the republic of Classico that its tax rates would be almost doubled in an attempt to "eradicate" the country's fiscal imbalance.

Government officials were out in force yesterday explaining to the public and to Classico's biggest trading partners (such as the US and China) that this policy was indeed necessary and that Classico's **(a)** <u>economy would not be affected by such a sharp tax hike</u>.

"We have always done the responsible thing in fiscal policy," intoned Antonio Hadrian, Class-ico's senior Finance Minister at a press reception on the palace grounds. "Our fiscal excesses last year were due to massive spending on dams and waterworks to prevent a recurrence of the flooding that took place two years ago. But these huge fiscal outlays **(b)** <u>came at the expense of business spending</u>."

He added that the nation had just emerged from an incredible infrastructure building campaign before the floods hit, and this had caused national budget deficits to be **(c)** <u>"larger than we think prudent."</u>

The President himself weighed in with some appropriate comments at the ball to honor a visiting delegation of academics, businesspersons, and MBA students from the US. "I can assure everyone that the **(d)** <u>plan-ned tax increases will raise tax revenues</u> without slowing down our economy. We have the assurance of the Classical Bureau of Economists," and with that everyone visibly relaxed, and the ball featuring the famous Classico Symphony was a huge, rowdy success.

However, not all were nearly that sanguine. Media consultant Monica Swanson worried that, "From the macro I know, **(e)** <u>this policy will be deflationary</u>. This is not good for my business...I am worried."

The following day, Valerie Ericsson, CFO of Classico Pharmaceuticals, was kind enough to talk to us. She agrees with Monica's analysis. "Yes, we can expect prices to fall and confidence, too. Our growth shouldn't falter—but expect housing, stock prices, and **(f)** <u>also wages to be heading down</u>."

Upon relating this analysis, Daniel Ladd, a nutritionist accompanying the visiting MBA delegation, commented, "Well, **(g)** <u>if prices fall and wages fall, then we are at the same place....right?</u>

Article 8.2   WHEN BUMPER STICKERS SAY IT ALL

James Wilson, Richmond Econometric Analysis

"Look, I'm no rocket scientist," says Prof. Claus Elderberry to the crowd of reporters gathered outside his university office, "but I know that **(a)** if our central bank lowers interest rates, we will be able to borrow more to build more houses and factories, and to hire more workers. The economy will finally be able to drag itself out of this two year recession."

He then ends his presentation by passing out bumper stickers that say Lower Rates NOW! and by disseminating the central bank's email address. "Be interest rate activists," he attempts to shout, his hoarse voice now barely audible. "You have a right to a central bank that puts jobs first—email the bankers to lower rates."

Claus hardly looks the activist— just another typical professor in a rumpled tweed jacket. Professor Elderberry is also not an economist. "They're too cautious—I don't care for them," is his summary dismissal of that profession. He is, instead, a marine biologist with a "passionate hobby for economics and finance".

And he is not alone. Several prominent business leaders, large numbers of students, and several prominent politicians have climbed aboard his bandwagon. Business students throughout the country, however, have been very reluctant to climb on.

"His policy just won't work," explains Rob Foley, an MBA student getting a joint MBA-MD degree at the St. Martin School of Management in Milwaukee.

(b) "(His policies) will only get us more inflation—and who needs that?" Rob adds, "Besides, the rates will surely go back up again in say 6-8 months."

His classmate Tina Cassandra resonates, "You see, if you are in a Classical economy, you will have higher wages too—this Claus guy just doesn't understand that!" Tina works at Zinard.Com, a media-consulting agency fran-chise, and **(c)** she also is worried that long-term interest rates would rise if the professor's policies are put into effect.

Last night at the Lampatt Business School in St. Louis, Dr. Erica Glassberg, Chairperson of the National Finance and Accounting Consortium, included the following comments in her address at the banquet honoring the graduating class. **(d)** "I am not convinced that interest rates would head back up following a cut by the central bank. It is a little more complicated. If consumer confidence falls, we could conceivably be in an economy where the central bank lowers rates that are stuck in the 'low position' due to a further deterioration of confidence in this country." She adds ominously, "growth will not increase. This is the dreaded 'liquidity trap' situation that plagued Japan in the early 2000s when its rates were virtually at zero percent and there was no growth. In fact, the US wrestled with a similar concern in the wake of 9/11, and then later in 2008."

Asked to comment after the conference, Vice Chairperson Jim Ziakus' enigmatic explanation to this reporter was, "It is tough to explain—

(e) she shifted two curves. Elderberry only shifted one."

Confused? You're not alone! Stay tuned for more macro reports in this column!

ANSWERS AND HINTS

Article 8.1 Tax Hike Planned in Classico

(a) Show the effects of a tax increase using an ISLM–ADAS framework. Use a Classical AS curve (hence, the thinly veiled name of the country). A fall in Classico's national income would translate to fewer imports from the US and China. With no change in final Y in Classico due to the results of the ISLM analysis with the Classical AS, Classico can claim that its imports from the US and China would not be affected.

(b) The increase in G resulted in 100 % crowding out in Classico. Businesses could not afford to borrow and spend because past increases in government borrowing (to finance the increase in G) had presumably driven up domestic interest rates in Classico.

(c) The deficits sound dangerously close to unsustainability. Refer to earlier discussions on this subject.

(d) In this case, with Y unchanged, an increase in the tax rate will lead to higher tax revenues.

(e) As AD drops left, P will fall.

(f) The crucial assumption here is that nominal wages and prices are indeed fully flexible.

(g) Yes, real wages remain unchanged.

Article 8.2 When Bumper Stickers Say It All

(a) Prof. Elderberry is referring to just the investment function in isolation. Incorporate his advocated policy in an ISLM–ADAS framework with a Classical AS to demonstrate the fallacy of Elderberry's comments. His comments illustrate the danger of looking at just one component and not at the whole picture (not at ISLM in its entirety).

(b) Show the LM "snap back" in the above ISLM–ADAS exercise. The increase in P and the consequent shift back in the LM occurs with a lag following the initial monetary expansion.

(c) The Fisher effect again (from Chap. 6).
(d) If C and I fall, the IS drops to the left, too. In this case, the LM may not need to "snap back." Interest rates remain very "low." The combined effect is a much lower final interest rate with no change in GDP growth, and a decrease in P. Determine the effect on capital investment and consumption.

After 9/11, 2001, confidence indexes in the US plunged. As the Fed aggressively increased M to lower rates, the final rates fell significantly due to simultaneous shifts in IS and LM, in this framework.

It was a similar story for Japan, with the difference being that the confidence terms plunged with the collapse of its financial sector beginning in the mid to late-1990s.

In the US, the massive increases in M after late 2007 in the wake of the "sub-prime mess" coupled with a collapse in confidence as home prices and stocks corrected, resulted in a situation analogous to the one described in this case.

In the next chapter we will discuss these scenarios from the Keynesian perspective.

(e) She "shifted" both IS and LM. Prof. Elderberry just shifted the LM.

Chapter 9
The Keynesian Model

John Maynard Keynes and the General Theory In Cambridge, England, as you walk up King's Parade keeping that late-medieval architectural gem, King's College Chapel, to your right, you will come to a fairly nondescript lane known as King's Lane.[1] It is not prominently marked; one could easily miss it. Leave the crowds behind by taking a right and turn down King's Lane, keeping King's College to the right. The lane ends in a sharp left to form an elbow where Queen's Lane begins. At this elbow in the lane, look up to your right at the row of windows located directly above a (usually locked) gateway into King's College. These windows belong to the room where macroeconomic history was made—Keynes' office at King's College in Cambridge University.[2]

One version of the story has John Maynard Keynes "looking out" of these famous windows to realize that the paradigm then in existence (the Classical model), was hopelessly defunct. He "saw" global depression, and, more importantly, in the long lines of unemployed workers he witnessed involuntary unemployment, a concept conspicuously missing from the Classical model.

Clearly, unemployment and growth rates were not at some fixed "natural" rates n_0 and Y_0, as specified by the Classicists. Something was dreadfully wrong. A paradigm shift had occurred and he, John Maynard Keynes, had discovered the new model.

---

[1]Cambridge is a highly recommended visit. This famous and exquisite university town, tracing its history to well before the Roman conquest, has a distinct "rural feel" which adds to its charm.

[2]The author remains grateful to Professor John Cathie of Cambridge University for pointing out "the window." This momentous event occurred soon after the Rutgers University Executive MBA students had just attended a private harpsichord recital by the renowned Dr. Gerald Gifford at King's College Chapel. The window is now a favorite pilgrimage destination during the annual Rutgers visit. While controversy swirls around the "authenticity" of the story pertaining to Keynes' office, the fact remains that Keynes is still considered to be one of our most globally influential and intriguing macroeconomists, and that he did indeed make history while at Cambridge.

© Springer International Publishing Switzerland 2016
F. Langdana, *Macroeconomic Policy*, Springer Texts in Business and Economics, DOI 10.1007/978-3-319-32854-6_9

At about this time (January 1935), he wrote a memorable letter to his father's friend, George Bernard Shaw, informing him in characteristic fashion, "…I believe myself to be writing a book on economic theory which will largely rationalize (not, I suppose, at once, but in the next few years), the way the world thinks about economic problems…." He had concluded earlier that his theories would "revolutionize the way the world thinks about economic problems."

His seminal work, <u>The General Theory of Employment, Interest and Money</u>, set against the backdrop of the Great Depression, was published in 1936, and is considered by many to be one of the most influential books of the twentieth century.

Nobel laureate Paul Samuelson had this to say about <u>The General Theory</u>:

It is a badly written book, poorly organized…it is arrogant, bad-tempered, polemical….it abounds in mare's nests and confusions….flashes of insight and intuition intersperse tedious algebra. An awkward definition suddenly gives way to unforgettable cadenza. When it is mastered we might find its analysis to be obvious and at the same time, new. In short, it is a work of genius.

Keynes' new paradigm, which would later bear his name, flew in the face of the Classical model. It did acknowledge and explain involuntary unemployment and recession and it did provide specific macroeconomic policies to alleviate them. And Keynes was right in his letter to George Bernard Shaw—it did revolutionize the way the world made macroeconomic policy.

* *Introducing Keynes, Peter Pugh and Chris Garratt,Totem Books, Cambridge, England 1994.*

We now turn to a diagrammatic derivation of the Keynesian AS curve followed by the usual sequence of policy experiments and simulated articles.

9.1   Keynesian Aggregate Supply: Diagrammatic Derivation

The <u>crucial assumption</u> underlying the Keynesian AS curve is:If labor demand (n_d) is greater than labor supply (n_s), nominal wages (W) adjust in proportion to the change in prices (P). But if n_d is less than n_s, nominal wages (W) do not adjust to changes in the price level and are said to be "sticky downwards."

The derivation is presented in the four diagrams in Fig. 9.1. The two diagrams on the left (from top to bottom) are the production function and the labor market with employment at n_0, real wages at W_0/P_0, and GDP growth (from the production function) corresponding to employment n_0 to be Y_0.

The two diagrams on the right (top to bottom) are the Y-Y reflector designed to reflect values of Y from the production function by 90° down to the lower diagram which is the (P,Y) space in which the Keynesian AS is to be derived.

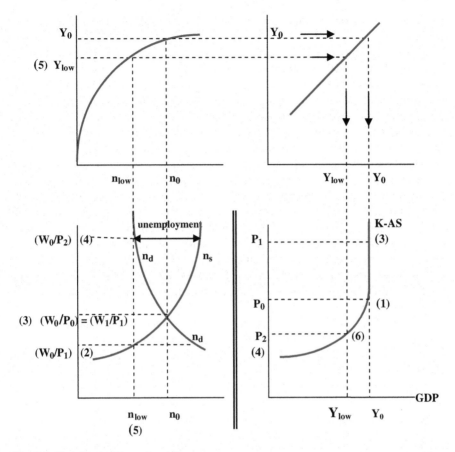

Fig. 9.1 Deriving the Keynesian AS curve

9.1.1 Derivation Sequence

The following steps match the corresponding numbers in Fig. 9.1.

(1) Plot the initial given point (P_0, Y_0) into (P, Y) space. The value of Y_0 is reflected over from the production function. The initial value of P_0 can be plotted anywhere; our objective is to determine how subsequent changes in price affect the P and Y values.

(2) Increase P_0 to P_1. Assumption: Price changes first and nominal wages W adjust after a lag, if $n_d > n_s$. If $n_d < n_s$ then, by Keynes' assumption, nominal wages W simply will not adjust. Since we now have W_0/P_1 as the current real wage, we find that $n_d > n_s$ along this real wage line in the labor market diagram. By Keynes' assumption, W_0 will adjust fully in this situation and increase to W_1 in the same proportion as the increase in prices from P_0 to P_1.

(3) This leaves the real wage unchanged: W_1/P_1 now equals W_0/P_0. We are back to where we started. Employment is still n_0 and GDP is still Y_0. So far, this is

reminiscent of the derivation of the Classical AS curve. We plot (P_1, Y_0) and join to (P_0, y_0).

(4) We now <u>decrease</u> P_0 to P_2. Note that prices had indeed decreased (collapsed by as much as 25–30 %) during the Great Depression when this AS curve was being formulated. The real wage in the very short run is W_0/P_2. We find that this gives rise to a situation where $n_d < n_s$, by examining the labor market. By Keynes' assumption, in this case, W_0 stays unchanged.

This was not a wholly preposterous assumption. Typically, as supply exceeds demand, nominal wages should fall or their rates of growth should decrease. But, as we shall see very soon, in the Great Depression a wage floor prevented this downward mobility in W, thereby rendering nominal wages "sticky downwards."

Employment n_0 now decreases to n_{low} as the number of workers employed will be determined by the labor demand at the higher real wage W_0/P_2. The number of workers seeking employment at W_0/P_2 will be determined by the labor supply curve. The difference between the number actually seeking work at W_0/P_2 and the number employed will be the amount of "involuntary unemployment" which was conspicuously missing in the theoretical framework of the Classical model.

(5) From the production function, output falls to y_{low} corresponding to n_{low} in the labor market.

(6) We reflect this lower output value over to the bottom right diagram and plot (P_2, Y_{low}) and join to (P_0, Y_0) to get the Keynesian AS curve.

The AS curve derived here should look familiar. This was the AS encountered in Chap. 5, where concepts such as demand-pull inflation, overheating, and soft landing were discussed. The same phenomena will be revisited in an ISLM–ADAS framework in this chapter. This time, we will use a labor market to illustrate the explicit effect on employment and real wages, and the production function will be linked to output.

The following Survival Guide will assist us in analyzing macroeconomic policy in an ISLM framework involving the Keynesian AS curve.

9.2   Survival Guide for Islm with Keynesian as (K-AS)

1. Make all moves in (i,Y) space. Make all shifts to IS and LM here.
2. "Drop down" the final Y value into (P,Y) space. The AD shifts accordingly to ensure that the Y values in (i,Y) and (P,Y) spaces are consistent—the Y values must "line up." At this stage, one obtains the "final" P and Y values of the policy exercise.
3. Simply adjust the expenditure line to ensure that goods market equilibrium is consistent with the final value of Y.[3] Once again, determine if consumption and

---

[3]Here steps 3 and 4 of the survival guide are different from those of the Classical model. While prices may have changed, we do not bother going back to "adjust" the LM, even though technically the LM will shift with a change in P. The crucial effects here, namely the changes in P and in Y, are indeed captured and reflected by the model in its diagrammatic analysis. Incorporating

capital investment (I) have changed relative to C_0 and I_0, using the consumption and investment functions. Examine the labor market. If final real wages are such that labor supply exceeds labor demand, then nominal wages will not change with the change in prices. A change in unemployment will occur. If final wages are such that labor supply is less than labor demand, nominal wages will adjust in proportion to the change in prices. The final level of employment must match that of the final output in the production function. (The employment rates in both the labor market and the production function must again "line up.")

4. Present your results boldly.

Armed with the survival guide, we proceed to the following policy exercises incorporating the Keynesian AS curve.

9.2.1 Policy Exercise I: Increase in G

The government launches a massive infrastructure spending campaign to jump-start the economy and put people back to work. Huge power plants, thousands of miles of roads and railways, a new port, an extension of the subways for the nation's largest cities, and several new airports are planned. Using an ISLM-ADAS in a Keynesian paradigm, analyze the effects of this policy on all the key macro variables.

The steps below are represented by corresponding numbers in Fig. 9.2.

Note that the starting point $(W_0/P_0, n_0)$ in the labor market in Fig. 9.2 lies on the labor demand curve. At this initial point we have initial unemployment denoted un_0, depicted as the difference between the available labor supply at the initial real wage and the existing labor demand. As long as the initial point in (P,Y) space lies on the positively sloped portion of the AS curve, we always start at this point in the labor market. The intuition is that initially, at (P_0, Y_0), the economy is still far from attaining Y_{max} at full employment and maximum capacity. There is still room to grow the economy from Y_0 to Y_{max}. This initial level of slack in the economy therefore implies some initial level of involuntary unemployment un_0 which will steadily shrink as we approach the kink in the AS curve at Y_{max}.

Proceeding with the exercise, as G increases on infrastructure outlays:

1. The IS_0 curve shifts to the right to IS_1. Interest rates increase to i_1, GDP growth increases to Y_1.
2. We drop down into (P,Y) space. The Y value in (P,Y) space must match the Y_1 in (i,Y) space. The AD_0 shifts out to AD_1. Inflation now increases to P_1, and GDP increases to Y_1.

(Footnote 3 continued)

the final LM shift would make a diagrammatic representation somewhat intractable. While purists may disagree, the final twitch in LM does not add any additional value from a macroeconomic policy perspective, and is disregarded here in the interest of pedagogic convenience.

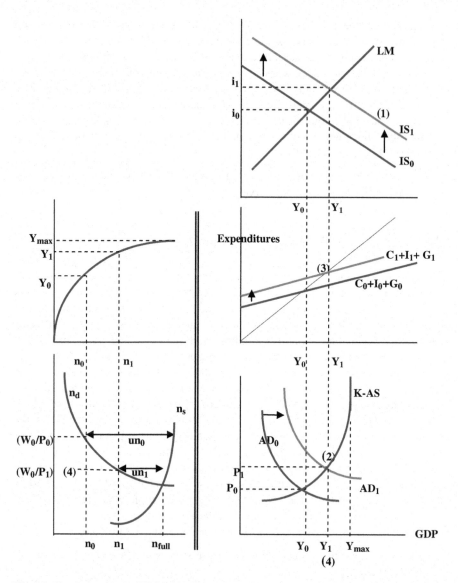

Fig. 9.2 Survival guide for ISLM with Keynesian AS (K-AS)

3. The expenditure line shifts to the right to be consistent with Y_1—after all, the IS and the expenditure line both represent the same (goods) market in different spaces. The goods market is now at a higher equilibrium consistent with equilibrium in ISLM space. Once again, we abstract from the trade sector.

   How does C_1 compare to C_0? Since $C = \underline{C} + bY$, as Y_0 increases to Y_1, C_1 will therefore be larger than C_0. Private consumption has increased. Is $I_1 > I_0$? Since

$I = \underline{I} - \text{fi}$, and since interest rates increase from i_0 to i_1, capital investments will decrease to I_1. That is, $I_1 < I_0$. Private capital investment has been crowded out.

4. In the labor market, as P_0 increases to P_1, nominal wages will not adjust since labor supply exceeds labor demand at both W_0/P_0 and W_0/P_1. So the real wage drops as the denominator increases (to P_1) while the numerator (W_0) stays unchanged.

With this fall in real wages we see (in the labor market) that unemployment shrinks to un_1. Here labor demand increases as real wages fall while labor supply falls.

Employment increases to n_1, determined by the labor demand at the new lower real wage, and this coincides with GDP of Y_1 in the production function. Note the "firewall" between the labor market and (P,Y) space designed as a reminder that the two diagrams have different vertical axes.

The values Y_{max} in the production function and n_{full} in the labor market are included in Fig. 9.2 for completeness, at this stage. In the following section, their presence will be justified as we revisit overheating in the context of ISLM–ADAS.

The final results are radically different from the neutrality results obtained in the previous chapter. An increase in government spending in an economy characterized by a Keynesian AS curve result in:

- The famous Keynesian multiplier effect. GDP growth increases from Y_0 to Y_1.
- Interest rates increase to i_1 as a result of the demand for loanable funds necessary to finance the bond-financed deficits.
- Private consumption increases to C_1. After all, this increase in consumption drives the multiplier effect.
- The rise in interest rates adversely affects—crowds out—private capital investment, which falls from I_0 to I_1.
- Inflation increases from P_0 to P_1.
- The rise in inflation erodes real wages. They fall to W_0/P_1. Nominal wages do not change.
- Unemployment decreases to un_1—employment increases to n_1.

Here, an increase in G jump-starts the economy. Both GDP growth and employment rates increase, and we obtain the Keynesian output-inflation tradeoff. In stark contrast to the laissez faire role for government in the Classical world, activist discretionary government spending does indeed make a difference as multipliers are unleashed. Unlike in the Classical world, in the Keynesian world there is a role for government in stabilizing the economy.

Large infrastructure spending by China (and Japan) through the early 2000s, and in the United States following the subprime crisis of 2008, has attempted to generate such effects and to revive growth.[4] Following the Great Depression, the US had its own version of early infrastructure spending in the form of the TVA (Tennessee Valley Authority), a construction project that included a vast complex

---

[4]In a later exercise in this chapter, we will examine why these policies have not been nearly as successful as the one in the example just discussed.

of dams, power stations, canals, and roads. Another post-depression example is the CCC (Civilian Conservation Corps) that hired involuntarily unemployed workers to undertake the reforestation of many major national parks, as well as road construction, flood control and public works. In fact, it was finally the massive increase in G due to the defense buildup before and during WW2 that enabled the nation to finally emerge from the Great Depression.

The early version of the stimulus package in the wake of the 9/11 was a textbook Keynesian policy recommendation. A bond-financed $100 billion increase in G included spending on reconstruction in New York and Washington D.C. This was the first of a series of spending packages on anti-terrorism and infrastructure. Later, the Obama administration, faced with an impeding recession in the US following the financial meltdown of Fall 2008, unleashed a plan for a massive and vintage Keynesian increase in G of about $500 billion on infrastructure—ostensibly on roads, airports, bridges, high-speed trains, alternate fuel and power, and environmental control. (Unfortunately, most of this "stimulus" was whittled away by the States on nonproductive programs). At about the same time (November 2008), China rapidly put its own Keynesian stimulus plan into action. It announced a staggering four trillion yuan increase in G ("fixed asset spending") on infrastructure, education, housing, water purification, transportation and environmental cleanup.

9.2.2   Policy Exercise II: Increase in Monetary Growth

Under pressure from the government the central bank increases M and lowers interest rates to attempt to revive economic growth and employment.

1. Following the guide and using the same initial points as the previous exercise, we see in Fig. 9.3 that initially, as M_0 increases to M_1, LM_0 shifts to the right.[5] Interest rates drop to i_1 and GDP growth is at Y_1. Note that when central banks "lower interest rates," this usually implies an initial increase in monetary growth.
2. We "drop down" to (P,Y) space, and adjust AD so that AD_1 is consistent with Y_1 in (i,Y) space. Inflation has increased to P_1.
3. Closing the goods market, the expenditure line shifts to the right. C_1 is greater than C_0, since Y_0 has increased to Y_1. I_1 is greater than I_0, since interest rates fell. There is no change in G_0, by policy. In the labor market, as price increases the real wage dips to W_0/P_1, resulting in higher employment at n_1 and lower unemployment, un_1. (Note that since labor supply is greater than labor demand, nominal wages W_0 do not change).
4. A monetary expansion has jump-started this economy. GDP growth has increased to Y_1, interest rates have fallen to i_1, private consumption and investment have both increased, and employment has also increased to n_1.

---

[5]The exact mechanism by which the major central banks change the money supply will be discussed in the Chap. 11.

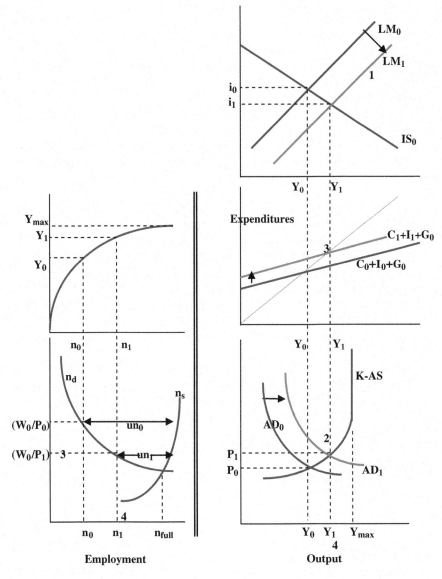

Fig. 9.3 Monetary stimulus in ISLM ADKeynesianAS

The ease and speed with which monetary policy can be enacted usually makes it the first choice of policymakers attempting to revive their sluggish economies with demand-side stabilization.[6]

---

[6]Recall that other instruments are cuts in taxes and, of course, increases in G, both of which take much longer to implement, given the necessary approval processes in government. On the other

From Stage 2 to Overheating

If monetary stimulus continues to be applied, the LM will shift further to the right, driving down interest rates as presented in Fig. 9.4. The value of Y also increases as AD mimics the most recent LM and shifts further to the right. As the AD pushes the economy towards the kink and the point of maximum sustainable growth, the economy begins to overheat.[7]

As prices increase, real wages keep falling from W_0/P_0 to W_0/P_1, and so on. Employment consequently increases while unemployment progressively decreases (the horizontal gaps between labor supply and labor demand keep shrinking).

Eventually, output growth hits Y_{max} at full employment as the AD reaches the Keynesian kink amidst full-fledged overheating. Interest rates have fallen to i_{final}.[8] Here, the real wage Wo/P_{high} is at the intersection of labor supply and demand. There is no involuntary unemployment. The labor market is at full employment, n_{full}, which also corresponds to Y_{max} in the production function.

The economy has transitioned from a nice Stage II recovery at Y_1, where there was still room for the economy to grow (see Fig. 9.3), to an overheated economy as a result of "too much" demand-side stimulus. Output growth is raging out of control, inflation is rising rapidly, skilled labor is virtually impossible to find, and commodities and futures prices are probably climbing. In all likelihood, dangerous SAP bubbles may be developing in the equities and real estate markets, as well as in wages and benefits of certain kinds of high-skilled labor as discussed earlier in Chap. 5.

It is important to note that, as discussed earlier in Chap. 5, actual "overheating" may not always look like this textbook diagram any more. Over the last 15 years or so, overheating has really been relegated to just one specific sector in the form of a SAP bubble. The rest of the economy is typically calm while one sector explodes; the "overheating" is mostly asymmetric. For example, overall inflation in the US was 2.2 % in 2000, while the SAP bubble in dotcoms was raging. And later, same story when the housing market was in the stratosphere in 2008. In China too, when the stock and property markets were raging SAPs, overall inflation lay dormant.

(Footnote 6 continued)

hand, monetary policy, especially in an economy characterized by an autonomous central bank, can be enacted very rapidly without being hindered by a lengthy and debate-ridden approval process.

[7]Here the overheating is being caused by relentless monetary stabilization. It needn't always be the case. The overheating could also be caused by excessive fiscal stimulus in the form of mammoth and ongoing increases in G and/or huge tax cuts, or some combination of all three "policy buttons." Finally, an "irrational exuberance" could also trigger overheating. Increases in the confidence parameters (perhaps in conjunction with any of the policies cited here) will also shift the IS remorselessly to the right, resulting in the AD being pushed towards the kink.

[8]The interest rates in ISLM space are short-term rates. Soon we will examine the effects of these policies on long-term rates when we revisit the role of expectations in the Fisher effect.

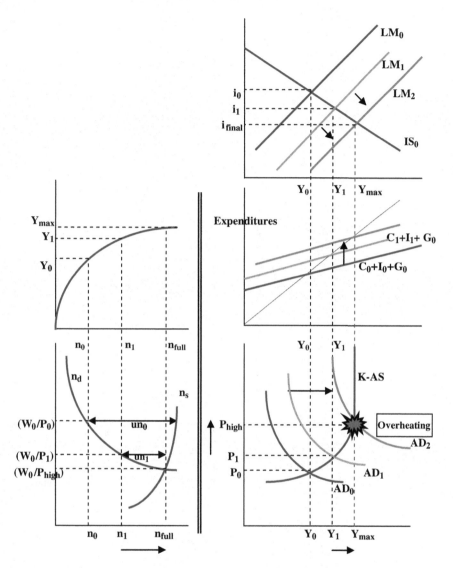

Fig. 9.4 From stage II to overheating

9.2.3 Policy Exercise III: Engineering a Soft Landing

The next logical exercise is to cool down this overheated economy by engineering a soft landing using ISLM–ADAS. The result of the exercise just completed in Fig. 9.4 is now taken as the starting point at which the central bank "taps the brakes" and increases interest rates by contracting monetary growth.

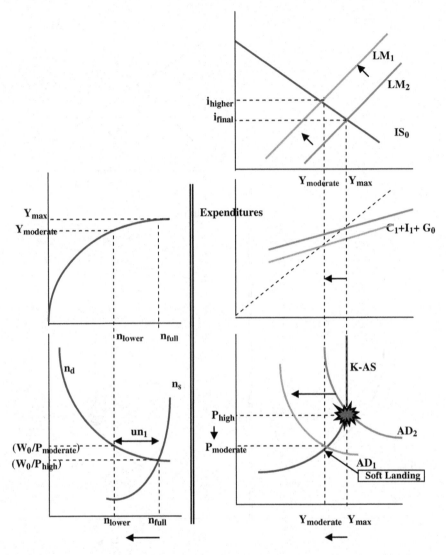

Fig. 9.5 Engineering a soft landing

1. In Fig. 9.5, LM_2 shifts to the left to LM_1 as the central bank contracts monetary growth and "drives up" interest rates from i_{final} to i_{higher}. GDP growth falls from Y_{max} to $Y_{moderate}$. This process can take from 6 months to 2 years—monetary policy acts with "long and variable lags" as Milton Friedman said.

2. AD shifts left to line up with $Y_{moderate}$ in (i,Y) space. Inflation now falls to $P_{moderate}$ from P_{high}.

3. The expenditure line drops left. Consumption decreases as Y falls. Capital investment decreases as the higher interest rates slow down interest-sensitive sectors. Government spending is unchanged here.

In the labor market as the rate of inflation (P) falls, the real wage rises. The level of employment now falls to n_{lower} and unemployment actually increases. The red-hot labor market has been cooled down. If the economy can indeed be finally stabilized at $Y_{moderate}$, $P_{moderate}$ and n_{lower}, then a soft landing has been successfully engineered.

While decreases in government outlays and tax increases can also eventually slow growth, they involve long-term decision making and implementation lags. Contractionary monetary policy, however, can be enacted at very short notice by an autonomous and responsible central bank at the first whiff of overheating. Hence, monetary contraction remains the policy of choice for engineering soft landings.

Examples of perfect soft landings are few. Such deliberately planned slowdowns are fraught with macroeconomic risk. Often, it is impossible to separate deliberate increases in unemployment (and expected unemployment) from large accompanying declines in consumer and investor confidence. These falling confidence levels cause the AD to be driven <u>further</u> leftward due to the confidence-induced leftward shift in IS, thereby turning an intended soft landing into a hard landing.

For example, when the Fed attempted to calm down the SAP bubble in housing in 2006, the whole economy came crashing down. Unbeknownst to the Fed, it had to contend with not just one SAP bubble in housing but two more in private credit card debt and mortgage-backed securities!

9.2.4   Policy Exercise IV: When Low Interest Rates Don't Work—Increasing M Against a Backdrop of Collapsed Confidence

We are given that confidence has crashed in this economy. It may be due to a bursting SAP bubble, resulting in sharply deflated stock prices, plunging real estate values, and a weakened banking sector. The central bank is now under pressure to jump-start the economy by increasing M and lowering interest rates. But despite this, confidence remains unmoved. Expectations are at rock-bottom since the near-term future, for whatever reason, continues to look bleak.[9]

The following steps match those in Fig. 9.6.

---

[9]A good example of this exercise is Japan in the 1990s and early 2000s. The case of the US Fed with its massive Quantitative Easing program from 2008 to 2015 would be the perfect example here. This scenario, which was briefly discussed earlier, is now being revisited in the context of a fully articulated ISLM-ADAS model.

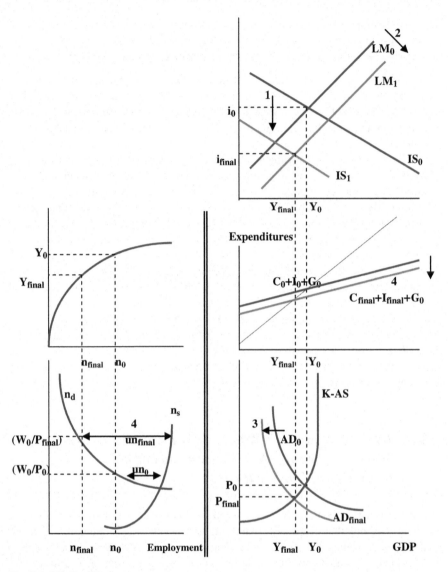

Fig. 9.6 The liquidity trap

1. IS_0 falls left to IS_1 as confidence (consumer and investor) falls. Interest rates fall and GDP drops.
2. Against this "given" backdrop of falling confidence, the central bank increases M and lowers rates further to revive growth. Interest rates are now very low at

i_{final} and growth is increased, to some degree, to Y_{final}.[10] Note that the final location of Y_{final} depends on the magnitude of the IS shift to the left, relative to the LM shift to the right. In this case, Y_{final} happens to be lower than Y_0. The economy is still in recession compared to the initial rate of growth, Y_0.

3. We drop into (P,Y) space and AD_0 shifts left to AD_{final}. Inflation is lower at P_{final} and growth has fallen to Y_{final}. For diagrammatic clarity, only the initial and final AD curves have been shown in (P,Y) space in Fig. 9.6; the AD shift stemming from the initial drop in IS to the left is not presented.

4. The expenditure line in the goods market shifts left to be consistent with Y_{final}. C_{final} is significantly less than C_0 since both Y and $\underline{C}$ have fallen. Capital Investments I_{final} are also lower than I_0. Technically, the effect on final capital investments is ambiguous since we have falling interest rates which tend to increase I, as well as falling investor confidence ($\underline{I}$) which tends to decrease I. Generally, in an economy characterized by plunging confidence, the effect of falling $\underline{I}$ on capital investments is found to dominate that of falling interest rates. Hence, while the algebraic effect on investments is ambiguous, in all probability I_{final} will be less than I_0.

As prices fall, we may see an increase in the real wage and a decline in employment from n_0 to n_{final} (and a rise in unemployment to the higher rate un_{final}).

The impotence of expansionary monetary policy against a backdrop of collapsing confidence is analogous to the **liquidity trap** described previously. The US scenario by late 2008, with $\underline{C}$ and $\underline{I}$ in collapse following the demise of the SAP bubbles in housing and in mortgage-backed securities, is an excellent example. Repeated attempts by Fed Chairman Bernanke to keep the economy alive by increasing M frantically, drove interest rates close to zero. The only legacy of the furious increase in M was a plunge in prices, close to deflation, and almost-zero interest rates.

9.3 Tax Inversion, Statutory Taxes, and Effective Taxes: 50 Foot Walls and 51 Foot Ladders

Tax "inversion" is the process by which US companies move their headquarters overseas to other rival countries where the corporate tax is lower. Famous examples include US drug-giant Pfizer's merger with Allergan, headquartered in lower tax Ireland, to bring down Pfizer's tax bill in one quick stroke.

In the latest iteration of tax inversion, one company acquires another rival company that is headquartered in a tax-light economy. It then "reincorporates" by relocating its headquarters to the tax-light economy, in this case from the US to Ireland. Other cases abound, as in Burger King to Canada, and Chiquita Banana to

---

[10]This is reminiscent of the very low short-term interest rates experienced by Japan in the early 2000s and in the United Sates from 2008–15—virtually zero percent interest rates!

Ireland. Often, the operational business nerve center remains in the original country, but the firm must 'play along' with the appropriate number of board meetings and board members, etc., in its new location.

The main reason for the high rate of inversion by US companies, is, of course, taxation. Domestic earnings in the United States are taxed at the high 39.1 % rate, and earnings repatriated from foreign subsidiaries are taxed at this rate too, as explained below

> For example, a US firm with a subsidiary based in Dublin pays the 12.5 % headline rate of corporation tax in Ireland. The US taxman then levies a 26.5 % rate on earnings from that subsidiary that flow back to America. That means the company's overall tax bill has effectively been topped up to the domestic rate of up to 39 %.
>
> Most other countries impose a much lower rate than the US on repatriated earnings. If a company can shift its country of incorporation, the US taxman loses the right to take a slice of income from foreign subsidiaries.
>
> This system has led American firms to stash an estimated $2tn (£1.32tn) overseas, rather than repatriate the money. It is also seen as a key motivation behind most tax inversions.

Pfizer Takeover, <u>The Guardian</u>, 11/23/2015

Complicating this further is the fact that "statutory tax rates" must be distinguished from "effective tax rates." While America has the highest corporate tax rate of 39.1 % in the Organization for Economic Co-operation and Development (OECD), a group that includes most advanced and mature economies, this high tax rate is really the "statutory rate;" the OECD average is 24.1 %. The statutory tax rate is the base tax applied to corporate profits.

However, most companies are not actually taxed at the statutory rate. Tax deductions, such as pensions, health insurance, and returns on investments allow corporations to reduce the pool of taxable profits. Thus the "effective rate" at which corporations are typically taxed is quite lower.

But whereas the statutory rate is relatively straightforward and uncontroversial, the "effective taxes" may vary significantly by industry, sector, state, and company. In spite of this, however, the United States is till close to the top in the OECD countries. According to the World Bank and International Finance Commission, for 2014, the effective tax rate for the US was 27.9 % behind #1 New Zealand. In 2011, a study by the Congressional Research Service pegged the US effective tax rate at 27.1 %, slightly below the OECD average of 27.7 %.

The range of effective taxes varies significantly within and across countries, with the biggest driver of this variance being the generosity of the schedule of depreciation. The faster a company can depreciate its assets, the better, of course, for tax purposes, and the depreciation schedule varies significantly based on the nature and scale of the equipment (asset) in consideration.

In the case of Pfizer, the company announced that its effective tax rate would be slashed from 25 % in 2014 to as low as 17 % in the first year of the deal. The US attempted to regulate away this "loophole" by placing tighter restrictions on inversions where the US company ends up with a combined stake of between 60 and 80 % of the foreign takeover target. This was intended to stop US firms buying much smaller foreign rivals simply to relocate to a tax-light country and shave millions off their tax bills. However, the terms of the Pfizer–Allergan merger pre-empted this regulation by ensuring that the US firm will own 56 % of the new company, which put it just below the 60 % limit at which inversion could be blocked!

This brings to mind one of those perfect Chinese expressions: Regulations, by themselves, do not 'work. According to the Chinese, if you build a 50-foot wall, someone will invent a 51-foot ladder! In fact Adam Smith said much of the same in his classic, The Wealth of Nations. Regulations by themselves will not work. The incentive–structure must be so designed to allow consumers and producers to "behave" in the desired manner and to be allowed to maximize their utility in doing so. In other words, the best method of preventing inversion would be the removal of the underlying cause—high tax rates—thereby making it "worthwhile" for companies to stay at home in a more fair-tax climate.

Bottom line: While US effective taxes are lower than the much-touted high 39.1 % statutory taxes, they are still high enough to warrant inversion. And, besides, the time and cost expended by companies to minimize their statutory taxes is a drain on productivity that could be better deployed in more productive endeavors.

A Simple Example of Inversion

Reginald Crisanto, Rutgers EMBA, 2016 The firm I worked for took advantage of lower income taxes in Belgium on products manufactured in the United States but sold to certain countries, while maintaining corporate citizenship in the United States. This was achieved through the set up of a principal company in Belgium, which is responsible for managing global manufacturing, supply chain strategy, and commercial operations of international businesses. The principal company bears most of the financial and operational risks of the firm.

Under IRS rules, the principal company has to maintain "substantial contribution" in the manufacture and commercialization of products from the United States to certain countries. Maintaining "substantial contribution" is critical to the success of this company structure. This arrangement also requires that the principal company has distribution agreements with affiliates that are deemed limited distributors in countries where the firm has commercial operations, licensing agreements for the intellectual property, and supply agreements for the manufacturing of the products, among others.

As a result, the products manufactured in the United States can be transferred to the principal company and not subjected to US income taxation. The taxation occurs in Belgium when the principal company sells the products to the limited distributor affiliates. The firm enjoys 5 % effective tax rate on income earned in Belgium for a period of time. This company structure provides the firm up to 35 % of potential savings on net sales of the principal company to limited distributor affiliates.

Fig. 9.7 The Phillips Curve

9.4   The Phillips Curve

If we were to plot the changes in the rate of inflation against changes in the
unemployment rate in Exercises I and II in Figs. 9.2 and 9.3, we would find that as
P (rate of inflation) increases from P_0 to P_1, the unemployment rate—the laterally
measured "gap" between labor supplied and labor demanded—decreases from un_0
to un_1. This, of course, is accompanied by the increase in the employment rate
(n) and output growth (Y).

A.W.H. Phillips, a New Zealander, plotted and studied British inflation and
unemployment data in order to plot the above relationships in a curve which today
bears his name. As presented in Fig. 9.7, the Phillips Curve illustrates an inverse
relationship between the rates of inflation and unemployment, with increases in
inflation accompanied by decreases in the unemployment rate (and, presumably,
increases in output) and vice versa. This was the quintessence of the Keynesian
model, depicted now as an exploitable relationship between inflation and unemployment, and known as the famous (and later controversial), output-inflation
tradeoff.

In this Keynesian paradigm, if the unemployment rate is considered to be "high,"
increases in demand-pull inflation caused by shifting the AD to the right by
appropriate fiscal and/or monetary stimuli would be the remedy. On the other hand,
if unemployment is "too low" and overheating is imminent, contractionary
demand-side policies would lower the inflation rate, increase unemployment, and
soft-land the economy. All this is validated by the empirically observed relationships embedded in the Phillips curve.

> **Emerging Economies and the Keynesian Paradigm** Most emerging and
> newly industrialized economies (NICs) display strong Keynesian character-
> istics. Typically, their labor markets are individually characterized by excess
> labor supplies at existing real wages. These economies have endemic rates of
> high "initial" unemployment. One could make a strong case for the starting

points in labor markets to resemble point n_0 in ISLM exercises I and II of this chapter.

Usually, in these economies, an x percent increase in the inflation rate may not necessarily induce the same x percent increase in nominal wages. For instance, if inflation were to go from 3 to 5 % in China, it is unlikely that average nominal wages (W) for the whole economy would leap by 5 % in the near-term.

The significant excess supply of labor, the absence of sophisticated bond markets, the resulting lack of accurate information pertaining to current and expected inflation, and the inability to manage real wages by collective bargaining or negotiation allow for a degree of nominal wage stickiness in these economies.

This accounts for the fact that emerging and newly industrialized economies are usually Keynesian in nature, even though specific wage floors of the kind used in the Great Depression may be conspicuously absent.

9.5 The Yield Curve and the Keynesian Paradigm

The shape of the yield curve ranges from the "normal" upward sloping curve discussed in Chap. 6 and replicated in Fig. 9.8, to the "inverted" yield curve presented in Fig. 9.9.

The **upward sloping yield curve**, with long-term interest rates higher than the short-term ones, is often thought to be indicative of an economy in the early stages of a sustained recovery. As discussed earlier, the interest rates in the (i,Y) space in the ISLM-ADAS analyses are <u>short-term rates</u>, corresponding to the left end of the yield curve. If the economy were initially in some late-Stage I or early Stage II recovery, the rate of inflation would eventually increase as the AD is shifted right presumably by some combination of fiscal and monetary stimulus. Demand-pull

Fig. 9.8 The yield curve

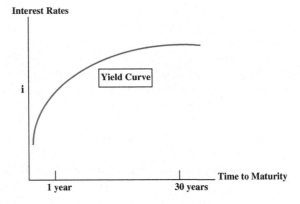

Fig. 9.9 Inverted yield curve

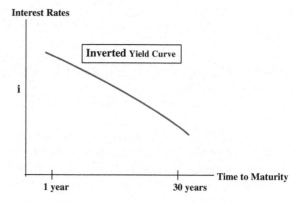

inflation is, after all, procyclical; the rate of inflation increases along with GDP growth. As expectations of an economy growing into Stage II increase, so do expectations of future accompanying increases in inflation.

In the current time period, the efficient bond market incorporates these expectations of future macroeconomic growth, thereby adding on these increases in expected inflation premiums to long-term loans. As explained by the Fisher effect (see Chap. 6), bonds do "know best" and lenders will indeed incorporate expectations of future inflation rates while making long-term loans in the current period. This forward-looking feature results in final long-term nominal interest rates being higher than short-term ones, giving the yield curve its "healthy" upward slope, indicative of vibrant Stage 2 growth expected in the not too distant future.

On the other hand, an **inverted yield curve** is often thought to be indicative of an impending recession or, at the least, an expected slowdown in the near-term.

ISLM-ADAS Exercise III, where an overheated economy was soft-landed using monetary policy, helps explain this sentiment. Using the overheated economy as our starting point, as in the exercise, we have the central bank engineering a soft landing by contracting monetary growth and driving up interest rates, in the present time period.

Since these are short-term rates, the "short" (left) end of the yield curve rises up sharply in Fig. 9.9 as the central bank "steps on the brakes" to slow the economy down fast (China in 1995, US in 1999–2000 and then again in 2006). This action causes GDP growth to slow from Y_{max} to Y_1 in the near future, and the overheated inflation rate to fall from a dangerous P_{high} to a manageable P1 in the near future, as depicted earlier in Fig. 9.5.

Once again, in the current period, the bond market sees all this activity in its forward-looking macroeconomic "radar." Individuals know that the central bank is driving up short-term rates—the only rates that central banks can influence directly—and this, in turn, will eventually decrease inflation in the future to P_1 as the economy slows to some Y_1.

Lenders in the current period expect less inflation in the future. According to the Fisher effect and a competitive market for loans, this expectation results in their charging lower long-term nominal interest rates for long-term loans made in the current period, thereby resulting in a fall in the "long" end of the **yield** curve. In the current period, with the short end rising due to current central bank's contractionary monetary policy, and the long end falling due to falling long-term expectations of future inflation as investors expect a recession (or at the least, a slowdown) in the near future, the yield curve adopts the inverted shape.

It is very important to understand that long-term rates, typically for bonds of maturity greater than 5 years, <u>are endogenously driven</u>—it is <u>only</u> the very short-term rates, the overnight lending rates known as the Federal Funds rates (Chap. 10) that are exogenously controlled by the Fed. In the 2008–15 period, the Fed under Chairman Ben Bernanke launched **Operation Twist** in which the Fed actively manipulated the long end of the yield curve in an attempt to artificially lower long-term interest rates to keep the economy alive. In doing so, the Fed stripped away all the endogeneity of the bond market and deprived the US economy of its most vital long-term "radar;" Operation Twist was macroeconomically heretical to bond vigilantes. The results of this move by the Fed are controversial at best.

Both the cases discussed here linking the shape of the yield curve to expected macroeconomic performance are, at best, "most likely" scenarios. By no means is an inverted yield curve always a harbinger of an impending recession or slowdown. As we will see in Chap. 10, a positive productivity shock—cost-push inflation in "reverse"—caused by, say, a new breakthrough technology such as the advent of the internet, would result in a rightward shift in the AS with an increase in growth

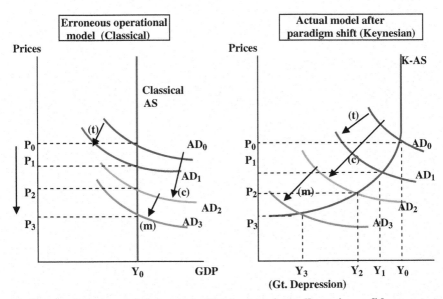

(t) = tax increase and decrease in G; (c) = ongoing collapse in confidence;
(m) = effective monetary contraction

Fig. 9.10 The Great Depression: The Paradigm Shifts

and an expected future decrease in inflation. Yield curve inversion could occur in this scenario too, but the implications would be in marked contrast to the previous dismal scenario of impending slowdown.

By the same token, as discussed earlier in chapter 6, a rise in the long end of the yield curve, depicted in Fig. 6.1, it is not necessarily always synonymous with expected strong growth. For example, in the case of a rising long-term interest rates, other factors besides policy-induced demand-pull inflation could be driving up future inflation.

The culprit may be cost-push inflation due to an expected oil crisis (Chap. 5). This would drive-up expectations of future increases in inflation, thereby raising the long end of the yield curve. And we know that cost-push inflation is inversely correlated with GDP growth; it is countercyclical. In this case, an upward sloping yield curve would certainly not be a prologue to healthy growth in the near future but, instead, an early warning for cost-push inflation and slower growth!

Yet another scenario pushing up the "long end" of the yield curve, discussed earlier, could be an increase in future inflation stemming from the rampant monetization of unsustainable deficits.

Hence, recapping from Chap. 6, the bottom line is that movements in the yield curve, such as the rising of the "long end," by themselves, signify that future (expected) inflation/risk is increasing; that is all. Any further deductions pertaining to the specific underlying macroeconomic causality of this movement—expected hyperinflation, strengthening/overheating economy in the future, impending cost-push inflation—can only be obtained with further analysis. Instantaneous macro-predictions based solely on the changing shape of the yield curve, without accompanying analyses of the factors underlying the shape, need to be treated with a certain degree of caution.

9.6   The Agony of a Paradigm Shift: The Great Depression

The year 1929 began on a glorious note. US real GDP exceeded potential GDP, and unemployment was a low 3.2 %. The 1920s had witnessed years of economic strength that included tremendous booms in housing and in new technology. In fact, the period was optimistically labeled the "New Era." But all that was about to change.

Following the crash in October 1929, the stock market had lost more than one-third of its value in 2 weeks. And this was only the beginning. By the time the stock market crash had deteriorated into the Great Depression by 1933, real GDP had fallen by 29 % relative to its 1929 level. Prices had collapsed, with deflation at 24% compared to prices in 1928. Twenty-five percent of the work force was involuntarily unemployed with virtually no social security or unemployment benefits in place, and unemployment remained above 14 % until 1940. Only the arming of the US, preparatory to its entry into WW2, finally shook off the vestiges of the lingering unemployment from the Depression.

The Great Depression was an inconceivable macroeconomic meltdown that remains permanently seared in the minds of those unlucky enough to have experienced it. And it was aggravated by four huge policy mistakes that, remarkably, turned a bad stock market correction into a singularly devastating macroeconomic calamity.

This book sidesteps the ongoing controversy between Keynesians and Monetarists regarding the primary causes of the Great Depression. Instead, the approach here focuses primarily on the effect of the four policy mistakes, compounded by a paradigm shift.

Mistake 1: Wage Floors

The operational model employed in 1929 was of course the Classical model with its vertical AS curve and with no role for discretionary fiscal and monetary policy. But this model was rendered defunct when President Hoover, in a well-meaning attempt to prevent workers' real purchasing power from falling, introduced wage floor legislation. These wage floors prevented nominal wages from <u>falling in the same proportion</u> as the collapsing prices in the months following the Crash. By legislating a system of minimum wages (wage floors) that did not adjust downwards with falling prices, Hoover inadvertently created Keynes' "sticky wages!" Nominal wages fell from 57 cents an hour in 1929 to 44 cents an hour in 1933, while prices fell by a significantly larger percentage. This wage floor—the first mistake—prevented W from falling in proportion with P, quickly demolished the fundamental assumption of full flexibility of W and P which was absolutely necessary for the vertical AS curve of the Classical Model. In fact, with "sticky wages," the AS curve quickly transformed into the familiar kinked Keynesian AS curve derived earlier in this chapter.

Unfortunately, this change in paradigm from Classical to Keynesian was not immediately obvious.[11] Policy makers were blind-sided—they continued to prescribe macropolicy based on the "wrong" (Classical) model, while in fact their world had changed to one where the AS had now taken on the positively sloped, kinked, Keynesian shape! They were unaware that the paradigm had shifted.

As confidence continued to plunge following the crash and the ensuing margin calls (at that time investors could borrow up to 90 % of the value of the stock), the IS, and hence the AD, kept falling left along the Keynesian AS. As GDP thus fell to Y_{low}, and with national income falling, so did the tax base. Tax revenues fell, resulting in a small budget deficit.

Mistake 2: Tax Increases and decreases in G

At this point, policy makers made their second mistake. Continuing to operate in the now-defunct Classical AS model, they rapidly moved to increase tax rates to "do something" about the budget deficit. Tax rates were savagely increased. The

---

[11]In a following chapter, the Identification Problem will help explain why it is econometrically very difficult even today to identify the "real" model when dealing with time-series data.

Tax Revenue Act of 1932 nearly doubled income taxes (the highest tax bracket jumped from 25 to 63%), imposed excise taxes, and boosted corporate taxes from 12 to 13.75 %.

As depicted in Fig. 9.10, with a vertical AS, these increases would indeed generate a larger slice of tax revenues, given that national income was supposedly "fixed" at some natural rate. However, with the Keynesian AS, the sharp tax increases proved to be terribly contractionary. The recession only worsened as the IS pivoted clockwise with the AD matching this leftward movement over the sloping AS curve as depicted as (t) in Fig. 9.10. GDP growth and inflation fell even further, and, with the sticky wages, unemployment began to increase rapidly. In addition, government spending, although modest, was reduced in an attempt to respond to the deficits, further pushing the IS to the left! All along, as jobs were lost and unemployment soared and expenditures plunged, continuously collapsing consumer and investor confidence formed a terrible backdrop to the crisis, further pulling the IS and AD to the left, denoted as (c) in Fig. 9.10.

Things progressively got worse. The recession deteriorated inexorably. American social worker Frances Perkins wrote in 1934:

> But with the slow menace of a glacier, depression came on. No one had any measure of its progress; no one had any plan of stopping it. Everyone tried to get out of its way.

Mistake 3: Liquidity Crisis

Banks began to fail; almost 33 % of all banks failed by 1933. Before the Crash in October 1929, bank loans had over expanded due to booming stock and property markets, but following the stock collapse, many borrowers could not make the interest payments on their loans or the repayment schedules. Panic spread as banks failed; there were "runs" on banks. Depositors rushed to pull their money—uninsured deposits in the era before FDIC—out before the banks went under.[12] There was a severe decline in the money stock, with M1, the most liquid measure of money, falling by 26.5 % from 1929 to 1933, and M2, a less liquid measure, falling by 33.3 % over the same period.[13]

While the Federal Reserve did not deliberately enact a contractionary monetary policy, its reluctance to rush in, increase monetary growth, and inject liquidity to the liquidity-starved economy resulted in an <u>effective</u> reduction in M, depicted as (m) in Fig. 9.10. Once again, policy makers believed that the only result of this effective decrease in M would be more deflation, since the model was still supposed to be

---

[12]The Federal Deposit Insurance Corporation (FDIC) was a result of the Great Depression. Established in 1933, the FDIC insures bank deposits for up to $100,000 per deposit. This (it was hoped) would ensure that depositors no longer fear bank failures and thus recessions and depressions would not precipitate panics and provoke runs on banks.

From The Macmillan Book of Business and Economic Quotations, Michael Jackman, 1984.

[13]The monetary aggregates, M1-3 will be defined in Chap. 11. For now, M1 includes all cash and demand deposits, and M2 includes all of M1 plus interest bearing checking accounts.

Classical. Andrew Mellon, head of the Federal Reserve, was a deflationist. He believed that the increase in prices during the 1920s was the primary cause of the macroeconomic malaise, and he therefore wanted prices to fall to pre-World War I levels! He commented in 1930:

> Let the slump liquidate itself. Liquidate labor, liquidate stocks, liquidate the farmers, liquidate real estate....It will scourge the rottenness out of the system. High costs of living will come down. People will work harder, live a more moral life. Values will be adjusted, and enterprising people will pick up the wrecks from less competent people.

The tragic, erroneous implication of using the "wrong" model was that P would further fall as M fell, and Y would be unaffected since the AS was still supposed to be Classical (see Fig. 9.10). So the Fed did nothing—it did not inject liquidity into the system by increasing M. Its silence was terrifying. The third giant mistake had been made.

In reality, the huge monetary contraction once again resulted in an AD shifting even further to the left over a sloping AS, depicted as (M) in Fig. 9.10. The economy had now reached Great Depression status. Confidence was in total free-fall. Unemployment and GDP growth had reached their Great Depression levels with the economy contracting by 30 %. Rampant deflation had set in, with prices collapsing to P_3 in Fig. 9.10.

Milton Friedman and Anna Schwartz, in their Monetary History of the United States, have argued that the effective monetary contraction was, in fact, the proverbial straw that broke the economy's back. While we shy away from debates involving the principal factor responsible for the Great Depression, the result of this huge monetary contraction, coming on the heels of a major tax hike and a sharp drop in confidence, cannot be overstated.

Against this backdrop, President Hoover's 1931 comment epitomizes the sentiment of policy makers unknowingly trapped in the now-defunct Classical model. The laissez faire role for government intervention with a conspicuous absence of any role for G or M is clearly apparent:

> Economic depression cannot be cured by legislative action or executive pronouncement. Economic wounds must be healed by the action of the cells of the economic body, the producers and consumers themselves.

Mistake 4: Smoot-Hawley

As if these mistakes were not enough, a strong contender for the title of the principal factor was the Smoot-Hawley Act of 1930. This was a tariff (tax on imports), imposed on about one-third of US imports, resulting in a tariff increase from 45 % in 1930 to 60 % by 1933. Naturally, European exporters placed retaliatory tariffs on US exports, resulting in a global trade war that essentially shut down world trade. By 1933, the bottom had been reached. The inconceivable had happened—full-fledged depressions ravaged the US and its major trading partners worldwide.

Here we not only analyze the policies that caused the Great Depression, as most other texts do, but we place these policies against a backdrop of a paradigm shift. In this context the "mistakes" that led to the greatest macroeconomic cataclysm in US history may not seem completely preposterous. Policy makers were simply operating in the wrong model. By the time Keynes "looked out his window" and concluded that the "model had changed," it was too late. The Great Depression was in its darkest throes, laboring in the agony of a paradigm shift.

Could a Great Depression Happen Again?

First and foremost, it is clear that the Federal Reserve is extremely unlikely to ever again make Mistake 3. In times of great and grave national crises, the Fed has moved with amazing and impressive alacrity to inject liquidity into an economy in distress.

A striking example was the response following the terrorist attacks on the World Trade Center and the Pentagon on 9/11. With thousands of flights loaded with uncleared checks stranded on the ground, and domestic and global financial institutions desperately in need of large infusions of funds, the Fed promptly injected liquidity into the system. Within 3 days of the attack, over $108 billion was lent to banks and investment dealers. Prior to September 11, 2001, injections of funds to the banking system had seldom exceeded $6 billion.

Another example of decisive Fed injections was the 14 % increase in monetary growth in the days following the October 19, 1987 stock market correction—in fact, liquidity was being injected into the system on the very afternoon of the correction! Over a longer duration, from late 2007 to early 2008, the Fed under Chairman Bernanke drove-up the money supply and flooded the US economy with liquidity in a desperate attempt to prevent contagion from the collapsing housing market bubble to the rest of the economy (more on this in the article following this chapter). Other examples are the infusions of liquidity following the 1995 Mexican Peso crisis and the 1997 Asian currency crisis.

Other positive factors that make a recurrence of the Great Depression unlikely are deposit insurance in the US (FDIC) that reduces bank panics and "runs" on banks, and unemployment insurance and benefits which would prevent sharp collapses in confidence and in spending at the first hint of unemployment. Furthermore, Mistake 4—despite the backlash against global trade—would be unlikely given the fundamental benefits of free trade in goods and services and in unrestricted global capital flows.

On the negative side, however, Mistake 2, unfortunately, keeps recurring. Policymakers find it difficult to understand that by increasing tax rates they may not be necessarily increasing tax revenues; the notion of output endogeneity is often lost in the analysis; in fact, taxes were increased again in 1937! More recently, this tax mistake was made in the US in 1990–1991 even after the "No New Taxes" pledge of President Bush, and was (mistakenly) prescribed by the IMF to ravaged Asian economies in the wake of the 1997–1998 currency crisis. Japan has made this mistake at least thrice between 1995 and 2015.

All in all though, the chance of the concurrence of all four policy mistakes, discussed here, against a backdrop of a sharp collapse in stock prices and confidence, triggering another Great Depression seem unlikely.

During the post-World War II era, the world became Keynesian and exploited the Phillips curve relationship quite effectively. This was the era of "fine-tuning" and discretionary demand-side policy making. Economies were jump-started and soft-landed successfully and the "real world" cooperated with the model. But then, in the late 1970s, something went wrong. The Phillips curve relationship crumbled into a meaningless jumble of points. Suddenly, there was no clear unified model, and macroeconomic analysis and policy appeared to be irrevocably changed. A new and emerging group of macroeconomists insisted that the paradigm had changed yet again and that "Keynes was dead." Needless to say, the Keynesians strongly disagreed and continue to do so.

Before we come to yet another exciting phase in the evolution of macroeconomic policy, a discussion of key questions and a review of "media articles" to allow us to fully understand the Keynesian model is in order.

9.7 Discussion Questions

1. *It looks as if the vertical portion of the K-AS curve is identical to the vertical Classical AS curve. Are they essentially the same curves?*

They are "similar" in that they are both vertical segments, derived by the fact that W and P are fully flexible. But the similarity ends there. The Classical AS is vertical at some "natural" rate of output growth, Y_0, corresponding to some rate of employment n_0. The vertical segment of the K-AS curve, on the other hand, is at an overheated Y_{max}, corresponding to full employment and virtually no excess capacity in the economy.

2. *Is Stage 3 inflation (the rapid increase in inflation beyond the overheated stage) the same as hyperinflation?*

No. Hyperinflations are usually caused by unsustainable deficits that necessitate monetization. Overheating and Stage 3 inflation are caused by excess demand that rapidly drive-up wages and prices given the finite (maximum possible) aggregate supply.

3. *From a previous chapter, we know that foreign income, Y*, can shift the global IS to the right, also driving the AD to the right. Why is this not listed under factors that can stimulate an economy?*

We only list changes in G, M, and tax rates, t, as factors that can jump-start or soft-land an economy because these are the three policy instruments available to us. Foreign income Y* is an exogenous variable which is taken as given by the domestic economy. It certainly affects domestic IS and AD, but is not a policy variable that can be readily controlled by domestic policy makers to shift IS and hence, AD.

4. *Wasn't it fairly obvious that the paradigm had shifted during and after the Great Depression? What would it have taken to convince the Classical economists that the model had changed?*

In hindsight and retrospect, yes, paradigm shifts seem obvious. But in reality, they are extremely difficult to detect during the contemporaneous time period. In Chap. 10, we will discuss a time-series problem known as the Identification Problem. This problem makes it extremely difficult to pinpoint the "correct" model, since several different models may "explain" the real-world data equally well. But in addition to this problem, there are the lags to consider—policy ineffectiveness may be misinterpreted simply as the lag before the policies actually show effects. In addition, data is often not very accurate and needs to be revised several times. And finally, there may be a sense of denial on the part of policy makers that the model that had worked so impeccably well in the past may now be defunct.

Please relate the underlined passages in the following articles to material covered in this chapter as well as in preceding ones. Use diagrams (ISLM–ADAS) liberally.

ARTICLE 9.1 "WE HAVE OPTIONS," PM TELLS CABINET

Michael Sadler, Belgravia Policy Review

As the latest economic data hit the stands, Dr. Norton Jones, Prime Minister of Belgravia, moved swiftly to assure the nation that plans were already afoot to counter the impending macro-economic problems.

"It is clear that our present (a) slowdown is attributed to long recessions in our two biggest trading partners, the United States and Japan, but we have many tricks up our sleeve to counteract that," he told the powerful Belgravian Association of Model Train Builders at the National Hobby Convention in the tiny mountain principality of Luray.

The audience was not impressed. Zenobia Mistry, an expert in Swiss train models, said, "I know something about finance; (b) when the yield curve points the other way, I know that a recession is coming." But Kevin Morgenstern, an American model train veteran spe-cializing in early generation diesels conceded, "At least the guy (the PM) is trying. He has a plan that makes sense to me, and (c) let's just wait to see if he gets us through this. But now I have to get my Roanoke-built 611 off the main-line before that high speed TGV slams into it..." and with that he clambered hurriedly onto the tracks.

When questioned about his "plans" the PM stated, (d) "We have a budget surplus, and that allows us huge policy options. Given the fact that (e) we are still an emerging economy, fiscal expansion which includes a new expanded subway system, seven new power plants and dams, and, of course, the intercity high-speed train system will be the key."

He dismissed concerns from political opponent Bill Macla-shovsky regarding the financing of the new infrastructure spending. The PM said, "Since we are running national budget surpluses, a (f) sustainable deficit is not a problem. In fact, it is part of the solution. I also expect a strengthening of our currency and capital inflows in the near future."

Dr. Jones has two other 'tricks' up his sleeve. The Belgravian central bank will cooperate by (g) lowering interest rates, and he is lobbying for an across-the board tax cut of 28% to stimulate consumption and capital investment. He also hopes that once investors see that these plans are in the works (h) the current trend of defeatism and gloom will be reversed.

"All in all, this is a (i) three-pronged Keynesian offensive," re-marked Sophie DeSalle of France Poly-technique, a Loire Valley consul-ting house. "This is quite a standard package, actually. The important thing is that Dr. Jones has been quick to recognize the peril and quick to launch this stimulation package. We are quite sanguine about Belgravia in the near-term."

At the hobby conference, Al Silverman, a 77-year old model train buff, may have said it best. "While the 'locomotive' of the economy may need to be jump-started, and then later cooled down and all that—my trains need nothing! They run perfectly all the time!" More power to him (pun intended).

ARTICLE 9.2 THE GOOD NEWS: ECONOMY IS SLOWING!

Mary Torres, <u>Newark World Business Weekly</u>

A recent visit to the kingdom of Bardoli is a study in contrasts. Just four weeks ago, this reporter spoke to Mr. Sudhir Gupta, owner of the Sea Breeze chain of hotels, who lamented that **(a)** <u>he had to "import" students from overseas during the busy summer months to staff the front desks of his hotels.</u> "It was my only option. Our labor market dried up months ago!"

The entire country had been desperate for workers until very recently. Employees for the ser-vice industries—hotels, amuse-ment parks, general tourism, outdoor recreation—as well as sectors such as nursing, IT hardware and software specialists, engineers of all kinds, and high school teachers were virtually impossible to find.

"Personally, we have been riding this big high," says Bernice Fitzpatrick, a software engineer. "I know other engineers who changed jobs every two months for **(b)** a salary increase of <u>at least 25 percent with every change.</u> It was a crazy time," she says, shaking her head.

Professor Umbotu Ulundi of Bardoli Medical School added, "The **(c)** <u>over-inflated stock market and housing market added to the crazy salaries</u> that some sectors were getting. The **(d)** <u>cen-tral bank had to put an end to the madness.</u> It was really impossible to replace nurses as we couldn't afford the salaries demanded by new nurses. Sheer madness!"

The central bank certainly put an end to the "madness". **(e)** <u>Six interest rate hikes have cooled down the torrid labor market. The stock market is down by 19% relative to its high last year, and housing prices are also 24% lower.</u> And talk of a sharp cutback in defense spending is adding to expectations for further GDP slowdowns. The current GDP growth rate of 4.1% (down from the supercharged 7.8% last year) is expected to be down to 3.5% by this time next year, according to our survey of the nation's top economists. **(f)** <u>The price of gold has fallen by 32%, and other commodities futures have displayed similar drops in price.</u>

(g) <u>The rate of imports has also slowed, with the current account deficit posting its slowest increase</u> in six years. "This is all in line with macro theory," said Karen Chang, a recent MBA graduate from New Market University in Omaha, **(h)** "<u>I also expect long-term rates to fall over the next six months</u>".

Maximillan Porshe of the gian German real estate consortium, Haus, concurs. "I expect this to be a good time for mortgage purchases and re-financing. **(i)** <u>However, new home sales aren't just functions of interest rates. The question is how low will disposable incomes fall and how will the consumer feel</u> as the central bank taps the brakes? Hopefully this will not be a hard landing."

ARTICLE 9.3 ICELANDIC SAGA: THE MACRO VERSION

© Prof. Farrokh Langdana, Rutgers Business School,

The author is most grateful to his MS in Finance students at the University of Iceland, and to Prof. Vilhjalmur Bjarnason, and Mary Langdana for comments and suggestions.

To fully understand the macroeconomic "Icelandic Saga" of 2008, one must first analyze

(i) the sequence of macro-events in Iceland from 2003 to the present, and (ii) the nature of the "three-bubble-scenario" in the United States from September 2007 to the current period.

Beginning in 2003, Iceland put into motion a series of expansionary macro-policies that eventually earned the country the title of The Nordic Tiger. Chronologically, in 2003, the Central bank of Iceland dropped the reserve ratio from 4% to 2% resulting in a strong monetary stimulus. In 2004, Iceland witnessed a significant increase in government spending on its massive energy-intensive projects. At this point, thanks to these monetary-fiscal stimuli, GDP was racing to over 6% annual growth with inflation at 2.5%, the latter in line with the Central Bank of Iceland's inflation target.

Then in 2005, even more expansionary policy, as income taxes were cut from 38.58% to 37.37%, followed by additional tax cuts in 2006 to 36.72%. These measures further powered the economy—the Nordic Tiger was on fire and the envy of the world. Capital was pouring in. And why not? A high-skilled labor force, surging consumer and investor confidence, powerful stock markets, low taxes and low regulations—Iceland was the poster country for macroeconomic growth and listed as #5 in Global Competitiveness by the prestigious Heritage Foundation in 2007.

As the stock market soared and as housing prices inflated, the "wealth effect" resulted in a sharp spurt in private consumption. This, coupled with globally increasing food, commodity, and energy prices driven-up by the emerging economies, resulted in inflation ominously increasing to over 8.6% in 2006. Finally in the summer of 2007, the central bank hit the brakes and raised interest rates to calm down the housing market and to force a gentle slowdown and to engineer a soft-landing.

But by then the Nordic Tiger was in no mood to slow down—it brushed aside the feeble attempts by its central bank to soft-land the economy. And as foreign capital lined-up to invest in Iceland, the super-strong ISK allowed its citizens to borrow in foreign currency, thereby neatly side-stepping any domestic central bank attempts to engineer a soft landing.

In the Summer of 2007, as the Land Rovers and Toyota 4x4s clogged the pretty streets of Reykjavik, as high-end restaurants such as Vox were packed to capacity, and as expensive golf clubs posted 2-year wait-lists, the Icelandic Vikings were on the prowl again—unstoppable and magnificent.

Then in 2008, even more expansionary policy! Corporate taxes were dropped from 18% to 15% in January. The economy was now racing ahead and overheating strongly.

Now while the super-heated Summer of 2007 was happily progressing in Iceland, just over five flying hours away in the United States, something was going dangerously wrong. The American soft-landing was in deep trouble. Its repercussions would be felt around the world, and most definitely in Iceland, which by then was thriving on internationally borrowed money.

As Federal Reserve Chairmen, Alan Greenspan and then Ben Bernanke attacked the housing bubble in the US by pushing up interest rates to 5.25% from a low bubble-fostering 1%, and as the US housing bubble began to deflate, a shocking revelation manifested itself—America was not just deflating one bubble in housing, but two additional bubbles! The dotcom bubble of the late 1990s had eventually led to three bubbles by 2005—a bubble in housing prices, another giant bubble in mortgage backed securities, and yet a third bubble in revolving private credit-card debt with every American family owing over $8,200 by June 2008 (Indexcreditcards.com).

The mortgage-backed securities, the key element of 'the sub-prime crisis', were, very simply, "bundles" that contained good solid loans as well as lots of very dubious ones. These packaged bundles were gobbled up by hungry hedge-fund managers. The dubious component of these mortgage-backed securities, known as the sub-prime loans were mortgage loans made to low-credit, or 'sub-prime' borrowers, many of whom were often not even required to substantiate their exaggerated incomes with documentation (hence the term, 'liar loans' or 'no-doc loans').

As the US Fed drove up interest rates to calm the housing bubble, the three bubbles began to collapse quickly, and financial institutions in the US, Western Europe, and even in China were in trouble as their losses mounted. As the banks and investors faltered, they needed capital to restore their positions at home. In addition, since higher rates at home (in the US) made the "carry trade" to Iceland less profitable, the hot capital rushed out of Iceland. *(Carry trades were made by investors borrowing cheaply in Japan and the US and investing in Iceland thanks to its high interest rates).* So investors sold their positions in ISK and converted back to US$ and euro, thus weakening the ISK in 2008.

With its very low hard-currency reserves (reportedly under 2.5billion US$), the CBI could not defend its currency by buying it back and by selling dollars. In fact, this low-reserve position of the central bank coupled with the inescapable fact that the Icelandic economy was (and is) still fundamentally strong with practically no direct exposure to subprime loans, a budget surplus, and very low government debt may have even resulted in a speculative raid on the ISK, further causing it to depreciate. From November 2007 to May 2008, it fell by 27% against the dollar, which itself was taking a beating compared to the euro and other currencies.

(A speculative raid of this kind is typically conducted by investors who attempt to "short" a currency, in that

they bet that the currency will weaken in the near future. Simply put, they convert out of the currency (ISK in this case) to US$ and then after the Krona plunges, reconvert back, thus making quick gains in the arbitrage.)

In summary, this Icelandic saga was a combination of contagion from the US crisis coupled with the inevitable feature of an overheated economy. Super-hot Iceland was bound to have a soft landing, or, in this case, a hard one. Perhaps this slowdown is a good thing in aiding the bubbles in housing to calm down. Perhaps this painful hard landing will result in the frenzied consumption (akin to that of the US) to abate to a more stoic Nordic rate of growth? Perhaps Icelanders will heed the warnings of fellow countrymen like, Ragnar Onundarson, who has been warning Icelanders since 2005 of the impending hard-landing caused by bubble addiction.

By late 2008, the situation had taken a turn for the worse. The hot capital exodus left the country bereft of reserves, and the big three Icelandic banks, on the verge of collapse, had to be rescued by nationalization. The country, deep in debt denominated in US dollars, was further hammered by contagion caused by the dollar reversal of late 2008. Iceland had to be thrown a life-line of emergency fund transfers/loans by its neighbors, the IMF and the US.

In spite of this, I remain confident that Iceland, with its highly-skilled workforce, huge energy resources and competitive economy, will power back in the very near future.

ANSWERS AND HINTS

ARTICLE 9.1 "WE HAVE OPTIONS," PM TELLS CABINET

(a) Denote Y* as the foreign income (US and Japan) and show how recessions in these two countries affect the IS and hence the AD of the domestic economy. (You may need to refer to a previous chapter to review the effect of foreign recessions on the domestic economy.)

(b) Is Zenobia Mistry's conclusion incontrovertible? Explain why an inverted yield curve is thought to presage a slowdown and also explain why this may not necessarily be the only conclusion one could draw from an inverted yield curve.

(c) Kevin Morgenstern may be referring to the lags with which macroeconomic policies manifest themselves. Policies take time to make themselves felt.

(d) Yes, this allows Belgravia to increase G with impunity, and hopefully to reap multiplier effects. In other words, Belgravia has many fiscal "policy bullets" left in its arsenal of macroeconomic stimulus policies.

(e) Emerging economies are typically Keynesian, with the percentage change in prices usually far greater than the percentage change in nominal wages. This condition is necessary for a positively sloped Keynesian AS curve that will yield convenient multiplier effects stemming from the increase in G on infrastructure.

(f) Bond financing will inject the "idle" loanable funds back into the income expenditure stream and jump-start growth, as discussed in several earlier chapters beginning with the NSI in Chap. 3. Assume here that Belgravia is a safe haven country and, using the earlier NSI discussion, briefly discuss how and why Belgravia may experience a strengthening of its currency as well as a capital inflow.

(g) These are the other two policy buttons—cuts in tax rates and monetary expansion. Compare this exercise to the simpler case discussed in Chap. 5 (pre-ISLM) without the labor market and (i,Y) space and note the increase in sophistication post-ISLM.

(h) Consumer and investor confidence have apparently collapsed. However, a bold stimulus package may hopefully "turn around" the confidence parameters and further assist in shifting IS.

(i) Sophie DeSalle is referring to the three Keynesian macroeconomic policy instruments, namely changes in G, M, and tax rates.

ARTICLE 9.2 THE GOOD NEWS: ECONOMY IS SLOWING!

(a) Clearly, the labor market was tight—the service industry, and particularly the tourism industry, was in dire need of workers. The economy seemed to be close to overheating.

(b) Sounds like a SAP bubble existed in high-skilled labor

(c) SAP bubbles in equity and real estate markets had created a dangerous wealth effect (discussed in earlier chapters) which, in turn, drove-up demand for skilled workers.

(d) and (e) A soft landing and a deflation of SAP bubbles was engineered with contractionary monetary policy.

(f) Expectations of future inflation are now lower, given the monetary contraction and the 'cooling down' of the economy. Hence, the attractiveness of gold and precious metals as inflation hedges has gone down, resulting in a drop in the price of gold.

(g) As national income (Y) falls during a soft landing, imports also fall as consumers now seek to purchase fewer foreign (and domestic) goods in a slowing economy. The current account (from Chap. 3) is defined as exports minus imports. If imports exceed exports, the nation incurs a current account deficit that increases at a slower rate when the growth in imports begins to slow.

(h) Include the Fisher effect and the inverted yield curve in this answer.

(i) Use the investment function to answer this. The effect of the slowing economy on investor confidence is the key.

Chapter 10
The Supply-Side Model and the New Economy

By the early 1980s, the macroeconomic landscape had changed significantly for the United States and several other Western European economies. Once, successful Keynesian discretionary demand-side stabilization policies appeared to be ineffective. The output-inflation tradeoff seemed to be no longer in evidence—expansionary fiscal and monetary stimuli only yielded additional inflation with no accompanying increase in GDP growth or employment. The Phillips curve, for all intents and purposes, appeared to be dead.

According to the rational expectationists, the emerging school of macroeconomics at that time, these changes was clearly indicative of the demise of the Keynesian model. They claimed that, once again, the paradigm had shifted and that the model best described the economy, had changed from Keynesian to Rational Expectations.

Leading this revolution were economists such as Robert E. Lucas, Thomas Sargent, Robert Barro, Joanna Gray, and E.S. Phelps, who ushered in the rational expectations paradigm with its attendant supply-side policy implications. These economists fundamentally believed in an optimizing, market-clearing approach to macroeconomics. A greater role of expectations, uncertainty, and asymmetric information, accompanied by more sophisticated time-series analyses, were the hallmarks of this school of thought.

This chapter begins with an examination of the causes underlying the so-called demise of Keynesian macroeconomics. We explore the transition from the Keynesian to the rational expectations paradigm by deriving the expectations-augmented aggregate supply curve (AE-AS). This will be followed by an analysis of the supply-side policy implications of the rational expectations model.[1] A case

---

[1] In this chapter and the remainder of this book, rational expectationists and supply-siders will be used interchangeably. Technically, in the context of this chapter, rational expectationists were the theoretical macroeconomists who constructed fundamental mathematical models that validated the paradigm shift. Their supply-sider colleagues then prescribed real-world macroeconomic policies consistent with this new rational expectations model.

© Springer International Publishing Switzerland 2016
F. Langdana, *Macroeconomic Policy*, Springer Texts in Business and Economics, DOI 10.1007/978-3-319-32854-6_10

will then be made to link these supply-side policies to the advent of the New Economy in the United States, the reformist attempts made by Germany and France from 2007–2008, the policies adopted by the European Central Bank (ECB), and espoused by China in 2016.

The latter half of the chapter includes a discussion of the Keynesian response to the alleged paradigm shift propounded by the rational expectationists. This is followed by a Keynesian analysis and explanation of the "so-called" New Economy and the outlook pertaining to its longevity. Interestingly, the Keynesian explanation of the second paradigm shift, as well as the transition to the productivity-driven New Economy, may be as compelling as that provided by the supply-siders.

We then discuss the identification problem, which helps to explain how and why both the Keynesian as well as supply-sider models can legitimately co-exist in the United States and other developed economies. Finally, this chapter explores whether the two paradigms can be reconciled—even in the short run. Robert E. Lucas' well-known 'islands' model will be overviewed here in the context of the ability of policy makers to exploit perceived output-inflation tradeoffs in an economy characterized by imperfect information.

10.1   The Expectations-Augmented AS Curve: An Explanation of the Paradigm Shift

In Fig. 10.1, we derive the Joanna Gray/Phelps expectations-augmented aggregate supply curve. This is a positively sloped AS curve that bears a resemblance to the positively sloped Keynesian AS curve of the previous chapters and has similar policy implications. Fiscal and monetary policies will indeed affect GDP and inflation, but the similarity ends there. The expectations-augmented AS, as the name implies, incorporates a significantly higher degree of sophistication pertaining to expectations formation over time. It is this feature that explains how this AS may have transitioned into the rational expectations AS curve by the early 1980s to usher in the shift from the Keynesian era to the supply-side model.

The four diagrams in Fig. 10.1 should be familiar from earlier AS derivations. The two plots on the left are the production function and the labor market, while the two on the right are the y–y reflector and (P,Y) space in which the expectations-augmented AS is to be derived.

The crucial assumption that "drives" this derivation is that <u>information is asymmetric</u>.[2] Here, demanders of labor (employers) are assumed to know the changes in contemporaneous prices as well as nominal wages. That is, they "see"

---

[2]The model presented here is a synthesis of the Joanna Gray/Phelps class of asymmetric information models that were key in the early development of the paradigm shift. Once again, in keeping with the policy-driven focus of this book, the theoretical aspects are de-emphasized to make way for expositional convenience and intuition.

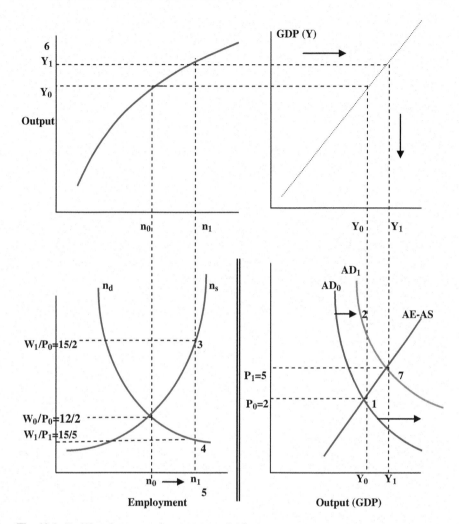

Fig. 10.1 Deriving the expectations-augmented AS curve

changes in both P and W in the current time period. Suppliers of labor (workers), on the other hand, do not see/know changes in both P and W in the current period; they are only aware of the change in their nominal wages (W). In this sense, information in the labor market is asymmetric—workers know only one piece of information (changes in nominal wages, W), while employers know both pieces of information (changes in W and P) in the current time period.

Employers know both (all) pieces of information, not because they are necessarily any smarter than the "workers," but rather because employers have access to more information by interacting with wholesalers and subcontractors, and have more knowledge about imported goods, inventories, transportation costs, etc.

We now turn to the derivation of the AS curve that will explain the paradigm shift and lead the way to the controversial New Economy. The New Economy has always generated a storm of controversy from the Keynesians who insist that the "old" paradigm is alive and well, and the whole business—the "so-called" paradigm shift in the 1980s to the "New Economy"—fits well into their original framework without necessitating a paradigm shift.

10.1.1   Diagrammatic Derivation: Expectations-Augmented Aggregate Supply Curve

Steps 1–7 are represented by corresponding numbers in Fig. 10.1.

1. Initially, the economy is at Y_0 and prices are at P_0. We plot this point in (P,Y) space. For pedagogic simplicity, let $P_0 = 2$, and nominal wages, $W_0 = 12$. Equilibrium exists in the labor market at n_0. Let the initial Y_0 be some recessionary rate of growth that warrants stabilization.
2. We are given some demand-side stabilization, that is AD_0 shifts right to AD_1, causing P0 to increase to P1, from 2–5, and nominal wages to increase from W_0 to W_1, from 12–15.
3. Given the assumption that information is asymmetric, employers know that prices have more than doubled but nominal wages have only gone from 12–15. However, workers "see" only the change in nominal wage from 12–15, and consequently think that they are "better off" as their salaries (W) have now increased. They are inadvertently "fooled" into believing that they are better off, and they supply more labor.[3]
4. This information asymmetry leads to an increase in demand for labor as well. Employers discern correctly that they are now paying only 3 in real wages (15/5), as opposed to 6 earlier (12/2), and they demand more labor (point 4, in Fig. 10.1). In this stylized version of the Gray/Phelps model, point 3 in Fig. 10.1 is where workers "think they are" in terms of real wage and labor supply, while point 4 is where producers "know" they are.
5. This increase in labor supply driven by asymmetric information on the part of suppliers of labor (workers), coupled with the increase in demand on the part of demanders of labor (producers), leads to employment increasing to n_1 in the labor market, in Fig. 10.1.
6. As employment increases to n_1, GDP growth increases to Y_1 as seen in the production function.

---

[3]The numbers used for P_1 and W_1 are purely for discussion. The point is that increases in nominal wages do not match increases in prices, and this disparity leads to an erosion of the real wage.

7. Reflecting this higher Y_1 into (P,Y) space and plotting, we obtain the second point, (P_1,Y_1). Joining this point to the initial given point (P_0,Y_0), we obtain the expectations-augmented AS curve.[4]

The expectations-augmented AS curve is indeed positively sloped like its Keynesian counterpart of an earlier chapter. The Keynesian AS was positively sloped by virtue of nominal wages being "sticky" and not changing in proportion to prices. The expectations-augmented AS, on the other hand, is positively sloped due to imperfect—asymmetric—information which leads workers to mistakenly interpret observed nominal wage increases for real wage increases and, hence, to supply more labor.[5]

The expectationists argue that this asymmetric information approach best explains the positively sloped AS curve which generated the successful output-inflation tradeoffs from the 1950s to the late 1970s in the US. After all, since nominal wage freezes were primarily in effect only during the Depression (1929–33), and given an exploitable Phillips curve that was indeed in effect during the 1950s–1970s, the imperfect information theory would be the only viable explanation for the positively sloped AS.

In addition to explaining the output-inflation tradeoff, the heightened sophistication of the intertemporal expectations-formation structure also provides for a cogent explanation of Paradigm Shift II from the Keynesian to the supply-sider paradigm in the United States in early 1980s, and then, perhaps, again by 2016.[6]

10.1.2   Paradigm Shift II: An Expectations-Augmented Explanation

How long can a tradeoff driven by imperfect information be exploited? Do workers misinterpret observed nominal wage changes for real wage changes only in the short- and medium-term? Would not suppliers of labor (workers) eventually realize that their real wages had actually deteriorated (from 6 to 3) over repeated episodes of demand-side stabilization policy?

Turning to Fig. 10.2, we pick up where we left off in Fig. 10.1. The positively-sloped, expectations-augmented AS curve facilitates output-inflation

[4]This AS is also called the adaptive expectations AS curve.

[5]The asymmetric information theory for a positively sloped AS is only one of several theories. Another explanation is the rigidity in long-term nominal wage adjustments caused by long-term wage contracts. According to this theory, unexpected increases in inflation in a labor market characterized by fairly rigid long-term contracts will have the same effect as in our model. Once again, nominal wage increases will not match increases in inflation, resulting in a positively sloped AS.

[6]This is the view propounded by the expectationists. Later, in this chapter, the Keynesian explanation of the "so-called" paradigm shift will be discussed.

tradeoffs. But, over time, the relentless pursuit of expansionary fiscal and monetary policies with successive recessions result in workers, eventually realizing that their observed increases in nominal wages (12–15) have not been in proportion to the actual increases in the price level (2–5).

In other words, workers now "catch on;" they update their information sets and revise their expectations. When another round of fiscal and monetary stabilization is anticipated, workers/unions now indulge in proactive long-term contracts to ensure that the real wage is not eroded by the next series of stabilization policies.

Thus, in our example here, workers/unions now contract for a nominal wage of $W_1 = 30$. This nominal wage W_1 ensures that real wages remains unchanged from $W_0/P_0 = 12/2 = 6$ initially, to $W_1/P_1 = 30/5 = 6$, once again.

At this point, information has become symmetric. Both suppliers as well as demanders of labor now accurately identify changes in all pieces of information, W and P. In Fig. 10.2, this full (symmetric) knowledge on the part of both demanders and suppliers of labor translates to equilibrium employment n_0 once again corresponding to a real wage of 6. And, from the production function, GDP growth corresponding to employment n_0 is back to Y_0.

If we reflect this final Y_0 over to (P,Y) space and plot (P_1,Y_0) to join with the original point (P_0,Y_0), we obtain the rational expectations AS curve (RE-AS), which is the theoretical centerpiece of the new supply-side paradigm (Fig. 10.2). Since the RE-AS is a vertical line similar to the Classical model which predates the Keynesian paradigm, the RE-AS is also known as the new classical aggregate supply curve.

Economies that transition from the positively sloped expectations-augmented AS to the vertical RE-AS are typically those with (i) sophisticated labor forces with market power capable of influencing long-term nominal wage contracts, and (ii) fully-articulated and efficient bond markets that accurately "signal" expected inflation to workers as well as employers. Typically, developed economies are more likely to have these two criteria in place compared to emerging economies. The latter may be burdened with larger pools of excess labor incapable of affecting nominal wage contracts (as in parts of China, India, Eastern Europe, South America, Africa), and often lack well-developed government bond-markets.

Remember that Keynesian discretionary fiscal and monetary policies have no effect on real GDP growth or employment in a classical-type model. In fact, demand-side stabilization, the mainstay of Keynesian policy, is neutral to real variables and affects only nominal variables such as inflation and nominal wages. This is now the case, as depicted in Fig. 10.3 where expansionary demand-side stabilization is attempted. Changes in G or M change only the rate of inflation— GDP growth remains at Y_0. The output-inflation tradeoff has vanished. The Phillips curve relationship, vital for jump-starting or soft-landing economies, is conspicuously absent. The paradigm has now "shifted" from K-AS to RE-AS.[7]

---

[7]Paradigms, in the context of this chapter, are basically differentiated by their AS curves. ISLM space and the AD curve are identical for both Keynesian as well as RE-AS models. It is only the AS curves derived from crucial assumptions in their respective labor markets that separate the two major paradigms.

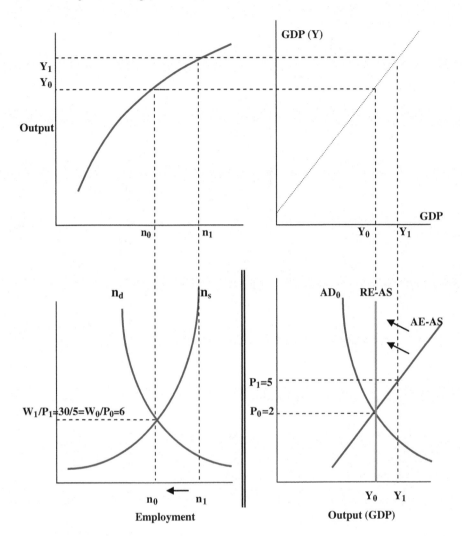

Fig. 10.2 Asymmetric information becomes symmetric

Against this new backdrop, if Y_0 is indeed some recessionary "low" rate of growth, how can GDP and employment be stimulated if expansionary fiscal and monetary policies have no effect? Since, shifting the aggregate demand affects only inflation, leaving Y_0 unchanged, clearly the only viable policy option would be *to shift the aggregate supply* to the right to increase GDP growth. This radical emphasis on policies designed to shift the aggregate supply curve instead of the aggregate demand led to the aptly named "supply-side" model.

According to this theory, as once successful aggregate demand-side policies began to fail in developed economies possessing more sophisticated labor markets

Fig. 10.3 The futility of demand-side stabilization in a rational expectations paradigm

that are characterized by forward-looking information in efficient bond markets, policy makers began to focus their attention to shifting the aggregate supply.

10.2   Supply-Side Economics

Three main elements of effective supply-side policy are:

(1) Significant income/personal tax cuts
(2) Sweeping corporate/business tax cuts
(3) Massive deregulation.

10.2.1   Significant Income Tax Cuts

The crucial assumption here is that in addition to stimulating after-tax consumption as discussed earlier, income tax cuts also impact the labor market. Tax changes now also result in shifts in labor supply and demand curves.

The Labor supply is now defined as:

$$\textbf{Labor Supply} = f\left(\underset{(+)}{\text{real wage}}, \underset{(-)}{\text{personal tax rates}}, \underset{(+)}{\text{macroeconomic outlook}}\right).$$

Here, labor supply is positively related to the real wage and macroeconomic outlook, and negatively related to personal tax rates.

An intuitive explanation of a tax-cut-induced increase in labor supply is as follows. There is a sense on the part of suppliers of labor that these tax cuts are temporary, and hence currently employed workers may avail themselves of such tax cuts by working more hours. In addition, individuals not currently in the work force (not actively seeking employment, as discussed earlier), may now find it worthwhile to seek employment, thereby becoming a part of the civilian labor force, and increasing the participation rate. The pool of available workers increases as more and more disenfranchised individuals now "come back" into the active labor market, thereby shifting the labor supply to the right. These new entrants to the labor force now find it worthwhile to re-enter the work force, given that, with the tax cuts, the government is not siphoning away a disproportionate share of any additional income in the form of high taxes.

Conversely, personal tax increases result in shifts in labor supply to the left as individuals realize that, at the margin, it is not worthwhile to enter the labor force. For example, former homemakers and turned workers might now choose to remain at

Fig. 10.4 Labor supply and changes in income tax rates

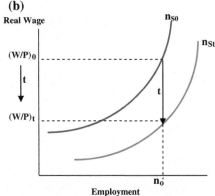

home if higher income tax rates lead to very insignificant (if any) real income gains after incorporating expenses such as childcare, housekeeping, and transportation.

An alternative explanation linking labor market shifts to tax changes is as follows. As presented in Fig. 10.4a, initially at employment n_0 the real wage was $(W/P)_0$ and the initial labor supply curve is n_{so}. Let the government impose a tax of t. Income tax increases, in effect, decrease the after-tax real wage. In this situation, what increase in real wages would the workers have to be offered so that, once again, they supply n_0 labor? The answer is the after-tax real wage would have to be the same as it was before the tax increase. Thus, to induce employment of n_0 again, the real wages would have to rise by t to offset the tax increase. This translates to an upward shift in labor supply by t. This exercise holds true for any and all levels of employment, thus resulting in the labor supply curve shifting up ("left") from n_{so} to n_{st}.

The opposite holds for tax cuts; the labor supply shifts down (to the "right"), as presented in Fig. 10.4b. Here, to maintain the original level of employment n_0 following the tax cut, the real wage would have to decrease by t to ensure that the after-tax real wage matches that before the tax cuts. Once again, this mechanism holds for all levels of employment thus shifting the labor supply down, or to the right.

While tax changes also affect disposable income and consumption as in the Keynesian model, one key difference between the two paradigms is that in the case of the rational expectations paradigm, taxes also influence the labor market.

The next main element of supply-side policy pertains to business tax cuts.

10.2.2   Sweeping Corporate/Business Tax Cuts

Here, labor demand, depicted in Fig. 10.5, is given by:

$$\textbf{Labor Demand} = f\left(\underset{(-)}{\text{real wage}}, \underset{(-)}{\text{business tax rates}}, \underset{(+)}{\text{macroeconomic outlook}}\right).$$

Fig. 10.5 Labor demand and cuts in business tax rates

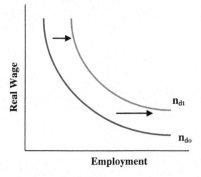

Labor demand is negatively correlated to real wages and business tax rates, and positively correlated to the macroeconomic outlook.

The assumption here is that with business tax cuts such as investment tax credits, and with accelerated depreciation, firms (demanders of labor) increase labor demand. Once again, the sense that the tax cuts are "temporary," coupled with an opportunity to increase shareholder wealth, leads employers to demand more labor.

Hence, cuts in corporate/business taxes shift labor demand to the right, from n_{d0} to n_{dt} as presented in Fig. 10.5, while increases in these taxes do the opposite.

Changes in the third term, "macroeconomic outlook," also shift the labor demand and supply curves. As the outlook improves, both labor demand and supply curves shift right, and vice versa. This term, unlike tax rates, is not an exogenous policy instrument, but is, instead, determined by endogenously formed expectations. Discussions pertaining to stagflation and recessions, later in this chapter, will activate this term that lies dormant at this stage.

10.2.3 Deregulation

According to the supply-siders, government intervention is perceived to be intrusive and excessive and is believed to retard the productivity of the private sector, with "productivity" defined as output per worker per unit time. An economy unfettered by such excessive government regulation, therefore, is likely to experience an increase in productivity.

Figure 10.6 represents an economy with a sharp decrease in unproductive government regulation. With massive deregulation, at each and every unit of the labor force a higher output is now possible—n_0 labor now results in the higher Y_{dereg} as opposed to the initial output level Y_0 when the economy was highly regulated due to the increase in productivity.

For example, upon deregulation, industries such as airlines and trucking would now determine optimal routes, prices, and stops based on market forces, and not on required schedules and limits imposed by government. Similarly, financial institutions and utilities would determine their rates and fee-structures based on market-driven competition, and not on some government-imposed mandate. All these sectors would experience increases in productivity.

Fig. 10.6 An Increase in Productivity

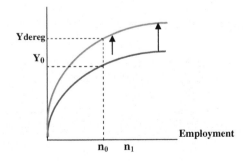

The United States embarked on an active deregulatory policy beginning in the later years of the Carter administration, followed aggressively by President Reagan and his successors to the present. Examples of deregulated industries in the US are airlines, trucking, financial services, telecommunications, and utilities. Western Europe, the United Kingdom, France, and Germany have all seen deregulation adopted with varying degrees of intensity from the early 1990s to the present.

According to the supply-siders, an excessively regulated economy retards productivity in that private enterprise will not be "unleashed" to maximize the creative and risk taking instincts present in inherently dynamic economies. In this case, the reverse of Fig. 10.6 occurs; the production function "bends down" with lower output produced at each and every level of employment.

Emerging economies have also embraced the concept of "less government," to some extent. However, these cases usually involve a two-stage process beginning first with privatization, eventually followed by gradual deregulation. Once again, with varying degrees of success, Mexico, Argentina, India, China, and Chile (to name a few) have, in fits and starts, attempted privatizations of industries once considered safely within the government domain. (Please refer to the discussion of State Owned Enterprises, SOEs, from Chap. 6.)

10.2.4 Supply-Side Stabilization

Integrating the three major supply-side policies, Fig. 10.7 displays the essence of shifting the AS curve to the right. Initially Y_0 is some low recessionary rate of growth corresponding to employment at n_0. The AS is a rational expectations AS curve in an economy characterized by symmetric information.

A combination of personal and business tax cuts set against a backdrop of government deregulation of key industries results in a final shift to the right in the RE-AS. Here, both labor supply and demand curves shift right due to the tax cuts, and the production function rises due to the surge in deregulation-driven productivity. This supply-side stimulus results in GDP growth increasing from Y_0 to Y_1 and employment from n_0 to n_1 as depicted in Fig. 10.7.

In this case, the increase in output growth is not matched by an increase in inflation, as was the case in the Keynesian paradigm. Here, the rate of inflation actually falls from P_0 to P_1. There is no output inflation tradeoff in this paradigm—the Phillips curve relationship is gone. Instead, increases in output and employment growth are accompanied by convenient decreases in the rate of inflation!

Ireland and Information Technology: A Supply-Side Story Beginning in the late 1990s, Ireland embarked on a serious supply-side policy that may well have contributed to its re-engineered status as the Information Technology (IT) powerhouse of Europe into the early 2000s.

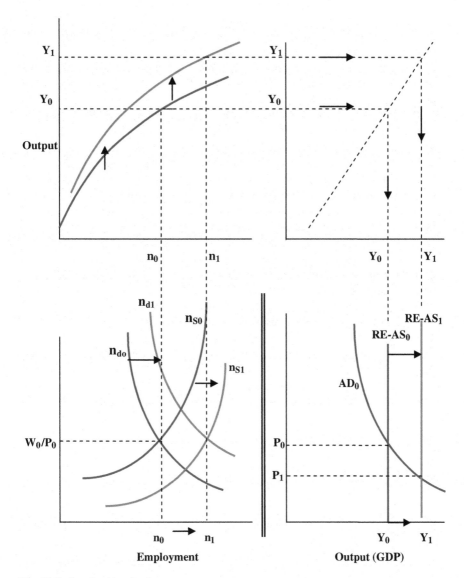

Fig. 10.7 Supply-side stimulus

Corporate tax rates as low as 10 %, coupled with a well-educated labor force, a five-year "tax holiday" for new foreign investment in IT, and a conspicuous absence of "meddlesome" government regulation, resulted in a huge global capital inflow primarily in the IT sector. More than 45 % of American investment in Europe's electronic industry in the late 1990s was absorbed annually by Ireland. Consequently, by the late 1990s, Ireland was making one-third of all personal computers sold on the Continent, and GDP growth at times exceeded an annual rate of 10 %.

The supply-side policies adopted by Ireland were not popular with continental Europe, where large government spending coupled with higher taxes dominated macroeconomic policy.

By 1998, the European Commission had labeled Ireland's policy of giving a preferential tax rate of only 10 % to its financial services and manufacturing sectors as "unfair" to European Union (EU) members with higher tax rates (almost 32 %). The Commission claimed that attracting global investment with low tax rates was tantamount to a hidden State subsidy to its champion sectors and, therefore, technically illegal.

Ireland responded to this pressure in the late 1990s by agreeing to eliminate the 10 % rate for its few "championed" sectors. It then announced, however, that *all* its sectors would be taxed at a new uniform rate of 12.5 %, one-third the average corporate tax rate in Europe! Ireland was determined to keep the continental penchant for taxation at bay, and to retain its hard-won title of "Celtic Tiger."

Update: With the progress, came the challenges. Massive capital inflows accompanied Ireland's resurgence, and with capital flows came inflows of high-skilled labor too. The runaway capital inflows and confidence pushed Ireland into vicious SAP bubbles in housing and equities, and Ireland did not fare well in the subprime crisis of 2008–2014. But by 2016, the fundamental supply-side, low-tax, low-regulation bedrock of the Irish economy was resulting in Ireland being one of the earliest Eurozone economies to recover.

10.3 Stagflation

An economy in the throes of stagflation is characterized by a rising rate of inflation and an ominously falling rate of GDP growth and employment as described in Fig. 10.8. Typically, "stagflation" brings to mind the severe episodes experienced by the US, Japan, and Western Europe in the 1970s which coincided with the oil crises.

Oil shocks slammed into the world economy following the October 1973 Yom Kippur War, when the Arab oil-producing nations sharply restricted oil exports. Another shock followed shortly thereafter in 1979, this time related to the Iranian revolution and the deposition of the Shah. Inflation rates soared to double digits coupled with similar rates of unemployment and shrinking national GDP rates.

Further, aggravating the situation may have been the paradigm shift from the Keynesian to supply-sider (rational expectations) model, in progress in many developed economies from the mid- to late-1970s. According to the expectationists, policies designed to jump-start economies stuck at Y_{low} and mistakenly still

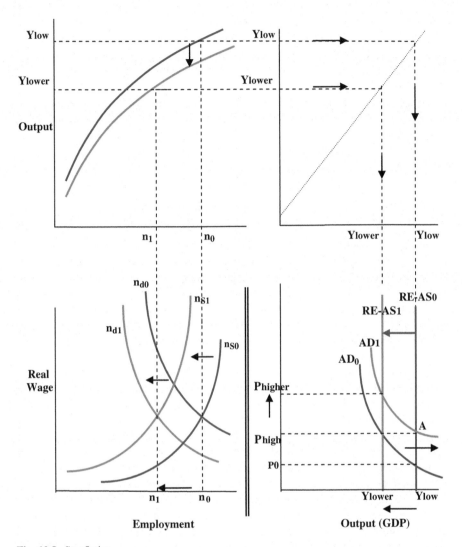

Fig. 10.8 Stagflation

considered Keynesian only served to worsen the rate of inflation. Rightward shifts in the AD due to frequent and desperate attempts at fiscal and monetary stabilization only increased P_0 to P_{high}, labeled A in Fig. 10.8, without any accompanying relief in GDP or employment.

Superimposing the effects of the oil shocks and the accompanying reduction in productivity as production was forced to move to non-optimal, secondary sources of energy, resulted in a downward shift in the production function.[8] Additional

---

[8]Both oil shocks have been combined into one "composite" shock as shown in the diagram.

leftward shifts in labor demand and supply caused by the deteriorating outlook, completed the dismal picture. The final toll of stagflation was an even higher rate of inflation at P_{higher} and a worsening recession at Y_{lower} as presented in Fig. 10.8.[9] Higher inflation coupled with stagnating or deteriorating output finally resulted in the paradigm-busting Stagflation.

By late 2008, the specter of Stagflation was again starting to emerge—not just in the US after the subprime crisis (described in Article 11.3), but in many Asian economies and certainly in Western Europe, as policy makers shuddered at the prospect of slowing growth and rising prices.

10.4   From the Supply-Side to the New Economy

From a macroeconomic perspective, the 1990s could be characterized as the era of the New Economy in the US. Following the minor recession of 1990–1991, and before 2001, the US economy displayed an amazing nine years of very strong GDP growth, productivity gains, and record low unemployment, set against a backdrop of virtually no inflationary pressure. The Europeans were quick to adopt such a performance as a policy goal, and in Singapore, Japan, and China policy makers became determined to put their own respective versions of the New Economy into operation.

According to the expectationists, the New Economy traces its roots to the supply-side policies put in place in the early 1980s. The massive deregulations, it is argued, paved the way for the eventual breakthroughs in technology. Firms and individuals were free to respond to market pressures, and to seek out market opportunities. The climate fostered risk-taking, massive private capital investment, and entrepreneurship. The unleashed creativity of US enterprise (according to this argument), in turn led to the inevitable internet-assisted economy, resulting in permanent structural increases in productivity (see the following box).

Technological growth, fostered in part by the early deregulations, shifted the production function up. Over time, labor demand and supply curves also shift right due to a stronger "macroeconomic outlook" fueled by expectations of yet more growth, thereby increasing equilibrium employment.

These combined labor-market and productivity effects resulted in a rightward shift in the RE-AS, resulting in the hallmark of the New Economy—growth in GDP without an accompanying increase in inflation. In fact, during the heyday of the New Economy in the US in the mid-1990s–2000, quarterly GDP growth at times exceeded 5 % with unemployment in the 3 % range and with hardly any appreciable change in the rate of inflation.

---

[9]US macroeconomic statistics during the stagflationary bouts in the 1970s were indeed bleak, and included double-digit inflation and unemployment. Relate stagflation to the earlier discussion on cost-push inflation, where similar countercyclical movements in prices and GDP were discussed.

The diagram depicting the New Economy is identical to Fig. 10.7, which presents the supply-sider paradigm. The only difference is that the production function in the New Economy is shifting up not to deregulation *per se*, but rather to a <u>result</u> of the deregulation—gains in productivity stemming from breakthroughs in technology. Additionally, in the labor market of the New Economy, the labor demand and supply curves do shift to the right but not due to large personal and business tax cuts. Instead, the curves shift right because of endogenous expectations of strong growth.

Labor demand also increases due to increased productivity, since this increased productivity implies an increase in the marginal product of labor. While this feature is not explicitly incorporated in our labor market for expositional convenience, we assume that the "outlook" term captures this shift in addition to expectations of future real growth. Indeed, the "outlook" term is positively correlated to productivity gains, and productivity has a strong procyclical component as discussed below.

The New Economy and the Productivity Puzzle The New Economy lives and dies by its ability to influence overall productivity. Faster GDP growth with lower inflation, higher profits, and budget surpluses is vitally dependent on high and increasing productivity. While, the US may be at the early stages of a more sustainable New Economy (Phase 2, if you will), the numbers from Phase 1 have been truly quite impressive. Labor productivity, defined as output per worker per hour, jumped from 1.4 % during 1975–1993, to over 3 % during 1995–2000 in the US, by even the most conservative estimates. In the nonfarm business sector, for example, growth of output per hour accelerated to a 2.8 % annual rate during 1996–2000 as the New Economy blossomed, compared to just 1.6 % for the previous 25 years.

The crucial question then is how much of this increase in productivity is structural (long-term/permanent), and how much is cyclical. After all, during boom times, employers do tend to work their employees harder to keep pace with additional demand, thereby contributing to increased productivity statistics. Conversely, as the economy slows, employers who are reluctant to shed employees at the first sign of a slowdown, keep them on the payroll but have them producing less output commensurate with the falling demand. This results in falling productivity numbers as the economy slows. This feature may account for a procyclical—moving "with" the business cycle—component of measured productivity.

Robert Gordon, long an outspoken skeptic of the New Economy, finds (from an ongoing series of empirical studies) that the productivity gains touted as "permanent" New Economy features exist only in the manufacture of computers (hardware) and a few other durable goods. The remaining productivity increases, he concludes, are cyclical. On the other end of the spectrum, however, New Economy proponents at the Federal Reserve find evidence that across-the-board labor productivity increases since the early 1990s have indeed been structural, implying a conservative rate of growth at just over 3 %.

Superimposed on this vitally important debate is the enormous expenditure in the 1990s in the US on IT. Large capital spending on IT can influence labor productivity in two ways, by either (i) "capital deepening" which essentially increases the amount of capital available per worker, or (ii) affecting "total factor productivity" (TFP) which increases the efficiency with which units of labor and capital generate increases in output.

Very simply, total factor productivity is a residual defined as:

TFP = Percentage increase in real output per unit time−(percentage

increase in labor + percentage increase in capital, per unit time)

Interestingly, by the early 2000s, several studies had found evidence to indicate that almost half of the acceleration in productivity growth between the first and second halves of the 1990s in the US was, in fact, due to capital deepening and not due to an increase in TFP. If capital deepening were indeed the case, a cut-back in IT spending would have serious ramifications for the New Economy by virtue of the rapid ensuing decrease in the sup-posedly large "capital deepened" component of productivity. Proponents of this theory point to the US experience in the early 2000s as evidence.

Accurate measures and determinants of productivity are absolutely vital in estimating the longevity and intensity of the New Economy. After all, with fiscal and monetary policy deemed ineffective, and given the advanced stage of deregulation in the US, macroeconomic growth (in this model) would now be dependent solely on productivity gains.

This crucial subject will be revisited when we summarize the outlook and nature of "Phase 2" of the New Economy toward the end of this chapter.

So how does the Keynesian paradigm reconcile itself to the observed "New Economy" behavior, namely the increases in productivity and growth without any accompanying increases in inflation during the late 1990s–early 2000s? How would the Keynesians explain the apparent demise of the Phillips curve and the "failure" of demand-side stabilization, as claimed by the supply-siders during this period?

To answer these questions and to discuss the Keynesian response, a brief overview of the identification problem in analyzing time-series data is in order.

10.5   The Identification Problem

Figure 10.9a, b present two pairs of observed real world data points, (P_0,Y_0) and (P_1,Y_1), represented by A and B. The rates of inflation, P_0 and P_1, and the rates of GDP growth, Y_0 and Y_1, are two sets of observed inflation and output growth rates, respectively. (P_0,Y_0) and (P_1,Y_1) can be interpreted as rates of inflation and GDP

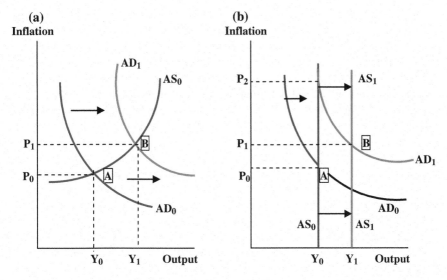

Fig. 10.9 The Identification Problem

growth at two points in time, with (P_0,Y_0) being in Period Zero and (P_1Y_1) in some later time (Period One).

While the points A and B in Fig. 10.9a, b are directly observable, the <u>actual models</u> explaining how the economy progressed from (P_0,Y_0) to (P_1,Y_1) are not. In other words, while we "see" points A and B, we do not actually "see" the respective underlying AS and AD curves. It is up to macroeconomic theory to construct mathematically consistent models that can explain the movement of the economy from point A to point B, and in doing so, to form a "template" within which *all* future policies can be analyzed.

From Fig. 10.9a, b we can see that two drastically different models can explain the observed path of the economy from A to B equally well. In Fig. 10.9a, a Keynesian paradigm with expansionary demand-side policy (increasing G, M, or cuts in taxes) has jump-started this economy, taking it from point A at (P_0,Y_0) to point B at (P_1,Y_1). In this case, the output-inflation tradeoff has been realized.

However, in Fig. 10.9b the <u>same points A and B</u> can now be linked within the context of a supply-side paradigm. Here the initial AS curve, AS_0, is shifted to the right, presumably by tax cuts, deregulation, a surge in productivity, and/or expectations of strong future growth. The AD is also shifted to the right by the same demand-side policies as in Fig. 10.9a (increases in G or M or cuts in taxes). This combination of AD and AS shifts results in an economy transitioning from A to a new equilibrium at B in Fig. 10.9b.[10]

---

[10]The AD shifts are independent of the AS curve, and hence are identical in Fig. 10.9a, b.

Both paradigms, irrespective of their underlying philosophies and policy prescriptions, provide us with perfectly reasonable explanations of an economy moving from A to B. Herein lies a fundamental reason for the ongoing debate and confusion pertaining to "the" right model in developed economies—both paradigms legitimately co-exist because both fit the observed data equally well.[11] This is one very intuitive explanation of the **identification problem**, prevalent in the analysis of serially correlated time-series data, making it extremely difficult to identify the single "correct" model within which macroeconomic policy must be analyzed, prescribed, and conducted.

While the two paradigms diagrammatically "explain" the shifts from points A to B equally well, the policy implications remain radically different. In Fig. 10.9a, for example, stimulative demand-side policy—increases in G or M or cuts in taxes—is solely responsible for the increase in national output from Y_0 to Y_1. Here, the shift in the AD "drives" real economic growth.

In Fig. 10.9b, on the contrary, the demand-side shift by itself, without an accompanying supply-side shift in the AS, would only result in an increase in inflation from P_0 to P_2, with output growth stuck at Y_0. It is only when the AS curve is shifted to the right due to some combination of deregulation, business tax cuts, and increases in productivity that output increases from Y_0 to Y_1. In sharp contrast to Fig. 10.9a, the boost to real economic growth in Fig. 10.9b is solely due to the AS shift.

10.6   A Keynesian Explanation of the "New" Economy

Figure 10.10a presents the Keynesian response to what has been labeled the "new" economy. The Keynesians claim that there is nothing "new" about the economy, but that, once again, the confusion (according to this school of thought) may have been shown by the identification problem.

Keynesians do not deny the inescapable fact that productivity has increased in the US starting in the 1990s. While the exact nature and composition of this increase in productivity—structural versus cyclical, and "capital deepening" versus TFP—are vigorously debated in the academic and policy literature, the increase in productivity, powered by the internet economy, cannot be denied.

However, the Keynesians point out that all aggregate supply curves, whether they are vertical or kinked, will shift to the right as the production function bulges up with an increase in labor productivity. In Fig. 10.10a, Keynesians demonstrate

---

[11]The problem exists primarily in developing economies because these economies are almost certainly Keynesian. Developing economies are characterized by excess labor supply and the inability of this excess labor supply to enforce and influence nominal wage contracts. Information is imperfect and asymmetric, and there is an absence of efficient bond-markets that signal expected inflation. All these characteristics point to Keynesian models as "default" paradigms for emerging and even for newly industrialized economies.

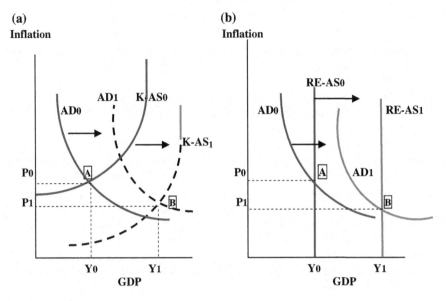

Fig. 10.10   Keynesians fight back

that even a Keynesian AS, shifted to the right by productivity gains, will replicate the exact same observed "New Economy" results of increasing Y and falling P.

Figure 10.10b reproduces the conventional expectationist view of the New Economy discussed earlier, with IT gains driving productivity increases and shifting a vertical AS to the right. Once again, thanks to the identification problem, both paradigms seem to fit the New Economy mantra of "growth without increasing inflation" equally well. Once again, the two sets of observed data, A and B in Fig. 10.10a, b, are identical, and the debate continues to rage.

The major difference between the two explanations, however, is that the Keynesians believe that the "new" economy spawned in the 1990s was an episodic, one-off shift in the kinked K-AS curve. They argue that once this somewhat dramatic shift to the right of the K-AS slows down, and increases in technology and productivity eventually stabilize to some lower "more sustainable" level, the K-AS curve's rightward shift will be arrested.

They claimed that, once again, demand-side stabilization, with its attendant Phillips curve and its symptoms of overheating and soft-landing will reassert itself with a vengeance. Once again, discretionary fiscal and monetary policies will stabilize output and employment. It is only in this transitional phase, they argue, that atypical results such as growth without accompanying increases in inflation are to be observed.

The expectationists contend that while the identification problem technically leaves the door open for ongoing debate regarding the legitimacy of the New Economy, the episodes of stagflation were evidence enough that information had in fact become symmetric in developed economies. Fiscal and monetary stabilization would not have real <u>long-term</u> effects given the vertical nature of the rational expectations AS curve.

They insist that, in the long run, any and all increases in real output and employment growth can only come about through shifts to the right in a vertical AS, driven by ongoing breakthroughs in technology-powered productivity gains. Shifting the AD, <u>without</u> any accompanying shift to the right in the vertical AS, would, according to their paradigm, only result in increases in inflation with no change in output or employment.

While the New Economy proponents attribute most of the increases in productivity to policies put in place in the formative days of supply-side economics in the early 1980s, Keynesians emphasize that the coincidental influence of a host of other contributing factors cannot be denied. For example, the strength of the US dollar from the early 1990s served to keep prices of imports down and to some extent may have mitigated incipient inflationary pressure. The Asian crises of 1997–1998 followed by the rapid relative strengthening of the US dollar did much to lower prices of imports, and the drop in semiconductor prices through the 1990s was certainly a contributing factor. Furthermore, they point out that the worldwide glut in global commodities—not to mention fuel—also kept inflation in check. Keynesians stress that these factors, and not just supply-side initiatives, went a long way to contribute to the "growth without inflation" that has come to characterize the New Economy of the late 1990s and the early 2000s.

In the Keynesian view, GDP growth in the "new" economy was largely a result of a conventional textbook Keynesian stimulus—expansionary monetary policy. The significant monetary expansion in the US in the mid- to late-1990s was the primary source of GDP growth, plain, and simple. The AD was shifted to the right in a fairly standard Keynesian expansion, over a Keynesian AS due to an increase in M, thanks to a generally looser Fed monetary policy for much of the 1990s. This, coupled with a <u>one-time shift</u> to the right in the Keynesian AS (presented in Fig. 10.10a) due to the permanent increase in productivity stemming from the internet-powered economy, resulted in the so-called "growth without inflation" that was, in the Keynesian view, erroneously attributed to some permanent paradigm-shattering New Economy.

The new economists and their supply-side ancestors have argued that the Phillips curve was "dead." The Keynesian response is that the Phillips curve was simply lying dormant in the heyday of the New Economy. It was temporarily masked by the one-time rightward shift in the Keynesian AS due to the growth in productivity.

In fact, during the early 2000s, the not-so-soft landing by the Federal Reserve, followed by repeated attempts to jump-start growth by increasing monetary growth and decreasing interest rates, led many analysts to wonder if the Keynesian paradigm was indeed back on center-stage. These moves, followed by the fiscal and monetary stimulus package in the US since 2002, smacked clearly of vintage Keynesianism. And then, the massive post-2008 stimulus plans and the Quantitative Easing unleashed by the Fed (discussed earlier in this book), were textbook Keynesian stimuli.

10.7 Contrasting the "New" Economy with the "Old" One

The "old," or "traditional," economy is loosely interpreted to be the Keynesian model, while the New Economy is seen as the most recent iteration of the technology-driven version of the supply-side, rational expectations, vertical AS model. The differences between the two models go way beyond the obvious theoretical and diagrammatic ones. As discussed, the two paradigms clearly have very strong policy implications that are fundamentally polar extremes of each other.

The following Table 10.1 will help recap and overview all the differences in the two paradigms.

Table 10.1 Comparing and contrasting the two paradigms

"New" economy (vertical AS) supply-side	"Old" economy (Keynesian AS)
1. Changes in fiscal and monetary policies (increasing G or M, for example), result in no real effects. Only the rate of inflation is affected with no change in Y or employment. There is no role for activist fiscal or monetary policy in this economy, much like the earlier classical paradigm	Expansionary fiscal and monetary policies generate multiplier effects. Rates of Y and employment increase, as do C and I. Conversely, contractionary policies can engineer soft landings. There is a distinct discretionary role for activist fiscal and monetary policy
2. There is no output-inflation tradeoff. In fact, increases in output are matched by decreases in the rate of inflation	There is a very evident output-inflation tradeoff. The Phillips curve relationship is evident. Increases in inflation are accompanied by increases in GDP growth and decreases in the unemployment rate
3. Increases in GDP growth and employment are driven by technology-enhanced productivity growth that result in a supply-side stimulus. Furthermore, this productivity growth can be traced back to deregulation and the ensuing climate of risk-taking and entrepreneurship that it fosters	Growth in GDP and employment are driven by demand-side policies that stimulate the aggregate demand (AD). Deregulation will also shift the K-AS to the right and may certainly increase productivity in some areas, but the rightward shift in the AS would be episodic—a one-time shift
4. Large infusions of global capital are vital to fund the disparity between total demand for loanable funds and the total supply of loanable funds. Massive capital inflows finance high-technology startups fostered by the explosion in creativity and entrepreneurship. Please refer to discussion on the NSI (national savings identity) in Chap. 3	Typically, as shown in the NSI discussion, large infusions of global capital are essential to fund bond-financed budget deficits. These deficits are caused by large increases in government spending necessary to generate Keynesian multiplier effects
5. Changes in nominal wages and prices are (with short lags) fully flexible. Information is symmetric. Long-term government bonds operating in highly efficient bond markets signal future inflation effectively.	Nominal wages do not change fully in proportion to changes in prices. Some combination of excess supplies of labor (in emerging economies), imperfect information, or nominal wage rigidities, yield the

(continued)

Table 10.1 (continued)

"New" economy (vertical AS) supply-side	"Old" economy (Keynesian AS)
Labor markets are relatively more deregulated, and workers have more market power. This allows them to negotiate long-term wage contracts and to maintain their real wages	positively sloped AS curve. Labor markets are relatively more regulated, and workers do not have the ability to negotiate real wage contracts—they have relatively less market power
6. Inflation pressures are now harder to detect as increases in inflation are not positively correlated to GDP growth. Conventionally measured inflation may appear benign, but dangerous speculative asset price (SAP) bubbles in the stock market, the IT sector, and real estate may develop	Overheating is easier to detect. Inflationary pressures are evident in conventionally measured indexes. Since inflation here is procyclical, an overheated economy "growing too fast" will exhibit dangerously rising inflation across the board. Long-bonds in this economy are good indicators of expected inflation
7. In summary, this economy is driven by continuous increases in productivity in a highly deregulated economy, represented by ongoing rightward shifts in the vertical AS. There is no role for fiscal and monetary policy in influencing GDP growth or employment. There is no rapid-action "emergency package" to rescue a traumatized economy. For instance, there could be no supply-sider response on September 12, 2001, in the wake of 9/11 and the ensuing drop in confidence	In summary, these economies are primarily stabilized by active demand-side fiscal and monetary policies. Many Keynesian regimes would advocate privatization and eventual deregulation of large inefficient SOEs. Regarding productivity increases, constant (flat) productivity growth is usually viewed as the norm, with occasional, episodic, rightward shifts in the K-AS. This paradigm allows for an emergency stimulus package of rapid increases in M and planned increases in G when the economy is in crisis, as exemplified by the US $100 billion stimulus package immediately following 9/11

10.8   Can the Two Models Be Reconciled?

Purists from both camps would recoil at the suggestion. In the long run, given the fundamental structural differences driving the two paradigms, any chance of a "compromise" model reconciling the two polar views would be extremely unlikely in developed economies. (Emerging economies are typically Keynesian, as discussed earlier.)

By the early 2000s, however, an increasing number of analysts along with mainstream policy-oriented economists, have proposed a model of a developed economy transitioning from a Keynesian-type AS curve in the short-run to a supply-side model in the long-run.[12] This quasi-paradigm, which could also be

---

[12]Mainstream macroeconomics texts by authors such as Michael Parkin and Richard Froyen also propose short-term and long-term AS and Phillips curves.

labeled the "synthesis view", is composed of "long-term" New Economy adherents who believe that, although the AS is eventually vertical, there is indeed room for short-term, demand-side stabilization. For example, in the very short term, the central bank may need to quickly "hit the brakes" to stem runaway growth or to re-ignite growth and confidence. This would provide the correct short-term impetus, but may not be a viable long-term policy.

Theorists point to the expectations-augmented AS curve discussed earlier as one explanation for the time-dependent change in the slope of the AS. As explained by the Joanna Gray-Phelps model, in the short-term, in a world characterized by asymmetric information, when expectations of inflation do not actually match actual inflation, workers supply more labor. This additional labor, in turn, results in increases in output and employment that accompany increases in inflation, yielding the positively sloped expectations-augmented AS curve.[13]

However, overtime, workers "catch on" and contract for higher nominal wages to keep their real wages constant. Information becomes symmetric and, as discussed, the AS becomes vertical, yielding the Rational Expectations AS curve. Furthermore, according to Robert E. Lucas' seminal "islands" models (please see the following box), the rate at which the AS snaps back to its vertical position—the rate at which information becomes symmetric—is directly a function of the degree of attempted stabilization in an imperfect information environment.

This "synthesis view," combining short-term Keynesian behavior with a long-term vertical AS curve, may explain why demand-side policies, such as changes in monetary growth that attempt to jump-start and soft-land economies, may be successful only for short periods in developed economies. Typically, these policies may be successful only at inflection points in the business cycle when growth is just about to lose momentum or the economy is on the verge of a recovery. Eventually, however, only structural changes in taxes, deregulation, and technology-induced productivity would be remedies for long-term macroeconomic growth. (Keep in mind, this "synthesis" view is espoused by long-term expectationists/supply-siders.)

Lending credence to this synthesis view are the actions of the Federal Reserve and the ECB. After all, the attempt by the Federal Reserve to engineer a US soft-landing in 2000, and to deflate the housing bubble in 2004, by contracting monetary growth and increasing interest rates were "text-book" Keynesian policy prescriptions. So were the almost frantic attempts to jump-start growth with a sequence of significant interest rate cuts, beginning in 2001 and then in 2007 to prevent contagion from the rapidly deflating SAP bubbles. (The whole sub-prime saga and Fed policy traced back to 2000, is presented in detail in Article 11.3, in the following chapter.)

---

[13]In the example where prices went from 2–5 while wages only went from 12–15. Here workers did not "see" the increase in price—they only "saw" their nominal wage increases from 12–15 in the short-run, and responded by supplying more labor. Thus, output increased with increases in price, resulting in a positively sloped AS.

The European Central Bank, too, in spite of strident claims of <u>only</u> inflation control as its policy objective, has at times indulged in decidedly Keynesian behavior. It has lowered interest rates on several key occasions to invigorate growth in the larger German and French economies, despite strong signals of impending increases in inflation in the Eurozone. Since, the ECB's well-publicized policy objective is to ensure that inflation in the Eurozone is at most 2 %, these actions have led a growing body of central bank watchers to wonder if the major central banks, such as the ECB and the Fed, are indeed subscribing to a "synthesis" model that combines a Keynesian AS in the short-run and a vertical AS in the long-run.

Keynes famously said, "in the long-run we are all dead." In the context of this section, it might appear that "in the long-run we may be either die-hard Keynesians or supply-siders, but in the short-run we are all Keynesians."[14] But Robert E. Lucas put an end to all that. In his view, presented next, even in the "short-run" there was no possibility of any Keynesian output-inflation tradeoff. Such a tradeoff was only a perceived tradeoff—any attempts to exploit it would only hasten the evolution to the vertical AS curve.

Explaining the Synthesis: Robert E. Lucas and his 'Islands' economy[15]

In, "Some International Evidence on Output-Inflation Tradeoffs," (AER 1973), Robert E. Lucas cleverly introduced the notion of imperfect information by constructing a radically new model—the "islands" economy—that soon spawned a whole new body of macroeconomic modeling. Here, producers scattered randomly over individual "islands" are independently able to observe price changes. They cannot, however, distinguish relative changes in prices from economy-wide nominal changes in prices. For example, when producer X sees an increase in price, he/she does not know if this change results from a real increase in excess demand for the product on the producer's island, or if the price increase is simply due to an increase in inflation that affects all islands.

In the Lucas model, the producers cannot communicate with any other islands. Hence, given this imperfect information, they must hedge. If the price increase is indicative of excess demand for the product, then increases in output are warranted. In this case, the observed price increase would be accompanied by an increase in output, resulting in a positively sloped AS curve.

If, on the other hand, the price increase is perceived as simply due to an "ocean-wide" inflation that affects all islands, producer X would have no

---

[14]In this section, we deliberately shy away from specific definitions of short- and long-run. The point is that information asymmetry can exist only for so long. Eventually, workers will know all pieces of information. And besides, this process may be of different duration in different economies. An economy with a more sophisticated labor market will go from short- to long-run far more quickly than one with a less-developed economy possessing a less sophisticated labor market.

[15]**Robert E. Lucas Jr., of the University of Chicago, was the recipient of the Nobel Prize for Economics in 1995.**

incentive or motivation to respond to this observed increase in price with an increase in supply. In this case, islanders promptly attribute any observed price increases to inflation caused by central bank monetization. Consequently, they do not increase output, resulting in a vertical AS curve.

Borrowing the concept of signal extraction from electrical engineering, Lucas found that economies with very disciplined monetary policies were indeed represented by AS curves that were positively sloped. (Monetary discipline was characterized by a central bank that had a history of not indiscriminately and constantly attempting to tweak the money supply or resort to vast debt monetization.)

On the other hand, in economies where monetary discipline was low, Lucas found that islanders attributed most (if not all) of the observed price increase simply to inflation, and the AS was indeed found to be steeper depending on the degree of monetary variance. In other words, in the Lucasian economy the slope of the AS was found to be inversely proportional to the degree of monetary discipline.

Perhaps most interestingly, Lucas' model also demonstrated how expectations adjusted rapidly and efficiently. Positively sloped AS curves in economies known for their high monetary discipline would mercilessly adapt and get steeper at the first sign of a deterioration in monetary discipline. The AS curve would snap back to vertical, with the rate of adjustment directly proportional to the rate of deterioration in monetary discipline!

In terms of policy these findings have huge implications. Some economies may indeed be characterized by positively sloped AS curves by virtue of asymmetric information. However, the output-inflation tradeoffs are only perceived tradeoffs—they are not exploitable. Any attempts to exploit these tradeoffs would quickly result in the AS becoming vertical. The perceived tradeoff would rapidly disappear.

Many years later, this model was experimentally reconstructed with live "producers" in a simulated islands economy by the author (Journal of Economic Behavior and Organization 1994). The "producers" (MBA and EMBA students) were located on "islands" characterized by imperfect information and subjected to prices from both disciplined as well as undisciplined monetary policies. The Lucas results were faithfully replicated. As in the Lucasian economy, the greater the monetary discipline, the flatter the AS, and the greater the perceived output-inflation tradeoff. As monetary discipline progressively deteriorated, the slope of the AS curves predictably increased. Eventually, producers simply began to ignore posted price increase, and the AS curves became vertical.

In conclusion, according to the synthesis view, there may be apparent tradeoffs in the short-run driven by asymmetric information. The AS curve in the short-run may indeed look like a conventional Keynesian AS curve, but the similarity ends there. Unlike its Keynesian counterpart, there is no long-run exploitable Phillips curve relationship. Instead, only a shimmering mirage of a Phillips curve is perceived here. The faster we attempt to approach this mirage, the more quickly it disappears. Therein lies the theoretical elegance of the Lucas islands model.

10.9   The Outlook for the New Economy

Is the New Economy a one-time episodic event as claimed by the Keynesians, or is this a paradigm that is here to stay, albeit in a more sustainable version compared to the late 1990s? At the epicenter of this discussion lies the issue of the longevity of the productivity gains. These, after all, "drive" the New Economy.

How long will the productivity gains last? Have we entered a "phase 2" of the New Economy since 2001, with lower yet more sustainable productivity gains? Economic research has provided several insights into the matter.

1. The first issue, discussed earlier in this chapter, pertains to the nature of the productivity gains. Are they structural or cyclical? While the evidence is mixed and controversial, the general consensus is that until the economy has completed one real business cycle—boom followed by a real recession—it will be extremely difficult to sift out cyclical changes in productivity from structural ones.
2. A huge contributing factor to the New Economy was the massive drop in semiconductor prices in the early–mid-1990s. To some extent, this may have prevented inflation from increasing in proportion to the explosion in growth. Annual multifactor productivity growth (defined earlier) in the semiconductor sector was 30.7 % from 1974–1990, and 22.3 % from 1990–1995, and then it exploded to 44.0 % from 1996–1999 (Oliner and Sichel 2000). Industry experts (Jorgensen 2001) expect price declines to continue well into the second decade of the new millennium.
3. The IT revolution, the centerpiece of the New Economy, may be just another breakthrough in a long series of technological revolutions. By the end of the nineteenth century, the widespread adoption of electricity was followed by the internal combustion engine. These inventions revolutionized travel (land and air), and manufacturing. In the twentieth century, these breakthroughs were followed by others in medicine (vaccines, antibiotics) and communications (radio, television). If the IT revolution was then just another in a series of technological developments, expectations of a trend increase in the rate of growth may be unjustified. Rather, the IT economy could be interpreted as simply ensuring the sustainability of recent growth rates.
4. Finally, even if the IT economy is indeed different from preceding technological revolutions, it is not clear if the economy's long-term growth rate will be higher, or if just the level of national income will be ratcheted up, followed by the same long-term post World War II trend rate of growth (3–4 %). Evidence from

"phase 2" of the New Economy since 2001 seems to indicate a return to the long-term post World War II real rate of growth of the US economy. Once again, data from a full business cycle would be necessary to obtain any meaningful empirical estimates.

10.10 Which Model for Developed Economies?

The fact of the matter is that, in the United States, productivity numbers reminiscent of the 1960s were evidenced again in the late 1990s (the heyday of what has been labeled the "New Economy"). The causes and prospects of the New Economy have generated considerable interest from research as well as policy perspectives. Due to the identification problem, both paradigms, Keynesian as well as supply-sider, offer equally plausible explanations for the phenomenon labeled as the "New Economy." In addition, both models can also be found to fit a range of other macroeconomic outcomes in developed economies.

Against this macroeconomic backdrop, it remains to the reader to decide not just which model best explains the "New Economy," but also which model consistently explains all macroeconomic behavior in the developed economy that is being analyzed. In my macroeconomics classes, both paradigms are discussed in detail, and finally the students have to decide for themselves. While analyzing developed economies, they can choose to be either long-term Keynesians or long-term supply-siders; they can all be Keynesians in the short-run. (The choice is clear for emerging economies where the Keynesian paradigm applies in the short-term and the long-term.)

In some cases, the long-term choices for developed economies are based on the plausibility of the theoretical and technical assumptions underlying the derivation of the model, or the logical and intuitive elegance of one paradigm relative to the other. The richness of the labor market and the clear policy implications of the Keynesian model are admired by many. Others are impressed by the elegant simplicity and the bold, uncluttered, policy strokes of the supply-side paradigm.

In other cases, individuals choose their model based on their own real-world experiences and instincts, or on moral and/or philosophical grounds. For example, the absence of a role for government intervention in macroeconomic stabilization may be seen by some to be highly desirable. The fundamental belief that market forces and not government intervention should determine business decisions, and that private enterprise must be allowed to compete freely and to succeed or perish in such an environment, resonates with the expectationists.

Others, however, may strongly believe that it "ought" to be government's responsibility to be involved in activist macroeconomic policy, especially to cure unemployment. And there "should" be a minimum level of regulation to ensure that environmental, moral, and non-commercial concerns are not swept aside by unregulated businesses interests.

Both paradigms would agree that privatization and deregulation can indeed increase productivity. Both emerging and developed economies have pursued privatizations. While the intensity and determination with which privatizations are undertaken may be higher in supply-sider regimes, in enlightened emerging economies (China, India, Mexico, Brazil, to name a few), there is a growing conviction that state-owned enterprises (SOEs) eventually have to be allowed to "sink or swim" in the sea of global competition; a rightward shift in a Keynesian AS has undeniable merits.

After all the discussion throughout this book, and armed with the two diametrically different paradigms and their implications, the reader is finally equipped with all the tools for choosing the long-term paradigm for analyzing developed economies.

We now turn to questions that clarify and discuss some key concepts, followed by simulated media articles. The next chapter discusses the mechanisms by which central banks change interest rates, along with the objectives (and challenges) of prudent central bank policy in the global economy.

10.11   Discussion Questions

1. *Does the "synthesis" view imply that one need not adopt a polar model—Keynesian or Supply-sider—but could, instead, comfortably adopt the compromise version just described?*

   The synthesis version is purely a <u>short-run</u> compromise driven by observed real-world macropolicy—especially monetary policy. As long as short-run imperfections and asymmetries in information exist, or as long as wage-contracts remain "sticky" (rigid) in the short-term, such tradeoffs will be successful. According to the expectationists, however, as the asymmetries disappear, the vertical AS will re-emerged along with its attendant supply-side oriented policies. As discussed earlier, Robert E. Lucas constructed his "islands economy" in 1973 to demonstrate that the greater the attempts to try and exploit information imperfections in the short-run, the faster the convergence of the economy to a vertical AS curve, and the quicker the demise of any perceived short-term tradeoff.

   Of course, die-hard Keynesians would have no problem with the "synthesis" view in the short-run. In the long-run, however, they would advocate simply a continuance of the Keynesian policies. After all, for them the AS is positively sloped in both the short-run as well as the long-run.

2. *If there are two diametrically different paradigms for developed economies, why do the bond market and often the stock market behave in a predominantly "Keynesian" fashion? For example, monetary policy announcements are immediately assumed to be fully capable of attaining the desired objectives regarding GDP, employment, and inflation.*

Bond markets in the US and in Europe certainly tend to display "Keynesian" tendencies. An announcement by the central bank that the short-term rate will be lowered by, say, 50 basis points, is often seen as an indicator of greater GDP growth, greater employment, and an accompanying increase in the inflation rate. These indicators, after all, are hallmarks of Keynesian output-inflation tradeoffs. Typically, the yield curve might get steeper soon after the central bank's announcement, as long bonds incorporate higher expected inflation resulting from the rate cut. Anticipation of renewed economic growth often results in a stock buying frenzy as investors reenter the equity market, which may result in a spike in stock prices following a central bank announcement of looser monetary policy.

Conversely, immediately following an announced rise in interest rates, yield curves often get flatter as bond markets recognize the attempt by the central bank to cool down the economy by means of a monetary contraction. Expected inflation falls as a soft landing is expected, driving down long-term rates. Investors may take profits and sell out of a market on the verge of being slowed down, thereby causing a drop in stock prices, in this instance.[16]

One can indeed make a case that stock and bond markets in most developed economies either are "mostly Keynesian," or that these markets subscribe to the "synthesis" view and are Keynesian in the near-term.

3. *How would you explain a recession in the supply-side (New Economy) paradigm?*

The labor market is the key to explaining a recession in the New Economy paradigm, presented in Fig. 10.11. In the version done in this chapter, both labor supply and demand were functions of the real wages, tax rates, and a term labeled "macroeconomic outlook.".We discussed how cuts in taxes (personal and/or business) either shifted labor supply or labor demand to the right, and vice versa. To explain recessions, we now need to activate the "outlook" term.

Simply, the "macroeconomic outlook" is composed of forward-looking consumer and investor confidence. If the future looks bleak, the "outlook" term will decrease and labor demand will shift to the left as presented in Fig. 10.11. The effect on labor supply is uncertain. Discouraged workers may simply opt out of the labor market, thereby removing themselves from the civilian labor force, or they may work more hours in anticipation of leaner financial times ahead. Hence, we leave labor supply curve unchanged. Equilibrium employment in the labor market will fall as labor demand shifts left. (The other shifts are described following Diagram 11.)

From the production function diagram, as employment falls, output falls too, and this causes the vertical AS to shift to the left. Furthermore, the production function itself drops as the economy worsens. Typically, employers tend to hold on to most

---

[16]This assumes that all other macroeconomic factors—tax rates, government spending, confidence, foreign GDP—remain constant and dormant. This is a purely linear, simplified causality from interest rate announcements to typical long-bond and stock market behavior, immediately following the Fed's announcement.

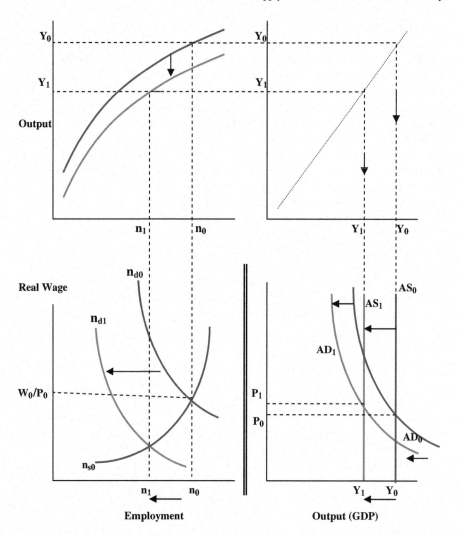

Fig. 10.11 A recession in the supply-side paradigm

of their workers until a recession is well under way. In doing so, each worker's output per hour (productivity) drops since the demand for the product has fallen in the slowing economy. Worsening macroeconomic conditions will also affect conventional consumer and investor confidence terms, C and I, which account for the drop in AD, as shown in Fig. 10.11.

The final effect on inflation is ambiguous and depends on the relative magnitude of the AD and AS shifts.

In the following articles, please comment on the underlined passages using material presented in this and preceding chapters. Use diagrams liberally.

Article 10.1   SHIKOKU NEEDS LESS STIMULUS

Rohit Gupta, Aberdeen World News

Last weekend, Mr. Keichi Nagumo, Minister of Finance of the Republic of Shikoku, unveiled the country's most recent "economic stimulus" package. The event followed the graduation ceremony of the prestigious National Engineering Institute at the Koda Hotel. Even though the event was studded with the usual luminaries, there was something missing—a real expectation of success was conspicuously absent from the proceedings.

In spite of the eighth stimulus package in six years, Shikoku, one of the most formidable economies of the recent past, remains mired in recession with no end in sight. A total of 400 trillion units of domestic currency have already been (a) spent on gigantic infrastructure projects ranging from the Kaga desalination complex to one of the most modern airports in the world, not to mention the super high tech magnetic levitation (maglev) train system currently under development. But all these huge expensive projects have only managed to (b) nudge the economy from its severe bouts of deflation, up to about 2 percent inflation for short periods, before sinking back down again..

We interview Mr. Mitsubishi, who is enjoying a walk in the Fujimoro lotus gardens with his 5-year-old grandson. "We spend and spend, and I know that my hard earned savings are (c) being borrowed by our government to build expensive toys. But these are toys that we can't use, and this is not what we need now. I have not worked in 18 months, and all my close friends are now out of work; all six of us once designed the best ships in the world. What will become of us?" he says keeping one watchful eye on his grandson who is feeding the ducks by the water's edge.

Dr. Midori Konda, well-known author of Shikoku's Agony stresses that "Its not just fiscal profligacy." She points out, "They have (d) constantly hit the 'money button' to revive their economy, with the result that (e) interest rates are virtually at zero percent! But nothing is happening! The central bank and the government are praying for a Keynesian recovery (f) but they're praying in the wrong temple. It's the wrong model, and the sooner they accept this the better!"

On Monday, at the Eastern Heaven Ice Cream Bar, we ran into owner, George Haromi, "Listen guys, I don't need a PhD to figure this. The (central) bank (g) brought down the stock market with those crazy interest rate hikes four years ago, remember? And the country (h) went into chronic depression when the stock market collapsed. People's entire retire-ments evaporated overnight—can you imagine? The elderly are wiped out— my wife's mother had to move in with us. Why would you take a loan at a time like this—I'm an experienced bus-inessman and (i) I'm not borrowing anything for a LONG time!" He then excused himself to scoop out

Mango Mayhem ice-cream for two school-girls.

Now, Shikoku has yet another stimulus package, but there are no expectations of success. Des-pondency is epidemic. The bond market's reaction did nothing to help; (j) rates sprang to 12 percent, as the government deficit/GDP ratio crossed over 10 percent. The (k) currency continues to plunge, hitting its 20-year low last Tuesday. So what can be done?

"Throw away the old model," says Dr. Konda. "Politically this will be tough, but we have to let all the sick companies and institutions die. We can't and shouldn't keep spending trillions to bail them out. Unemploy-ment will get worse before it can get better. (l) Get government out of de-cisions on manufacturing, trade, and specialization. No more

government subsidies, directives, or 5-year national plans. Order the (m) central bank to stop printing money at once. Shikoku needs less stimulus. Let the free market rule. (n) Unshackle the labor market by scrapping all the employment regu-lation—this is vital. And most important, slash all business taxes significantly."

Dr. Konda then flies off to Scotland for a conference in Aberdeen. This reporter and his camera crew decide to walk by the Eastern Heaven. There are no customers. It is a nice evening. A cool breeze blows in from the bay. George Haromi sees us and waves us in. "Here, have some free Mango Mayhem," he beams, as he hands us small ice cream cones. Maybe things are looking up after all.

Article 10.2   IMPLICATIONS OF THE "NEW" ECONOMY

Jesse Cohen, Kansas City Financial Examiner

"The implications go way beyond academic discussion," intones Dom Panelli, at the National Policy Bureau's Conference on the New Economy in Flemington, NJ. "What we have here is a fundamental sea change in policies prescribed by respective governments and in the way we do business."

With the elections never too far away in the US, this opinion has profound implications. Panelli's comment is countered by an article published by Policy Today that insists that it was

(a) low interest rates, cheaper imports, and a "one time boost in productivity" that resulted in the New Economy. This kind of thinking is immediately chall-enged by last month's Engi-neering Outlook which presents rigorously measured productivity numbers in virtually all major sectors. Most areas show a huge jump since the late 1990s, and all (b) indicate no slowdown in their growth rates. In view of this backdrop of conflicting data, believers on both sides remain adamant.

As the experts debated the issues, this newspaper took the matter to the practitioners. Art Vandalay, Director of JKV, an Oklahoma-based wireless bio-metric equipment manufacturer, says, "This whole industry basically grew overnight, and we haven't even scratched the surface. Technology has a long way to go, and we are coming up with more potentially path-breaking innovations literally on a daily basis." He vehemently adds, "I have been an engineer for 34 years, and I know that we are in a new phase since the IT explosion of the 1990s. My only problem is getting enough skilled labor to keep pace with the new ideas."

Jerry Kitsmiller, controller at Cyber Lock, an encryption company in Richmond, adds an ominous note. "This new world of e-commerce fueled by the internet is real. No doubt about that. But it can come crashing down if these folks in Washington enact (c) even more legislation to regulate our industry. It worries me a lot .... stagflation would be terrible."

But at StatsOnLine, the global statistical analysis giant, Perin Guzder admits, (d) "We can't say for sure if it was monetary policy against a backdrop of favorable world events that 'caused' the New Economy, or some big tech-nological revolution set in a new paradigm".

This was not good enough for Isabella Soprano, researcher at the Carson Mountain Radio Telescope in Colorado. "We can detect an object as small as an electric golf cart at the edge of the universe, and those (e) folks can't write a program to find out which 'model' works? Come on! Get serious!"

In Ireland, a similar debate has long been under way. (f) Did huge transfers from the rich European Union countries "cause" Ireland's remarkable growth, or was it textbook supply-side economics leading to the New Economy? "I admit that the transfer did help enormously. And the tax cuts could also be called 'old economy,' but (g) I really think that huge pro-business initiatives and the fact that our government has stopped meddling in the economy may have given us our miracle," says Mike Kelly, bartender at the Celtic Rebel pub in Dublin, as we waited for the heads on our glasses of Guiness to stop rising.

The mood has spread globally. In China, Jiao Xianquan, President of the Shanghai Consortium of Business told us, "We really must (h) privatize our key sectors, force them to compete globally, allow our bright young men and women to take risks and unleash their minds and energies."

All are not convinced. Dr. Mica Fischer, Chairman of the Dresden Group in Dresden, Germany, scoffed at the debate in a television debate last night.
(i) "There is nothing to debate. We raise interest rates, things slow down, and unemployment goes up. We lower rates, the opposite happens. End of story. Nothing 'new' about this New Economy!"

The following are major discussion topics/issues pertaining to the supply-side paradigm.

(1) "The supply-sider model is just a transitory fix. Once the deregulation is all done, then what happens? What drives the growth then?" True/False? Comment.

(2) "This emphasis on technology is misplaced. Keep in mind, we have diminishing returns to technology—I mean, how small a mobile phone will we finally make? Will I rush out and buy a new laptop just because it might be just a little faster? Or a new Ipod just because the new design looks prettier and can store a million tunes?" True/False? Comment.

(3) "How can supply-siders explain bubbles and overheating at some 'Y max'? In their world there is no such thing as maximum capacity! But we all know that bubbles and capacity constraints do indeed exist!" Comment.

(4) "The supply-side model is useless. Note how the US went totally Kyenesian after 9/11!" Comment.

(5) "Why do giant companies like Dell and Walmart insist that they are products of the supply-side paradigm? What is this connection with the supply-side model and supply chain management (SCM)?"

(6) "Free trade is vital to supply-siders. But how can we trade freely if other countries copy our knowledge-intensive products such as new software, R&D, music, etc.?" Comment

(7) "If free trade is vital to the supply side paradigm, then we should use tax revenues to subsidize key sectors and to champion new exports. By this strategy, we will capture global market share, and these champion products and technologies will be the vanguard of our growth for the next ten years or so." Comment.

ANSWERS AND HINTS

Article 10.1 Shikoku Needs Less Stimulus

(a) This illustrates the basic Keynesian fiscal multiplier driven by large infrastructure spending.

(b) As AD is shifted right, inflation is pushed up as the economy barely enters Stage 2 of demand-pull inflation ... but then the AD drops back down ... why is this happening? (Please be sure to read through the whole article before answering.)

(c) This is typical bond-financed government deficit spending. What may be some factors causing manufacturing and heavy industry to bear the brunt of the slowing economy?

(d) and (e) Monetary stimulus has also been relentlessly applied. As money supply has increased, interest rates have progressively fallen, until apparently they are now close to zero. Both G and M were increased to attempt a rightward shift in AD. Use diagrams to explain how these policies were supposed to have revived Shikoku's economy.

(f) Could Shikoku be in the throes of a paradigm shift? Use diagrams to explain.

(g) Sounds like the central bank contracted monetary policy to deflate a potential SAP bubble in the stock market—and succeeded. Apparently, the contraction in M was severe. Use diagrams here.

(h) It is hardly surprising that the collapse in perceived wealth following the central bank's bursting of the SAP bubble has led to plunges in C and I.

(i) This relates to low I. A healthy demand for loanable funds is crucially dependent on investor confidence and not just on interest rates, as discussed in earlier chapters. Even though interest rates are close to zero in this economy, expectations of future growth are dismal. Investor confidence is at rock bottom, and businesspersons like George are not even contemplating any borrowing.

(j) Central bank policy directly influences very short-term interest rates. However, long-term rates, as discussed in earlier chapters, are endogenous. Use this fact, coupled with Shikoku's deficit/GDP ratio, to explain the rise in "rates" to 12 %.

(k) An exodus of capital into safer and healthier economies results in investors selling domestic currency to purchase assets denominated in foreign (hard) currency. This causes the domestic currency to plunge.

(l) A smaller role for government is advocated here; deregulation is the mantra. This is clearly a supply-side proposal.

(m) Further emphasis on the supply-side. Basically, demand-side fiscal and monetary stabilization is not effective any more. The paradigm has shifted. The emphasis ought to be on attempting to shift the aggregate supply curve instead of the aggregate demand curve. Illustrate, using diagrams.

(n) These are textbook supply-side policies. Deregulation is vital—especially in the labor market. And tax cuts are absolutely necessary to a supply-side stimulus. Illustrate, using diagrams.

Article 10.2 Implications of the "New" Economy

(a) Dom Panelli is referring to the Keynesian explanation for the New Economy. Use diagrams to explain.

(b) This is the supply-side perspective. Productivity growth is real, ongoing, and here to stay. The New Economy is not an episodic one-time event.

(c) Use the set of four diagrams (production function, labor market, reflector and (P,Y) space) to show how, in this supply-sider perspective, an increase in government regulation could result in stagflationary effects.

(d) Why can't statistician Perin Guzder "say for sure"? Use diagrams.

(e) It is not technical deficiency, but the nature of the time-series data that results in the problem.

(f) Was it just an increase in donor-funded government spending in Ireland that produced a nice Keynesian recovery in that country?

(g) Or was it a genuine supply-side stimulus? Refer to the chapter.

(h) Here is an example of attempts to generate a shift in the AS even though the economy may almost certainly be Keynesian.

(i) In the short-run we can all be Keynesians. But in some economies, we cannot perpetually exploit short-run tradeoffs based on imperfections or rigidities. If the AS eventually becomes vertical (according to long-term supply-siders), the output-inflation tradeoff ceases to exist. Furthermore, according to Robert E. Lucas, in this case the more we try to exploit short-term tradeoffs, the faster they will converge to vertical AS world.

Chapter 11
Central Banks and Monetary Policy

After analyzing monetary policy in both Keynesian and rational expectations paradigms, and across emerging and developed economies, the time has finally come to explore the exact mechanism by which central banks enact monetary growth.

We begin by reviewing the institutional structure of major central banks that include the US Federal Reserve (the Fed) and the European Central Bank (ECB). This will be followed by a discussion of the three major methods by which monetary growth, and hence, short-term interest rates are changed. The discussion pertaining to the instruments of monetary policy includes the conventionally accepted ("textbook") version of changing monetary growth followed by the empirically observed reality of current monetary policy.

We then explore and evaluate the objectives of monetary policy in both emerging and developed countries. How should monetary policy be conducted? Sect. 11.3 begins with a discussion of Keynesian stabilization, followed by the Friedmanian x-percent rule, and ends with the Taylor rule. The ECB's attempts to maintain an inflation target (discussed earlier) will also be revisited in this context.

Issues such as the implication and attainment of monetary discipline, and the policy of pegging one's currency to the hard currency of another country to enable monetary discipline, will be covered towards the end of this chapter. The "impossible trinity", the undoing of the East Asian economies during the currency crises of 1997–98, Argentina's 2001–02 crisis, Switzerland's ordeal in 2015, and the pressures of pegging to a falling US dollar in 2007–08 and then to the rising dollar with the "Taper Tantrum" in 2013, are also discussed in some detail.

© Springer International Publishing Switzerland 2016
F. Langdana, *Macroeconomic Policy*, Springer Texts in Business
and Economics, DOI 10.1007/978-3-319-32854-6_11

11.1   Institutional Framework: The Federal Reserve

The Federal Reserve (the Fed), the central bank of the United States, was founded in 1913 by an act of Congress. It should be noted that in the early years of the 20th century, there was strong resistance to the idea of one central bank in the US. However, a series of banking panics culminated in a particularly vicious run on banks in 1907, and this finally led to a consensus for a central bank. The objective (at that time) was to manage the nation's money supply more effectively and allow it to be more flexible in times of monetary crises.[1]

The key bodies within the Federal Reserve are the **Board of Governors** and the **Federal Open Market Committee (FOMC)**. The Board of Governors is based in Washington, D.C., and is composed of seven governors who have non-renewable 14-year terms, staggered by two years. The governors are appointed by the President and confirmed by the Senate. The Chairperson and the Vice Chairperson have renewable 4-year terms, and are both designated by the President and confirmed by the Senate.

The fairly long terms serve to insulate the Board of Governors from political pressure and to ensure that the Federal Reserve (and therefore monetary policy) is indeed independent of government pressure to either monetize a runaway deficit or to indulge in excessive and possibly detrimental changes in money growth and interest rates. The 2-year staggering is to limit the number of Presidential appointments to the board to a maximum of four members—presumably this would reduce the possibility of a certain president "stacking" the board of governors with individuals that subscribed only to his/her macroeconomic paradigm.[2]

Some economists believe that this provision also reduces the possibility of "political business cycles" (PBCs) wherein a "government-friendly" Federal Reserve attempts short-term stimulation by lowering rates shortly before an election, allows the incumbent to get re-elected as growth temporarily picks up, and then, months after the election, lets society incur the costs of the ensuing inflation and the original lower rate of growth.

As a result of the relatively long terms and the staggering by two years, the Board of Governors is basically a quasi-independent body. The Federal Reserve is, of course, a creation of Congress, and the chairperson is required to report to Congress on a regular basis and to be subjected to long afternoons of demanding grilling. Nonetheless, the Federal Reserve remains independent in that it takes monetary action first and later explains and reports its actions to Congress.

The **FOMC** is primarily responsible for the course and conduct of monetary policy in the US. By law, the FOMC is required to meet at least four times a year in

---

[1]The "compromise" solution was to have 12 Federal Banks representing different regions of the US, instead of just one central bank in the capital, as in most other countries.

[2]If governors cannot finish their terms, and if more than four slots become available, the President has to leave those unfilled. The President can appoint only a maximum of four members to the board of governors over a 2-term Presidency.

Washington, D.C., but since 1980 they have met at least eight times a year. The committee comprises the 7-member Board of Governors plus five of the presidents of the 12 regional Federal Reserve banks. The President of the New York Federal Reserve is always included since the New York Federal Reserve is always an integral part of the money supply process. The other four presidents are rotated into the FOMC every January 1. All 12 Federal Reserve presidents are invited to participate in the deliberations, but the final voting on the course of monetary policy is done only by the 12 members (7 Governors + 5 Presidents).

The presidents of the regional Federal Reserve banks are selected by the directors of their respective banks. Each Federal Reserve bank has nine directors, six of whom are elected from the member banks in the district while the three others are appointed by the Board of Governors in Washington, D.C.

Ever since the system of the Board of Governors and the FOMC was instated in 1935, there has been an ongoing debate regarding the independence of the central bank and the influence of the Federal Reserve presidents on the course of monetary policy. However, advocates of central bank autonomy have prevailed, with the result that the Fed, along with the German Bundesbank (and possibly the ECB in the years to come), is among major central banks that have acquired strong reputations for monetary discipline over the last few decades.

The **Federal Advisory Board** is another component of the Federal Reserve. It is composed of 12 prominent bankers who represent the interests of the financial services in their respective districts, and, as the name implies, their role is purely advisory.

In addition to prescribing and implementing the course of monetary policy, the Federal Reserve also regulates and supervises all the financial institutions that transact money. These institutions range from around 8000 commercial banks to small savings and loans. In addition, the Fed is also a major lender of last resort (as discussed later in this chapter), and it also provides financial services such as clearing interbank payments, managing wire transfers, and managing exchange rates and reserves.

We now turn to a discussion of how money policy is implemented by central banks. In the previous 10 chapters we deftly increased or decreased M and shifted the LM back and forth to analyze the effects of monetary policy. Now we examine the mechanism by which M is actually changed.

11.2 The Money Creation Process: How the Federal Reserve Changes the Money Supply

Central banks use three methods to change a nation's money supply:

   (i) **Open Market Operations (OMOs).**
  (ii) **Discount Rate Policy**
 (iii) **Changing the Reserve Requirement (RR)**

Prior to discussing these, a description of one aspect of the implementation mechanism of major central banks—reserve requirements (reserve ratios)—is in order. In the following two sections, we discuss the widely accepted "textbook" version of the theoretical working of the money multiplier and Open Market Operations (OMOs). This is followed by the reality of the state of OMOs in Sect. 11.2.2.1.

11.2.1 Reserve Requirements and the Money Multiplier: The Theory

Under this system, all depository institutions are required by law to hold a minimum fixed percentage of deposits as reserves. The Reserve Ratio (RR) is defined as the ratio of reserves to deposits.

RequiredReserveRatio = Reserves/Deposits

Although in the US the Federal Reserve determines the required ratio for each type of deposit, we assume a flat RR of 10 % in this chapter, for convenience.[3] Hence, a deposit of $1000 made to the First Bank of New York by Person 1 would result in the First Bank putting $100 in reserves and being able to loan out $900, in this simplified example in which we have multiple banks. This loan is made to Person 2 in Florida who then buys computer hardware from a store in Orlando for $900. The store owner deposits this check into the Bank of Orlando, which then has to hold $90 in reserve and be able to lend out only $810 to Person 3 who needs to remodel her home office, and so on.[4]

We can write the string of total deposits generated by the initial $1000 of deposits, given the 10 % RR, as:

$$\$1000 + \$900 + \$810 + \$729 + \cdots \tag{11.1}$$

Since each successive bank obtains only 0.9 of the deposits of the previous bank, the above string of numbers can be re-written as:

$$\$1000 \left(1 + 0.9 + 0.9^2 + 0.9^3 + \cdots\right) \tag{11.2}$$

---

[3]This is actually very close to the reserve ratio in the US. Please note that "reserve requirements" and "reserve ratios" will be used interchangeably in this chapter.

[4]Note that the reserves earn no interest. In this simplified Federal Reserve example, we also assume that no funds are simply held by the banks and individuals as cash. Such holdings would affect the magnitude of the final result as explained in the next section.

Since the sum of the infinite series $1 + x + x^2 + x^3 + x^4 + \cdots = 1/(1 - x)$, the series in our example works out to be:

$$(1 + 0.9 + 0.9^2 + 0.9^3 + \cdots) = 1/(1 - 0.9) = 1/(0.10) = 10 \qquad (11.3)$$

In other words, the infinite sum is equal to $1/[1 - (1 - R)]$ where R is the RR. This simplifies to simply $1/(R)$, which is $1/(0.10) = 10$

Substituting the result from (11.3) into (11.2), we obtain the total increase in checking account balances throughout all the banks to be:

$$(\$1000)(10) = \$10,000 = (\text{Initial Deposit})(1/\text{Reserve Ratio})$$

In general:

The total increase in deposits $= (\textbf{Initial Deposit})(1/\textbf{Reserve Ratio}) \qquad (11.4)$

Economists refer to the term 1/Reserve Ratio as the money multiplier, and in some ways it is identical to the fiscal multiplier of the earlier Keynesian chapters.

11.2.2 Open Market Operations (OMOs)

With the review of reserve ratios and the money multiplier, we now explore Federal OMOs, the most frequently used method by which the Federal Reserve and other major central banks change money supply.

The FOMC meets in Washington. The setting is splendid; white and gold wallpaper dating back to the art deco era graces the walls. The committee sits on plush brown-colored swivel chairs around an immense oval 27-foot Honduran mahogany table. A green light is switched on whenever the proceedings are being taped. Large numbers of staffers, statisticians, econometricians, and technical assistants are also present prior to the main deliberations. Until the mid-1990s, the announcements of FOMC meetings had been typically relegated to inside columns of inner pages of business newspapers. But things changed in the mid-1990s—since then, FOMC meetings have often attracted as much media attention as royal weddings.

We begin with the case where the FOMC meets and decides that the economy needs a looser monetary policy (lower interest rates), and decides to increase M by $1000, in this simplified example.

The committee then instructs the Trading Desk at the New York Federal Reserve to buy $1000 worth of government securities (US Treasury bills and notes) from a Government Securities Dealer (GSD). "GSD" is a prestigious designation reserved for only a few highly regarded financial institutions. The Federal Reserve then pays the GSD with a check for $1000 drawn on itself. The GSD then deposits this check in its account at its commercial bank (New Jersey National Bank, for example).

Fig. 11.1 Monetary growth

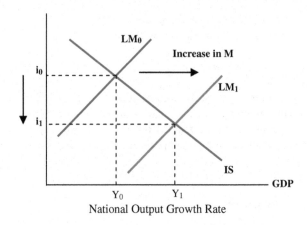

National Output Growth Rate

The New Jersey bank then sends this check to the Federal Reserve for credit. The Federal Reserve "pays" New Jersey National Bank by crediting this bank's account at the New York Federal Reserve by $1000. In other words, the Federal Reserve increases the <u>reserves</u> of the New Jersey bank by $1000.

Assuming a RR of 10 %, the New Jersey Savings bank must place $100 in reserve and can now lend out $900, and the effect of the initial injection of $1000 now ripples through the economy as discussed. As the money "changes hands", a string of successively smaller deposits and loans are made in the process described in the preceding section.

As banks now have a greater supply of loanable funds, competition between them to lend these newly-available funds rapidly translates to a lowering of interest rates.[5] Throughout the book we deftly shifted the LM to the right to signify an increase in the money supply M, resulting in a lower interest rate as presented in Fig. 11.1. Now, finally, the mechanism has been described.[6]

The rate lowered by the Federal Reserve in our example is the short-term rate— the **federal funds rate**. This is the overnight rate that banks and other depository institutions charge each other while trading their non-interest bearing reserves. Banks, whose reserves may have fallen below the ratio required by the Fed, borrow at this overnight lending rate from other banks that happen to have excess reserves. In our example, as the FOMC authorizes an open market purchase of government

---

[5]Remember that the Federal Reserve has most influence on very short-term (overnight) interest rates, by monetary policy. Short-term rates are exogenously determined. Long-term rates, on the other hand, are endogenously determined by expectations of future risk and inflation formed by processing information efficiently in forward-looking bond markets that "know best" (Chap. 6).

[6]In the US recession of 1990–91, despite several interest rates cuts, the confidence levels were so low that the only "borrowing" was from homeowners who already held mortgages but were attempting to refinance them at the prevailing lower rates. A similar lack of borrowing existed in the low rates in 2008, after Chairman Bernanke pushed down rates in the Sub-prime Crisis (Article 11.3).

bonds, and as reserves generally increase, the federal funds rate, perhaps the best indicator of current Federal Reserve policy, tends to fall.

While the money multiplier implies that the total loans generated (money "put into circulation"), should be ($1000)(10) = $10,000, the actual money multiplier for the US is not 10 but lies between 2 and 3. This difference is due to the fact that our formula assumes that there is no "leakage" in the money creation process and that all the loans make their way directly into other checking accounts which are then promptly deposited into banks 2, 3, 4, and so on. However, this process ignores the fact that individuals tend to hold a portion of their loans in cash. This tendency to hold cash constitutes the "leakage" in our example as deposits held as cash are not available for other banks to lend out. As cash holdings increase, the money multiplier decreases as successive shrinking bank deposits in turn rapidly decrease future loanable funds.

From this discussion, it becomes clear that an efficient market with large volumes of tradeable government bonds is a necessary condition for effective OMOs. Economies not possessing such bond markets and, more importantly, such relatively risk-free and easily traded government debt would certainly be unable to readily change the growth of the money supply and short-term interest rates using OMOs.

To decrease money growth and to increase short-term rates, the reverse process takes place. The FOMC instructs the Trading Desk at the New York Federal Reserve to sell bonds to a GSD, resulting finally in a removal of reserves from the GSD's commercial bank (New Jersey Bank). The ensuing decrease in the supply of loanable funds in New Jersey Bank and its competition results in a rapid increase in the interest rates. In previous chapters, this was evidenced when we contracted M and shifted the LM to the left, thereby increasing interest rates.

In summary, open market purchases of government securities from the private sector result in an increase in bank's reserves and the resultant increase in national money supply, accompanied by a drop in short-term rates. An open market sale of government securities does the opposite: banks' lending abilities decrease as their reserves fall. The money supply shrinks, resulting in higher interest rates in the short-term.[7]

Typically, the media announce the FOMC's decision in terms of the final intended change in the federal funds rate.[8] In reality, though, the FOMC sets the target range for the intended federal funds rate, and then indulges in OMOs to attain it.

We now turn to the empirical reality of OMOs and the money multiplier. Unfortunately, the money growth process is, in reality, not nearly as clinical and convenient as that presented in the pedagogic-academic literature, and in this and the preceding section.

---

[7]These processes assume that all other factors, including the demand for loanable funds, remain unchanged.

[8]The federal funds rate changes are usually expressed in terms of basis points, with each point being 1/100th of a percent. Thus, 25 basis points will be a change of 0.25 %. Note that the "prime rate" is simply the rate that commercial banks charge their biggest and best (prime) customers.

11.2.2.1   Reserve Ratios and the Money Multiplier: The Empirical Reality

The author is most grateful to the late Prof. Giles Mellon of Rutgers Business School, with whom he co-authored and presented "Effective Monetary Policy in a World of Non-Binding Reserve Requirement," at the National Business and Economics Conference, 2002. This section (updated to 2016) incorporates portions of the working paper.

Monetary legislation in the 1990s has caused fundamental changes in the way that money/credit creation results from OMOs. In 1990, the Fed abolished completely all reserve requirements on time deposits for US banks. (Similar regulations also went into effect in Japan, the UK, Canada, Australia, and in several Western European economies.) Since time deposits for US banks made up some 80 % of total deposits, the result of this legislation was to free-up the bulk of US bank net deposits from reserve requirement obligations.

Reserve requirement on demand deposits were retained, though the ratio was lowered to 10 % in the US in 1992. But even this moderate system of reduced legal reserve obligations soon ceased to be a binding constraint on bank expansion of deposit and credit for two reasons; (i) The rapid expansion of ATM systems containing huge amounts of cash, and (ii) the institution of "sweep accounts" where the banks moved large amounts of demand balances into time accounts with legal reserve requirements.

As a result of these developments, the great majority of US banks now hold no reserves at all at the Fed to meet reserve requirements, and, indeed, can satisfy their reserve requirements with only a portion of the cash balances in their ATM systems which count as legal reserves. Following the sub-prime crisis in the US, by 2016, most banks in the US were holding significant excess reserves on a permanent basis, well in excess of the legally binding minimum amount—legal reserve requirements have ceased to exert any binding limit on monetary expansion.

It should not, however, be thought that under this new system, OMOs are useless, or, alternatively, any injection of new reserves through OMOs would allow the banks to expand deposits and credit without limit.

The cash holdings of banks in ATM machines, though they far exceed legal required reserves, are not "excess" in the operational senses. The reserves are "excess" only in the sense of the legal RR. In reality, they may be optimal reserves at "desired" levels necessary for the banks to do business. In other words, "effective" although not legally established reserve ratios are now found to exist—an injection of reserves via OMOs will still increase the rate of monetary growth, and vice versa.

In fact, the concept of **negative interest rates** adopted since 2015 is primarily designed to be a "rental cost" on private banks when they "park" their money at their central banks. Central banks of Japan, the Eurozone, Denmark, Sweden and Switzerland–economies that account for almost 25 % of global GDP—cut their interest rates to below zero by early 2016, essentially forcing large financial institutions to pay a rental fee to central banks for parking their money overnight.

Following the subprime crisis and the massive liquidity generated by years of Quantitative Easing (QE, discussed earlier), and given the liquidity trap situation in existence for much of the post-subprime period, financial institutions, awash in excess reserves, deposited heavily at their central banks. Now, with negative interest rates, it costs them to do so, and thus, at least in theory, private banks will be induced to make more loans, and therefore, stimulate the economy instead of safely parking their deposits in stable central banks.

The key issue is, however, the computation of the size of the so-called money multiplier, now that the clean conventionally-accepted mechanism of the multiplier presented in Sect. 11.2.1 has been muddied by the recent events and legislation pertaining to reserves. The existence of "effective" and non-binding reserve ratios does indeed complicate the conventional money multiplier and significantly increases the difficulty in accurately determining its magnitude.

However, this sub-section does not invalidate this chapter's discussion on open market operation and the general money creation process. Instead, this discussion places OMOs in a real-world context and emphasizes the formidable challenges faced by modern central banks in exercising at least some discretionary control on the rate of monetary growth. By early 2016, there was a definite sense that the Fed had largely lost control over money in circulation, with the culprits being the vast and highly sensitive global flows of hot capital that could negate any domestic monetary fine-tuning by the Fed.

Before we transition to the second method of changing monetary growth, we briefly discuss the very important distinction between OMOs and the monetization of outstanding government debt discussed earlier in Chaps. 3 and 6.

OMOs, the Federal Reserve and the Treasury The operations are considered to be "open market" because transactions involving government securities are conducted by the Federal Reserve in an open market with commercial banks and the general public, but not with the government. The exclusion is to ensure that there is no possibility of monetization of national budget deficits incurred by the government.

The Fed's open market purchases and sales of government securities (OMOs) should not be confused with the Treasury's sales of government debt to individuals and institutions. The Treasury issues new debt to finance large increases in government spending (G) and to finance the ensuing budget deficits. As discussed in detail in the national savings identity (NSI) in Chap. 3, these sustainable bond-financed budget deficits are linked to current account deficits and to large accompanying capital inflows.

In sharp contrast, the government securities that are bought and sold in OMOs by the Federal Reserve to change the money supply, (M), are not new securities, but instead are outstanding (pre-existing) government securities.

A central bank that buys new bonds directly from the US Treasury effectively "prints money", and this could be the dangerous first step on the road to eventual hyperinflation. In fact, by late 2007 and through 2015, during the financial meltdown, the Federal Reserve began a "Monetization Plus" program known as QE described in earlier chapters. Here, instead of buying unsellable new Treasury debt directly from the Treasury (which is the conventional definition of "monetization"), the Fed bought the "toxic" mortgage-backed securities (explained further in Case 11.3), and the problematic outstanding debt from failing financial institutions, investment banks, and insurance companies. The massive and controversial bailout plan from 2007-15 included monthly purchases by the Fed of $42 billion of toxic mortgage-backed securities, and resulted in unprecedented money creation, flooding the global economy with liquidity.

Another difference between Treasury issues of new debt and Federal Reserve OMOs lies in the nature of the transaction. Domestic and foreign investors voluntarily purchase the Treasury's new issues of government bonds at national bond auctions; this is an endogenous purchase of sovereign debt. Not so in the Fed's OMOs.

The "Broken Rhombus" presented in Fig. 11.2 helps to demystify and eradicate any confusion between the transaction in government securities and Treasury-financed government spending (G), changes in the monetary growth rate driven by the Federal Reserve (M), Monetization of both the outstanding debt and the toxic mortgage-backed instruments of the Subprime Crisis, and the flow of funds between private institutions/individuals and private banks, for capital investments (I).

There are two "legs" of the rhombus represented as "broken". The first one is the so-called "firewall" between the central bank (The Fed) and the Treasury. This leg has been severely compromised since 2007. This firewall had ensured that the money creating authority (the central bank, the Fed) was totally independent and autonomous of the spending authority (the Treasury). As previously discussed, the objective was to prevent a rogue government from rampantly monetizing nonsustainable spending. Well, as also discussed earlier and in article 11.3, this was clearly not the case in the United States since 2007.

The other "broken leg" of the rhombus pertains to the flow of funds between private banks and borrowers. This flow of funds has been strongly dysfunctional from 2008 to 16, due to the liquidity trap discussed in earlier chapters. In this case, borrowers were not inclined to borrow due to the bleak macroeconomic outlook and excessive government regulation and taxation in the US. And at the same time, lenders (private banks) were not eager to lend, given the damage done to some of their balance sheets. Hence, the "broken rhombus," broken in two places.

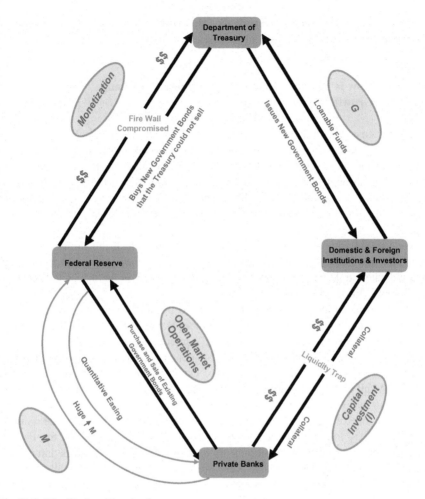

Fig. 11.2 The 'Broken Rhombus'

11.2.3   *Changing the Discount Rate*

The rate at which the Federal Reserve lends reserves to banks is called the **discount rate**. In this section we begin with the conventional discussion of how discount-rate policy is, theoretically, designed to be a tool of monetary policy—that is, how discount rate policy is supposed to work. This will be followed by a discussion of the actual effectiveness of discount rate policy in the US.

11.2.3.1 How is Discount Rate Policy Supposed to Change Money Growth?

If a major customer in the private sector requires a loan from, say, Valley National Bank, and if Valley National does not have the amount on hand, it is reluctant to turn away the major customer. Generally, Valley would first try to borrow from other banks through the federal funds market, at the federal funds rate, discussed earlier. If this rate is too high, or the reserves are simply not available from other banks, then Valley can borrow directly from the Federal Reserve at the discount rate.

By changing this discount rate, the Federal Reserve affects the amount borrowed by banks and signals a change in monetary policy. Announced raises in discount rate indicate a tighter money-growth policy, while drops in the discount rate imply an "easier" (looser) money-growth policy.

While federal funds rate policy is conducted by the 12-person FOMC, the discount rate is administered only by the 7-member Board of Governors. Discount rate changes are highly visible signals of the Fed's intent regarding near-term changes in monetary growth. Even though discount rate changes are not made as frequently as changes in the federal funds rate, they are usually synchronized with appropriate OMOs. A fall in the discount rate, for instance, is usually accompanied by an open market purchase of government securities, and vice versa.

Perhaps one of the largest infusions of liquidity using the discount rate window was on the day following 9/11. On Wednesday, September 12, 2001, the Federal Reserve lent a staggering $45 billion from its discount window to banks that needed to finance uncleared checks that were stuck in grounded aircraft all over the country. In sharp contrast, lending for the whole week prior to the attack was just under $200 million.

11.2.3.2 How is Observed (Actual) Discount Rate Policy Different?

Aside from significant discount window activity in such times of crisis, the discount rate in recent times has not been a proactive tool of monetary policy. Borrowed reserves have constituted an extremely small percentage of total member bank reserves from the late 1990s to the present. In fact, on average, since the mid-1990s, borrowed reserves have only constituted less than 1/200th of total bank reserves!

In addition, there is strong empirical evidence that the discount rate actually follows the 3-month Treasury Bill (T-Bill) rate, which is the interest rate paid by the government when it borrows from the public for a period of three months. Typically, the Fed is almost never proactive in its discount rate policy, with the discount rate closely mimicking or, at times, lagging, the short-term T-Bill rate.

The reason for adopting the T-Bill rate as a benchmark is that if the discount rate were to fall below the T-Bill rate, a clear arbitrage opportunity would present itself. Banks could now borrow reserves from the Federal Reserve at this low discount rate, and then lend these out risklessly to the government at the 3-month T-Bill rate for a guaranteed profit. Conversely, if the discount rate were to exceed the T-Bill rate, borrowing from the Fed would rapidly shrink. Barring national crises such as the attacks on 911, only banks in dire financial straits would be forced to borrow reserves from the Fed under these circumstances.

As a consequence, instead of using discount rate policy as a proactive monetary policy instrument as the conventional wisdom indicates, the Fed has been found to adopt a discount rate policy that very closely mimics the 3-month T-Bill rate.

11.2.4 Changing the Required Reserve Ratio

This is the least frequently used method of changing the money supply. By changing the required RR, the Federal Reserve changes the quantity of deposits that can be supported by a given level of reserves. For instance, increasing the RR from 10 to 12 % would increase the reserves to be held "at the Fed" by local banks, thus lowering their lending ability, and vice versa.

In our earlier example, the theoretical final money multiplier would now drop to $1/(0.12) = 8.33$, thus lowering the eventual amount of deposit creation that would eventually ripple through the economy.

Changes in the RR are disruptive as banks have to undergo a sudden, finite change, whereas they can now lend out more/less of their deposits, and hence the RR is changed very infrequently. Increases in the RR, in particular, are uncommon and are highly unpopular with banks since reserves are non-interest-bearing.

Following this discussion of the institutional structure of the Federal Reserve and the three methods by which the money supply can be changed by central banks, the next logical question explores the objectives of effective monetary policy.

11.3 The Role of the Central Bank: How Should Monetary Policy Be Conducted?

In addition to making discretionary changes in the money supply, the Fed has several functions. These include clearing interbank payments, supervising and regulating the banking system by reviewing the quality of loans and ensuring that the banks are maintaining the RR, managing exchange rates and the nation's foreign exchange reserves, and acting as the **lender of last resort** for the banking system.

This last role is perhaps the most dramatic. The Federal Reserve must quickly inject liquidity into an economy during times of great national crisis. Following 9/11, the Fed moved with impressive speed and determination to rapidly pump funds into a system that was suddenly in a grave liquidity crisis. Within two days of the attack, the Federal Reserve had injected a total of over $108 billion to meet demands from banks to cover uncleared checks that were in planes stranded on the ground in airports all over the country.

Such rapid injections of liquidity are typically done by overnight (short term) repurchase agreements (known as RPs or repos). Here the Fed buys securities from banks and provides liquidity to them, with the agreement that on a specified date (usually the next day) the banks will repurchase the securities back from the Fed at a fixed price. In other words, this arrangement enables the Fed to make a short-term loan to financial institutions in need of short-term liquidity. While repos are usually for one-day (overnight) lending, such an agreement could span a 2-week period.

A similar injection (though on a much smaller scale), followed the stock market correction in October 1987, when a liquidity crisis prompted a money growth increase of 14 % during the week following the correction. Other examples are monetary infusions following the 1995 Mexican peso crisis and the 1997 Asian currency meltdown.

Chairman Bernanke frantically injected money into the US economy in the "subprime crisis". As the housing bubble was deflated by Fall 2007, fears of contagion from a falling W (wealth holdings) to $\underline{C}$ and $\underline{I}$ and then eventually to household consumption (C) led the Fed to inject liquidity rapidly. Federal Funds rates plunged from 5.75 % in October 2007 to 1 % by December, 2008. (The chronology of Fed responses from the dotcom bubble of 2000 to the subprime crisis of 2007–08, are presented in Article 11.3.)

While the Federal Reserve has to perform the functions described above, its single most important responsibility remains the control of the growth of the money supply in the United States. How should this be done? What policy should the Federal Reserve adopt for changing M? And what about central banks of emerging economies? How is their policy prescription different?

To answer these questions, we begin with Milton Friedman's role for monetary policy, followed by the Taylor rule and the Humphrey Hawkins legislation, the bane of the US Federal Reserve. An overview of the ECB is followed by a discussion of challenges for monetary policy within the Eurozone.

11.3.1 Milton Friedman and the Role of Monetary Policy

Long before the advent of a formally recognized "New Classical" AS curve, decades before the arrival of the rational expectations paradigm, Milton Friedman outlined a role for monetary policy consistent with a vertical aggregate supply curve (Fig. 11.3) for developed economies.

Fig. 11.3 Milton Friedman
and the Role of Monetary
Policy

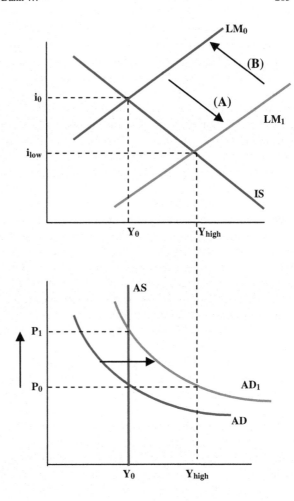

In Friedmanian doctrine, monetary policy would be <u>unable</u> to <u>consistently</u> attain the following objectives on a long-term basis:

1. Full employment
2. High GDP growth.

In Fig. 11.3, we establish interest rates, output, and employment "targets" for monetary policy.[9] Note the vertical AS curve implicit in Friedmanian monetary doctrine. An increase in money growth (an open market purchase) leads to a rightward shift in LM_0 to LM_1, resulting in attainment of the interest rate target,

---

[9]The employment target is not specifically displayed in Fig. 11.2, as the labor market is not displayed here. We assume that employment is positively correlated to output growth.

i_{low}, and output target, Y_{high}, depicted as (A) in Fig. 11.3. (The employment target is also attained, but the labor market diagram from Chap. 9 is not reproduced here).

However, these would be just the immediate short-term impact effects of monetary policy. Milton Friedman pointed out that, in developed economies, prices would increase from P_0 to P_1, thus resulting in the LM "snapping back" to LM_0, presented as (B) in Fig. 11.3. As discussed earlier in Chap. 8, in a classical AS curve model, nominal wages would adjust with prices, rendering the real wage unchanged. The labor market would be finally at the original rate of employment, and GDP growth corresponding to the original rate of employment would still be the same. Thus, with the shift (snap-back) in LM, GDP growth would again fall back to Y_0 in the long-run.

The only lasting effects of the monetary expansion in this case would be an increase in inflation from P_0 to P_1 (accompanied by an increase in nominal wages as discussed earlier), and no long-term increase in output growth or in employment. Interest rates would also "snap back" to i_0. In fact, by the Fisher effect (Chap. 6), long-term rates would rise right away due to expectations of future impending inflation.

Clearly, according to Friedman, monetary policy cannot and should not be used to try and attain long-term output, interest rate, and employment targets. The results would only be progressively increasing cycles of higher inflation and long-term rates.

So how should monetary policy be conducted?

Milton Friedman advocated an **"x percent money-growth rule"** for developed economies. Here, the central bank resolutely maintains a publicly announced and rigidly adhered-to fixed money growth rule that would not be sacrificed to attempt any futile demand-side stabilization. In this case, the central bank makes it very clear that drops (changes) in GDP growth and employment will not, and cannot, be cured by expansionary monetary policy. While the magnitude of the announced growth rate in money could be tied to the real trend growth rate of the economy, the exact percentage growth is not nearly as important as the unwavering nature of the x-percent rule, and the implied determination of the central bank to adopt a non-interventionist monetary policy with regard to output and employment.

In the US, such a policy was adopted by Fed chairman Paul Volcker, who finally succeeded in eradicating the ravaging inflationary legacy of the 1970s. Inflation consequently fell from 10.5 % in 1980 to under 3 % by the mid-1980s, thanks to a resolutely-fixed 2 % money growth rule, single-mindedly aimed at attaining the well-announced money growth rate. While Keynesian critics may argue that the recession of 1980–81 may have been exacerbated by such determined Fed policy, inflation ceased to be an ongoing macroeconomic concern.

The Volcker monetary policy is, however, an exceptional episode and an unpopular one, given the attendant accompanying recession of 1980-81. In reality, central banks that adopt x-percent money-growth rules often come under intense pressure from the public (and governments) to lower interest rates and to "do something" to spur employment and growth. For central banks, a Friedmanian x-percent money rule can be, understandably, a lonely and unpopular policy objective.

Therefore central banks settle instead for a more practical or "second-best" version of the x-percent rule, wherein monetary policy's only objective is inflation control instead of an unwavering money-growth rule. Here, monetary policy attempts to target the only major endogenous variable that it can actually influence over the long-term—inflation. The central bank's sole objective is to hit the inflation target, P_{target}. The objective of monetary policy is to continuously make appropriate changes in monetary growth to offset any shifts in the AD from domestic or global exogenous shocks or changes in fiscal policy, and to thereby ensure that the inflation rate P_{target} is constantly attained.

The ECB, perhaps, epitomizes this policy of inflation targeting. In fact, it comes closest to adopting a true Friedmanian monetary policy by adopting two targets—an inflation target as well as an x-percent money growth target (please see following box).

However, the fact remains that even while both the hard-core x-percent rule as well as the slightly gentler "inflation-only" policy may be academically sound in a vertical AS paradigm, they are likely to be politically difficult and, at times, distinctly unpopular. This may be true even when the central bank enjoys a high degree of autonomy, as experienced by the ECB in the late 1990s and in the early 2000s.

The European Central Bank: Trials and Tribulations While membership in the Eurozone with its one common monetary policy and common currency is subject to the Maastricht criteria discussed in Chap. 6, the policy objective of the ECB itself is fraught with controversy.[10] The ECB's only policy objective is to manage the money growth of the member countries to attain and ensure an inflation target. The ECB has unambiguously and adamantly announced that a target of less than (or equal to) 2 % inflation is the only macroeconomic goal that it will attempt to attain.[11]

---

[10]As discussed earlier, the Maastricht convergence criteria include upper limits on the deficit/GDP ratio (3 %), debt/GDP ratio (60 %), long-term interest rates, and inflation. Prior to 2001, new member countries joining the European Union (EU) had an option—if they qualified, they could choose to also participate in the monetary union (the Eurozone). The UK, Sweden and Denmark are members in the EU, but they chose to "opt out" of the monetary union in the early 2000s. However, after 2001, if a new country (Poland, Hungary, Czech Republic) joins the EU, and its macro-statistics satisfy the Maastricht convergence criteria, then it has no choice—it has to be part of the monetary union (Eurozone) along with the European Union. Before a new country can be formally inducted into the Eurozone, it must lock its currency to the Euro for two years and demonstrate that it can indeed sustain the fiscal and monetary discipline entailed in joining the Eurozone.

[11]In addition to the inflation target, the ECB also has a concurrent monetary aggregate target. The inflation target, however, is the binding constraint and apparently grabs all the attention of both the public as well as policy makers. Nevertheless, both targets add to monetary policy being clearly prescribed for an economy with a vertical aggregate supply curve.

During the formative years of the ECB, potential member countries' governments were "right-of-center," but by the time the ECB came "on line" in 1999, most of the countries in the Eurozone (and in the European Union) were labor governments and socialist regimes that were decidedly "left-of-center". These governments, almost uniformly Keynesian, believed in the power of monetary policy to alleviate unemployment as well as sluggish growth via lower interest rates.

The ECB, on the other hand, with its publicly-declared "inflation-only" target set in a vertical AS curve paradigm, found itself in a clash of paradigms with Keynesian governments and the public when it repeatedly refused to "do something" to increase jobs and growth by lowering interest rates. The notion that monetary policy in certain economies may be ineffective in stabilizing output growth and employment is not intuitive, not fully-understood, and understandably unpopular in high-unemployment economies.

Compounding the matter further is the German Stability and Growth Pact, adopted by the Eurozone countries. Basically, this pact prohibits the use of government spending to jump-start economies. Upper limits on government spending and deficits are specifically prescribed by the Pact, and any violation of these upper bounds may result in severe fines that may equal 0.5 % of GDP!

The Stability Pact, as it is usually referred to, is based on a vertical AS paradigm, and hence it ascribes no benefit to GDP and employment resulting from increases in government spending, since fiscal multiplier effects are claimed to be non-existent in this paradigm. Hence, the Eurozone economies can rely on tax changes only if they are to attempt demand-side stabilization —changes in M and G are not possible. The ECB's inflation-only target prevents monetary fine-tuning, while the Stability Pact precludes changing (increasing) government spending to manage growth and employment.

As the Eurozone economies slowed along with the US economy by late 2001, policy makers, under increasing pressure from an exasperated public, increasingly wondered if, perhaps, the Stability Pact could be relaxed somewhat to allow at least some increase in government spending to explore if multiplier effects were truly non-existent. As unemployment increased by 2001, it was becoming increasing untenable to "do nothing" to attempt to stabilize the economy aside from the usual supply-side prescriptions of tax cuts and deregulation, that would, eventually, result in endogenous increases in productivity.

And the ECB's one-size-fits-all policy (Chap. 5) has remained controversial. By late 2008, contagion from a slowing United States finally began to drag down the Eurozone economies. In addition, strong interest rate gradients between the Eurozone and the United States resulted in the euro strengthening significantly against the dollar from 2006-mid-2008, and causing pain to its export sectors. Compounding this was the fact that Southern Europe needed monetary stimulus—Italy, Spain and Portugal were either flat or contracting in real GDP growth by late 2008, while France and Germany were preoccupied in fighting inflation, the primary (and official) objective of the EDB. The one-size-fits-all policy was (again) trying the patience of the suffering Southern European economies.

Another challenge faced by the ECB is more fundamental than a "clash of paradigms"; it pertains to the institutional design of the ECB and to the administration of its OMOs. The 6-member Executive Board of the ECB is equivalent to the Board of Governors of the Federal Reserve. The Executive Board members based in Euro Towers in Frankfurt have 8-year non-renewable appointments, and consist of the President, Vice-President, and four other members. Monetary policy is formulated and implemented by the Governing Council (similar to the FOMC), comprising 18 members; 6 Board members plus the 12 governors of the central banks of the member countries.[12]

Unlike the FOMC, where only 5 out of 12 Fed Presidents vote, all 12 central bank governors of the respective member countries are involved in the voting process in the ECB's Executive Board. This has caused some concerns among academic circles. By virtue of allowing all 12 governors to vote, the "center," composed of the Executive Board in Frankfurt, can be outvoted—in fact, blocks of countries could collude to determine the course of monetary policy for the Eurozone independent of "Frankfurt".

This was the case in the US before the Great Depression. All 12 Fed Presidents were included in the FOMC, with the result that the Board of Governors was often paralyzed when it came to enacting policy that might adversely affect one sector of the nation or the other; the 12 Fed Presidents would outvote the Governors, thereby neutralizing any central control of national monetary policy.

With more countries soon to enter the Eurozone, analysts fear that the ability of the ECB's Executive Board to direct and enact monetary policy may be further jeopardized.

Central banks of emerging economies are, of course, not constrained by inflation-only targets. In the Keynesian paradigm, monetary stabilization is indeed an effective tool for macroeconomic stabilization. Monetary policy is effective in attaining higher GDP growth and higher employment, or in engineering soft landings. China and the East Asian economies (possibly excepting Japan), Central Europe, India, Africa, and Latin and South America are examples where central banks may be successful in demand-side stabilization. However, these economies

---

[12]In addition to the inflation target, the ECB also has a concurrent monetary aggregate target. The inflation target, however, is the binding constraint and apparently grabs all the attention of both the public as well as policy makers. Nevertheless, both targets add to monetary policy being clearly prescribed for an economy with a vertical aggregate supply curve.

run the risk of relying excessively on monetary policy. Without accompanying fiscal reform and discipline, the specter of surging inflation and permanently high long-term rates that accompany excessive demand-side stabilization lurks in the background.

11.3.2   Is Monetary Discipline Worth the Pain?

Proponents of an inflation-only rule, conducted by a central bank that resolutely adopts a New Classical paradigm (vertical AS curve), would list the benefits as follows:

1. Lower inflation rates. This is the one variable that the central bank can consistently control in the long run using monetary policy.
2. Lower long-term interest rates. Since expectations of inflation will be curtailed given the policy of adopting some low to moderate inflation target, long-term nominal rates will be consequently lower, by the Fisher effect. Low long-term rates are vital in the formation of long-term capital growth (housing, new plant and equipment, for example.)
3. With lower inflationary expectations, unions may be more agreeable to lower increases in nominal wages, thereby breaking any wage-price spiral.
4. Stable exchange rates. This is particularly important for small economies with large exposure to the trade sector (Singapore, Taiwan, Hong Kong). A fixed money growth rule will yield less volatility in nominal exchange rates and hence in the prices of tradeable goods (imports as well as exports).
5. Monetary discipline breeds fiscal discipline. Empirically, countries with highly disciplined (tight) monetary policies have been positively correlated with low and highly sustainable budget deficits. With no possibility of monetizing away any fiscal profligacy thanks to a tight money-growth rule, policy makers are forced to incur only the deficits that they can bond-finance.
6. Monetary and fiscal discipline is the necessary condition for the "safe haven" status that attracts global capital inflows. An economy incurring a bond-financed deficit and/or a current account deficit must also be a safe haven economy to attempt NSI-type financing as discussed in Chap. 3.

Now that we have discussed how monetary policy ought to be conducted and having listed the benefits of monetary discipline, it quickly becomes evident that the Federal Reserve (as well as the ECB, to some extent) may really not be adopting inflation-only targets. There is clear evidence of attempts to engineer a soft landing in the US in 2000 to deflate the tech sector's SAP bubble, and then to attempt to jump-start the US economy with thirteen interest rate cuts from 2001 to 2003. This was followed by seventeen increases in Federal Funds rates to calm the SAP bubbles, followed by sharp drops again by 2008, to prevent contagion (please see

Article 11.3). And then from 2007 to 2015, the Fed (as discussed earlier) adopted the massive monetization known euphemistically as QE.

Instead of an inflation-only rule, the Fed seems to have displayed decidedly Keynesian behavior. Why? The answer lies in a discussion of the bane of the Federal Reserve—the 1978 Humphrey Hawkins Act.

11.3.3 The "Curse" of Humphrey–Hawkins

In the **1946 Employment Act**, Congress declared that it was the "...responsibility of the Federal Government to...promote maximum employment, production, and purchasing power". Congress then went one step further in 1978 with the Full Employment and Balanced Growth Act, commonly referred to as the **Humphrey–Hawkins Act (H–H)**, which specified unemployment targets for the Federal Government. Every year, around the 20th of every February and July, the Fed Chairperson has to testify before the Senate Banking Committee regarding the degree to which the H–H targets were achieved and to forecast the course of monetary policy over the next 18 months.

At first glance, Humphrey–Hawkins seems like a perfectly reasonable set of policy objectives. Closer examination yields just the opposite—Humphrey–Hawkins is macroeconomically inconsistent and fundamentally unsound. From both a theoretical and a monetary policy perspective, simultaneously attaining the H–H targets of low unemployment and low inflation by implementing monetary policy, is an exercise in futility.

In Chap. 10, we discussed how both Keynesian and supply-sider models could legitimately co-exist in the US due to the identification problem. We now analyze the implications of H–H for each of the two paradigms in turn.

We begin by assuming that the US is operating in a Keynesian paradigm. This model is characterized by the output-inflation tradeoff and the Phillips curve. Demand-side stabilization resulting from an expansionary monetary policy would increase GDP growth, decrease unemployment, but also increase the rate of inflation! Clearly, in a Keynesian model, Humphrey–Hawkins targets of low unemployment and low inflation would be impossible.

We now assume that the US is operating in a supply-sider paradigm with the vertical rational expectations aggregate supply curve. In this paradigm, increases in output growth (due to a rightward shift in the AS) and decreases in unemployment are accompanied by falling rates of inflation. In this case it may appear that the Humphrey Hawkins targets of low inflation and unemployment have been attained.

However, on closer examination, it becomes clear that these results are not the results of monetary (demand-side) policy. They are, instead, the products of shifts in the aggregate supply curve due to increases in productivity, deregulation, and so on. A monetary stimulus by itself (a shift in AD), without any accompanying supply-side stimulus (shift in AS), would only result in a higher rate of inflation at the same rate of GDP growth, as discussed in the previous chapter.

Therefore, from a monetary policy perspective, Humphrey–Hawkins is a macroeconomic impossibility. No matter what the paradigm, the targets are fundamentally impossible to hit using monetary policy. It is no wonder that several policy makers have undertaken the abolishment of H–H as a personal agenda. In fact, ECB officials consider themselves lucky to have just one policy objective— keeping inflation below 2 %—instead of the impossible challenge of Humphrey– Hawkins.

11.3.3.1 Is the Humphrey–Hawkins Act really a liability?

Cynics point out that despite its fundamental macroeconomic inconsistency, Humphrey–Hawkins may actually benefit the Fed by giving it some "wiggle room". Instead of single-mindedly having to direct monetary policy towards attaining a highly visible monetary aggregate target or an inflation target, H–H actually allows the Fed some discretion by prescribing both an unemployment/output target as well as an inflation target.

If the economy were to slip into recession and actual unemployment were to rise above the target employment target, H–H would legitimize monetary loosening by the Fed and the subsequent lowering of interest rates. On the other hand, if the economy were to signal imminent overheating, the Fed could legitimately contract money growth to engineer a soft landing.

Hence a case could be made that, conveniently, Humphrey–Hawkins allows the Federal Reserve to indulge in short-term discretionary policy. Unlike its European counterpart, the ECB, the Federal Reserve isn't constrained by an official, rigid and transparent inflation-only policy.

Cynics further contend that, unlike the ECB that agonizes every time it deviates from its policy objective to lower interest rates under pressure from slowing economies in the Eurozone, the Federal Reserve has no such compunction, thanks to the (inadvertent) flexibility provided by the "impossible" Humphrey–Hawkins.

Hence, given the discussion presented on H–H, it is hardly surprising that the ultimate significance of Humphrey–Hawkins, whether curse or convenience, remains open to debate.

11.3.4 The Taylor Rule

What is the Federal Reserve's policy response given the dual unemployment and inflation objectives? The answer lies in the **Taylor Principle** and the **Taylor Rule**.

Named after John Taylor of Stanford University, the Taylor Principle (1993) states that changes in the central bank's policy interest rate must be disproportionally larger than changes in the inflation rate.

An increase in the inflation rate of one percent, for example, should result in a monetary policy response whereby interest rates increase by greater than one percent. According to the Taylor Principle, this action would increase the real interest rate, defined as the nominal rate minus inflation in Chap. 6. The rise in the real rate, in turn, reduces spending, slows down the economy, and with the implicit leftward shift in aggregate demand, results in the inflation rate dropping back down to its target.[13]

The Taylor Principle is not without its hazards. Using the expression for the Fisher effect from Chap. 6, $r = i - \pi$, we can see that if the increase in the policy interest rate (i) is not disproportionally larger than the increase in inflation (π), real rates will actually fall, thereby stimulating the economy and hence pushing the inflation higher. Hence, the exact amount by which the policy interest rates need to be changed, is crucial to the final outcome.

In response to these policy hazards, John Taylor formulated the **Taylor Rule.** This rule enables policymakers to determine exactly how much the Fed should change the policy interest rate (the Federal Funds rate) in response to deviations of actual inflation and output/employment from their specified H–H targets.

While several versions and extended forms of the Taylor Rule exist, we begin by discussing an early and simplified version, expressed as:

$$\textbf{Federal Funds Rate} = \textbf{i}_t = \textbf{2} + (\textbf{p}_t) + \textbf{0.5}(\textbf{p}_t - \textbf{p}_t*) + \textbf{0.5}(\textbf{Y}_t - \textbf{Y}_t*)$$

where
$\textbf{i}_t$ the Federal funds rate, the policy interest rate controlled by the FOMC, in the current period t
π_t Prior 4-quarter inflation rate
π_t* FOMC's inflation target
$\textbf{Y}_t$ Current rate of real GDP growth
$\textbf{Y}_t*$ Trend rate of growth of real potential GDP (long-term target)

According to this simple Taylor rule, the FOMC contracts monetary growth and increases short-term interest rates (Federal Funds rates) if actual inflation π_t exceeds the target π_t*, or if real GDP growth Y_t exceeds the long-term trend rate Y_t*. The $(Y_t - Y_t*)$ term is also referred to as the "output gap".

The constant term, 2, is the assumed long-term average of the real interest rate defined as the long-term average difference between the nominal interest rate i and the rate of inflation, and the coefficients of magnitude 0.5 are the degrees to which the FOMC responds to the deviations of inflation and output from their "targets". Taylor contends that since 1999, the FOMC has responded more vigorously to deviations in inflation from the target rate of inflation, thereby implying that the coefficient is probably higher than 0.5 at the present.

Taylor assumed that the equilibrium long-term real rate was 2 %, and that the long-term output gap is zero, on average. By substituting the expression $i = r + \pi_t$,

---

[13]Clearly, the Taylor principle attempts to exploit short-term output inflation tradeoffs. Please see Carl E. Walsh, "The Science and Art of Monetary Policy", FRBSF, Economic Letter, May 2001, for an excellent overview.

with r = 2 into the Taylor Rule, we obtain a long-run target inflation rate equal to 2 %. That is, $\pi_t* = 2$.

Extended Taylor rules are more sophisticated versions of the rule discussed here, with targets that include the S&P 500 stock price index (as well as exchange rates and long-term interest rates). In the case of a stock price index, if a dangerous SAP bubble were to develop, with average stock prices exceeding some implicit target, the Taylor Rule would advocate an open market sale of government bonds, leading to an increase in short-term (Federal Fund) interest rates along the lines of the Fed's deflation of the perceived SAP bubble in technology stocks in 2000.

11.3.5   Exchange Rate Pegging, Currency Crises, and Sterilization

As introduced in the pre-ISLM Chap. 6, in economies where the central bank has no significant institutional autonomy, and where legislation pertaining to monetary discipline is absent, exchange rate pegging has often been the only option left to central bankers hoping for some modicum of monetary independence from the government. Here, the country seeking monetary discipline (Country A), locks—pegs—the exchange rate between its currency and that of another country with a longstanding reputation for monetary discipline (Country B). In this case it announces that monetary policy in A would be directed <u>only</u> towards ensuring that the exchange rate remained fixed (pegged) at 10 units of A's currency to 1 unit of B's currency.[14]

Such a well-announced peg would allow the central bank, presumably striving for some form of independence from fiscal pressure in the conduct of monetary policy, to reject pressure to increase M to "do something". Perhaps more importantly, under a self-enforced system of pegged exchange rates, the central bank now has a mechanism by which it can resist pressure from the government to monetize non-sustainable deficit spending.

With a peg of 10A = 1B, if the central bank were to buckle under pressure from a fiscally irresponsible government and increase monetary growth to finance large deficits, the domestic currency would immediately weaken and the peg would be instantly threatened. Instead of 10A = 1B, it would tend to drop to 12A = 1B (in this simplified example), and this would immediately signal, to domestic and foreign investors, a breakdown in A's monetary discipline. With interest in A lower than in B due to the increase of monetary growth in A, and coupled with the loss in

---

[14]We adopt 10A = 1B as the peg here, purely as an example for discussion. Such a "fixed" peg is known as a "hard" peg. Thailand's peg to the US dollar in the mid-late 1990s, before the 1997–98 East Asian currency crisis, is a good example. Most pegs, however, are "managed" as in the case of Singapore and the US. The ratio of A's currency relative to B's is managed within certain target ranges by A's central bank by continuously buying and selling the currencies of A and B on global foreign exchange markets.

confidence in A's ability to maintain monetary discipline, capital would rapidly flow out of A to B as soon as it becomes evident that the 10A = 1B peg is about to "break".

If, however, the peg is viable and if A does indeed successfully pursue a disciplined monetary policy aimed only at managing the 10:1 currency ratio, domestic and foreign investors will increasingly see A as a safer haven. Global capital flows into A, and foreign investment increases as it becomes evident that A's monetary policy basically mimics that of a high-monetary-discipline country, B. Good examples include the incredible capital inflows experienced by Mexico in the early 1990s and later that decade by the East Asian economies. Expectations of growth combined with signals of macroeconomic discipline resulted in massive inflows into these economies that were pegged to the US dollar.

In a sense, from a central bank perspective the adoption of a hard peg would be a "pre-emptive strike" against any attempts at fiscal profligacy. Hopefully, the scenario describing a breaking peg (from 10A = 1B to 12A = 1B) would be only a hypothetical warning of the dire consequences of losing macroeconomic discipline. Central bankers would make clear to those advocating unrestricted monetization that the peg would indeed be broken if the central bank were pressured to increase money growth to pay for excessive and non-sustainable government spending. Country A would experience a traumatic hot capital outflow, resulting in a sharp spike in domestic interest rates.[15] Capital investment would, subsequently, fall due to the rise in domestic interest rates, threatening the country with recession.

Perhaps most damaging, any monetary credibility attained by Country A after adopting the peg and after enduring the subsequent macroeconomic straightjacket over a significant period of time would be, unfortunately, wiped-out "in an afternoon." The long end of the yield curve for Country A would, in all probability, begin to rise as nervous (and disappointed) lenders now began to add additional risk premiums to long-term debt issued by that country.

However, the policy of pegging is fraught with questions. Given the benefits of pegging and despite the dire macroeconomic consequences of forsaking the peg, are there any drawbacks to designing monetary policy solely towards managing the exchange rate? Why do pegs often "blow apart" with severe consequences for the country attempting to "import" monetary discipline from a type-B country? Why did the Mexican and East Asian attempts at pegging their currencies to the US dollar come to naught?

In our initial example, monetary policy in A was solely directed to ensuring that 10 units of country A's currency were pegged to one unit of B's currency. In a world economy characterized by global capital mobility, a hard peg implies that A's central bank must ensure that domestic interest rate changes match those in Country B. In other words, if B's bonds were to yield higher interest rates, A would experience a capital outflow as domestic and foreign investors quickly switched to

---

[15]As discussed in the section on Hot Capital outflow in Chap. 3, the supply of loanable funds curve shifts left as capital rushes out of country A.

B's higher-yielding bonds. As investors sold A's currency to invest in B, this would put downward pressure on A's currency and threaten the peg of 10A = 1B. To prevent such a result, A's central bank would have to quickly increase its own interest rates to match the increase in the interest rates in B.

As long as both A and B are in similar phases of their respective business cycles, interest rate changes in A can indeed mimic those in B. If both A and B are in recessions, then lower rates in B will certainly be welcomed by matching lower rates in A and the peg will remain intact. Likewise, if both A and B were to overheat, interest rate hikes in B would be gladly matched by similar hikes in A and both economies would soft-land with the peg intact. But if their two economies were to be in different phases of their business cycles, the peg would come under severe pressure. For example, an overheated B would prescribe higher interest rates, but if A were in a recession, then A would find it impossible to increase rates to match B's rates.

Country A's central bank would have to make a hard choice—to increase rates to match the rise of rates in Country B and to maintain the integrity of the peg, or to lower rates at home and provide domestic relief to an economy in the throes of recession. Usually the second option dominates. As Country A lowers domestic interest rates with interest rates rising in Country B, the peg snaps. The domestic currency typically loses significant value as mobile capital rushes out. Vital imports into Country A become significantly more expensive and its domestic interest rates spike as the supply of loanable funds drops, and macroeconomic credibility, attained at such great cost, collapses.

Pegging, therefore, is a temporary measure of attaining monetary independence and discipline. It works only as long as the economies of both A and B are in similar phases of their respective business cycles. As real GDP growth slowed in Mexico and East Asia, while the US economy supercharged its way into the New Economy in the mid-late 1990s, their respective pegs were eventually doomed.

More recently, in 2007–08, the US adopted a loose money policy to attempt to stem potential contagion in the wake of deflating bubbles (see Article 11.3). As interest rates in the US plunged, economies with managed pegs to the US$ had to essentially also lower their interest rates to ensure the integrity of their pegged exchange rates. As the US attempted to revive its faltering economy by increasing M and pushing its AD to the right, pegged economies such as Kuwait, Saudi Arabia, the UAE, Vietnam, and Hong Kong, that were already close to overheating, had to make some very difficult choices. They could (i) either mimic US policy, lower their interest rates, and thrust their overheated AD curves further to the right, consequently superheating their economies, (ii) they could re-adjust their pegs (allow their currencies to appreciate), or (iii) they could simply break their pegs and allow their currencies to float. By late 2008, the "pegs were on fire," straining under the pressure of declining US interest rates as America struggled to stave-off a recession.

If option (i) were to be adopted, it should be noted that some pegged countries attempt to **sterilize** their foreign exchange (FX) operations to prevent, or, "sterilize", their exchange rate management from affecting their domestic economies. In the above case, if one of the pegged countries (Kuwait, for example) were to mimic US policy and try and maintain its peg to the dollar as it weakened, the Kuwaiti central bank would actively buy US dollars and sell its own currency. This process would artificially weaken the home currency and strengthen the US dollar, and bring the peg back in line.

However, managing the price of anything—and this includes currencies too—to deviate from the endogenously-driven market-price, is not without consequences. As pegged countries actively indulge in FX operations and buy US dollars and sell their own currencies, they flood their economies with domestic money. Their money supplies surge and could prove disastrous if their economies were already close to overheating (as was the case by 2008). At this point, the central bank attempts to **sterilize** the FX operations by actively indulging in open market contractions with the domestic local banks. In other words, the central bank attempts to "mop up" the huge liquidity created—the increase in money supply (M) created by pegging—and it sells the same denomination of government bonds to the local banks, thereby attempting to retract the increase in M, and to alleviate overheating pressures in the economy.

China did indeed manage to insulate its economy to some degree, by sterilizing its FX interventions. Till 2005, by some estimates, almost 70 % of the increase in domestic money created to manage its peg with the US, was sterilized. However, by 2006, the process was wearing thin. The state banks were maxxing-out with their purchases of Chinese government securities, and more open market sales of bonds were getting harder to accomplish. Compounding this further was the fact that by 2006–07, there was increasing foreign ownership of the four big Chinese State banks (Citigroup and Guangdong Development Bank, for example), and this made sterilization even harder. Consequently, the PBoC finally realized that there was really no other option—the yuan would have to be allowed to appreciate and to converge towards its endogenous market price. The price of pegging over the long run was proving entirely too prohibitive.

Currency Crisis: Europe 1992 The precursor to the Euro, the European Currency Unit (ECU), was based on a system of pegged exchange rates within 12 European economies. Basically, the European currencies were quasi-locked in managed pegs to the German currency, the Deutsche Mark (DM). Economies were bound to the DM by a narrow band and allowed ±2.25 % fluctuation with respect to the DM. British, Italian and Spanish currencies, on the other hand, needed more monetary flexibility and adopted a "wide band" with fluctuations of ±6 %.

This system, known as the Exchange Rate Mechanism (ERM), worked very well from its inception in 1979 till the early 1990s. The managed pegs to the German currency resulted in Teutonic monetary discipline in the other European economies. Inflation plummeted and wage growth was contained. Monetary discipline, in turn, bred fiscal discipline as governments now realized that monetization of runaway spending was not possible any more. The central banks' only policy objective was to transact domestic and foreign currencies to manage the exchange rate within the prescribed bands with respect to the DM.

And then The Wall came down. Massive infrastructure expenses in the former East Germany resulted in a German budget deficit that looked dangerously non-sustainable. Adding to their woes, monetary growth increased by a staggering 19 % in the year following German unification as East German currency was swapped at a 1:1 rate with the DM in a burst of political euphoria. Faced with rapid monetization and non-sustainable deficits, the Bundesbank drove up interest rates to send a clear signal to the German fiscal authority that monetization would not be forthcoming.

As German rates shot up, to ensure the integrity of the peg the other member nation of the ERM would also have had to contract monetary growth and drive up their respective interest rates. But this move would have been problematic. Several member economies were actually dangerously close to recession. They needed the exact opposite interest rate prescription—monetary loosening and lower interest rates! As the peg was tugged by the German economy at one end and by the slowing British, Austrian, Spanish, and Italian economies at the other, the ERM blew apart in Fall 1992. The Bank of England actually lowered rates, and the British pound subsequently fell by as much as 20 %.

Once again, the peg (ERM) had worked well as long as all 12 economies moved together, in the same phase of their respective business cycles. However, after 13 years, when the interest rate requirements inevitably differed, domestic considerations (such as the alleviating of domestic recessions), clearly dominated any attempts to preserve the peg.

Before we leave the section on pegging, it must be noted that not all pegs are designed and implemented to "import" monetary discipline from some country B. Countries like Singapore, for example, adopt managed pegs to reduce fluctuations in their domestic currencies. Since global trade is the primary engine of Singapore's growth, stable export and import prices are imperative. To prevent this relatively small country's currency from being constantly buffeted by global exogenous factors and market forces, a peg to the more shock-resistant US currency has been adopted and expertly managed, since the early 1980s. In fact, before China abandoned its hard peg of 8:24 yuan to 1US$ in 2005, the People's Bank of China (PBoC) sent a team of economists to the Monetary Authority of Singapore

(MAS) to study how Singapore managed its peg to a trade-weighted basket of global currencies. A similar system was then adopted by the PBoC in 2005.

11.3.5.1 The Impossible Trinity

The concept of the "impossible trinity" is linked to the effects on domestic discretionary monetary policy in an economy where capital is globally mobile and where the central bank has had to adopt a system of pegged exchange rates.

The "impossible trinity" lists three macroeconomic features that cannot simultaneously exist from a theoretical perspective.

An economy cannot:

(1) **Exist in a regime characterized by perfectly mobile capital,**
(2) **Have its exchange rates pegged to that of an economy with monetary discipline, and**
(3) **Have the ability to influence its own interest rates using monetary policy.**

Any combination of two of the three macroeconomic features listed above may be possible—but not all three, and hence the "impossible trinity".

For example, as discussed in the previous section, in a world of perfectly mobile capital an economy (Country A) pegged to, say, the US dollar would find that any attempts on its part to unilaterally change—decrease, for example—its domestic interest rates, would result in an outflow of capital, causing an accompanying incipient depreciation of the domestic currency, thereby breaking the peg.

In other words, Country A would be unable to change domestic interest rates with perfectly mobile capital flows and with its peg intact. Features (1) and (3) hold, while (2) is not possible; all three together are impossible.

We now turn to discussion questions followed by the articles that highlight key topics covered in this chapter.

11.4 Discussion Questions

1. *In the Past, Currencies Were "Backed by Gold". What Backs the World's Major Currencies Now?*
   All that "backs" the strength and value of a nation's currency today is the credibility of that country's macroeconomic policies. An economy perceived as a safe haven for its longstanding fiscal and monetary discipline and political stability is considered an economy with a "hard currency".

2. *Since the New York Federal Reserve bank is always directly involved in open market operations, isn't it unfair to always allow the New York district area to be the first beneficiary of newly created money?*
While the New York Fed is indeed a vital cog in the money creation process, there are around 64 government securities dealers (GSDs) spread over the US. Hence, the injection of new funds is spread over the country, and market forces cause the interest rate effects of the monetary change to be spread very rapidly through the economy.

3. *While H–H has been criticized as macroeconomically "impossible", weren't the two targets of low unemployment and low inflation attained for most of the 1990s, during the era of the New Economy?*
While the two targets were indeed hit, they were not achieved by monetary policy only as H–H directed, but instead by combinations of monetary and fiscal policy. In the New economy explanation, the increase in GDP growth was due to the explosion in productivity stemming from the internet-assisted economy, which was, in turn, unleashed by earlier deregulation. In essence, a shift in AS, not a shift in AD, was the principal driver of the "growth without inflation" result.

4. *The PBoC and the MAS are not endowed with high degrees of institutional autonomy. Yet, over several decades, they have conducted monetary policy that ranges from good to exemplary. How can this record be reconciled with no/little independence?*
These central banks have been blessed at critical times in the past with central bankers (Zhu Rongji, Dr. Richard Hu) who had a firm grasp on the essentials of effective monetary policy. The system, however, cannot depend on a perpetual stream of accomplished individuals, and must insure against the possibly of errant macropolicy. Hence, the safeguard of central bank autonomy becomes important.

5. *In attempts to change monetary growth, why do most emerging economies eschew OMOs in favor of policies that resemble changes in reserve ratios or discount rate policies?*
The essential ingredients for OMOs are risk-free national government bonds and an efficient forward-looking bond market. Many emerging economies are in the process of building globally recognized national bond markets and bringing national deficits to sustainable proportions over a significant time period. But the existence of efficient bond markets also implies relatively high degrees of capital mobility, more importantly pertaining to capital outflows, and attaining this mobility remains one of the greater challenges for emerging economies.

The following simulated articles that highlight some key concepts. Please relate the underlined passages to material covered in this and in preceding chapters.

Article 11.1   THE ROLE OF EFFECTIVE MONETARY POLICY

Justin Chen, <u>Michigan Business Quarterly</u>

At the recent symposium on monetary policy conducted by the Economic Research Group in Portland, Oregon, the role and effectiveness of monetary policy was discussed passionately. Opinions ranged from the effectiveness of Federal Reserve policy to claims of monetary policy impotence. Participants included mid to high-level executives, academics, entrepren-eurs, financial analysts and, of course, economists. In addition, there was a strong showing from attendees of the National MBA Conference, also being held at the same complex.

This paper interviewed several participants at the coffee break. Christina Hansen, senior purchasing executive of the Far Hills department store in Knoxville, Tennessee, said, "Honestly, that last seminar was an eye-opener—if the **(a)** <u>discount rate policy is really a lagged effect</u> of market-determined rates, then why this fuss over Fed announcements regarding the discount rate!"

At this comment, Jeff Caruso, a hospital executive chimed in, "and we now realize that **(b)** <u>even long-term rates are really not controlled by the Fed</u>—hey, I was in shock..." But, at this, Melinda van Eyksson, pharmaceutical marketing VP for Europharma in Morristown, New Jersey, muttered, "Folks, it's the **(c)** Fed <u>Funds rates that we must watch— over long periods</u>", and she shot us a meaningful look, "right?   That will

tell us what the Fed is trying to do to the monetary base over a sustained period of time."

"Yes, yes," added Dr. Fred Waterstone, of the Carmella Graduate school in Dayton, Ohio, as he got emotionally worked-up and threatened to spill his coffee, "Watch the short rates and you will see the Fed's hand on the steering wheel—and keep in mind who **(d)** <u>came to your rescue after the terrorist attacks on September 11</u>!"

With this, the pendulum again swung in favor of the Fed, till we ran into Michael Smithkline, CFO of the Jamaica Coffeebean Company. "With all these countries pegged to the US, I wonder **(e)** <u>how this affects our (US) monetary policy</u>." He then grimaced as he sipped the coffee, "awful coffee—they should try the coffee we make in Jamaica. Now <u>that's</u> coffee!"

"Well, it is clear to me that the Humphrey Hawkins legislation is a 'necessary evil' for monetary policy. **(f)** <u>It is 'impossible'</u> as the speaker indicated, but **(g)** <u>it allows the Fed some wiggle room</u>. But this was not clear to me before this conference! I always thought that one clear monetary policy goal was best!" remarked Arijit Bose, President and owner of the Bose Trading company in San Fran-cisco, "now please excuse me, I need to see how I can import that Jamaican coffee...."

"All in all, even though China does not have the huge quantity of government debt outstanding as the US does, we have done pretty good in terms of monetary policy," remarked Xiao-Min Wang, of Beijing Techsat, a technology research institute focusing on medical/laser systems, **(h)** "<u>But the point about institutional autonomy is well taken.</u>"

Conversation was lively. Participants clearly felt that the seminars were most enlightening. But Michael was right. The coffee could have been better....

Article 11.2   HOSINTAHL IN TROUBLE. END IN SIGHT?

Armelle Vernet, <u>Macroeconomic Times</u>

The Republic of Hosintahl has its back to the wall. Its currency, the Hosin, is pegged to the US dollar, and it is beginning to hurt.

Last week, the Prime Minister, Larbuz Xindal, announced that, "Lord Keynes taught us that **(a)** <u>multipliers occur due to large government spending.</u> But Ms. Wadine Gystro (Central Bank President) insists that <u>she will not increase money growth to pay for this</u>! This is unpatriotic!"

This sentiment has found strong support. Walso Komtree, **(b)** <u>president of the textile workers union, urged the government to spend more</u> and to force the central bank to "print a little money to fund the new highway project so our poor can get employed." He even accused Ms. Gystro of "caring more for her equations than for her people and not really relating to the working class."

In a related interview with the news agency, All-World, Ms. Gystro responded to these charges against her. She said, **(c)** "<u>they can obviously fire me if they want to, but as long as I am the head of the central bank we will maintain the integrity of the peg</u> at the announced rate of 250 Hosins to 1 US dollar."

General Nuypal, head of the air force remarked, "we should **(d)** <u>increase money growth and re-peg at say, 300 Hosins to the dollar.</u> This will give us a realistic peg, and create jobs!"

Upon hearing this, Gystro exploded in a TV interview, "What? No way! That would be the **(e)** <u>4th time we have 're-adjusted' the peg since we adopted it</u> two and a half years ago. We started at 150 (Hosins) to 1 US$ and now look where we are." She added that the **(f)** <u>whole experiment with pegging was to bring back the global investment that had fled</u> after the hyperinflation and the coup by General Nuypal several years ago.

"With the **(g)** <u>deficit/GDP ratio already at 9.9 percent, I cannot sanction this.</u> Fire me if you like—the peg stays as long as I'm in charge. **(h)** <u>We will create more jobs with foreign capital investment, and that will only happen if we are serious about both monetary and fiscal discipline</u>," she told the Prime Minister in a televised statement last Tuesday.

She also reminded the TV audience that her father was a sheet-metal worker, and she could relate to the "working class" better than her critics.

In the meantime, as the debates and public accusations continue, (i) more foreign invest-ors are selling Hosins and pulling out capital. This is straining the peg even further. Unemployment inches up, angry demonstrations by laid-off workers are now a daily feature, resentment mounts, and, most ominously, (j) long-term rates continue to increase—the last four weeks have already seen a 5% gain in long-term rates!   And no compromise seems likely between the Prime Minister and his Generals and the Central Bank President.

Alas, the perils of macro-economic discipline. (k) Is it worth all this pain?

Article 11.3   FEDERAL RESERVE POLICY FROM THE DOTCOM BUBBLE TO THE "SUBPRIME MESS": A STORY OF TWO UPS AND TWO DOWNS

Prof. Farrokh Langdana, Rutgers Business School, NJ, USA

To understand the whole rollercoaster saga of vast swings in US monetary policy, one has to really go back to December, 1999. After trying unsuccessfully to "talk down" the market in 1996 with his "irrational exuberance" comment, Chairman Greenspan was determined not to follow the path taken by Japan in the late 1980s.

As the Japanese housing and asset-price bubbles reached Overheating and then stormed into Stage Three of demand-pull inflation (Chapters 5 and 9), the Bank of Japan did nothing. In silent fascination, it watched the bubbles stretch larger, until they ultimately popped. When bubbles explode, they evaporate huge portions of an entire generation's savings and consequently, C and I in Japan have crashed for over a decade.

So Al Greenspan, determined not to "do a Japan," finally lashed-out at the SAP bubbles from December 1999 through the year 2000 with four monetary strikes, pushing very short-term interest rates—Federal Funds rates—up from 5.25% to 6.5%.

The ensuing soft landing of the technology sector in 2000 was controversial because overheating over the previous decade has been asymmetric. In conventional text-books, an overheated economy is manifested by an increase in overall inflation. As discussed earlier, this model has changed—overheating today is mainly a sectoral and not an economy-wide phenomenon. For instance, in 2000, overall inflation stood at only 2.2%, and yet dangerous bubbles existed in the dotcom sector. Similarly in China when the housing bubbles first appeared in 2005, overall inflation was benign—in fact, parts of the nation were actually experiencing deflation!

As the SAP bubbles in technology deflated by 2000 in the US, it seemed that all was going according to plan—till 9/11. The massive exogenous shock slammed the AD to the left and threatened to make the soft landing a very hard one.

The Fed moved with impressive and vigorous alacrity. On 9/11 itself, the Fed, in a desperate attempt to shore-up confidence and to flood the economy with much-needed liquidity, reversed course and began a series of cuts in interest rates. In fact, in Confidence Credibility and Macroeconomic Policy, Giles Mellon and the author mathematically prove that a massive monetary infusion can indeed stabilize faltering C and I if, and only if, the liquidity is injected in the very early stages of weakening confidence. Any delay only renders such an infusion impotent.

Just when the US economy was recoiling from the shock of 9/11, an additional succession of confidence-battering shocks slammed into the economy--the scandal of Enron, the space shuttle Columbia disaster, the war in Iraq, and hurricane Katrina. To counter each shock the Fed lowered rates even more. By July 2003, after thirteen cuts, Federal Funds rates had dropped as low as 1%.

At this stage we have a "one up and one down" policy regarding interest rates. "Up" to calm the SAP bubbles in technology from December 1999-2000, "down" from 2001 to restore liquidity and jump-start growth following 9/11, and then to restore faltering confidence in the wake of each additional exogenous shock.

As interest rates fell to record lows and as the Fed was preoccupied with managing the exogenous shocks hitting post-9/11 America, the housing market bubble began to inflate. And this bubble was accompanied by an episodic change in private consumption in the US. Post 9/11, consumption in the US went from 66% of GDP in 2000 to 72% by 2005. Not only did C/Y increase, but the marginal

propensity to consume (the MPC, discussed in Chapter 4) increased from a steady 0.88 that existed for several decades till 2000, to 0.92 after 9/11. The US began a long and vigorous consumption spending binge driven in part by the massive positive wealth effect of real estate, which in turn was propagated by the astonishingly low mortgage rates and lax lending regulation.

Finally—and a little too late according to the Fed's critics—interest rates were driven up again beginning in July 2004 from 1.25% to 5.25% by July 2006. Chairman Greenspan began the second round of interest rate hikes and Chairman Bernanke put the final icing on the cake by raising Federal Funds rates further. They were pushed up a total of seventeen times to finally hit 5.25%. We were back at the races, determined to deflate yet another SAP bubble. The tally on interest rates at this point, was two up and one down.

At about this time, this well-ordered scenario that was often repeated and well understood (or so it seemed), began to break apart. With a sudden and sickening realization it became apparent that we were not just deflating one bubble in the housing market but actually three bubbles! There were two more unwanted bubbles that were deflating too. It became gradually clear that the housing bubble had also led to a bubble in mortgage-backed securities, a hot favorite of hedge fund managers, and yet another bubble in private credit card debt; each American family owed about $9,000 by late-2008 on credit cards. If the three bubbles deflated, then confidence would go into free-fall thus shutting-down private consumption which accounted for 72% of the economy. Something had to be done and done fast—or so it seemed at that time.

At this point it is important to understand the "psyche" of the Fed by going back to the Great Depression and Mistake 3 (discussed in Chapter 9). Both Greenspan and Bernanke, avid students of the Great Depression, knew full well that the lack of a vigorous and rapid response from the Fed to the liquidity crisis was the cause of most of the contraction. The Fed did not restore liquidity and consequently M fell by 33% thereby dragging the recession into the Depression.

This profound and poignant monetary policy blunder has always loomed in the subconscious of the Fed and indeed in the subconscious of its Chairpersons. In fact, in a shocking revelation at Milton Friedman's 90th birthday party, Chairman Bernanke declared to Milton and Anna Friedman, "Regarding the Great Depression. You're right. We did it. We're very sorry. But thanks to you we won't do it again."

The main task at hand then seemed to be to inject liquidity rapidly and to prevent "contagion" – that is, to prevent collapsing wealth holdings (from the plunging housing market) from "infecting" $\underline{C}$ and $\underline{I}$. If there were to be contagion from the rapidly deflating bubbles, overall consumption would falter, taking the whole economy down. So the rates frantically headed back down again— short term rates were rapidly pushed down from 5.25% to 2% by May 2008.

As rates progressively fell, the dollar hemorrhaged. Global capital inflows slowed due to the combination of lower US interest rates plus a deteriorating long-term macro outlook (as discussed in Chapter 3).

As interest rates fell along with investor confidence, there were increasing concerns that the US was about to follow Japan in a version of the "liquidity trap". As discussed earlier, this is a situation in which even very low interest rates—they were close to zero in Japan in the late 1990s—do nothing to jump-start growth due to the fact that investor confidence is also dead.

By mid-2008, the "two up, two down" swings in monetary policy had played themselves out. Contagion from collapsing wealth holdings had spread to $\underline{C}$ with the index recording its lowest-ever reading in November 2008, then to $\underline{I}$, and finally to private consumption, C. Given the enormous impact of consumption on overall output, the country braced for its first consumption-driven recession since 1982. The concept of "decoupling" was a laughable myth as contagion spread globally due to (i) foreign holdings of mortgage-backed securities, and to (ii) the sharp drop in US imports that virtually shut down whole regions of export-driven production in China, for example.

Paradoxically—and reassuringly—as virtually all the major economies began to slow rapidly, the US once again became the "safest haven" thanks to its size and its history of impressive resilience in the face of macroeconomic calamity. The ensuing "flight to safety" of much-needed global capital resulted in the dollar reversal. And as the dollar rebounded fast, countries that had shorted the US (bet on the dollar's continued future fall) and denominated most of their borrowing in US$, were traumatized; Iceland and South Korea, for example, buckled under this sudden dollar-driven contagion.

By late 2008, the $700 billion bailout—monetization on an unprecedented scale—was announced. The Obama administration planned a vintage Keynesian stimulus, but the ability to increase government spending is limited given the size of the budget deficits. However, this stimulus, huge though it seemed at the time, was just the tip of the iceberg.

The liquidity trap precludes further monetary stimulus, and tax cuts, while effective, are controversial.

Even the monthly $42 billion in quantitative easing (QE), between 2007 and 2015 (discussed earlier in this text) did not dramatically jump-start the economy.

Finally, it will, once again, be up to the US to re-invent herself as she has done after every major macroeconomic convulsion. The extraordinary resilience of the US economy remains its most paramount and its most globally-envied asset, and it is this, unfettered by excess government regulation, and enhanced by bold tax cuts spurring innovation, that will spark the next recovery.

ANSWERS AND HINTS

Article 11.1 THE ROLE OF EFFECTIVE MONETARY POLICY

(a) Explain why this is so. Describe the clear arbitrage opportunities that would arise if the Fed allowed its discount rate to be significantly out of line with the 3-month T-bill rate.

(b) Long-term rates are endogenously determined. They embody market driven expectations of future risk and inflation a la the Fisher Effect.

(c) The federal funds rates are exogenously determined by Fed policy, and long-term sustained trends in fed funds rates would indeed indicate the intent of US monetary policy.

(d) Perhaps the most crucial role of the Fed is to be the "lender of last resort", and to inject huge amounts of liquidity in times of great crisis, as following 9/11.

(e) Having a number of countries wouldn't affect US monetary policy, per se, aside from the fact that the FOMC would have to, at the least, consider the ramifications of its proposed policy on other economies pegged to the dollar.

(f) This discusses the fundamental infeasibility of Humphrey–Hawkins.

(g) Here Mr. Bose is referring to the options available to the Fed. It can indeed adopt the Taylor rule and attempt to tweak output and inflation in the short run, unlike the ECB that has one unequivocal policy objective.

(h) Ms. Wang is referring to the discussion pertaining to the dependence on enlightened policy makers in regimes where the central bank has very little institutional independence.

Article 11.2 HOSINTAHL IN TROUBLE. END IN SIGHT?

(a) Ms. Gystro does not want to monetize government spending. It seems that bond-financed increases in government spending are not an option. Clearly Ms. Gystro and PM Xindal are operating in two different paradigms.

(b) There is huge pressure to increase government spending and alleviate the suffering of unemployed workers. Ideal macroeconomic policy that may benefit the whole economy is often overshadowed by more pressing local interests.

(c) This is exactly what the peg is designed to do in an economy where the central bank obviously has no institutional autonomy—the peg allows the central bank to resist pressure to increase monetary growth. In this case, apparently not for much longer, given the pressure on Ms. Gystro.....

(d) This form of "managed" peg allows the central bank to loosen monetary growth, and re-peg at a new rate, with the domestic economy now worth considerably less in terms of foreign currency. However, ...

(e) ... repeated "adjustments" of the peg—four times in a little over two years, in this case—defeat the purpose of pegging! When domestic and global investors realize that the peg is indeed very "soft" and subject to buckling under government pressure, it will be a peg "without teeth" and will not be treated seriously.

(f) In this case, pegging was supposed to signal a new era characterized by monetary discipline. As we saw in Chap. 3, capital inflows–the 'global investments' referred to in this paragraph–flow towards safe havens, often irrespective of interest rate differences. In Hosintahl's case, this peg would signal a move away from its irresponsible hyperinflation days, and towards responsible money creation, with the country pegged to (presumably) another economy of sound monetary virtue.

(g) This answers the question posed in the answer (a) above—the deficits cannot be bond-financed any more. They are non-sustainable. Lenders are not forthcoming for obvious reasons, and hence the severe pressure on Ms. Wadine Gystro.

(h) A clear signal to global investors that Hosintahl is swallowing some bitter medicine to adopt fiscal and monetary discipline would make it a "safer haven" and perhaps induce capital investment back into its textile and mining sectors.

(i) The outflow has begun. Perhaps this is the beginning of a hot capital outflow as investors realize that it is just a matter of time before Ms. Gystro is fired and the peg is broken. As investors sell Hosins to divest themselves of their Hosintahl assets, the downward pressure on that currency increases.

(j) Bonds know best, after all. Even the fledgling Hosin bond market is signaling risk and inflation warnings in the near future. Monetization is very likely at this stage, and the bond market is flashing red.

(k) The benefits of monetary discipline have been listed in this chapter.

References

Aghion, P., & Howitt, P. (1998). *Endogenous growth theory*. Cambridge, MA: MIT Press.

Bank of Canada. (1996). *The transmission of monetary policy in Canada*.

Bank of Japan. (1995, May). Reserve requirements system and their recent reforms in major industrialized countries: A comparative perspective. *Quarterly Bulletin*, 54 – 75.

Barro, R. J. (1976). Rational expectations and the role of monetary policy. *Journal of Monetary Economics, 11*, 1–32.

Bartolini, L. B., & Prati, A. (2000, September). Day to Day monetary policy and the volatility of the federal funds interest rate. Staff Report No. 110, Federal Reserve Bank of New York.

Burdekin, R. C. K., & Laney, L. (1988). Fiscal policymaking and the Central Bank institutional constraint. *Kyklos, 41*, 647–662.

Burdekin, R. C. K., & Langdana, F. K. (1992). *Budget deficits and economic performance*. London: Routledge.

Burdekin, R. C. K., & Langdana, F. K. (1993). War finance in the Southern Confederacy, 1861-65. *Explorations in Economic History, 30*, 352–376.

Burdekin, R. C. K., & Langdana, F. K. (1995). *Confidence credibility and macroeconomic policy: Past, present, future*. London: Routledge.

Burdekin, R. C. K., & Weidenmier, M. D. (2001, December). Inflation is always and everywhere a monetary phenomenon: Richmond vs. Houston in 1864. *American Economic Review*.

Case, K. E., & Fair. R. C. (2016). *Principles of macroeconomics* (9th Ed.). Upper Saddle River: Prentice Hall.

Clarida, R., Gali, J., & Gertler, M. (1999). The science of monetary policy: A new Keynesian perspective. *Journal of Economic Literature, 37*, 1661–1707.

Cox, W. M., & Alm, R. (1999). *Myths of rich and poor: Why we're better off than we think*. New York: Basic Books.

Cox, W. M., & Alm, R. (2000). Information age economics: Good news on inflation. May 11, 2000. IntellectualCapital.com.

European Central Bank. (2001). *The monetary policy of the ECB*, Frankfurt.

Federal Reserve Bank of New York. (1993, April). *Reduced reserve requirements: Alternative for the conduct of monetary policy and reserve management*.

Feinman, J. N. (1993, June). Reserve requirements: history, current practices, and potential reforms. *Federal Reserve Bulletin*, 569–589.

Friedman, M., & Schwartz, A. J. (1963). *A monetary history of the United States*, Princeton: Princeton University Press.

Friedman, M. (1968). The role of monetary policy. *American Economic Review, 58*, 16.

Froyen, R. T. (2008). *Macroeconomics: Theory and practice* (9th Ed.). Upper Saddle River: Prentice Hall.

Fuhrer, J. C. (1993). What Role does Consumer Sentiment play in the US Macroeconomy? *New England Economic Review*, 32–44.

© Springer International Publishing Switzerland 2016

F. Langdana, *Macroeconomic Policy*, Springer Texts in Business and Economics, DOI 10.1007/978-3-319-32854-6

Gavin, W. T., & Mandel, R. J. (2001, July) Economic news and monetary policy. *National Economic Trends*, Federal Reserve Bank of Saint Louis.

Goodhart, C. (2000, June). Can Central Banks survive the IT revolution? *Institutional Finance*, 189–200.

Gordon, R. J. (1999a). US economic growth since 1870: What we know and still need to know. *American Economic Review, 89*, 123–128.

Gordon, R. J. (1999b). Does the new economy measure up to the great inventions of the past. *Journal of Economic Perspectives, 14*, 49–74.

Grey, J. (1976). Wage indexation: A macroeconomic approach. *Journal of Monetary Economics, 2*, 221–235.

Henke, S. (1999). Yugoslavia destroyed its own economy. *Wall Street Journal*.

Hertzel, R. L. (Spring 2000). The Taylor rule: Is it a useful guide to understanding monetary policy? *Economic Quarterly*, Federal Reserve Bank of Richmond.

Jackman, M. (1984). *The Macmillan book of business and economic quotations*. London: Macmillan.

Jorgensen, D. W., & Stiroh, K. J. (1999). Information technology and growth. *American Economic Review, 89*, 109–115.

Keynes, J. M. (1936) (reprinted 1964). *The general theory of employment, interest and money*. Harcourt, Brace and Jovanovich, London.

King, M. (1994, August). Monetary policy instruments: The U.K. experience. *Bank of England Quarterly Review*, 268–276.

Katona, G., & Mueller, E. (1953). *Consumer attitudes and demand, 1950-52*. Michigan: University of Michigan Press.

Langdana, F. K. (1990). *Sustaining budget deficits in open economies*. London: Routledge.

Langdana, F. K. (1994). An experimental verification of the Lucas 'Islands' approach to business cycles. *Journal of Economic Behavior and Organization, 25*, 271–280.

Langdana, F. K., & Giles, M. (1995, October). Fiscal and monetary stabilization in a confidence-driven rational expectations economy. *International Journal of Finance*.

Langdana, F. K., & Murphy, P. T. (2014). *International trade and global macropolicy*. New York: Springer Press.

Lucas, R. E. (1972). Expectations and the neutrality of money. *Journal of Economic Theory, 4*(1–3), 24.

Lucas, R. E. (1973). Some international evidence on output-inflation tradeoffs. *American Economic Review, 63*, 326–334.

Lucas, R. E. (1977). Understanding business cycles. *Carnegie-Rochester Series on Public Policy, 5*, 7–29.

Lucas, R. E. (1981). *Studies in business cycle theory*. Cambridge: MIT Press.

Meyer, L. H. (2001). The future of money and of monetary policy. Address Delivered at Swarthmore College, December 5, 2001: Federal Reserve System, Release of same date.

Oliner, S. D., & Sichel, D. E. (2000). The resurgence of growth in the late 1990s. *Journal of Economic Perspectives, 14*(4), 3–22.

O'Sullivan, A., & Sheffrin, S. M. (2001). *Macroeconomics: principles and tools*, Upper Saddle River: Prentice Hall.

Pakko, M. (2000, May). Capital Deepening. National Economic Trends, The Federal Reserve Bank of St. Louis.

Pakko, M. (2001, May). Accounting for computers. National Economic Trends, The Federal Reserve Bank of St. Louis.

Parkin, M. (2007). *Economics* (8th Ed.). New York: Addison Wesley.

Phelps, E. S., & Taylor, John. (1977). Stabilizing powers of monetary policy under rational expectations. *Journal of Political Economy, 85*, 163–190.

Pugh, P., & Garratt, C. (1994). *Introducing Keynes*. Cambridge, England: Totem Books.

Santomero, A. (2001). Second quarter. Review, Federal Reserve Bank of Philadelphia.

Sargent, T. J. (1979). *Macroeconomic theory*. New York: Academic Press.

Sargent, T. J., & Wallace, N. (1981). Some unpleasant monetarist arithmetic. Quarterly Review, Federal Reserve Bank of Minneapolis 5, 1–17.

Sellon Jr., G. H., & Weiner, S. E. (1996). Monetary policy without reserve requirements: Analytical issues. Economic Review, Federal Reserve Bank of Kansas City, pp. 5–24.

Sellon, G. H., & Weiner, S. (1997). Monetary policy without reserve requirements: Case studies and options for the United States. Economic Review, Federal Reserve Bank of Kansas City, pp. 5–29.

Stevens, R. J. (1993). Required clearing balances. Federal Reserve Bank of Cleveland, Economic Review, pp. 2–14.

Stiroh, K. (2001). What drives productivity growth? Economic Policy Review, Federal Reserve Bank of New York, March 2001.

Taylor, J. B. (1993). Discretion versus policy rules in practice. In *Carnegie Rochester Conference Series on Public Policy* (pp. 195–214), December 1993.

Taylor, J. B. (1999). The robustness and efficiency of monetary policy rules as guidelines for the interest rate setting by the European Central Bank. *Journal of Monetary Economics, 43*, 655–679.

Walsh, C. E. (2001). The science and art of monetary policy. Economic Letters, Federal Reserve Bank of San Francisco, May 4, 2001.

Index

CPSIA information can be obtained
at www.ICGtesting.com
Printed in the USA
LVOW06*1751190717

541896LV00001B/2/P